ELEMENTS OF *Literature*

LITERATURE OF THE UNITED STATES
FIFTH COURSE
TEST BOOKLET

HOLT, RINEHART AND WINSTON
Harcourt Brace & Company
Austin • New York • Orlando • Atlanta • San Francisco • Boston • Dallas • Toronto • London

Staff Credits

Project Director: Kathleen Daniel

Executive Editor: Mescal K. Evler

Managing Editor: Robert R. Hoyt

Project Editor: Amy Strong

Level Editors: A. Maria Hong, Ruth McClendon Linton

Editorial Staff: Joel Bourgeois, Roger B. Boylan, Dana Chicchelly, Teresa Diaz, Jeffrey T. Holt, Katherine E. Hoyt, Constance D. Israel, Jamie Jones, Renee Lloyd, Carrie Laing Pickett, Jael Polnac, Darleen Ramos, Atietie O. Tonwe, Michael A. Webb

Editorial Support Staff: Roni Franki, Ruth A. Hooker, Kelly Keeley, Margaret Sanchez, Pat Stover

Editorial Permissions: Ann B. Farrar, Janet Harrington

Designers: Janet Brooks, Julie Ray

Production Coordinator: Rose Degollado

Manufacturing Coordinator: Mike Roche

Contributing Writers

Mary Ellen Higgins
Drew Johnson
Phil LeFaivre
Tara McCarthy
Bruce Mulkey
Robert D. Reynolds
Jo Zarboulis

The following selections were excerpted from their original sources for instructional purposes:

from "What is an American?" from *Letters from an American Farmer*
  by Michel Guillaume Jean de Crèvecoeur, page 36
from a letter written by Herman Melville to Nathaniel Hawthorne, page 84
from *Adventures of Huckleberry Finn,* Chapter 5, by Mark Twain, page 122
from *The Glass Menagerie,* Scene 1, by Tennessee Williams, page 209
from *Bone* by Fae Myenne Ng, page 276

Printed in the United States of America

ISBN 0-03-095588-2

2345 022 99 98

The copying masters in the *Test Booklet* have been organized by literary period, corresponding to the eight literary periods covered in the Pupil's Edition. Within the literary period division, copying masters are organized by collection; within the collections, worksheets are organized by selection or by other features within the collection. Standardized Test Preparation copying masters are located at the end of the booklet, followed by the Answer Key for all tests in the *Test Booklet.*

As a general rule, teachers may want to designate Selection Tests or Collection Tests that cover poetry selections as "open book tests," since these tests often require students to respond to the exact wording, rhythm, or meter of the poetry.

LITERARY PERIOD INTRODUCTION TESTS

An objective, multiple-choice test is provided to accompany each literary period introduction in the Pupil's Edition. The tests cover the key events and concepts in each period and assess critical reading skills.

SELECTION TESTS

Selection Tests include objective questions, expanded-response questions (enhanced multiple-choice questions and graphic organizer activities), and essay questions. Based on state-of-the-art assessment practices, the Selection Tests provide teachers with an authentic tool for evaluating individual performance.

COLLECTION TESTS

These summative end-of-collection tests may include up to three sections. In the first and longest section, students complete graphic organizer activities about characters and events, and they respond to application-level essay questions on the collection theme and the collection's featured element of literature. The second section tests vocabulary retention using selected Words to Own from the collection. The final section, which usually appears only in the last collection test within a literary period, assesses student mastery of the specific language skill taught in the literary period's Language Workshop feature.

THE AMERICAN LANGUAGE

For each of The American Language features in the Pupil's Edition, a multiple-choice critical reading test is provided.

LITERARY PERIOD TESTS

Each of these end-of-unit assessments allows students to apply their newly acquired skills to a literary selection not included in their textbooks. Students are asked to read a brief literary passage and to respond to vocabulary questions, objective multiple-choice questions, and expanded-response and essay questions. The literary selection on each test is from the literary period that students have just studied, and students are challenged to make connections between the test selection and the other selections from the same literary period.

STANDARDIZED TEST PREPARATION

This section of the Test Booklet provides students with a comprehensive overview of the types of standardized test items commonly encountered at upper grade levels. Verbal expression and critical reading and thinking items are presented in brief lessons, which are followed by sample items. Words to Own from the Pupil's Edition of *Elements of Literature* are featured in the critical thinking items.

ANSWER KEY

The Answer Key provides answers to objective questions in the *Test Booklet,* as well as model responses for all expanded-response items and criteria for evaluating all essay responses.

TABLE OF CONTENTS

COLLECTION 4:
THE TRANSFORMING IMAGINATION

Selection Tests

THE AMERICAN RENAISSANCE
A LITERARY COMING OF AGE

COLLECTION 5:
THE LIFE WORTH LIVING

Selection Tests

COLLECTION 6:
THE REALMS OF DARKNESS

Selection Tests

A NEW AMERICAN POETRY
WHITMAN AND DICKINSON

COLLECTION 7:
THE LARGE HEARTS OF HEROES

COLLECTION 8:
TELL IT SLANT

THE RISE OF REALISM
THE CIVIL WAR AND POSTWAR PERIOD

COLLECTION 9:
SHACKLES

COLLECTION 10:
FROM INNOCENCE TO EXPERIENCE

THE MODERNS

COLLECTION 11:
LOSS AND REDEMPTION

COLLECTION 12:
THE DREAM AND THE REALITY

COLLECTION 13:
NO TIME FOR HEROES

COLLECTION 17:
REACHING FOR THE DREAM

CONTEMPORARY LITERATURE

COLLECTION 18:
THE WAGES OF WAR

COLLECTION 19:
DISCOVERIES AND AWAKENINGS

SELECTION TEST

Here Follow Some Verses upon the Burning of Our House,
July 10, 1666   Anne Bradstreet   Pupil's Edition page 69
Huswifery   Edward Taylor   Pupil's Edition page 73

Thoughtful Reading *(40 points)*
On the line provided, write the letter of the *best* answer to each of the following items.
(5 points each)

_____ **1.** In her poem, Bradstreet mostly criticizes herself for
   a. losing her faith in God's goodness
   b. failing to react quickly in an emergency
   c. not taking proper precautions against fire hazards
   d. valuing material possessions too much

_____ **2.** Bradstreet emphasizes both the things she has lost and
   a. the people who escaped in the fire
   b. the new home that neighbors are building for her
   c. her memories of happy occasions in the house
   d. the items she has rescued from the flames

_____ **3.** When Bradstreet writes "I blest His name that gave and took . . .," she implies that
   a. she is being punished for the sin of vanity
   b. material objects are ultimately God's and not hers
   c. she secretly wants all her possessions to vanish
   d. God will be appeased if she says a prayer to him

_____ **4.** Which of the following ideas does Bradstreet find most consoling?
   a. God has prepared a rich home for her in heaven.
   b. Through the fire, she has atoned for her sins.
   c. She has emerged unharmed from the fire.
   d. Her relatives will give her temporary shelter.

_____ **5.** In "Huswifery," the speaker compares God to a
   a. homemaker making skeins of yarn
   b. teacher instructing a weaver
   c. judge weighing evidence
   d. person building a spinning wheel

_____ **6.** The speaker in "Huswifery" seems to imagine himself or herself as
   a. an instrument that God can shape
   b. a person who has no goals or desires in life
   c. a wagon wheel endlessly turning in place
   d. a favorite child who deserves special treatment

_____ **7.** Which phrase *best* illustrates the speaker's wish in "Huswifery"?
   a. All the speaker's words and actions reflect God's purpose.
   b. God relieves the speaker of his or her boring, day-to-day tasks.
   c. The speaker learns how to prosper from making cloth.
   d. The speaker proves his or her faith by mastering a difficult craft.

_____ **8.** Which of the following quotations is the *best* example of inversion?
   a. "And make thy Holy Spirit, Lord, wind quills . . ."
   b. "Then mine apparel shall display before ye . . ."
   c. "My Conversation make to be thy Reel . . ."
   d. "Then weave the Web thyself. The yarn is fine."

Expanded Response *(30 points)*

9. Choose the option that *best* completes the following statement. On the lines provided, write the letter of the answer you choose and briefly defend your choice. There is more than one possible answer. Use at least one example from the selection to support your ideas. *(15 points)*

After the burning of her house, Bradstreet discovers that
a. she was more deeply attached to her home than she imagined
b. the catastrophe has enhanced her faith
c. God will replace her possessions with better ones
d. she has the strength to cope with tragedy

_____

_____

_____

_____

_____

10. Edward Taylor uses an extended metaphor to illustrate his idea of serving God. Suppose Taylor were writing today and he decided to use a modern machine, such as a computer, television, or telephone, to convey his notions about an ideal spiritual life. In the space below, sketch a rough diagram of a modern machine. Make labels for the various parts of the machine, telling how Taylor might use each of its parts as a metaphor for God's influences on a Puritan's life. *(15 points)*

Written Response *(30 points)*

11. Both Bradstreet and Taylor use extended metaphors to illustrate ideas about their Puritan faith. On a separate sheet of paper, describe one of these extended metaphors and explain what the metaphor suggests about the speaker's religious beliefs. Make at least two references to specific details in the poem to support your ideas.

SELECTION TEST

from Sinners in the Hands of an Angry God
Jonathan Edwards

Pupil's Edition page 78

Checking Vocabulary *(20 points)*
Match each word in the left-hand column with its meaning in the right-hand column. Place the letter of the correct meaning in the space provided. *(2 points each)*

_____ **1.** abhors

a. attributed to a certain cause

_____ **2.** abominable

b. all-powerful

_____ **3.** ascribed

c. scheme; plan

_____ **4.** appease

d. scorns; hates

_____ **5.** constitution

e. unimaginable

_____ **6.** contrivance

f. enraged; angered

_____ **7.** inconceivable

g. to persuade; force

_____ **8.** induce

h. physical condition

_____ **9.** omnipotent

i. disgusting; loathsome

_____ **10.** provoked

j. to calm; satisfy

Thoughtful Reading *(25 points)*
On the line provided, write the letter of the *best* answer to each of the following items.
(5 points each)

_____ **11.** In his sermon, Edwards mainly taps into his audience's fear of
    a. their minister's wrath
    b. burning forever in a fiery pit
    c. associating with sinners
    d. floods and other natural disasters

_____ **12.** When Edwards refers to the "unconverted persons in this congregation," he chiefly addresses the
    a. men and women who do not believe in God
    b. church visitors who are followers of other religions
    c. parishioners who don't want Edwards as their leader
    d. members who do not accept Christ as their Savior

_____ **13.** Edwards presents God as a being who
    a. enjoys human suffering and misery
    b. continually redefines the universe
    c. is often angry and vengeful
    d. easily forgives repentant sinners

____ **14.** Edwards builds a sense of urgency and peril by suggesting that
   a. death and damnation may occur at any moment
   b. the church is being persecuted by unholy forces
   c. ministers alone can determine who is to be saved
   d. the end of the world is coming soon

____ **15.** Which of the following quotations is the *best* example of a figure of speech?
   a. ". . . the flames gather and flash about them . . ."
   b. "In short, they have no refuge, nothing to take hold of . . ."
   c. ". . . the mere arbitrary will, and uncovenanted, unobliged forbearance of an incensed God."
   d. "The bow of God's wrath is bent, and the arrow made ready on the string . . ."

Expanded Response *(30 points)*

16. Choose the option that *best* completes the following statement. On the lines provided, write the letter of the answer you choose and briefly defend your choice. There is more than one possible answer. Use at least one example from the selection to support your ideas. *(15 points)*

The "unregenerate" members of the congregation who literally interpret Edwards's sermon may be
   a. convinced that their own salvation is impossible
   b. terrified by the God that Edwards describes
   c. persuaded that in the eyes of God everyone is forgiven
   d. impressed by Edwards's use of figures of speech

_____

_____

_____

17. Edwards evokes images of fire and water to portray God's power and anger. In the chart below, describe each image and explain how it is used. *(15 points)*

	Image	How It Is Used
Fire		
Water		

Written Response *(25 points)*

18. In your opinion, what are the primary messages conveyed by Edwards's sermon? On a separate sheet of paper, describe two major ideas Edwards expresses in the selection. Make at least two references to specific details in the selection to support your ideas.

SELECTION TEST

from The Autobiography
Benjamin Franklin

Pupil's Edition page 85

Checking Vocabulary (20 points)

Match each word in the left-hand column with its meaning in the right-hand column. Place the letter of the correct meaning in the space provided. *(2 points each)*

____ 1. abate   **a.** correctness

____ 2. arbitrary   **b.** difficult

____ 3. arduous   **c.** lack of care in speech or action

____ 4. assert   **d.** to declare; claim

____ 5. eradicate   **e.** following

____ 6. facilitate   **f.** to eliminate

____ 7. indiscreet   **g.** based on whim

____ 8. itinerant   **h.** traveling

____ 9. rectitude   **i.** to simplify

____ 10. subsequent   **j.** to lessen

Thoughtful Reading (25 points)

On the line provided, write the letter of the *best* answer to each of the following items. *(5 points each)*

____ 11. Franklin leaves Boston mainly because he
     a. wants to live a quiet life in the countryside
     b. yearns for the life of a sailor
     c. is engaged to marry Miss Read in Pennsylvania
     d. has left his apprenticeship and needs to find work as a printer

____ 12. In this selection from his autobiography, Franklin seems most eager to portray his
     a. ability to work steadfastly toward his goals
     b. willingness to break away from convention
     c. deep resentment of people who have wronged him
     d. frugality in financial matters

____ 13. Franklin considers moral perfection to be
     a. an illusion promoted by ministers and religion
     b. an annoying claim made by hypocrites
     c. a state attainable through study and practice
     d. a pathway to heaven and God's grace

_____ **14.** In developing a method for examining virtues, Franklin reveals his
     a. doubt that real goodness can be attained
     b. logical and orderly mind
     c. scorn for traditional philosophy
     d. deeply emotional side

_____ **15.** Franklin ranks the virtues in an order according to
     a. how the clergymen of his day ranked them
     b. the popularity of individual virtues among his friends
     c. the idea that the mastery of one virtue facilitates the next
     d. the belief that the most difficult virtues must be developed first

Expanded Response *(30 points)*

16. Choose what you believe is the *strongest* response to the following question. On the lines provided, write the letter of the answer you choose and briefly defend your choice. There is more than one possible answer. Use at least one example from the selection to support your ideas. *(15 points)*

Which of the following statements describing Franklin *best* illustrates how he became a self-made success?
a. He emphasizes that human beings can improve themselves.
b. During a storm at sea, he acts as the captain of the ship.
c. Following his troubles in Boston, he devises an alternate plan of action.
d. He charms a variety of people during his journey.

_____

_____

_____

17. The following chart lists two of Franklin's precepts. In the space below each quotation, describe how Franklin does or does not live up to that precept, using an example from the selection to support your ideas. *(15 points)*

"**Resolution:** Resolve to perform what you ought; perform without fail what you resolve."	"**Humility:** Imitate Jesus and Socrates."

Written Response *(25 points)*

18. Based on what Franklin reveals about his habits and experiences, which of the thirteen virtues do you imagine would be the most difficult for him to master? On a separate sheet of paper, explain your opinion on this subject. Make at least two references to specific details in the selection to support your ideas.

COLLECTION 2 TEST

The Examined Life

Responding to Literature *(70 points)*

For each activity that follows, choose appropriate authors from the list below, and apply the activity to those authors. *(10 points each)*

Anne Bradstreet	Edward Taylor
Jonathan Edwards	Benjamin Franklin

1. Although Puritanism emphasized and valued eternal life over mortal experience, many Puritan writers of the period expressed a tension between the ideas of living a full life on earth and of focusing only on a spiritual afterlife. Choose two authors and, using the chart below, analyze their descriptions of the relation between earthly life and the afterlife.

Author	View of Earthly Life	View of Afterlife

2. In his *Autobiography,* Benjamin Franklin enumerates the thirteen virtues of temperance, silence, order, resolution, frugality, industry, sincerity, justice, moderation, cleanliness, tranquility, chastity, and humility. Choose two of these virtues and two Puritan authors. Based on their writings, analyze what each author would say either in agreement or disagreement with Franklin, using the chart below.

Author	Virtue	Agreement with Franklin	Disagreement with Franklin

Respond to each of the following questions. Attach an extra sheet of paper if necessary.
(25 points each)

3. The writers in Collection 2 are concerned with universal questions about existence and the nature of being. Both in their lives and in their writings, they seek answers to questions such as: What is my purpose in life? How can I influence the course of my life? What happens when I die? Choose two authors from Collection 2 and compare and contrast their views about one of these universal questions. Make at least two references to the selections to support your ideas.

_____

_____

_____

_____

_____

_____

_____

_____

_____

_____

_____

_____

_____

_____

_____

_____

_____

_____

_____

_____

_____

_____

4. The three Puritan writers in Collection 2—Anne Bradstreet, Edward Taylor, and Jonathan Edwards—all use metaphors to convey their messages. Discuss the use of metaphor and its effects in two of the selections from Collection 2. Make at least two references to the selections to support your ideas.

_____

_____

_____

_____

_____

_____

_____

_____

_____

_____

_____

_____

_____

_____

_____

_____

_____

_____

_____

_____

_____

Vocabulary Review *(30 points)*
In the space provided, write the letter of the word that correctly completes the sentence.
(6 points each)

5. The sponsor for the student group explained that our goal as co-leaders is to _____ communication, making sure that each person has an opportunity to speak.
   a. appease   **b.** eradicate   **c.** facilitate   **d.** abate

6. Some of the first portraits painted in the Colonies were produced by _____ artists, who traveled frequently to the homes of the wealthy to paint their families.
   a. omnipotent   **b.** itinerant   **c.** arbitrary   **d.** subsequent

7. Mrs. Juarez was not easily _____ . To make amends for accidentally crushing her lilies, the gardener had to promise to supply and plant fifty new bulbs.
   a. appeased   **b.** provoked   **c.** ascribed   **d.** eradicated

8. Mom used a combination of reverse psychology and bribery, but her efforts were in vain. Nothing could _____ Brian to give up his ragged stuffed horse.
   a. abate   **b.** induce   **c.** assert   **d.** abhor

9. Although the trip down the switchback trails of the Grand Canyon takes only a few hours, the journey is much more _____ than it seems.
   a. subsequent   **b.** provoked   **c.** indiscreet   **d.** arduous

SELECTION TEST

Speech to the Virginia Convention
Patrick Henry   Pupil's Edition page 101

Checking Vocabulary (20 points)
Match each word in the left-hand column with its meaning in the right-hand column. Place the letter of the correct meaning in the space provided. *(2 points each)*

_____ 1. adversary   **a.** opponent

_____ 2. avert   **b.** warlike

_____ 3. inevitable   **c.** watchful

_____ 4. insidious   **d.** to prevent; turn away

_____ 5. inviolate   **e.** to comfort

_____ 6. martial   **f.** earnest plea

_____ 7. solace   **g.** uncorrupted

_____ 8. spurned   **h.** rejected

_____ 9. supplication   **i.** sly; sneaky

_____ 10. vigilant   **j.** not avoidable

Thoughtful Reading (25 points)
On the line provided, write the letter of the *best* answer to each of the following items.
(5 points each)

_____ 11. The main purpose of Patrick Henry's speech is to
   a. persuade his fellow delegates to fight against the British
   b. describe the history of British colonization in America
   c. seek revenge for personal injuries committed by the British king
   d. convince the delegates that he should be chosen to lead the revolution

_____ 12. Henry points out a contradiction between British
   a. claims of peaceful intent and their growing military presence in America
   b. settlement of America and maintenance of their government in Britain
   c. interest in the Colonies and neglect of the colonists' needs
   d. democratic tradition and the institution of royalty

_____ 13. Henry recounts several instances in which the colonists sought agreement and acceptable terms with the British. He does this to convince the delegates that
   a. it is treason to seek peace with the British
   b. the colonists have behaved in a cowardly way
   c. the British army is weak and can be easily defeated
   d. all peaceful options have been tried and have failed

_____ **14.** Henry states that the colonists have the advantage over the British of
    a. a more rigorously trained army
    b. a greater number of people
    c. moral correctness and conviction
    d. knowledge of the terrain

_____ **15.** Which of the following is the *best* example of persuasion through an emotional appeal?
    a. "There is no retreat, but in submission and slavery! Our chains are forged!"
    b. "They tell us, sir, that we are weak; unable to cope with so formidable an adversary."
    c. "I know of no way of judging the future but by the past."
    d. "Mr. President, it is natural to man to indulge in the illusions of hope."

Expanded Response *(30 points)*

16. Patrick Henry uses figures of speech to persuade the delegates to adopt his point of view. Which of the following images or references do you think *best* supports Henry's efforts to persuade his audience? On the lines provided, write the letter of the answer you choose and briefly defend your choice. There is more than one possible answer. *(15 points)*
    a. "I have but one lamp by which my feet are guided; and that is the lamp of experience."
    b. "Shall we acquire the means of effectual resistance, by lying supinely on our backs, and hugging the delusive phantom of hope . . . ?"
    c. "We are apt to shut our eyes against a painful truth, and listen to the song of that siren, till she transforms us into beasts."
    d. Other: _____

_____

_____

_____

17. In the statement in balloon 1, Patrick Henry urges his fellow delegates to follow a path that may cost them their lives. In balloon 2, write a fact that a delegate might use to support Henry's view. In balloon 3, write what a delegate might say to urge another course of action. *(15 points)*

1 "The war is inevitable—and let it come! I repeat it, sir, let it come!"

2

3

Written Response *(25 points)*

18. Imagine that you are a newspaper reporter covering Patrick Henry's speech. On a separate sheet of paper, write a lead paragraph for a news story about the speech. Describe the main point Henry makes, two ideas he uses to support it, and the delegates' different reactions to the speech.

SELECTION TEST

from The Crisis, No. 1
Thomas Paine

Checking Vocabulary *(20 points)*

Match each word in the left-hand column with its meaning in the right-hand column. Place the letter of the correct meaning in the space provided. *(2 points each)*

_____ 1. celestial   **a.** well-articulated, persuasive speech

_____ 2. consolation   **b.** given up

_____ 3. dominion   **c.** persistence

_____ 4. eloquence   **d.** comfort

_____ 5. impious   **e.** oppression

_____ 6. perseverance   **f.** false claim

_____ 7. pretense   **g.** divine; perfect

_____ 8. ravage   **h.** act of violent destruction

_____ 9. relinquished   **i.** irreverent

_____ 10. tyranny   **j.** rule

Thoughtful Reading *(25 points)*

On the line provided, write the letter of the *best* answer to each of the following items. *(5 points each)*

_____ 11. Paine argues that the best way to defeat the British is for
    a. each state to fight independently as the British approach
    b. the states to train their militias in guerrilla tactics
    c. the troops of all the states to join together in the fight
    d. the states to persuade the American Indians to join the revolution

_____ 12. Paine suggests that a state that surrenders its arms to the British would have to
    a. face destruction by the British troops
    b. send its own ambassadors to Britain
    c. suffer the hostility of the other states
    d. create its own government

_____ 13. Paine describes the Tories as
    a. preparing to leave America to return to Britain
    b. committing treason by spying on their neighbors
    c. being far wealthier than the average American
    d. possibly aiding and encouraging the British army

_____ **14.** By comparing the British king to a thief and a housebreaker, Paine suggests that
  a. British soldiers are using sneak attacks against the colonists
  b. the king is in dire need of money for his treasury
  c. the British are trying to take what is not theirs
  d. Britain has robbed America of its natural resources

_____ **15.** "The heart that feels not now, is dead: The blood of his children will curse his cowardice, who shrinks back at a time when a little might have saved the whole . . ." This quotation illustrates how Paine
  a. uses a dramatic rhetorical technique to convey ideas
  b. develops a family-based theme throughout the selection
  c. uses allusions to emphasize his points
  d. presents his thoughts using only plain, ordinary language

Expanded Response *(30 points)*
16. Choose the option that *best* completes the following statement. On the lines provided, write the letter of the answer you choose and briefly defend your choice. There is more than one possible answer. Use at least one example from the selection to support your ideas. *(15 points)*
In this essay, Paine strives to persuade the
  a. Americans to continue fighting despite military setbacks
  b. states to unite as a fighting force
  c. Colonial leaders to find and exile traitors to Canada
  d. colonists to resist giving in to British peace offers

_____

_____

_____

17. Read the following quotation from the selection. In the box below, explain what Paine may be referring to and how this quotation reflects his style. *(15 points)*

> "Is this the madness of folly, to expect mercy from those who have refused to do justice; and even mercy, where conquest is the object, is only a trick of war; the cunning of the fox is as murderous as the violence of the wolf; and we ought to guard equally against both."

Written Response *(25 points)*
18. Read the following lines from Paine's essay.

> ". . . I call not upon a few, but upon all; not on *this* state or *that* state, but on *every* state; up and help us; lay your shoulders to the wheel; better have too much force than too little, when so great an object is at stake."

On a separate sheet of paper, respond to the quotation by explaining how it reflects a theme in the selection. Note what Paine means by "lay your shoulders to the wheel" and what the "object" is to which he refers.

SELECTION TEST

from The Autobiography:
The Declaration of Independence
Thomas Jefferson

Pupil's Edition page 115

Checking Vocabulary *(20 points)*

Match each word in the left-hand column with its meaning in the right-hand column. Place the letter of the correct meaning in the space provided. *(2 points each)*

_____ **1.** abdicated

a. given up responsibility for

_____ **2.** acquiesce

b. seizure of property by authority

_____ **3.** candid

c. temporary; passing

_____ **4.** censures

d. forces

_____ **5.** confiscation

e. nobility of spirit

_____ **6.** constrains

f. unbiased; fair

_____ **7.** expunge

g. strong, disapproving criticisms

_____ **8.** magnanimity

h. to give up

_____ **9.** renounce

i. to agree or accept quietly

_____ **10.** transient

j. to erase; remove

Thoughtful Reading *(25 points)*

On the line provided, write the letter of the *best* answer to each of the following items. *(5 points each)*

_____ **11.** Jefferson states that the king has established tyranny over the colonies. To back up this statement, Jefferson
   a. cites lies that are self-evident
   b. portrays the king as a pawn of greedy British nobles
   c. describes Britain's colonization of other nations
   d. lists several specific actions of the king

_____ **12.** Jefferson emphasizes that the colonists
   a. desire a form of self-government
   b. expect guidance from the British Parliament
   c. want to rebel against all formal rules and regulations
   d. need an army to restore law and order

_____ **13.** The passage condemning Britain's involvement in the African slave trade was struck out of the original Declaration because
   a. Jefferson disliked the way the passage was worded
   b. not all the states were involved in the slave trade
   c. two states wanted to continue importing slaves
   d. the passage would have been especially offensive to the British

_____ **14.** Jefferson believed that the final version of the Declaration of Independence was
   a. perfect because it resolved all existing tensions
   b. worthless since all factions remained at odds
   c. disappointing because of its many omissions
   d. good publicity for his presidential campaign

_____ **15.** Which of the following is the best example of parallelism?
   a. "A prince whose character is thus marked by every act which may define a tyrant is unfit to be the ruler of a free people."
   b. ". . . we mutually pledge to each other our lives, our fortunes, and our sacred honor."
   c. "Prudence, indeed, will dictate that governments long established should not be changed for light and transient causes. . . ."
   d. "We hold these truths to be self-evident: that all men are created equal . . ."

Expanded Response *(30 points)*

16. Choose the option that *best* completes the following statement. On the lines provided, write the letter of the answer you choose and briefly defend your choice. There is more than one possible answer. Use at least one example from the selection to support your ideas. *(15 points)*

The most impressive aspect of the Declaration is
   a. the clarity with which it sets forth the offenses of the British
   b. the impassioned language urging Americans to form an army
   c. the philosophy it provides about the underpinnings of democracy
   d. its controlled eloquence of expression

_____

_____

_____

17. In his autobiography, Jefferson shows the original draft of the Declaration and how it was revised by Congress. On the lines provided, list three insights into the historical period you have gained from a study of this section of the autobiography. *(15 points)*

a. _____

_____

b. _____

_____

c. _____

_____

Written Response *(25 points)*

18. Congress first approached John Adams to write the Declaration of Independence. Adams turned down the assignment, saying that Thomas Jefferson should write it because Jefferson was the best writer among all the delegates. What do you think Adams admired in Jefferson's style? On a separate sheet of paper, respond to this question by describing at least two ways in which the Declaration displays the hallmarks of good writing.

THE AMERICAN LANGUAGE

"Revolutionary" English

Pupil's Edition page 127

On the line provided, write the letter of the *best* answer to each of the following items.
(10 points each)

_____ 1. Some of the differences that developed between the British and American
languages were caused by
   a. the addition of new words to British English
   b. the increasingly nasal pronunciation of British English
   c. the strong influence of American Indian languages on American English
   d. the physical separation of Britain and America

_____ 2. Changes in language usage occurred
   a. only in America
   b. only in Britain
   c. in both America and Britain
   d. in neither America nor Britain

_____ 3. The word *Americanism* identifies a word or expression that
   a. was adapted from an American Indian language
   b. describes the American lifestyle
   c. is used by the British to describe American attitudes
   d. originated in, or is peculiar to, the United States

_____ 4. Because they disliked Americanisms, some British purists
   a. believed the English language had reached perfection in the eighteenth
century and should not be changed
   b. believed a new American literature could supplant British literature as the
authority for usage
   c. were concerned that these phrases would contribute to political unrest
   d. were intimidated by the improvements made to British English

_____ 5. Many Americans and British feared that
   a. their languages eventually would change so much that the two peoples
would be unable to understand each other
   b. language differences would cause economic problems in America
   c. language differences would undermine the political power of both nations
   d. American English would corrupt British English

_____ 6. In eighteenth- and nineteenth-century America, the conflict between language
purists and advocates of linguistic change
   a. was strictly a linguistic matter
   b. became embroiled in politics
   c. led to the founding of an academy to regulate usage
   d. became an issue in international trade

_____ 7. Advocates of Federal English were convinced that
   a. Americans should imitate British English
   b. Americans should establish Latin as their official written language
   c. American English could become a pure and independent language
   d. American and British English should be united

_____ **8.** The greatest virtue of American English, according to its advocates, was its
    a. precise usage
    b. natural pronunciation
    c. logical spelling
    d. democratic character

_____ **9.** The most radical proposal regarding the language to be spoken in America suggested the
    a. creation of an American dialect
    b. adoption of Federal English
    c. establishment of a completely new language
    d. rejection of British authority in language

_____ **10.** An American who spoke in favor of the natural evolution of American English was
    a. Thomas Jefferson
    b. John Adams
    c. John Witherspoon
    d. Basil Hall

COLLECTION 3 TEST

The American Dream

Responding to Literature *(70 points)*

1. Persuasion influences opinion through a combination of logical reasoning and emotional manipulation. Choose two selections from Collection 3. In the following chart, jot down a phrase or an image from each selection and describe both the emotional overtones and the messages of these statements. *(10 points)*

Selection	Phrase or Image	Emotional Overtones	Message

2. Each of the writers in Collection 3 describes actions taken by the colonists during the period preceding the war, and British reactions to these actions. Choose one of the writers from Collection 3, and describe the writer's account of two of the colonists' actions and of the British reactions to them. *(10 points)*

Writer: _____

Colonists' Actions	British Reactions

Respond to each of the following questions. Attach an extra sheet of paper if necessary.
(25 points each)

3. The "American dream," associated with visions of freedom, prosperity, and hope for a better future, is a difficult concept to define because it means different things to different people. Choose two writers from Collection 3 and explain the ideas that each one has contributed to the concept of the "American dream." Support your ideas with at least two specific examples from the selections.

_____

_____

_____

_____

_____

_____

_____

_____

_____

4. The Age of Reason began in Europe during the seventeenth and eighteenth centuries with philosophers and scientists who called themselves rationalists. Rationalism is the belief that human reason should determine all opinions and courses of action. In your opinion, would Patrick Henry, Thomas Paine, or Thomas Jefferson be considered a rationalist? Choose one writer and respond to the question. Support your ideas with at least two specific examples from the selections.

_____

_____

_____

_____

_____

_____

_____

_____

_____

Vocabulary Review *(10 points)*
In the space provided, write the letter of the word that correctly completes the sentence.
(2 points each)

5. Despite elaborate precautions, the Shisedos were unable to protect their garden from the _____ of beetles.

   a. supplication   **b.** ravage   **c.** pretense   **d.** magnanimity

6. Dad was unwilling to buy Glen an electric guitar because he was tired of funding Glen's _____ interests.

   a. insidious   **b.** vigilant   **c.** celestial   **d.** transient

7. Interested more in school subjects than in social activities, Liza _____ the attention of her classmates and did her best to ignore them.

   a. spurned   **b.** relinquished   **c.** abdicated   **d.** acquiesced

8. The _____ of the president's speech impressed the delegates to the convention.

   a. consolation   **b.** perseverance   **c.** dominion   **d.** eloquence

9. Displaying _____ unusual in children so young, the first-graders at Pine Elementary School donated their favorite toys to the day-care center that had been damaged by fire.

   a. supplication   **b.** tyranny   **c.** magnanimity   **d.** pretense

Language Workshop Review: Coordinating Conjunctions *(20 points)*
Combine each pair of sentences with coordinating conjunctions. Make necessary minor changes or deletions that make the sentence read smoothly. *(4 points each)*

10. Thomas Jefferson would rise to eminence in America. He would become one of the country's most celebrated persons.

    _____

    _____

11. His beginnings were humble. Thomas Paine wrote some of the most memorable words in support of American independence.

    _____

    _____

12. Jefferson founded the University of Virginia. He believed that education was essential to democracy.

    _____

13. John Dickinson opposed the Declaration of Independence. The rest of the delegates signed it.

    _____

14. The colonists protested the "Intolerable Acts." They supported Patrick Henry's call to take up arms against the British.

    _____

    _____

Beginnings

Reading an Essay

One of the most famous tributes to America comes from the pen of a widely traveled French writer named Michel Guillaume Jean de Crèvecoeur. His comments helped to confirm the hopes of people disillusioned and burdened by history.

Read the essay carefully, and then answer the questions that follow.

FROM *"What Is an American?"*
Letters from an American Farmer
by Michel Guillaume Jean de Crèvecoeur

I wish I could be acquainted with the feelings and thoughts which must agitate the heart and present themselves to the mind of an enlightened Englishman when he first lands on this continent. He must greatly rejoice that he lived at a time to see this fair country discovered and settled; he must necessarily feel a share of national pride when he views the chain of settlements which embellishes these extended shores. When he says to himself, this is the work of my countrymen, who, when <u>convulsed</u> by factions, afflicted by a variety of miseries and wants, restless and impatient, took refuge here. They brought along with them their national genius, to which they principally owe what liberty they enjoy and what substance they possess. Here he sees the industry of his native country displayed in a new manner, and traces in their works the embryos of all the arts, sciences, and ingenuity which flourish in Europe. Here he beholds fair cities, substantial villages, extensive fields, an immense country filled with decent houses, good roads, orchards, meadows, and bridges, where a hundred years ago all was wild, woody, and uncultivated!

What a train of pleasing ideas this fair spectacle must suggest! It is a prospect which must inspire a good citizen with the most heartfelt pleasure. The difficulty consists in the manner of viewing so extensive a scene. He is arrived on a new continent; a modern society offers itself to his contemplation, different from what he had hitherto seen. It is not composed, as in Europe, of great lords who possess everything, and of a herd of people who have nothing. Here are no aristocratical families, no courts, no kings, no bishops, no ecclesiastical dominion, no invisible power giving to a few a very visible one, no great manufacturers employing thousands, no great refinements of luxury. The rich and the poor are not so far removed from each other as they are in Europe.

Some few towns excepted, we are all tillers of the earth, from Nova Scotia to West Florida. We are a people of cultivators, scattered over an immense territory, communicating with each other by means of good roads and navigable rivers, united by the silken bands of mild government, all respecting the laws without dreading their power, because they are <u>equitable</u>. We are all animated with the spirit of industry, which is <u>unfettered</u> and unrestrained, because each person works for himself. If he travels through our rural districts, he views not the hostile castle and the haughty mansion, contrasted with the clay-built hut and miserable cabin, where cattle and men help to keep each other warm, and dwell in meanness, smoke, and <u>indigence</u>. A pleasing uniformity of decent competence appears throughout our habitations. The meanest of our log houses is a dry and comfortable habitation.

Lawyer or merchant are the fairest titles our towns afford; that of a farmer is the only <u>appellation</u> of the rural inhabitants of our country. It must take some time before he can reconcile himself to our dictionary, which is but short in words of dignity and names of honor. There, on a Sunday, he sees a congregation of respectable farmers and their wives, all clad in neat homespun, well mounted, or riding their own humble wagons. There is not among them an esquire, saving the unlettered magistrate. There he sees a parson as simple as his flock, a farmer who does not riot on the labor of others. We have no princes for whom we toil, starve, and bleed; we are the most perfect society now existing in the world. Here man is free as he ought to be; nor is this pleasing equality so transitory as many others are. Many ages will not see the shores of our great lakes replenished with inland nations, nor the unknown bounds of North America entirely peopled. Who can tell how far it extends? Who can tell the millions of men whom it will feed and contain? For no European foot has as yet traveled half the extent of this mighty continent!

Understanding Vocabulary (20 points)
Each of the following underlined words has also been underlined in the selection. Reread those passages and use context clues to help you select an answer. On the line provided, write the letter of the word or words that *best* complete each sentence. *(4 points each)*

_____ **1.** People who are "convulsed by factions" are
   a. violently agitated
   b. denied upward mobility
   c. given extra responsibility
   d. ignored as troublemakers

_____ **2.** Equitable laws may be considered
   a. misleading
   b. heartfelt
   c. just and impartial
   d. cruel

_____ **3.** An unfettered spirit of industry is
   a. devious
   b. not restricted
   c. imaginary
   d. unworthy of serious attention

_____ **4.** People who experience indigence suffer from
   a. extreme poverty
   b. urban pollution
   c. complete isolation
   d. serious illness

_____ **5.** A person's appellation is his or her
   a. reputation
   b. political organization
   c. name or title
   d. equipment or gear

Thoughtful Reading (35 points)
On the line provided, write the letter of the *best* answer to each of the following items. *(7 points each)*

_____ **6.** Crèvecoeur believes an English person arriving in North America would probably feel
   a. envy
   b. pride
   c. hostility
   d. anger

_____ 7. The "national genius" that Crèvecoeur believes the Americans inherited from the British lies in their
    a. artistic taste
    b. literary ability
    c. industriousness
    d. sense of humor

_____ 8. According to Crèvecoeur, most people in America during this period
    a. were wealthy landowners
    b. experienced abject poverty
    c. traveled constantly to survive
    d. lived modestly and comfortably

_____ 9. Crèvecoeur describes the North American continent as
    a. wildly beautiful and rugged
    b. vast and unexplored
    c. crowded and overpopulated
    d. artistically inspiring

_____ 10. According to Crèvecoeur, an important difference between Europe and North America is that the latter lacks
    a. humble farmers
    b. aristocratic families
    c. lawyers or merchants
    d. religious leaders

Expanded Response (15 points)

11. How would you characterize Crèvecoeur's attitude toward the United States? On the lines provided, write the letter of the answer you choose and briefly defend your choice. Use at least one example from the selection to support your ideas.
    a. hostile
    b. hopeful
    c. admiring
    d. other: _____

_____

_____

_____

_____

_____

Written Response (30 points)

12. Both Michel Guillaume Jean de Crèvecoeur and Thomas Jefferson shared a vision of an agricultural society of virtuous, free, and proud individuals. What other similarities do you see in the philosophies of the two thinkers? On a separate sheet of paper, write an essay in which you compare Crèvecoeur's and Jefferson's points of view. Make at least two references to specific details in the selections to support your ideas.

SELECTION TEST

Rip Van Winkle
Washington Irving

Pupil's Edition page 153

Checking Vocabulary *(20 points)*
Match each word in the left-hand column with its meaning in the right-hand column. Place the letter of the correct meaning in the space provided. *(2 points each)*

_____ **1.** fidelity

a. likable; agreeable

_____ **2.** malleable

b. painstaking

_____ **3.** scrupulous

c. honest and careful

_____ **4.** vehemently

d. accuracy

_____ **5.** amiable

e. repeated

_____ **6.** conscientious

f. quiet; calm

_____ **7.** torpor

g. emphatically

_____ **8.** obsequious

h. submissive; obedient

_____ **9.** reiterated

i. capable of being shaped

_____ **10.** placid

j. inactive period

Thoughtful Reading *(25 points)*
On the line provided, write the letter of the *best* answer to each of the following items.
(5 points each)

_____ **11.** Many readers see "Rip Van Winkle" as a story of a wish come true. Which phrase below most accurately states the wish?
  a. to be free of both British and Dutch rule
  b. to stay young forever
  c. to find new friendships
  d. to escape domination and enjoy oneself

_____ **12.** The most momentous historical event that takes place during Rip's long sleep is
  a. the death of his wife
  b. the secession of New York
  c. Hendrick Hudson's arrival
  d. the American Revolution

_____ **13.** Rip Van Winkle is characteristic of the American Romantic hero in that he
  a. discovers great truths through intuition
  b. finds solace and comfort in the wilderness
  c. has profound insights into the limits of science
  d. meets supernatural beings in the forest

COLLECTION 4

_____**14.** From Irving's descriptions of the Kaatskill Mountains, you can conclude that he found this setting
    a. spooky and dangerous   **c.** majestic and wondrous
    b. humorous and unreal   **d.** spoiled and degraded

_____**15.** In his descriptions of Rip's hometown, Irving shows how a place and its people can change as a result of
    a. independence and commerce
    b. neglect and indifference
    c. the disappearance of one of its residents
    d. the destruction of the natural environment

Expanded Response *(30 points)*

16. Choose the option that *best* completes the following statement. On the lines provided, write the letter of the answer you choose and briefly defend your choice. There is more than one possible answer. Use at least one example from the selection to support your ideas. *(15 points)*
The story of Rip Van Winkle can be enjoyed mostly as
    a. a fantasy about the rewards of time travel
    b. an accurate view of late Colonial times
    c. a moralistic story about the dangers of escapism
    d. a humorous tale based on German folklore

_____

_____

_____

_____

17. Complete the chart below by describing the settings of the village where Rip Van Winkle resides, both before and after his long sleep. Focus on the differences in the mood of the village as well as on physical changes. *(15 points)*

Before Rip's Sleep	After Rip's Sleep

Written Response *(25 points)*

18. Everyone longs for escape from unpleasant or oppressive circumstances. Some of the things from which people wish to escape include dangerous political situations, painful relationships, and economic hardship. "Rip Van Winkle" is a classic story of wish fulfillment, in that Rip manages to escape from many different things. What do you think Rip escapes from? What makes this wish-fulfillment story appealing or unappealing to you? On a separate sheet of paper, respond to these questions in a complete paragraph that makes at least two references to specific incidents in "Rip Van Winkle."

SELECTION TEST

Thanatopsis
William Cullen Bryant Pupil's Edition page 170

Thoughtful Reading *(40 points)*
On the line provided, write the letter of the *best* answer to each of the following items. *(10 points each)*

_____ 1. In "Thanatopsis," nature urges the poet to find comfort in the
    a. fact that he is young and death is far off
    b. knowledge that death joins us with all others
    c. promise of resurrection after death
    d. idea that he will be famous after he dies

_____ 2. Which statement best summarizes the cycle described in "Thanatopsis"?
    a. The dead are replaced by the living, who in turn die.
    b. The natural world is constantly changing.
    c. We move from cheerfulness to sorrow and back again.
    d. Nature speaks to us gently, then harshly.

_____ 3. "Thanatopsis" strongly suggests that human beings are
    a. the highest form of living things
    b. doomed to live in dread of death
    c. an ongoing part of the earth itself
    d. incapable of improving their lives

_____ 4. Which facet of "Thanatopsis" makes it a good example of Romantic poetry?
    a. The natural environment has provoked deep emotions and insights in the speaker.
    b. The poem is written in unrhymed lines and focuses on the supernatural.
    c. The poet is absorbed in thoughts of dying.
    d. The poet applies logic and rational thinking to human concerns about life and death.

Expanded Response *(30 points)*
5. Different readers emerge from reading "Thanatopsis" with different feelings about the cycle of life and death it describes. After each word listed in the chart below, suggest the reasons a reader might react to the poem with that particular feeling.

Feeling	Reason
Gloom	
Reassurance	
Joy	

Written Response *(30 points)*
6. In "Thanatopsis," Bryant expresses his views on both the process of life itself and the nature of individual lives. On a separate sheet of paper, describe Bryant's views on the latter, making at least two references to the poem.

SELECTION TEST

The Ropewalk
The Cross of Snow
Henry Wadsworth Longfellow

Pupil's Edition page 176

Pupil's Edition page 178

Thoughtful Reading *(40 points)*

On the line provided, write the letter of the *best* answer to each of the following items.
(5 points each)

_____ **1.** "The Ropewalk" evokes both sunlight and shadow by
    a. showing ropes used in happy as well as dismal situations
    b. describing the up-and-down movement of a swing
    c. comparing the factory workers to spiders
    d. drawing a vivid verbal picture of a hangman's noose

_____ **2.** Many readers see in "The Ropewalk" an awakening of the writer's interest in social reform. Which of the following sentences *best* states the socioeconomic message of "The Ropewalk"?
    a. Factory workers need to be informed about the outcome of their work.
    b. Factories should develop machines to take the place of human labor.
    c. Factory workers perform labor that serves no real purpose.
    d. Factory workers perform labor that is dreary and dehumanizing.

_____ **3.** To which senses do these lines of imagery from "The Ropewalk" appeal?

> At the end, an open door;
> Squares of sunshine on the floor
>   Light the long and dusky lane;
> And the whirring of a wheel,
> Dull and drowsy . . .

    a. touch and hearing   **c.** smell and touch
    b. hearing and sight   **d.** sight and touch

_____ **4.** After reading "The Ropewalk," we can conclude that the speaker
    a. knows from firsthand experience what it is like to work in a rope factory
    b. is a labor activist who would like to organize the rope-factory workers to protest.
    c. has great admiration for the rope-factory workers and would like to be like them
    d. has a vivid imagination that enables him or her to see the rope factory in different lights

_____ **5.** What can we conclude about the female subject of "The Cross of Snow"?
    a. She is one of the few childhood friends of the speaker.
    b. She is a lonely person who lives in isolation from society.
    c. She is remembered fondly and is deeply missed by the speaker.
    d. She is very spiritual and in touch with the ways of nature.

_____ **6.** In "The Cross of Snow," the images of a halo, fire, and sunlight contrast with the
    a. image of a snowy, sun-capped mountain
    b. face of the speaker's dead wife
    c. image of a sunless mountain ravine
    d. recollection of a happy marriage

_____ **7.** In "The Cross of Snow," the cross the speaker wears is
     a. his guilt about the accident that killed his wife
     b. a medallion that his wife gave to him
     c. an emotional pain that has never healed
     d. his memento of a trip he took with his family

_____ **8.** What is surprising or unexpected about the image of the cross of snow in Longfellow's poem?
     a. Unlike real snow, it becomes dirty.
     b. It exists only in the speaker's mind.
     c. It refers to a sense of religious conviction.
     d. Unlike real snow, it persists through time.

Expanded Response *(30 points)*

9. Readers' opinions vary as to whether "The Ropewalk" and "The Cross of Snow" are sentimental or realistic. In the chart below, list some ideas that support both points of view. *(15 points)*

Poem	Sentimental	Realistic
"The Ropewalk"		
"The Cross of Snow"		

10. Choose the option that *best* completes the following idea. On the lines provided, write the letter of the answer you choose and briefly defend your choice. There is more than one possible answer. Use at least two examples from the two poems to support your ideas. *(15 points)*
Longfellow's imagery serves the following purpose:
a. to balance positive aspects of the human condition with negative ones
b. to express the speaker's reactions to personal experiences
c. to call attention to the inevitable sadness in life
d. to point out what can be learned from a study of nature

_____

_____

_____

_____

Written Response *(30 points)*

11. Judging from your reading of these two poems, how would you describe Longfellow's attitude toward life? Do you find him optimistic or pessimistic? On a separate sheet of paper, explain your point of view in one paragraph. Make at least two references to the poems to support your interpretation.

COLLECTION 4

SELECTION TEST

from Snow-Bound: A Winter Idyll
John Greenleaf Whittier   **Pupil's Edition page 182**

Thoughtful Reading *(40 points)*
On the line provided, write the letter of the *best* answer to each of the following items.
(10 points each)

_____ 1. Most of the imagery in *Snow-Bound* contrasts
     a. the bitterness of winter with the softness of spring
     b. a winter scene outdoors with a home scene indoors
     c. relying on oneself with cooperating with others
     d. the virtues of farming with the dangers of the city

_____ 2. A major reason for the popularity of *Snow-Bound,* both in its day and in the present, is its
     a. vivid portrait of a Romantic hero
     b. autobiographical sketch of a famous man
     c. picture of people from different backgrounds living in harmony
     d. description of people challenged by natural forces

_____ 3. The children described in the poem react to the storm with
     a. wonder and excitement   **c.** anxiety and tension
     b. bored nonchalance   **d.** anger and resentment

_____ 4. The speaker mentions an intense isolation. What makes this isolation a positive experience?
     a. The speaker has learned a great deal about himself during the storm.
     b. The emergency has helped the family to settle old quarrels.
     c. A storm-battered visitor has arrived to entertain the family.
     d. The snowbound family has risen to the challenge with merriment and enterprise.

Expanded Response *(30 points)*
5. *Snow-Bound* is full of sensory images. Respond to the imagery in the following lines by filling in the chart below them.

     The shrieking of the mindless wind, / The moaning tree boughs swaying blind, /
     And on the glass the unmeaning beat / Of ghostly fingertips of sleet. (lines 102–105)

1	2	3
The lines above appeal chiefly to the sense of:	Words that help develop the sensory imagery are:	The words in column 2 make the storm seem like:

Written Response *(30 points)*
6. Whittier uses imagery to describe how both the outdoor and indoor environments are transformed. On a separate sheet of paper, describe the transformations and explain how Whittier uses images to convey a sense of amazement toward these changed situations. Make at least two references to images in the poem to support your ideas.

SELECTION TEST

The Chambered Nautilus
Old Ironsides
Oliver Wendell Holmes

Pupil's Edition page 188

Pupil's Edition page 190

COLLECTION 4

Thoughtful Reading *(40 points)*

On the line provided, write the letter of the *best* answer to each of the following items.
(5 points each)

_____ 1. In "The Chambered Nautilus," the speaker implies that if he hadn't meditated on the nautilus, his life might have ended up being like
  a. a series of endless corridors leading nowhere
  b. a person who drowns in the sea
  c. the noise from an ancient sea god's horn
  d. the ever-changing and restless sea

_____ 2. The speaker finds the chambered nautilus remarkable because it is
  a. a rare shell seldom found on beaches
  b. broken and abandoned by its tenant
  c. evidence of how a living thing develops
  d. able to move through the water like a boat

_____ 3. In "The Chambered Nautilus," what does the speaker seem to wish for himself?
  a. an opportunity to live his life over again
  b. a carefree life by the seashore
  c. a fame that will endure long after his death
  d. a spirit that eventually will break free

_____ 4. In "The Chambered Nautilus," the poet develops an extended metaphor comparing the empty shell to
  a. the lack of meaning in his own life
  b. a body that once housed a soul
  c. a new building that will soon be occupied
  d. an estate that has been recently robbed

_____ 5. In "Old Ironsides," the metaphor of harpies plucking at an eagle refers to
  a. land birds attacking seabirds
  b. scavengers destroying something noble
  c. a story from Norse mythology
  d. the defeat of the British in 1812

_____ 6. In "Old Ironsides," the words *she* and *her* help to develop the metaphor comparing the ship to
  a. a valiant human being who has served gallantly in a war
  b. an old woman who has outlived her children
  c. a human being who has traveled throughout the world
  d. a mermaid who wants to return to the sea

_____ 7. The speaker in "Old Ironsides" wants to save the ship because it
  a. represents past glory
  b. still functions as a seagoing vessel
  c. is valuable as an educational tool
  d. is beautiful and well crafted

_____ **8.** When it was published, the poem "Old Ironsides" served a purpose similar to that of a
  a. newspaper editorial
  b. strikers' picket line
  c. birthday celebration
  d. sympathy note

Expanded Response *(30 points)*

9. Choose the option that *best* completes the following statement. On the lines provided, write the letter of the answer you choose and briefly defend your choice. There is more than one possible answer. Use at least one example from each poem to support your ideas. *(15 points)* The most striking similarity between "Old Ironsides" and "The Chambered Nautilus" is the
  a. poet's attempt to influence the reader's attitude
  b. use of oceangoing "vessels" as subjects
  c. tone of respect for the past
  d. statement of the poet's spiritual beliefs

_____

_____

_____

_____

_____

_____

10. In your opinion, which poem—"Old Ironsides" or "The Chambered Nautilus"—is more relevant to today's world? Write the title of your choice in the box provided. Then fill in the chart to explain that choice. *(15 points)*

Poem Title:
Major metaphors or symbols in the poem:
How the poem's message relates to life today:

Written Response *(30 points)*

11. On a separate sheet of paper, write a one-paragraph essay discussing how Holmes's two poems reflect the characteristics of American Romanticism. Make at least two references to specific details in the poems to support your ideas.

THE AMERICAN LANGUAGE

"Noah's Ark": Webster's Dictionary
Pupil's Edition page 195

On the line provided, write the letter of the *best* answer to each of the following items.
(10 points each)

_____ 1. In England, the ultimate linguistic authority traditionally rested with
    a. everyday usage
    b. the king
    c. the schools
    d. dictionaries

_____ 2. Determining matters of linguistic usage by common agreement is
    a. impossible in any society
    b. possible only where the social structure is fluid
    c. possible only in a relatively stable social structure
    d. possible under all conditions

_____ 3. In the eighteenth century, English schools introduced into their curriculum the study of
    a. English grammar
    b. Latin grammar
    c. Greek grammar
    d. German grammar

_____ 4. After the Revolution, a major impediment to establishing American linguistic independence was the fact that
    a. Americans were proud of their diversity
    b. there were no schools in the colonies
    c. most Americans could not read or write
    d. the only available grammar textbooks came from England

_____ 5. Until the late eighteenth century, the spelling of American English
    a. was regulated by an academy
    b. followed flexible rules
    c. copied British rules
    d. was influenced by Samuel Johnson's *Dictionary*

_____ 6. Noah Webster believed that accurate and uniform American spelling would promote
    a. clearer writing
    b. greater conformity with British English
    c. uniform American speech
    d. better language skills in the United States

_____ 7. Webster's first dictionary reveals that he
    a. appreciated fashionable and urban ways
    b. was conservative in matters of spelling and pronunciation
    c. was strict in matters of grammar and usage
    d. had had extensive training as a linguist

COLLECTION 4

_____ **8.** Webster's *American Dictionary* included frequent inaccuracies in
   a. pronunciation
   b. word histories
   c. usage
   d. grammar

_____ **9.** Webster's influence is evident today in our adoption of
   a. British spelling conventions
   b. his word histories
   c. some of his recommendations for spelling and pronunciation
   d. all of his recommended pronunciations

_____ **10.** Webster's *American Dictionary* was
   a. the first dictionary to include Americanisms
   b. criticized for its brevity
   c. praised by Samuel Johnson
   d. carefully researched by a team of scholars

COLLECTION 4 TEST

The Transforming Imagination

Responding to Literature *(70 points)*

1. Symbols and metaphors allow writers to express complex, many-layered ideas. These literary devices help readers make imaginative connections that go beyond the literal meanings of the words. In the chart below, write the literal description of the symbol or metaphor and its implication for the meaning of the poem. *(10 points)*

Selection Title	Symbol or Metaphor	Literal Description	Implication
"The Ropewalk"	factory workers as spiders		
"Old Ironsides"	the ship		
"The Chambered Nautilus"	the chambered nautilus		

2. While some literary critics consider Rip Van Winkle a model example of the Romantic hero and the prototype of the mythic American, others view him negatively as fulfilling a European stereotype of Americans. In the chart below, list three characteristics of the American Romantic hero. Then note which of Rip Van Winkle's qualities may be interpreted as reflecting such characteristics and which as representing the stereotype of the American in European eyes. *(10 points)*

Characteristics of the American Romantic Hero	Rip Van Winkle's Heroic Characteristics	Rip Van Winkle's Stereotypically American Characteristics

COLLECTION 4

Respond to each of the questions below. Attach an extra sheet of paper if necessary. *(25 points each)*

3. One hallmark of American Romanticism is its emphasis on looking to the wisdom of the past and distrusting progress. Choose two selections from Collection 4, and discuss how the writers develop this theme. In what ways are the selections similar and different? Support your ideas with at least two specific examples from each selection.

_____

_____

_____

_____

_____

_____

_____

_____

4. You have been asked to select the one poem or story that best represents the spirit of American Romanticism. In making your choice among the selections in Collection 4, look for the following concepts: individualism, innocence, reverence for nature, cultivation of the imagination, and respect for the past. Write an essay describing how the selection you have chosen exemplifies these characteristics of American Romanticism. Support your point of view with at least two examples from the work.

_____

_____

_____

_____

_____

_____

_____

Vocabulary Review *(10 points)*

In the space provided, write the letter of the word that correctly completes the sentence. *(2 points each)*

5. The inexperienced rider had no difficulty controlling his horse, an ancient and
_____ mare.
   a. conscientious   **b.** placid   **c.** reiterating   **d.** scrupulous

6. Aunt Lydia builds miniature dollhouses and designs their interiors with _____ detail.
   a. malleable   **b.** obsequious   **c.** amiable   **d.** scrupulous

7. "Of course, sir, whatever you say. Dinner will be served at 7 o'clock," responded the
_____ butler, as he bowed to his employer.
   a. obsequious   **b.** vehement   **c.** placid   **d.** malleable

8. Although Ayeesha likes to sculpt in wood, she prefers clay, which is _____ .
   a. vehement   **b.** amiable   **c.** scrupulous   **d.** malleable

9. The storyteller added flourishes, yet preserved the original story with _____ .
   a. reiteration   **b.** torpor   **c.** fidelity   **d.** vehemence

Language Workshop Review: Combining Sentences *(20 points)*

On the lines provided, combine each of the following groups of sentences into one sentence by inserting adjectives or phrases. The types of modifiers you need to use are specified in the brackets following each item. You may add, delete, or change word forms and add commas as necessary. *(4 points each)*

> **EXAMPLE:** William Cullen Bryant wrote about finding solace in nature.
> He wrote with nobility and dignity. *[phrase]*
>
> William Cullen Bryant wrote with nobility and dignity about finding solace in nature.

10. Henry Wadsworth Longfellow was the first American poet to earn a living solely by writing poems. He was also the first American to be honored with a bust in the Poet's Corner of Westminster Abbey. *[phrase]* _____

_____

11. John Greenleaf Whittier was a devout Quaker. He dedicated just as much of his life to the anti-slavery movement as he did to his poetry, sometimes risking his life for the cause. *[phrase]*

_____

_____

12. An idyll is a brief pastoral poem. It describes the picturesque in country life. *[phrase]*

_____

13. Applied to sentimental writing, the word *romantic* may take on negative connotations. It is a multifaceted word. *[adjective]* _____

_____

14. The first eight lines of an Italian sonnet describe a situation, and the last six lines describe a change in that situation. This is the form of most Italian sonnets. *[phrase]* _____

_____

COLLECTION 4

LITERARY PERIOD TEST

American Romanticism

Reading a Poem

The following poem was first published along with "Thanatopsis" in 1817. Read the poem carefully, and then answer the questions that follow.

Inscription for the Entrance to a Wood
by William Cullen Bryant

Stranger, if thou hast learned a truth which needs
No school of long experience, that the world
Is full of guilt and misery, and hast seen
Enough of all its sorrows, crimes, and cares
5   To tire thee of it, enter this wild wood
And view the haunts of Nature. The calm shade
Shall bring a kindred calm, and the sweet breeze
That makes the green leaves dance, shall waft a balm
To thy sick heart. Thou wilt find nothing here
10   Of all that pained thee in the haunts of men,
And made thee loathe thy life. The primal curse
Fell, it is true, upon the unsinning earth,
But not in vengeance. God hath yoked to guilt
Her pale tormentor, misery. Hence, these shades
15   Are still the abodes of gladness; the thick roof
Of green and stirring branches is alive
And musical with birds, that sing and sport
In wantonness of spirit; while below
The squirrel, with raised paws and form erect,
20   Chirps merrily. Throngs of insects in the shade
Try their thin wings and dance in the warm beam
That waked them into life. Even the green trees
Partake the deep contentment; as they bend
To the soft winds, the sun from the blue sky
25   Looks in and sheds a blessing on the scene.
Scarce less the cleft-born wildflower seems to enjoy
Existence, than the wingèd plunderer
That sucks its sweet. The mossy rocks themselves,
And the old and ponderous trunks of prostrate trees
30   That lead from knoll to knoll a causey rude
Or bridge the sunken brook, and their dark roots,
With all their earth upon them, twisting high,
Breathe fixed tranquillity. The rivulet
Sends forth glad sounds, and tripping o'er its bed
35   Of pebbly sands, or leaping down the rocks,
Seems, with continuous laughter, to rejoice
In its own being. Softly tread the marge,
Lest from her midway perch thou scare the wren
That dips her bill in water. The cool wind,
40   That stirs the stream in play, shall come to thee,
Like one that loves thee nor will let thee pass
Ungreeted, and shall give its light embrace.

Understanding Vocabulary *(20 points)*

Each of the italicized words below has also been underlined in the selection. Reread those passages, and use context clues to help you determine the meaning of each word. In the space provided, mark each true statement **T** and each false statement **F**. *(4 points each)*

_____ **1.** *Waft* refers to a species of tree.

_____ **2.** *Vengeance* may be a motive for aggressive action.

_____ **3.** Birds that sing in *wantonness* of spirit are swift.

_____ **4.** *Prostrate* describes trees that have collapsed under the burden of age or weight.

_____ **5.** A person who treads the *marge* walks along the margin.

Thoughtful Reading *(35 points)*

On the line provided, write the letter of the *best* answer to each of the following items. *(7 points each)*

_____ **6.** "Inscription for the Entrance to a Wood" focuses primarily on
   a. the premature death of heroes
   b. the comfort and inspiration of nature
   c. ambition as the highest human goal
   d. guilt as the chief cause of human misery

_____ **7.** At the end of the poem, the stranger is welcomed into the world of nature through
   a. religious teachings
   b. riddles
   c. reason
   d. love

_____ **8.** The poem portrays various elements of nature as
   a. living in a fragile state of coexistence with each other
   b. part of a cyclical pattern of life and death
   c. rejoicing in the comfort of their existence
   d. constantly battling the human world in order to survive

_____ **9.** The insects in the poem are described as
   a. a marginal part of the natural world
   b. the lowest form of living beings
   c. annoying but hard-working creatures
   d. reflections of sublime beauty and grace

_____ **10.** The speaker suggests that human beings should approach nature
   a. cautiously and warily
   b. with total abandon
   c. with a rational mind
   d. gently and optimistically

Expanded Response *(15 points)*

11. What word *best* describes the overall tone of the poem? On the lines provided, write the letter of the answer you choose and briefly defend your choice. Use at least one example from the selection to support your ideas.

    a. sarcastic

    b. angry and blaming

    c. calm and contented

    d. humorous

_____

_____

_____

_____

Written Response *(30 points)*

12. Many American Romantic poems emphasize the power of the imagination to transform experience. Write a one-paragraph essay discussing how "Inscription for the Entrance to a Wood" addresses this theme. Make at least two references to specific details in the poem to support your ideas.

_____

_____

_____

_____

_____

_____

_____

_____

_____

_____

_____

_____

_____

LITERARY PERIOD INTRODUCTION TEST

The American Renaissance
A Literary Coming of Age

Pupil's Edition page 204

On the line provided, write the letter of the *best* answer to each of the following items.
(10 points each)

_____ 1. The first flowering of a uniquely American literature, sometimes referred to as the American Renaissance, was directly influenced by
   a. intellectual and social ferment in New England
   b. an American version of an old philosophy called Aphorism
   c. the inspiration and lectures of Nathaniel Hawthorne
   d. the politics of the European Renaissance

_____ 2. Nathaniel Hawthorne and Herman Melville both
   a. had published books of lyric poetry
   b. were ex-seamen with little education
   c. explored the dark side of human existence in their work
   d. doubted that America would produce writers as good as Shakespeare

_____ 3. The philosophy embraced by Ralph Waldo Emerson's Transcendentalists had its roots in all of the following *except*
   a. Puritan thought exemplified by William Bradford, Anne Bradstreet, and Jonathan Edwards
   b. nineteenth-century Romantic thought exemplified by William Cullen Bryant
   c. Classical Greek idealistic thought exemplified by Plato
   d. eighteenth-century rational thought exemplified by Benjamin Franklin

_____ 4. In the Transcendentalist view of the world,
   a. everything is a reflection of the Divine Soul
   b. humanity's task is to conquer and tame the natural world
   c. people must struggle against the evil side of their nature
   d. human perfectibility is not an achievable goal

_____ 5. The Lyceum movement was an expression of New England's interest in
   a. the philosophy of Immanuel Kant
   b. self-improvement and intellectual inquiry
   c. the dark side of human nature
   d. eighteenth-century religious revivals

_____ 6. Which of the following statements about Ralph Waldo Emerson is true?
   a. He wrote a novel about sin and hypocrisy in Puritan New England.
   b. He traveled around the country giving sermons.
   c. He helped inspire numerous reform movements.
   d. He criticized a utopian group called "The Transcendental Club."

_____ 7. Utopian communities were founded with the intention of
   a. teaching philosophy to Romantic poets
   b. abolishing the institution of slavery
   c. funding the Lyceum movement
   d. creating a more perfect society

____ **8.** Reform movements during the first half of the nineteenth century included campaigns for
   a. building more factories
   b. improving public education
   c. improving living conditions for slaves
   d. limiting women's rights

____ **9.** The source of Emerson's optimism was
   a. his belief that we can directly find a benevolent God in nature
   b. the popularity of European writers in America
   c. the success of the Dark Romantic writers
   d. his belief that everyone would soon live in a utopian community

____ **10.** Both the Dark Romantics and the Transcendentalists
   a. saw signs and symbols in human events
   b. saw culture as a constant reminder of spiritual goodness
   c. valued logic and reason over intuition
   d. had an optimistic world view

SELECTION TEST

from Nature
Ralph Waldo Emerson

Pupil's Edition page 218

Checking Vocabulary *(20 points)*
On the line provided, write the Word to Own that *best* matches each definition that follows.
(2 points each)

perpetual	sublime	admonishing	manifold	indubitably
integrate	slough	perennial	blithe	occult

_____ 1. that which inspires awe

_____ 2. carefree

_____ 3. recurring yearly

_____ 4. outer layer of snake skin

_____ 5. unify

_____ 6. mildly warning

_____ 7. hidden

_____ 8. without a doubt

_____ 9. unchanging; constant

_____ 10. many different

Thoughtful Reading *(25 points)*
On the line provided, write the letter of the *best* answer to each of the following items.
(5 points each)

_____ 11. Which of the following quotations from the selection does **not** contain an example of sensory imagery?
    a. "The sun illuminates only the eye of the man, but shines into the eye and the heart of the child."
    b. "The stars awaken a certain reverence, because though always present, they are always inaccessible . . ."
    c. "Standing on the bare ground—my head bathed by the blithe air, and uplifted into infinite space—all mean egotism vanishes."
    d. ". . . the same scene which yesterday breathed perfume and glittered as for the frolic of the nymphs . . ."

_____ 12. According to Emerson, the person who can truly see nature is like a child because he or she
    a. no longer needs to rely upon either reason or faith
    b. perceives nature as a kind of toy
    c. is free of the burden of thought
    d. sees with the heart as well as with the eye

_____ 13. With which of the following statements would Emerson be most likely to agree?
    a. Human beings should attempt systematically to learn everything there is to know about nature and solve all its mysteries.
    b. The creations of human society, such as laws and cities, are as wondrous as the works of nature.
    c. Nature brings a sense of joy to the observer at all times, even to someone who is grieving.
    d. All elements of nature make a unified impression on those whose minds are open.

COLLECTIONS 5–6

_____ **14.** The third paragraph of the excerpt ends with this sentence: "This is the best part of these men's farms, yet to this their warranty deeds give no title." In the context of the paragraph, this sentence means
  a. the most valuable quality of the land is something that cannot be owned
  b. the deeds to the majority of the farms do not list the owners' names
  c. the work that farm owners perform does not entitle them to ownership of the land
  d. poets should be given deeds to the land, because only they can understand its worth

_____ **15.** Emerson's purpose in this essay is to
  a. express his disappointment with the society of his time
  b. explain and analyze the workings of natural phenomena
  c. describe a profound way of seeing nature
  d. persuade sinners to turn to nature and seek forgiveness from God

Expanded Response *(30 points)*

16. Which of the following quotations *best* represents Emerson's ideas about society and nature? On the lines provided, write the letter of the answer you choose and briefly defend your choice. There is more than one possible answer. *(15 points)*
  a. "The name of the nearest friend sounds then foreign and accidental. To be brothers, to be acquaintances—master or servant, is then a trifle and a disturbance."
  b. "To go into solitude, a man needs to retire as much from his chamber as from society."
  c. "The rays that come from those heavenly worlds, will separate between him and vulgar things."

  _____

  _____

  _____

17. Imagine that you work for a company that has a large piece of land to sell. You want to produce two brochures—one to appeal to someone with an Emersonian appreciation of nature, the other to appeal to someone who is looking for a good investment. Select three features of the land, such as a lake, a forest, or the climate. In the following layouts of the brochures, write a phrase to describe each feature for each brochure. *(15 points)*

Land for Sale **Emersonian Dream**	*Land for Sale* **Great Investment Opportunity**
• • •	• • •

Written Response *(25 points)*

18. On a separate sheet of paper, write a paragraph explaining how the following quotation from *Nature* exemplifies Emerson's intuitive (or emotional) style of thought. Then write a response that Benjamin Franklin, a rational thinker, might have had to Emerson's statement.

"Neither does the wisest man extort all her [nature's] secret, and lose his curiosity by finding out all her perfection."

SELECTION TEST

from Self-Reliance
Ralph Waldo Emerson

Pupil's Edition page 224

Checking Vocabulary *(20 points)*
On the line provided, write the Word to Own that *best* matches each definition that follows.
(2 points each)

proportionate	manifest	conspiracy	conviction	imparted
predominating	transcendent	benefactors	integrity	aversion

_____ **1.** secret plot with a harmful or illegal purpose

_____ **2.** surpassing; excelling

_____ **3.** belief

_____ **4.** having influence over

_____ **5.** balanced; having a correct relationship between parts

_____ **6.** revealed

_____ **7.** honesty; sound moral principles

_____ **8.** clear; plain

_____ **9.** intense dislike

_____ **10.** people who help others

Thoughtful Reading *(25 points)*
On the line provided, write the letter of the *best* answer to each of the following items.
(5 points each)

_____ **11.** Which of the following does **not** contain a figure of speech?
   a. "To be great is to be misunderstood."
   b. ". . . that envy is ignorance; that imitation is suicide . . ."
   c. "This sculpture in the memory is not without preestablished harmony."
   d. "Trust thyself: Every heart vibrates to that iron string."

_____ **12.** In the following metaphor, ". . . no kernel of nourishing corn can come to him but through his toil bestowed on that plot of ground which is given to him to till . . . ," which of the following *best* describes what "that plot of ground" represents?
   a. the duties an individual performs
   b. the results of an individual's actions
   c. the circumstances an individual is born into
   d. an individual's daily food

_____ **13.** When Emerson says we are "ashamed of that divine idea which each of us represents," which of the following *best* describes what he means by "that divine idea"?
   a. a wonderful and exciting plan of action
   b. an image of the world
   c. God, as we imagine him
   d. each person's uniqueness, as conceived by God

_____ **14.** Emerson states that the most sacred aspect of a person is the
   a. work that person accomplishes
   b. integrity of an individual's mind
   c. person's courage to be a nonconformist
   d. shadow that an individual casts on the world

COLLECTIONS 5–6

_____ **15.** According to Emerson, the "hobgoblin of little minds" is
    a. society   **c.** conspiracy
    b. cowardice   **d.** consistency

Expanded Response *(30 points)*

16. Which of the following quotations do you think *best* expresses Emerson's ideas about the importance of self-reliance? On the lines provided, write the letter of the answer you choose and briefly defend your choice. There is more than one possible answer. *(15 points)*
    a. "The power which resides in him is new in nature, and none but he knows what that is which he can do, nor does he know until he has tried."
    b. "Trust thyself: Every heart vibrates to that iron string."
    c. "Nothing is at last sacred but the integrity of your own mind."
    d. Other (paraphrase): _____

_____

_____

_____

17. Emerson uses the images in the left-hand column of the chart below to create metaphors. In the center column, tell what each image is compared to. In the right-hand column, tell what qualities are shared by each image and the thing to which it is compared. *(15 points)*

Image	What Image Is Compared To	Qualities That Are Being Compared
planting corn		
joint-stock company		
iron string		

Written Response *(25 points)*

18. On a separate sheet of paper, state the theme of Emerson's essay in one sentence. Then read the following quotation from "Self-Reliance." Do you think this quotation contradicts Emerson's theme? Provide at least two examples from the selection to support your answer.

"Accept the place the divine Providence has found for you; the society of your contemporaries, the connection of events. Great men have always done so and confided themselves childlike to the genius of their age. . . ."

SELECTION TEST

from Walden, or Life in the Woods
Henry David Thoreau

Pupil's Edition page 232

Checking Vocabulary (20 points)

On the line provided, write the Word to Own that *best* matches each definition that follows.
(2 points each)

pertinent	encumbrance	impervious	temporal	superfluous
effete	incessantly	derision	tumultuous	ethereal

_____ 1. without stopping

_____ 2. impenetrable; resistant

_____ 3. not earthly; spiritual

_____ 4. unnecessary

_____ 5. contempt; ridicule

_____ 6. sterile; unproductive

_____ 7. to the point; applying to the situation

_____ 8. burden; hindrance

_____ 9. worldly

_____ 10. turbulent; stormy

Thoughtful Reading (25 points)

On the line provided, write the letter of the *best* answer to each of the following items.
(5 points each)

_____ 11. Which of the following is the *best* interpretation of Thoreau's statement "In most books
the *I*, or first person, is omitted; in this it will be retained. . . . I am confined to this
theme by the narrowness of my experience"?
   a. Most authors forget to address their readers' interests.
   b. Most authors explain their feelings in their works.
   c. Most authors forget to write about themselves, the most important subject.
   d. Most authors' thoughts and feelings inform everything they write.

_____ 12. Which is the *best* interpretation of what Thoreau means when he says, " . . . we do like
cowbirds and cuckoos, which lay their eggs in nests which other birds have built, and
cheer no traveler . . . "?
   a. People who try to trick others into doing their work feel guilty.
   b. People who hire others to provide for their basic needs are left unfulfilled.
   c. People who are dishonest are unhappy.
   d. People who are cheerful are usually hard workers.

_____ 13. With which of the following statements would Thoreau agree?
   a. Most people's lives are too simple.
   b. The chief purpose of everyone's life should be to glorify God.
   c. Most people forfeit their lives by doing what society tells them to do.
   d. People need to learn to compromise in order to get along.

COLLECTIONS 5–6

_____ **14.** What reason does Thoreau give for going to live at Walden?
    a. He wanted to withdraw from life because he was depressed.
    b. He disliked people and wanted to get away from them.
    c. He wanted to prove that he did not need other people.
    d. He wanted to live life more fully.

_____ **15.** What reason does Thoreau give for finally leaving Walden?
    a. He wished to move on to other experiences.
    b. He did not find what he was seeking there.
    c. He got tired of working so hard for the essentials of life.
    d. He was lonely and missed the company of other people.

Expanded Response *(30 points)*

16. Which of the following experiences *best* illustrates Thoreau's doctrine of simplicity? On the lines provided, write the letter of the answer you choose and briefly defend your choice. There is more than one possible answer. Use at least one example from the selection to support your ideas. *(15 points)*
    a. cultivating the bean field
    b. watching the war between the ants
    c. building his own house
    d. other: _____

_____

_____

_____

17. At Walden, Thoreau set two goals for himself: to live deeply and to live simply. Use the following chart to analyze his experience. For each goal, shade in the scale to indicate how well you think he accomplished that goal while at Walden. (**1** means "not accomplished.") Then in the appropriate space, explain how he did or did not accomplish each goal (or how he fell short of a **10** on the scale). Support your response with evidence from the selection. *(15 points)*

Thoreau's Goals	Goal 1: To Live Deeply	Goal 2: To Live Simply
How Well Accomplished	1 10	1 10
How Accomplished or Not Accomplished		

Written Response *(25 points)*

18. In the section "Where I Lived and What I Lived For," Thoreau says, "I did not wish to live what was not life." On a separate sheet of paper, explain what he meant, supporting your answer with three specific examples of what Thoreau meant by "not life."

SELECTION TEST

from Resistance to Civil Government
Henry David Thoreau

Pupil's Edition page 248

Checking Vocabulary (20 points)

On the line provided, write the Word to Own that *best* matches each definition that follows.
(2 points each)

expedient	perverted	posterity	alacrity	inherent
insurrection	penitent	effectual	obstruction	impetuous

_____ 1. inborn

_____ 2. hindrance; blockage

_____ 3. revolt; rebellion

_____ 4. corrupted; misdirected

_____ 5. impulsive

_____ 6. generations to come

_____ 7. efficient; productive

_____ 8. eagerness; promptness in responding

_____ 9. sorry for doing wrong

_____ 10. means to an end; convenience

Thoughtful Reading (25 points)

On the line provided, write the letter of the *best* answer to each of the following items.
(5 points each)

_____ 11. Which of the following quotations from this selection is an example of paradox?
   a. "What is once well done is done forever."
   b. "*It* does not keep the country free. *It* does not settle the West."
   c. "That government is best which governs not at all."
   d. "I think that we should be men first, and subjects afterward."

_____ 12. Thoreau's major purpose in this essay is to persuade people to
   a. rebel against an unjust war
   b. follow their individual consciences
   c. call for an immediate end to the government
   d. devote themselves to the eradication of wrongs

_____ 13. In Thoreau's view, the practical reason the majority rules in a democracy is that
   a. this system satisfies more people
   b. the majority opinion is always the just opinion
   c. the majority opinion is more likely to be just
   d. the majority has more physical power on its side

COLLECTIONS 5–6

_____ **14.** Thoreau's hope for the democracy of his time was that it
     a. was one step along the route to a more perfect state
     b. would disappear as people ceased to vote
     c. would progress from an absolute to a limited monarchy
     d. would abolish poll taxes for all time

_____ **15.** Which of the following *best* describes Thoreau's attitude toward government after he was jailed?
     a. He was appalled that he was punished.
     b. He was angry about losing his freedom.
     c. He lost all respect for the government and pitied it.
     d. He worried that he would lose his voting privileges.

Expanded Response *(30 points)*

16. Which of the following quotations from the selection expresses the principle about government that is *least* possible to put into practice today? On the lines provided, write the letter of the answer you choose and briefly defend your choice. There is more than one possible answer. *(15 points)*
     a. "The only obligation which I have a right to assume, is to do at any time what I think right."
     b. "[The government] can have no pure right over my person and property but what I concede to it."
     c. "Let every man make known what kind of government would command his respect, and that will be one step toward obtaining it."
     d. Other (paraphrase): _____

_____

_____

_____

17. In his essay "Resistance to Civil Government," Thoreau, ever the idealist, describes features of the ideal government and the ideal individual. In the chart that follows, list three of these features in each column. *(15 points)*

Ideal Government	Ideal Individual
1.	1.
2.	2.
3.	3.

Written Response *(25 points)*

18. On a separate sheet of paper, summarize this selection by creating a list of five major points. As the first item in the list, describe Thoreau's purpose in writing the essay. The following four items in the list should summarize major points or incidents from the selection in a sentence or two.

COLLECTION 5 TEST

The Life Worth Living

Responding to Literature *(90 points)*

1. During the nineteenth century, Transcendentalists were at the forefront of the reform movement. They worked to abolish poverty and slavery, to extend the right to vote to more citizens, and to broaden human and civil rights. In the chart below, indicate from your reading the philosophical contributions that Emerson and Thoreau made to this reform movement. Mention at least three ideas contributed by each of the two writers. *(20 points)*

Emerson	Thoreau

2. Despite their different backgrounds and experiences, Emerson and Thoreau shared a number of ideas. Compare their views on nature, the individual, and conformity by filling out the chart below. *(20 points)*

	Emerson	Thoreau
Nature		
The Individual		
Conformity		

COLLECTIONS 5–6

Elements of Literature

Respond to each of the questions below. Attach an extra sheet of paper if necessary.
(25 points each)

3. In a letter to Emerson in 1843, Henry David Thoreau wrote that good writing is a multi-layered form of communication. It should at first appeal to the reader's common sense; then, upon deeper consideration, it should also convey both truth and beauty. From your perspective, did Thoreau follow his own observations? Write an essay in which you analyze the presence of common sense, truth, and beauty in his writings. Support your analysis with specific examples from *Walden* and "Resistance to Civil Government."

4. Both Emerson and Thoreau offer a recipe for living a productive, worthwhile life. Which of these men advances a philosophy that you might apply to your own experiences? Write an essay in which you discuss how and why you might adapt Emerson's or Thoreau's philosophy to your life.

_____

_____

_____

_____

_____

_____

_____

_____

_____

_____

_____

_____

_____

_____

_____

_____

_____

_____

_____

COLLECTIONS 5-6

Vocabulary Review *(10 points)*
In the space provided, write the letter of the word that correctly completes the sentence.
(2 points each)

5. Margo seems _____ to the taunts of her friends; she laughs at their snide remarks and continues to wear her beloved saddle shoes and bobby socks.
   a. sublime   **b.** proportionate   **c.** pertinent   **d.** impervious

6. Having heard rave reviews about Mrs. Byrd's gourmet cooking, Luis responded to the dinner invitation with _____.
   a. slough   **b.** alacrity   **c.** derision   **d.** posterity

7. Snow-capped peaks in the distance and meadows carpeted with wildflowers made visiting the Canadian Rockies in July a(n) _____ experience.
   a. blithe   **b.** predominating   **c.** sublime   **d.** effete

8. Judge Garcia has a long-standing reputation for _____ and fairness.
   a. integrity   **b.** encumbrance   **c.** insurrection   **d.** conspiracy

9. The factory owners hired an industrial consultant to make production more _____ and cost-effective.
   a. perpetual   **b.** occult   **c.** transcendent   **d.** effectual

SELECTION TEST

The Fall of the House of Usher
Edgar Allan Poe

Pupil's Edition page 262

Checking Vocabulary *(20 points)*

Match each word in the left-hand column with its meaning in the right-hand column. Place the letter of the correct meaning in the space provided. *(2 points each)*

____ **1.** demeanor

____ **2.** equivocal

____ **3.** morbid

____ **4.** pallid

____ **5.** palpable

____ **6.** prodigious

____ **7.** profuse

____ **8.** similitude

____ **9.** sojourn

____ **10.** stupor

a. pale

b. behavior; conduct

c. likeness

d. abundant

e. having more than one meaning

f. state of mental dullness

g. obvious; perceivable

h. diseased; unhealthy

i. short stay

j. of great size and power

Thoughtful Reading *(25 points)*

On the line provided, write the letter of the *best* answer to each of the following items. *(5 points each)*

____ **11.** The narrator's first impression of the House of Usher is of a building that
    a. promises the exciting adventure he longs for
    b. somehow stands in spite of obvious decay
    c. brings back bitter memories of his youth
    d. reminds him of pleasant times at school

____ **12.** Roderick Usher seems to be suffering mainly from
    a. a nervous disorder that affects his sensory reactions
    b. an inability to handle his household responsibilities
    c. poverty, resulting from poor business management
    d. guilt over the bad feelings between him and Madeline

____ **13.** Madeline's eventual fate is foreshadowed by
    a. her dislike of intrusions by visitors
    b. a disease which engenders deathlike trances
    c. a letter she has sent to the narrator
    d. a nightmare that reveals where she will eventually be buried

COLLECTIONS 5–6

_____ **14.** Which of the following statements *best* describes what eventually happens to the narrator?
  a. He grows in his awareness of the problems of aristocratic families.
  b. He heroically resolves to rescue Roderick from his fate.
  c. He is finally able to distinguish between reality and fantasy.
  d. He becomes enmeshed in the gloom of his surroundings.

_____ **15.** On a fateful night, in his bedroom, the narrator is strangely affected by ". . . the bewildering influence of the gloomy furniture of the room—of the dark and tattered draperies, which, tortured into motion by the breath of a rising tempest, swayed fitfully to and fro upon the walls, and rustled uneasily about the decorations of the bed." This passage is mainly intended to
  a. describe the effects of wind through an open window
  b. show the narrator's dislike of uncomfortable surroundings
  c. convey an atmosphere of unusual and ominous activity
  d. indicate that a malign intruder is in the room

Expanded Response *(30 points)*

16. After his sister dies and her body has been placed in a vault, Roderick becomes extremely agitated. Choose the statement below that *best* explains the reason for his agitation. On the lines provided, write the letter of the answer you choose and briefly defend your choice. Use at least one example from the selection to support your ideas. *(15 points)*
  a. His senses of sight and smell have become unbearably acute.
  b. He realizes suddenly that his family line will continue.
  c. He fears that Madeline has been buried alive.
  d. He strongly dislikes the story the narrator reads to him.

_____

_____

_____

17. At the climax of the story, Roderick twice shouts "Madman!" It is not clear to whom he is referring—himself or the narrator. In the chart that follows, explain how the word *madman* might describe either of the characters. Be sure to cite at least two examples from the selection to support your ideas. *(15 points)*

The madman is Roderick because . . .	The madman is the narrator because . . .

Written Response *(25 points)*

18. Whatever the gruesome furnishings of our nightmares, we may—strangely enough—choose to inhabit them for a while. The narrator of "The Fall of the House of Usher" remains for quite some time in the nightmarish atmosphere of the Ushers' home, in spite of the fact that he is gravely troubled. On a separate sheet of paper, suggest at least two reasons to explain why the narrator stays on at the house. Make at least two references to specific details in the selection to support your ideas.

SELECTION TEST

The Raven
Edgar Allan Poe   **Pupil's Edition page 282**

Thoughtful Reading *(40 points)*
On the line provided, write the letter of the *best* answer to each of the following items.
(8 points each)

_____ **1.** The speaker can best be described as a
    a. lonely elderly man longing for visitors
    b. magician conjuring up evil spirits
    c. melancholy person trying to forget a tragedy
    d. poet seeking inspiration for a new work

_____ **2.** At first encounter, the raven seems to be
    a. a frightening figment of the speaker's imagination
    b. a ghostly incarnation of a dead woman
    c. a symbol of darkness and death
    d. an entertaining and ungainly creature

_____ **3.** Approximately midway through the poem, the speaker's mood shifts from
    a. irritation to anger
    b. curiosity to melancholy
    c. despair to hope
    d. acceptance to vengefulness

_____ **4.** What effect does the raven's repetition of "Nevermore" have on the speaker?
    a. It plunges him into a deep despair.
    b. It helps him recall fond memories of Lenore.
    c. It reminds him that he can find the courage to go on.
    d. It does not distract him from his studies.

_____ **5.** In which lines below are the underlined words an example of **alliteration**?
    a. "Leave no black plume as a token of that lie thy soul hath spoken! /
    Leave my loneliness unbroken!—quit the bust above my door!"
    b. "Back into the chamber turning, all my soul within me burning, /
    Soon again I heard a tapping somewhat louder than before."
    c. "What this grim, ungainly, ghastly, gaunt, and ominous bird of yore— /
    Meant in croaking 'Nevermore.' "
    d. "On this home by Horror haunted—tell me truly, I implore— /
    Is there—*is* there balm in Gilead?—tell me—tell me, I implore!"

Expanded Response *(30 points)*

6. At the end of the poem, why does the speaker shift from apparent sanity into a wild frenzy? On the lines provided, write the letter of the answer you choose and briefly defend your choice. There is more than one possible answer. Use at least one example from the selection to support your ideas. *(15 points)*

   a. He is terrified of what will happen when he dies.
   b. He believes that the raven is an all-knowing demon.
   c. He realizes that he will never see Lenore again.
   d. He torments himself with sad thoughts.

   _____

   _____

   _____

   _____

   _____

   _____

   _____

   _____

7. What is realistic about the speaker's description of the raven in the poem? What is unrealistic about the description? Enter your ideas in the chart below, citing specific details from the selection. *(15 points)*

Realistic	Unrealistic

Written Response *(30 points)*

8. Edgar Allan Poe described the raven as being emblematic (symbolic) of "Mournful and never ending Remembrance" (see Pupil's Edition page 287). The bust of the Greek goddess Pallas Athena, upon which the raven perches, is symbolic of wisdom. On a separate sheet of paper, explore Poe's purpose in combining these symbols in the poem.

SELECTION TEST

The Minister's Black Veil
Nathaniel Hawthorne   **Pupil's Edition page 298**

Checking Vocabulary *(20 points)*
Match each word in the left-hand column with its meaning in the right-hand column. Place the letter of the correct meaning in the space provided. *(2 points each)*

_____	**1.** antipathy	**a.** wickedness
_____	**2.** iniquity	**b.** strong dislike
_____	**3.** obscurity	**c.** determined
_____	**4.** ostentatious	**d.** wise; keenly perceptive
_____	**5.** pensively	**e.** signify
_____	**6.** plausibility	**f.** conspicuous
_____	**7.** portend	**g.** outward appearance
_____	**8.** resolute	**h.** thinking deeply or seriously
_____	**9.** sagacious	**i.** something hidden or concealed
_____	**10.** semblance	**j.** believability

Thoughtful Reading *(25 points)*
On the line provided, write the letter of the *best* answer to each of the following items.
(5 points each)

_____ **11.** Mr. Hooper's sudden adoption of a black veil makes his congregation uneasy because
    a. they think he means to do them harm
    b. they can think of no explanation for his action
    c. it immediately reminds them of his sinfulness
    d. they believe he has had a terrible accident

_____ **12.** After permanently adopting the black veil, Hooper
    a. ignores his responsibilities as a minister
    b. frequently weeps and flies into rages
    c. accuses his congregation of terrible sins
    d. tends his congregation with his usual care

_____ **13.** The only individuals who readily understand the significance of Hooper's veil are
    a. little children
    b. the family of a young woman who has died
    c. people who are facing imminent death
    d. the family of Hooper's fiancée, Elizabeth

COLLECTIONS 5–6

_____ **14.** Though the story makes clear that Hooper is wearing the veil because of human sin, it is never entirely clear
   a. whose sins and what sins the veil stands for
   b. why the congregation continues to respect Hooper
   c. why Reverend Clark tries to remove the veil
   d. whether or not Elizabeth marries Hooper

_____ **15.** "The Minister's Black Veil" is a parable mainly because
   a. the characters and setting in the story are fictitious
   b. it is based on a famous story from the Bible
   c. it is up to the reader to draw a moral from the story
   d. the lesson in the story is plainly stated at the end

Expanded Response *(30 points)*
16. What does the black veil signify? On the lines provided, write the letter of the answer you choose and briefly defend your choice. There is more than one possible answer. Use at least one example from the selection to support your ideas. *(15 points)*
   a. the sins that all humans commit every day
   b. the false appearances we present to observers
   c. a belief that all people are doomed to eternal damnation
   d. a sin that Hooper believes he has committed

_____

_____

_____

_____

_____

17. Mr. Hooper's veil has a strong effect on people. Throughout his life, it elicits strong emotional responses and produces a variety of reactions. In the chart that follows, list positive and negative effects of the notorious veil that are experienced by Mr. Hooper and his parishioners. *(15 points)*

Positive Effects	Negative Effects

Written Response *(25 points)*
18. As Hooper lies dying, he cries out, "Why do you tremble at me alone? . . . Tremble also at each other!" On a separate sheet of paper, tell what you think Hooper means by this anguished cry. Support your opinion with at least two references to specific details from the story.

SELECTION TEST

The Quarter-Deck
Herman Melville   **Pupil's Edition page 313**

Checking Vocabulary *(20 points)*
Match each word in the left-hand column with its meaning in the right-hand column. Place the letter of the correct meaning in the space provided. *(4 points each)*

_____ **1.** imprecations   **a.** will

_____ **2.** inscrutable   **b.** answer

_____ **3.** tacit   **c.** curses

_____ **4.** volition   **d.** mysterious

_____ **5.** rejoinder   **e.** implied but not expressed openly

Thoughtful Reading *(25 points)*
On the line provided, write the letter of the *best* answer to each of the following items.
(5 points each)

_____ **6.** As Ahab paces the deck, the picture we get is that of
    a. a fastidious captain inspecting his ship
    b. a man with a disability exercising to regain his strength
    c. a man obsessed with his private dilemmas
    d. an old sailor who feels useless and misunderstood

_____ **7.** Ahab's search for Moby-Dick seems motivated mainly by his desire to
    a. train his crew to kill the most valuable of the whales
    b. prove that he is a competent commander
    c. obtain revenge for the loss of his leg
    d. enjoy dangerous adventures on the high seas

_____ **8.** Ahab's quarter-deck speech engenders in most of the sailors
    a. a distrust of their captain
    b. enthusiasm for finding the white whale
    c. happy memories of previous whaling trips
    d. a demand for extra pay

_____ **9.** After Ahab's speech on the quarter-deck, Starbuck murmurs, "God keep me!—keep us all!" With these words, Starbuck reveals his
    a. agreement with Ahab's goals
    b. regret at choosing the life of a sailor
    c. plans to encourage a shipboard mutiny
    d. horror at Ahab's apparent madness

_____ **10.** Captain Ahab's ceremony on deck
    a. resembles a religious communion
    b. resembles a common maritime ritual
    c. represents an appeal to the spirit of Moby-Dick
    d. represents concern for the crew's spiritual welfare

COLLECTIONS 5–6

Expanded Response *(30 points)*

11. Most of the sailors aboard the *Pequod* seem to support Ahab's quest for Moby-Dick. Considering what you have read thus far, what do you think is the main reason for this general concurrence? On the lines provided, write the letter of the answer you choose and briefly defend your choice. There is more than one possible answer. Use at least one example from the selection to support your ideas. *(15 points)*

a. They are motivated by the promise of a reward.

b. Each crew member remembers an injury that Moby-Dick has caused him.

c. They have sympathy for Ahab and want to help him.

d. Other: _____

_____

_____

_____

_____

_____

12. Ahab has shown himself to be both a skilled commander and a single-minded zealot. In the chart, support both views of Ahab with details from the selection. *(15 points)*

Skilled Commander	Single-Minded Zealot

Written Response *(25 points)*

13. Starbuck says, "Vengeance on a dumb brute! . . . that simply smote thee from blindest instinct! Madness! To be enraged with a dumb thing, Captain Ahab, seems blasphemous." What does Starbuck mean by a "dumb brute" and by "blindest instinct"? Why does he consider Ahab's rage "blasphemous"? Do you agree with Starbuck's opinions? Why or why not? On a separate sheet of paper, write a paragraph responding to these questions.

SELECTION TEST

from Moby-Dick
Herman Melville

Pupil's Edition page 321

Checking Vocabulary *(20 points)*
Match each word in the left-hand column with its meaning in the right-hand column. Place the letter of the correct meaning in the space provided. *(4 points each)*

_____ **1.** apparition

a. scholarly; well-informed

_____ **2.** erudite

b. fierce cruelty

_____ **3.** ferocity

c. disabled

_____ **4.** incapacitated

d. unexpected sight or ghostlike figure that appears suddenly

_____ **5.** ubiquitous

e. everywhere at the same time

Thoughtful Reading *(25 points)*
On the line provided, write the letter of the *best* answer to each of the following items.
(5 points each)

_____ **6.** As Ishmael recounts his memories of the voyage, he recalls how
  a. enthusiastically he joined Ahab's quest
  b. bitterly he reacted to Ahab's orders
  c. sympathetic he was toward Moby-Dick
  d. brave he felt during Moby-Dick's attack

_____ **7.** Moby-Dick has become a legend among whalers because he
  a. leads a huge pod of sperm whales
  b. shows a strange tolerance toward sailors who pursue him
  c. is rumored to appear simultaneously in different oceans
  d. represents the tremendous profits to be made from whaling

_____ **8.** In his calamitous first encounter with Moby-Dick, Ahab
  a. uses his willpower to drive the whale away
  b. attacks the whale with a six-inch knife
  c. flees in fear from the whale's attack
  d. experiences a religious conversion

_____ **9.** For some time after his tragic accident, Ahab manages to
  a. hide his vengeful obsession under a veneer of sanity
  b. openly share his feelings about his mishap
  c. avoid subsequent duties as a whaling captain
  d. transfer his anger with Moby-Dick to other whales

_____ **10.** In Ahab's mind, Moby-Dick represents
  a. the difficulties faced by all people who go to sea
  b. an element of the natural world that should be tamed
  c. a creature with virtues Ahab wishes to acquire
  d. evil forces that must be overcome and defeated

Expanded Response *(30 points)*

11. Why are whalers in awe of the great whales they hunt? On the lines provided, write the letter of the answer you choose and briefly defend your choice. There is more than one possible answer. Use at least one example from the selection to support your ideas. *(15 points)*

   a. The whales often seem to outwit and evade their hunters.

   b. Most sailors are convinced that whales are evil.

   c. Whales are at home in an environment hostile to humans.

   d. Legends and myths have sprung up about the behavior of whales.

_____

_____

_____

_____

_____

12. In this chapter, Ishmael, the narrator, describes Moby-Dick from several different points of view. In the chart below, record details about the whale from the perspective of the objective narrator, the superstitious sailors, and Captain Ahab. *(15 points)*

Perceptions of Moby-Dick		
Ishmael	**Sailors**	**Ahab**

Written Response *(25 points)*

13. Ahab is a leader who manages to convert many followers to his cause. On a separate sheet of paper, describe at least three personal characteristics that enable Ahab to draw others into his single-minded quest. Then compare and contrast these characteristics with those of a leader in today's world.

COLLECTION 6 TEST

The Realms of Darkness

Responding to Literature *(70 points)*

1. The characters listed below become involved in stressful, sometimes traumatic situations. Choose the character you believe copes *best* with the situation he or she faces, and the character you believe copes worst. Enter their names in the chart below. In the first column, briefly describe the situations. In the second column, note how the characters react. *(10 points)*

The narrator of "The Fall of the House of Usher"   Elizabeth, in "The Minister's Black Veil"
The speaker in "The Raven"   Ahab, in *Moby-Dick*

Situation	Character's Reaction
Character Who Copes Best:	
Character Who Copes Worst:	

2. The selections in Collection 6 involve characters with secrets. In the second column of the chart that follows, name a character from the selection and describe his or her secrets. In the third column, indicate whether your curiosity about these secrets has been satisfied. If so, how? If not, why not? *(10 points)*

Selection	Character and Secret(s)	Is Your Curiosity Satisfied?
"The Fall of the House of Usher"		
"The Raven"		
"The Minister's Black Veil"		
Moby-Dick		

COLLECTIONS 5–6

Respond to each of the questions below. Attach an extra sheet of paper if necessary.
(25 points each)

3. Write a paragraph explaining why you think stories and poems about the "realms of darkness" are popular with so many readers. Support your explanation with at least one example from each of the selections.

_____

_____

_____

_____

_____

_____

_____

_____

_____

_____

4. Write a paragraph discussing the major symbol in one of the selections listed below. Explain what the concrete symbol is, how it functions in the story or poem, and what it stands for.

"The Fall of the House of Usher"   "The Minister's Black Veil"
"The Raven"   *Moby-Dick*

_____

_____

_____

_____

_____

_____

_____

_____

_____

_____

Vocabulary Review *(10 points)*

In the space provided, write the letter of the word that correctly completes the sentence. *(2 points each)*

5. If a remark is _____, it can be interpreted in different ways.
   a. morbid   **b.** palpable   **c.** insipid   **d.** equivocal

6. Her _____ look showed that she was observing us carefully.
   a. obstinate   **b.** specious   **c.** tacit   **d.** scrutinizing

7. Was Ahab a(n) _____ captain, or was he blindly issuing foolish commands?
   a. sagacious   **b.** ostentatious   **c.** resolute   **d.** vivacious

8. The speaker in "The Raven" is _____, but all his learning cannot help him escape the raven's spell.
   a. prodigious   **b.** erudite   **c.** inordinate   **d.** ubiquitous

9. Tales from the Realms of Darkness often seem _____, but half the fun for the reader lies in deciphering their mysteries.
   a. incapacitated   **b.** emaciated   **c.** inscrutable   **d.** profuse

Language Workshop Review: Achieving Parallel Structure *(20 points)*

Rewrite the following sentences by expressing ideas of equal importance in the sentence using the same grammatical form. In most cases, more than one parallel structure is possible. You may have to add or delete words for clarity. *(4 points each)*

EXAMPLE: Mr. Hooper's parishoners began to doubt his skill as a minister and questioning his mysterious actions.

Mr. Hooper's parishoners began to doubt his skill as a minister and to question his mysterious actions.

10. Mr. Hooper's parishioners were bewildered by the black veil and asking each other what it meant. _____

_____

11. Ignoring what he heard was Roderick's way to deny what he knew was true—that Madeline was still alive. _____

_____

12. Captain Ahab's crew was enthusiastic about the hunt for Moby-Dick and eagerly wanting to kill the white whale.

_____

_____

13. Madeline's body had been put into the vault and they had shut the door tightly.

_____

_____

14. Captain Ahab's desire for revenge was all-consuming, and he was obsessed with it.

_____

COLLECTIONS 5-6

LITERARY PERIOD TEST

The American Renaissance: A Literary Coming of Age

Reading a Letter
Read the following letter that Herman Melville wrote to Nathaniel Hawthorne. Then answer the questions that follow the letter.

June, 1851

My Dear Hawthorne—

I should have been rumbling down to you in my pine-board chariot a long time ago, were it not that for some weeks past I have been more busy than you can well imagine,—out of doors,—building and patching and tinkering away in all directions. Besides, I had my crops to get in,—corn and potatoes (I hope to show you some famous ones by and by),—and many other things to attend to, all accumulating upon this one particular season. I work myself; and at night my bodily sensations are akin to those I have so often felt before, when a hired man, doing my day's work from sun to sun. But I mean to continue visiting you until you tell me that my visits are both supererogatory and <u>superfluous</u>. With no son of man do I stand upon any etiquette or ceremony, except the Christian ones of charity and honesty. . . .

I began by saying that the reason I have not been to Lenox is this,—in the evening I feel completely done up, as the phrase is, and incapable of the long jolting to get to your house and back. In a week or so, I go to New York, to bury myself in a third-story room, and work and slave on my "Whale" [the original title of *Moby-Dick*] while it is driving through the press. *That* is the only way I can finish it now,—I am so pulled hither and thither by circumstances. The calm, the coolness, the silent grass-growing mood in which a man *ought* always to compose,—that, I fear, can seldom be mine. Dollars damn me; and the malicious Devil is forever grinning in upon me, holding the door ajar. My dear Sir, a <u>presentiment</u> is on me,—I shall at last be worn out and perish, like an old nutmeg-grater, grated to pieces by the constant <u>attrition</u> of the wood, that is, the nutmeg. What I feel most moved to write, that is <u>banned</u>,—it will not pay. Yet, altogether, write the *other* way I cannot. So the product is a final hash, and all my books are botches. I'm rather sore, perhaps, in this letter; but see my hand! four blisters on this palm, made by hoes and hammers within the last few days. It is a rainy morning; so I am indoors, and all work suspended. I feel cheerfully disposed, and therefore I write a little bluely. . . . If ever, my dear Hawthorne, in the eternal times that are to come, you and I shall sit down in Paradise, in some little shady corner by ourselves; and if we shall by any means be able to smuggle a basket of champagne there . . . and if we shall then cross our celestial legs in the celestial grass that is forever tropical, and strike our glasses and our heads together, till both musically ring in concert,—then, O my dear fellow-mortal, how shall we pleasantly discourse of all the things <u>manifold</u> which now so distress us,—when all the earth shall be but a reminiscence, yea, its final <u>dissolution</u> an antiquity. Then shall songs be composed as when wars are over: humorous, comic songs,—"Oh, when I lived in that queer little hole called the world," or, "Oh, when I toiled and sweated below," or, "Oh, when I knocked and was knocked in the fight"—yes, let us look forward to such things. Let us swear that, though now we sweat, yet it is because of the dry heat which is indispensable to the nourishment of the vine which is to bear the grapes that are to give us the champagne hereafter.

But I was talking about the "Whale." As the fishermen say, "he's in his flurry" when I left him some three weeks ago. I'm going to take him by his jaw, however, before long, and finish him up in some fashion or other. What's the use of elaborating what, in its very essence, is so short-lived as a modern book? Though I wrote the Gospels in this century, I should die in the gutter.—I talk all about myself, and this is selfishness and egotism. Granted. But how help it? I am writing to you; I know little about you, but something about myself. So I write about myself,—at least to you. . . .

—H. Melville

HRW material copyrighted under notice appearing earlier in this book.

Understanding Vocabulary (20 points)

Each of the underlined words below has also been underlined in the selection. Use context clues in the selection to help you determine each word's meaning. Then, on the line provided, write the letter of the word or words that *best* complete each sentence. *(4 points each)*

_____ **1.** A visit is <u>superfluous</u> if it is
   a. beyond what is required   **b.** welcome and pleasing   **c.** emotional

_____ **2.** A <u>presentiment</u> is a
   a. ceremonial gift   **b.** fearful anticipation   **c.** happy recollection

_____ **3.** <u>Attrition</u> of an object occurs when the object is
   a. connected to a crime   **b.** lost because of carelessness   **c.** worn away by friction

_____ **4.** Things or circumstances are <u>manifold</u> when they are
   a. of many, varied kinds   **b.** obvious to all beholders   **c.** designed to mislead

_____ **5.** In the selection, the <u>dissolution</u> of earth refers to the earth's
   a. cruel indifference   **b.** basic evil   **c.** final extinction

Thoughtful Reading (35 points)

On the line provided, write the letter of the *best* answer to each of the following items. *(7 points each)*

_____ **6.** Melville's main excuse for not visiting Hawthorne recently is that he
   a. has been in New York working on his book *Moby-Dick*
   b. is frankly envious of Hawthorne's literary success
   c. has been occupied with farm and household work
   d. is convinced that he has a fatal illness

_____ **7.** Melville is discouraged about writing because
   a. his publisher has refused to read his manuscript
   b. he cannot please both himself and the public
   c. he is at a loss for a suitable subject
   d. his past mistakes distract and torment him

_____ **8.** Melville feels that the best environment for a writer is
   a. the excitement and stimulation of a big city
   b. a workshop with other dedicated writers
   c. a convivial, party-like atmosphere
   d. an atmosphere of peace and calm

_____ **9.** In speaking of "the dry heat which is indispensable to the nourishment of the vine," Melville is referring to the
   a. hardship that may be necessary to the creation of great writing
   b. idea that writers should take time out for hard physical labor
   c. harsh criticism that other writers have leveled at his work
   d. influence on his own work of Hawthorne's bitter views of life

COLLECTIONS 5-6

_____ **10.** In speaking of the "Whale," Melville says, "What's the use of elaborating what, in its very essence, is so short-lived as a modern book?" From a contemporary perspective, what is ironic about Melville's comment?
  a. Melville spent a great deal of time writing his book.
  b. The book has become a long-lived classic.
  c. Much popular fiction is soon forgotten.
  d. *Moby-Dick* is an extremely long and complex book.

Expanded Response *(15 points)*

11. Melville concludes his letter by saying, "I know little about you, but something about myself. So I write about myself,—at least to you. . . ." What aspect of himself does Melville display best in his letter? On the lines provided, write the letter of the answer you choose and briefly defend your choice. There is more than one possible answer. Use at least one example from the letter to support your ideas.
  a. his desire to abandon writing and become a full-time farmer
  b. his ability to view the writer's life with humor and objectivity
  c. his dislike of having to depend upon writing as a way of making a living
  d. his fear that his written works are of poor quality

_____

_____

_____

_____

Written Response *(30 points)*

12. In his letter to Hawthorne, Melville refers to the influence of nature on his immediate, day-to-day life. On a separate sheet of paper, write a paragraph that compares Melville's attitude toward nature, as seen in his letter, with the attitudes of Emerson and Thoreau, as seen in the selections in this unit. Make references to specific details from the selections to support your ideas. Use the chart below to organize your thoughts before you begin to write.

Attitudes Toward Nature		
Melville	**Emerson**	**Thoreau**

SELECTION TEST

I Hear America Singing
from Song of Myself, 10, 33, and 52
A Sight in Camp in the Daybreak Gray and Dim
Walt Whitman

Pupil's Edition page 351
Pupil's Edition pages 353–359
Pupil's Edition page 362

Thoughtful Reading *(40 points)*
On the line provided, write the letter of the *best* answer to each of the following items.
(5 points each)

_____ 1. In "I Hear America Singing," Whitman presents Americans as
   a. straining to break free of poor living conditions
   b. working industriously in a variety of occupations
   c. yearning for their old homelands and cultures
   d. competing vigorously to rise into the middle class

_____ 2. "I Hear America Singing" is a catalog because it
   a. lists related categories of people and events
   b. invites readers to choose items from a list
   c. organizes details about the tools needed in different trades
   d. appears in a volume describing the habits of Americans

_____ 3. In "Song of Myself," Number 10, the speaker
   a. presents herself or himself as an observer and a participant in several situations
   b. explains why life in the United States is filled with danger and sadness
   c. concentrates on his or her own trials and tribulations as a pioneer of American poetry
   d. presents a detailed argument why slavery is morally wrong

_____ 4. How could you demonstrate the cadence of "Song of Myself," Number 10?
   a. Read the stanza aloud to show how your voice rhythmically rises and falls.
   b. Point out how its images convey meaning.
   c. Explain the theme of brotherhood that underlies each line.
   d. Show how each line has end rhyme.

_____ 5. "Song of Myself," Number 33, presents heroes who
   a. are well known by name to most Americans
   b. have fought in wars to secure democracy and freedom
   c. represent the valiant deeds of ordinary people
   d. find inspiration through poetry

_____ 6. In "Song of Myself," Number 52, Whitman expresses the theme of the speaker's
   a. sense of wonder about America's new cities
   b. longing for simpler days gone by
   c. delight in her or his own mind and spirit
   d. dismay over the corruption of the wilderness

_____ 7. In "A Sight in Camp in the Daybreak Gray and Dim," Whitman stresses the
   a. fierceness of the soldiers in opposing armies
   b. reasons behind the war between North and South
   c. hardships he endured as a nurse during the war
   d. innocence of the war's individual victims

COLLECTIONS 7–8

_____ **8.** In general, Whitman's tone in these poems could *best* be described as
    a. detached and observant   **c.** emotional and subjective
    b. humorous and ironic   **d.** pessimistic and grim

Expanded Response *(30 points)*

9. Choose the option that *best* completes the following statement. On the lines provided, write the letter of the answer you choose and briefly defend your choice. There is more than one possible answer. Use at least one example from the selections to support your ideas. *(15 points)*
The power of Whitman's poetry derives from his
    a. focus on the day-to-day lives of ordinary Americans
    b. use of nontraditional forms
    c. ability to combine observation and personal reactions
    d. scholarly study of the causes of war

_____

_____

_____

_____

10. Walt Whitman made full use of the poetic elements of free verse: alliteration, assonance, imagery, onomatopoeia, and parallel structure. Read the following passage from "Song of Myself," Number 33. In the chart that follows, record the free verse elements employed in these lines. *(15 points)*

    I am the mashed fireman with breast-bone broken,
    Tumbling walls buried me in their debris,
    Heat and smoke I inspired, I heard the yelling shouts of my comrades,
    I heard the distant click of their picks and shovels, . . .

Alliteration	Assonance	Imagery	Onomatopoeia	Parallel Structure

Written Response *(30 points)*

11. In "Song of Myself," Number 52, Whitman writes

    "I sound my barbaric yawp over the roofs of the world."

On a separate sheet of paper, explain what you think Whitman means by this statement. Make at least two references to specific details in the selection to support your ideas.

SELECTION TEST

Poetry of Emily Dickinson

Thoughtful Reading (40 points)

On the line provided, write the letter of the *best* answer to each of the following items.
(5 points each)

_____ 1. Which phrase below *best* describes Dickinson's style?
    a. playful and careless
    b. unique and controlled
    c. free-flowing and wordy
    d. gloomy and pessimistic

_____ 2. To build metaphors and images in her poems, Dickinson draws mostly on
    a. her anger at the disappointments of romantic love
    b. the ideals and ideas of other New England poets
    c. her observations of her family's behavior
    d. her knowledge of the natural world

_____ 3. In "Heart! We will forget him!" and "I died for Beauty—but was scarce," Dickinson shows her gift for
    a. using poetry to solve the major problems of life
    b. setting up a dialogue between contrasting impulses
    c. incorporating formal religious beliefs into poems
    d. describing the deathbed agonies of a loved one

_____ 4. In "Success is counted sweetest," Dickinson implies that
    a. success is most valued by those who haven't attained it
    b. successful people take immense pride in their achievements
    c. she doesn't deserve the fame her poems have brought her
    d. real poets do not yearn for success and worldly praise

_____ 5. Dickinson arranges and punctuates her lines in a distinctive way to
    a. emphasize the pauses and transitions in her expressions
    b. make her true feelings difficult for readers to decipher
    c. obscure her lack of formal schooling
    d. introduce topics that other poets do not address

_____ 6. Many people consider Dickinson to have been a hermit because
    a. she did not tolerate ideas that were different from hers
    b. her poetry harshly criticizes society, especially urban life
    c. she lived a secluded life in a small town
    d. her poems show a lack of awareness of reality

_____ 7. In "Because I could not stop for Death," the speaker
    a. does not understand the full meaning of eternity until after he or she has died
    b. thinks that immortality is an illusion
    c. sees a kindly coachman turn into a gruesome skeleton
    d. recalls all the stages of life through which he or she passes

_____ 8. Dickinson's particular contribution to poetry can *best* be described as exemplifying how to
    a. share ideas with a wide audience
    b. stress thoughts instead of feelings
    c. edit work to make it verbose
    d. express ideas in original ways

COLLECTIONS 7–8

Expanded Response *(30 points)*

9. One theme in Dickinson's poetry is death. Choose the poem that you believe *best* illustrates Dickinson's concept of death. On the lines provided, write the letter of the poem you choose and briefly defend your choice, summarizing the poem's message about death. There is more than one possible answer. *(15 points)*

   a. "I died for Beauty—but was scarce"
   b. "Because I could not stop for Death"
   c. "I heard a Fly buzz—when I died"
   d. "Much Madness is divinest Sense"

   _____

   _____

   _____

   _____

10. Another of Dickinson's recurring themes concerns love. In the following web, note what you think Dickinson is saying about love in each of the poems. *(15 points)*

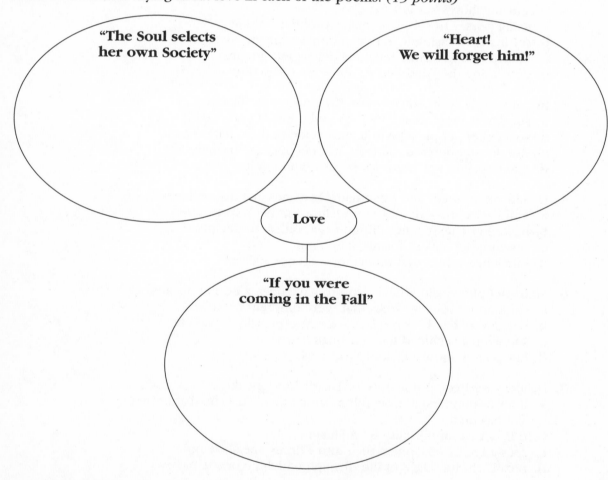

"The Soul selects her own Society"

"Heart! We will forget him!"

Love

"If you were coming in the Fall"

Written Response *(30 points)*

11. Can a reclusive, isolated person gather any wisdom about the world at large? On a separate sheet of paper, answer this question with regard to Dickinson and her poems. Make at least two references to details in the poems to support your ideas.

THE AMERICAN LANGUAGE

A Period of Vocabulary Growth

Pupil's Edition page 398

On the line provided, write the letter of the *best* answer to each of the following items.
(10 points each)

_____ **1.** One characteristic of the language of the backwoods was its
  a. use of precise syntax
  b. use of exaggerated slang and exuberant bragging
  c. closeness to British English
  d. blending of English and American Indian languages

_____ **2.** The Crockett almanacs are notable because they
  a. damaged Davy Crockett's political career
  b. set a new standard for American language
  c. brought backwoods language into Eastern homes
  d. supplied vital information about Tennessee

_____ **3.** In the first half of the nineteenth century, Americans called for an independent literature that would
  a. capture the distinctive American landscape and culture
  b. deal with the great themes of world literature
  c. copy the style and themes of English literature
  d. set a standard for national American usage

_____ **4.** Both Mark Twain and Walt Whitman made use of
  a. the King's English
  b. standard literary American language
  c. the language of American cities
  d. American vernacular

_____ **5.** From the political campaigns of the nineteenth century, we have inherited
  a. widespread use of the stump style
  b. colorful words and phrases coined by politicians
  c. the use of exaggerated language
  d. the tradition of long, rambling speeches

_____ **6.** Newspapers flourished in the late 1830s because
  a. improved printing methods made them cheap and profitable
  b. they were vastly improved in quality
  c. more and more people knew how to read
  d. the American population had increased greatly

_____ **7.** In the late 1830s, newspapers tried to attract readers by
  a. providing comprehensive news coverage
  b. including contests and puzzles
  c. offering special subscription rates
  d. using colorful language

_____ **8.** The language used in newspapers often involved the
   a. use of alliteration and assonance
   b. invention of whimsical abbreviations
   c. invention of adjectives and adverbs
   d. use of complex sentences

_____ **9.** An immigrant group that had a strong effect on the American language
   during the mid-nineteenth century was the
   a. Irish
   b. British
   c. German
   d. Polish

_____ **10.** The language that provided the greatest number of loanwords to the American language
   in the nineteenth century was
   a. German
   b. Spanish
   c. Polish
   d. Russian

LITERARY PERIOD TEST

A New American Poetry: Whitman and Dickinson

Reading Two Poems

Read the following two poems carefully. Then answer the questions that follow.

Aboard at a Ship's Helm
by Walt Whitman

Aboard at a ship's helm,
A young steersman steering with care.
Through fog on a sea-coast dolefully ringing,
An ocean-bell—O a warning bell, rock'd by the waves.
5   O you give good notice indeed, you bell by the sea-reefs ringing,
Ringing, ringing, to warn the ship from its wreck-place.

For as on the alert O steersman, you mind the loud admonition,
The bows turn, the freighted ship tacking speeds away under
   her gray sails,
The beautiful and noble ship with all her precious wealth speeds
   away gayly and safe.
10 But O the ship, the immortal ship! O ship aboard the ship!
Ship of the body, ship of the soul, voyaging, voyaging, voyaging.

The Moon is distant from the Sea
by Emily Dickinson

The Moon is distant from the Sea—
And yet, with Amber Hands—
She leads Him—docile as a Boy—
Along appointed Sands—

5   He never misses a Degree—
Obedient to Her Eye
He comes just so far—toward the Town—
Just so far—goes away—

Oh, Signor, Thine, the Amber Hand—
10 And mine—the distant Sea—
Obedient to the least command
Thine eye impose on me—

COLLECTIONS 7–8

Understanding Vocabulary *(20 points)*

Each of the underlined words below has also been underlined in one of the poems. Use context clues in the poem to help you determine the word's meaning. Then, on the line provided, write the letter of the word or words that best complete each sentence. *(4 points each)*

1. In the Whitman poem, a bell is ringing dolefully, or _____.
   a. cheerily   **b.** mournfully   **c.** hopelessly

2. The bell's admonition _____ sailors about a nearby reef.
   a. puzzles   **b.** warns   **c.** scolds

3. When applied to a ship, tacking means _____.
   a. suddenly sinking   **b.** moving toward land   **c.** changing direction

4. In the Dickinson poem, the sea is called docile because it is _____ to the moon.
   a. helpful   **b.** hostile   **c.** submissive

5. The Degree referred to in the poem is an _____.
   a. assigned direction   **b.** official rank   **c.** academic title

Thoughtful Reading *(35 points)*

On the line provided, write the letter of the *best* answer to each of the following items. *(7 points each)*

_____ 6. Both the Whitman poem and the Dickinson poem are examples of poetry that
   a. abandons conventional rhyme and meter
   b. stresses the pangs of unrequited love
   c. praises the work of ordinary people
   d. captures the cadence of public speakers

_____ 7. In the first stanza of the Whitman poem, the speaker describes
   a. the fear in the heart of an inexperienced sailor
   b. a rocky shore that inevitably wrecks ships
   c. a fog-bound ship approaching a reef
   d. the deceptive nature of many warnings

_____ 8. In the last two lines of the Whitman poem, the speaker suggests that
   a. all dangers can be avoided if we heed the warnings
   b. ocean voyages are filled with excitement
   c. the ship is loaded with pirated gold
   d. the human soul faces a difficult life journey

_____ 9. In the Dickinson poem, the moon and the sea are metaphors for
   a. uncaring and cold natural forces
   b. a strict teacher and a frightened pupil
   c. a loved one and the speaker
   d. the effect of a rising and falling tide

_____ 10. An example of slant rhyme in the Dickinson poem is
   a. Hands–Sands
   b. Eye–away
   c. Sea–me
   d. Along–appointed

Expanded Response (15 points)

11. What do you think is the most striking similarity between the Whitman and Dickinson poems? Choose what you believe is the *strongest* response to this question. On the lines provided, write the letter of the answer you choose and briefly defend your choice. There is more than one possible answer. Support your ideas with at least one reference to each poem.

    a. the use of sea imagery
    b. the free verse the poems employ
    c. the deep emotion expressed in the poems
    d. the use of central metaphors

    _____

    _____

    _____

    _____

    _____

Written Response (30 points)

12. Both the Dickinson and the Whitman poems celebrate and appeal to aspects of the human spirit. On the lines provided, explain which poem you consider to be more universal in its appeal, and show how this poem is like another you have read by the same writer.

    _____

    _____

    _____

    _____

    _____

    _____

    _____

    _____

    _____

    _____

    _____

    _____

    _____

    _____

COLLECTIONS 7–8

SELECTION TEST

The Battle with Mr. Covey
Frederick Douglass

Pupil's Edition page 425

Checking Vocabulary (20 points)
Indicate whether the following pairs of words are synonyms or antonyms by circling the **S** or **A** to the left of the item number. (2 points each)

S   A   **1.** intimated : proclaimed

S   A   **2.** comply : obey

S   A   **3.** interpose : withdraw

S   A   **4.** solemnity : lightness

S   A   **5.** render : make

S   A   **6.** singular : remarkable

S   A   **7.** attributed : dissociated

S   A   **8.** curry : groom

S   A   **9.** expiring : beginning

S   A   **10.** afforded : provided

Thoughtful Reading (25 points)
On the line provided, write the letter of the *best* answer to each of the following items.
(5 points each)

_____ **11.** During the course of this selection, Douglass shows how he
   a. is consumed by fear
   b. is reduced from defiance to submission
   c. moves from fear to defiance
   d. remains defiant throughout

_____ **12.** Which of the following statements is **not** true about Douglass at the conclusion of the selection?
   a. He regularly receives physical abuse from white men.
   b. He is still enslaved by Master Thomas.
   c. He vows that anyone who wishes to whip him must also kill him.
   d. He regains his sense of freedom and dignity.

_____ **13.** Douglass walks to Master Thomas's store to
   a. plot revenge
   b. visit friends
   c. seek help
   d. recover from his injuries

_____ **14.** Sandy advises Douglass to carry a root in his pocket that will
   a. make Covey a more humane, compassionate overseer
   b. secure his freedom if it is never removed
   c. heal the wounds that might be incurred during whippings
   d. make it impossible for any white man to whip him

_____ **15.** When Covey tries to bind Douglass's legs with a rope, Douglass
   a. bows down and begs Covey for mercy
   b. fights back by grabbing Covey by the throat
   c. escapes and runs away to St. Michael's
   d. rallies the other slaves to his assistance

COLLECTIONS 9-10

Expanded Response *(30 points)*

16. In the boxes below, briefly describe the events that precipitate Douglass's eventual rebellion against Covey. Be sure to record the events in the order in which they occur. The first box has been filled in for you as an example. *(15 points)*

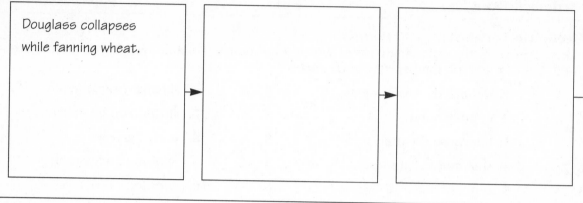

Douglass collapses while fanning wheat.

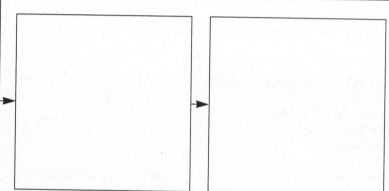

17. In your opinion, which of Douglass's actions involves the greatest risk? On the lines provided, write the letter of the answer you choose and briefly defend your choice. There is more than one possible answer. Use at least one example from the selection to support your ideas. *(15 points)*

a. traveling to St. Michael's
b. hiding in the cornfield
c. fighting with Mr. Covey
d. other: _____

_____

_____

_____

_____

_____

Written Response *(25 points)*

18. On a separate sheet of paper, write one paragraph that describes how Douglass was mistreated and how he responded to this abuse. Support your description with at least three examples from the selection.

SELECTION TEST

A Pair of Silk Stockings
Kate Chopin

Pupil's Edition page 436

Checking Vocabulary *(20 points)*
Match each word in the left-hand column with its antonym in the right-hand column. Place the letter of the correct antonym in the space provided. *(2 points each)*

_____	**1.** judicious	**a.**	lamenting
_____	**2.** appreciable	**b.**	imperceptible
_____	**3.** veritable	**c.**	unmoving
_____	**4.** acute	**d.**	irrational
_____	**5.** laborious	**e.**	easy
_____	**6.** reveling	**f.**	false
_____	**7.** fastidious	**g.**	easygoing
_____	**8.** preposterous	**h.**	dull
_____	**9.** gaudy	**i.**	sophisticated
_____	**10.** poignant	**j.**	reasonable

Thoughtful Reading *(25 points)*
On the line provided, write the letter of the *best* answer to each of the following items.
(5 points each)

_____ **11.** A wise use of her fifteen dollars, Mrs. Sommers thinks at the beginning of the story, would be to spend the money on
    a. kid gloves for herself   **c.** clothes for her children
    b. a nutritious lunch   **d.** a matinée at the theater

_____ **12.** At the beginning of the story, Mrs. Sommers is characterized as a
    a. dutiful, careful parent   **c.** flighty, irresponsible person
    b. neglectful mother   **d.** cheerful person

_____ **13.** Mrs. Sommers's new clothes make her feel
    a. guilty and ashamed of her selfishness
    b. fearful of her family's reaction
    c. self-assured, as if she belongs among the well dressed
    d. regretful that she does not dress this way every day

_____ **14.** The explanation for Mrs. Sommers's spending spree is that she
    a. thinks it won't matter   **c.** has plenty of money left at home
    b. is acting on impulse   **d.** has saved for the occasion

COLLECTIONS 9-10

_____ **15.** As she rides home on the cable car, Mrs. Sommers feels
- **a.** satisfaction and peace
- **b.** a terrible wave of remorse
- **c.** guilty about her children
- **d.** a certain longing to escape

Expanded Response *(30 points)*

16. This story tells us about Mrs. Sommers's current daily existence. In addition, we get a glimpse of what her life might once have been like and how she would like it to be in the future. In the chart below are three columns labeled *Once, Now,* and *Future.* In the column labeled *Once,* tell what you think Mrs. Sommers's life was like before her marriage. In the column labeled *Now,* describe what Mrs. Sommers's life is like currently. Then in the column labeled *Future,* tell what you think her life will be like in the years to come. For each category, provide at least two examples. A sample response is provided for each column. *(15 points)*

Once	Now	Future
She had fine clothes and accessories.	Her clothes and accessories are threadbare and simple.	Guilt will cause her to buy clothing for her children first, herself last.

17. On her shopping spree, Mrs. Sommers satisfies desires and needs that have long been repressed. Which of the following activities most thoroughly satisfies those desires and needs? On the lines provided, write the letter of the answer you choose and briefly defend your choice. There is more than one possible answer. Use at least one example from the selection to support your ideas. *(15 points)*
- **a.** purchasing the silk stockings
- **b.** having lunch at the restaurant
- **c.** attending the theater matinée
- **d.** other: _____

_____

_____

_____

_____

_____

Written Response *(25 points)*

18. On a separate sheet of paper, write one paragraph that explains why you think Mrs. Sommers spends the fifteen dollars in the way she does rather than in the way she had originally planned. Support your explanation with an example from the selection.

Elements of Literature

COLLECTION 9 TEST

Shackles

Responding to Literature *(70 points)*

1. In "The Battle with Mr. Covey" and "A Pair of Silk Stockings," people break free, if only temporarily, from the shackles that have held them in bondage. Use the chart below to explain the action each individual takes and the result(s) of his or her action. *(10 points)*

	Action Taken to Break Free from Bondage	Result(s) of Action
Frederick Douglass		
Mrs. Sommers		

2. In the Venn diagram below, note details about the character traits and circumstances of Frederick Douglass and Mrs. Sommers. In the overlapping space, indicate the character traits and circumstances they share. *(10 points)*

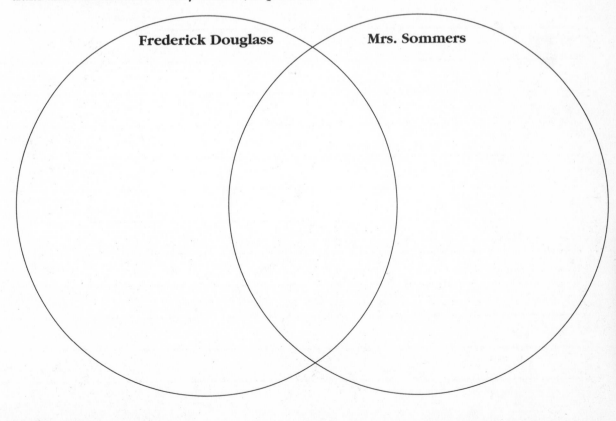

Elements of Literature

Respond to each of the following questions. Attach an extra sheet of paper if necessary.
(25 points each)

3. Explain how a person can be free even in the midst of a society that relegates him or her to slavery or to second-class status. Support your opinions with examples from the selections in Collection 9.

_____

_____

_____

_____

_____

_____

_____

_____

_____

_____

_____

_____

_____

_____

_____

_____

_____

_____

_____

_____

_____

_____

4. Choose a character from either "The Battle with Mr. Covey" or "A Pair of Silk Stockings" who changes as a result of the events that occur in the selection. Then write a paragraph that discusses how the character changes and why. Include from the selection at least two events that you believe led to the change.

_____

_____

_____

_____

_____

_____

_____

_____

_____

_____

_____

_____

_____

_____

_____

_____

_____

_____

_____

_____

_____

_____

_____

_____

_____

COLLECTIONS 9–10

Vocabulary Review *(30 points)*

In the space provided, write the letter of the word that *best* completes each of the following sentences. *(6 points each)*

5. Rather than stating them directly, Douglass sometimes _____ the conditions of his slavery.
   a. articulated   b. intimated   c. interposed   d. separated

6. Douglass's defiance was _____ at a time when few slaves resisted their master's authority.
   a. singular   b. expiring   c. acute   d. veritable

7. Slaves who failed to _____ with orders and instructions were severely punished.
   a. render   b. attribute   c. interpose   d. comply

8. Because she had very little money to spare, Mrs. Sommers initially wanted to make _____ use of the fifteen dollars.
   a. reckless   b. gaudy   c. judicious   d. recurrent

9. The _____ woman took all the time required to get an excellent and stylish fit.
   a. hedonistic   b. fastidious   c. obese   d. scandalous

SELECTION TEST

from Life on the Mississippi
Mark Twain   **Pupil's Edition page 452**

Checking Vocabulary *(20 points)*
Match each word in the left-hand column with its meaning in the right-hand column. Place the
letter of the correct meaning in the space provided. *(2 points each)*

_____ **1.** inanimate   **a.** to settle down

_____ **2.** complacency   **b.** empty

_____ **3.** subside   **c.** lifeless

_____ **4.** interminable   **d.** doubts; worries

_____ **5.** serenely   **e.** self-satisfaction

_____ **6.** benevolence   **f.** gloomy; dark

_____ **7.** misgivings   **g.** calmly

_____ **8.** blandly   **h.** mildly

_____ **9.** void   **i.** kindness

_____ **10.** somber   **j.** endless

Thoughtful Reading *(25 points)*
On the line provided, write the letter of the *best* answer to each of the following items.
(5 points each)

_____ **11.** Which of the following is the *best* example in the selection of an extended metaphor?
  a. Twain's comparison of Bixby to a smoothbore gun
  b. Bixby's comparison of Twain to an ass
  c. Bixby's comparison of a bluff reef to a wind reef
  d. Twain's comparison of the river to a book

_____ **12.** When Twain declares that he hasn't enough brains to be a pilot, he is reacting to
  a. the other pilot's threat to throw him through the window for offering unsolicited
     advice
  b. Bixby's comment that he must learn all of the shoal soundings and marks for each trip
  c. his inability to learn the names of the landmarks along the river
  d. the damage he had done to the boat by allowing it to run over a bluff reef

_____ **13.** Which of the following events in the selection indicates that Mr. Bixby believes that
   Twain is making progress in his apprenticeship?
  a. Bixby allows Twain to run several miles of the river by himself.
  b. Twain learns the names of all the landmarks along the river.
  c. Twain learns the shape of the river from St. Louis to New Orleans.
  d. Twain differentiates between a bluff reef and a wind reef to Bixby's satisfaction.

COLLECTIONS 9–10

____ **14.** When Twain states, "All the grace, the beauty, the poetry had gone out of the majestic river!" he
    a. has wearied of Mr. Bixby's "learning" and wants to become a roustabout
    b. has come into a fog so thick that he is unable to see the river or its banks
    c. is bemoaning the fact that his mastery of the river has come at a cost
    d. has grown tired of the river and wants to leave to pursue his writing

____ **15.** Twain compares the river to a book because he believes that
    a. every page is blank and tells nothing
    b. every page tells a different story
    c. you can't judge a book by its cover
    d. you can read the same story again and again

Expanded Response *(30 points)*

16. At various points in the selection, Twain believes he has almost mastered the art of piloting, only to have his complacency shattered by Mr. Bixby. In the sequence chain below, chart the progression of Twain's learning experiences from the beginning of the selection until he finally becomes a pilot. In each box, describe the extent of Twain's knowledge at the time. Then, in the same box, provide Mr. Bixby's response to Twain's insecurity or overconfidence. The first box has been completed as an example. *(15 points)*

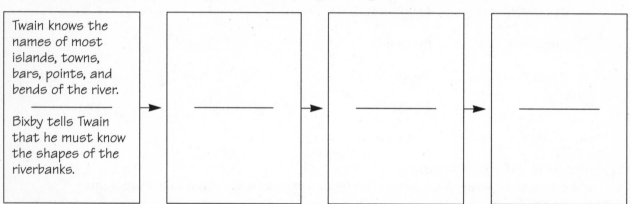

Twain knows the names of most islands, towns, bars, points, and bends of the river.

Bixby tells Twain that he must know the shapes of the riverbanks.

17. Based on the excerpt you have read, how do you think Twain felt after he achieved his goal of becoming a riverboat pilot? On the lines provided, write the letter of the answer you choose and briefly defend your choice. There is more than one possible answer. Use at least one example from the selection to support your ideas. *(15 points)*
    a. He was satisfied.
    b. He was disappointed.
    c. He was ambivalent.
    d. Other: _____

_____

_____

_____

Written Response *(25 points)*

18. On a separate sheet of paper, write one paragraph discussing Twain's use of extended metaphor in *Life on the Mississippi*, in which he compares the Mississippi River to a book. Support your explanation with three examples of this extended metaphor from the selection.

SELECTION TEST

An Occurrence at Owl Creek Bridge
Ambrose Bierce   **Pupil's Edition page 467**

Checking Vocabulary *(20 points)*
Match each word in the left-hand column with its meaning in the right-hand column. Place the letter of the correct meaning in the space provided. *(2 points each)*

____	1. sentinel	**a.**	central
____	2. deference	**b.**	harmful
____	3. chafed	**c.**	guard; sentry
____	4. perilous	**d.**	became impatient
____	5. oscillation	**e.**	dismaying
____	6. pivotal	**f.**	respect
____	7. appalling	**g.**	scrape
____	8. gyration	**h.**	back-and-forth movement
____	9. abrasion	**i.**	dangerous
____	10. malign	**j.**	whirling

Thoughtful Reading *(25 points)*
On the line provided, write the letter of the *best* answer to each of the following items. *(5 points each)*

____ 11. When Farquhar hears his watch ticking with an exaggerated intensity, the narrator is using the point of view known as
   a. second-person limited   **c.** objective
   b. third-person limited   **d.** subjective

____ 12. Which of the following *best* demonstrates the omniscient point of view?
   a. The narrator objectively describes the scene at the bridge.
   b. The narrator focuses only on Farquhar and his thoughts and feelings.
   c. The narrator reports that the gray-clad horseman was a Federal scout.
   d. The narrator gives a first-person account of the events.

____ 13. Which of the following statements about Peyton Farquhar is **not** true?
   a. He is a prosperous planter.   **c.** He longs to be a soldier.
   b. He is a supporter of slavery.   **d.** He has opposed secession.

____ 14. The Union soldiers in the selection are generally portrayed as
   a. merciless and deceptive   **c.** honorable and friendly
   b. benevolent and forgiving   **d.** selfish and distracted

____ **15.** The surprise ending of the story reveals that Farquhar's actual fate was
  a. a last-minute reprieve
  b. a successful escape
  c. death by drowning
  d. death by hanging

Expanded Response *(30 points)*

16. Which of the following statements do you think *best* describes what happens to the character of Peyton Farquhar in Bierce's story? On the lines provided, write the letter of the answer you choose and briefly defend your choice. There is more than one possible answer. Use at least one example from the selection to support your ideas. *(15 points)*
  a. He manages a brilliant escape from his executioners.
  b. He imagines a series of extraordinary events and sensations.
  c. He is tricked by a Federal soldier, with disastrous results.
  d. He sacrifices a comfortable life for the Southern cause.

  _____

  _____

  _____

  _____

17. In the chart below, list two examples of each of the three points of view used in "An Occurrence at Owl Creek Bridge": omniscient, objective, and third-person limited. One example has been completed for you. *(15 points)*

Omniscient	**1.** the description of Peyton Farquhar's background as a Southern planter **2.**
Objective	**1.** **2.**
Third-person Limited	**1.** **2.**

Written Response *(25 points)*

18. On a separate sheet of paper, write one paragraph that describes how Bierce provides hints about the real nature of Farquhar's "escape." Support your description with at least three examples from the selection.

SELECTION TEST

A Mystery of Heroism
Stephen Crane   **Pupil's Edition page 485**

Checking Vocabulary (20 points)
Correctly match each Word to Own in the first column with its *antonym* in the second column. Place the letter of the answer you choose in the space provided. *(2 points each)*

_____ 1. conflagration   **a.** motionless

_____ 2. stolidity   **b.** introduction

_____ 3. obliterated   **c.** noncombustion

_____ 4. prostrate   **d.** brightened

_____ 5. ominous   **e.** auspicious

_____ 6. gesticulating   **f.** emotion

_____ 7. provisional   **g.** upright

_____ 8. retraction   **h.** diligent

_____ 9. indolent   **i.** created

_____ 10. blanched   **j.** permanent

Thoughtful Reading (25 points)
On the line provided, write the letter of the *best* answer to each of the following items. *(5 points each)*

_____ 11. Which of the following events from the story is the *best* example of situational irony?
  a. In the midst of battle, an officer screams an order so loudly that it becomes a "falsetto shriek."
  b. The colonel and the captain cannot determine whether Collins really wants to fetch the water.
  c. After racing across the battlefield to the well, Collins must wait for the water to slowly fill the canteens.
  d. The terrified Collins returns to give the dying lieutenant a drink of water, but finds himself unable to do so.

_____ 12. The story's title includes the word *mystery,* probably because
  a. Collins wonders whether there is water in the well
  b. Collins behaves more like a coward than a hero
  c. the story is a type of detective story
  d. heroic behavior is not easy to define

_____ 13. The selection reveals that Collins does not consider himself a hero because he
  a. is merely going to the well to satisfy his thirst
  b. is terrified at the risk he is about to take
  c. believes that heroes have no shame in their lives
  d. turns his back on the wounded lieutenant

____ **14.** When the dying lieutenant asks for a drink of water, Collins's initial reaction is to
    a. refuse the request and keep running
    b. carry the wounded man back to his regiment
    c. leave the officer a canteen and keep running
    d. stop immediately and grant his request

____ **15.** At the end of the story, the only thing we know for sure is that
    a. Collins has spilled all the water while returning to his regiment
    b. the bucket is empty and lying on the ground
    c. the wounded lieutenant has drunk all the water
    d. the bucket has been spilled by the skylarking lieutenants

Expanded Response *(30 points)*

16. In the picture frame on the left, draw the scene from the selection during which Collins is most foolhardy, and on the right, draw the scene during which he is most heroic. On the caption lines beneath each frame, write a brief description of the scene. *(15 points)*

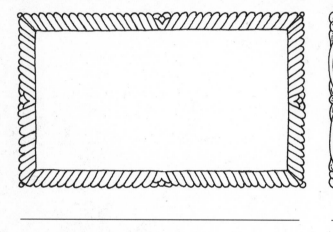 

_____   _____

_____   _____

_____   _____

17. Why do you think Collins makes his bold scramble for the water? On the lines provided, write the letter of the answer you choose and briefly defend your choice. There is more than one possible answer. Use at least one example from the selection to support your ideas. *(15 points)*
    a. He is thirsty and wants a drink.
    b. He is reacting to the provocations of his comrades.
    c. He is uncertain of his motives.
    d. Other: _____

_____

_____

_____

Written Response *(25 points)*

18. On a separate sheet of paper, write one paragraph that explains whether you think Collins's daring act is ultimately heroic, foolish, or a combination of both. Support your explanation with at least two examples from the selection.

SELECTION TEST

To Build a Fire
Jack London

Pupil's Edition page 496

Checking Vocabulary *(20 points)*
Indicate whether the following pairs of words are synonyms or antonyms by circling **S** or **A.** The first word in each pair is a Word to Own. *(2 points each)*

S   A   **1.** intangible: definite

S   A   **2.** undulations: wavelike motions

S   A   **3.** protruding: sticking out

S   A   **4.** solidity: liquidity

S   A   **5.** imperative: compulsory

S   A   **6.** extremities: limbs

S   A   **7.** recoiled: drew back

S   A   **8.** imperceptible: obvious

S   A   **9.** excruciating: mild

S   A   **10.** ensued: preceded

Thoughtful Reading *(25 points)*
On the line provided, write the letter of the *best* answer to each of the following items. *(5 points each)*

_____ **11.** Which of the following events in the selection describes the ultimate outcome of the man's struggle against the frigid weather?
   a. He realizes the danger of traveling in such weather and turns back.
   b. He builds a fire to dry his wet feet, then continues his trek.
   c. He runs all the way to the camp, even though his feet are frozen.
   d. He stops running, falls asleep, and freezes to death.

_____ **12.** Which of the following statements about the man in the selection indicates the level of his respect for the power of nature?
   a. The strangeness of the day makes no impression on him.
   b. He fears falling through the snow and getting wet.
   c. He travels alone in tremendously cold temperatures.
   d. He pays no attention to the instinctive reactions of his dog.

_____ **13.** Naturalism, as reflected in "To Build a Fire," holds that
   a. animals and human beings can learn to respect each other
   b. nature is a source of comfort and inspiration
   c. close observation of nature requires a scientific approach
   d. human beings are subject to forces beyond their control

_____ **14.** When the fire the man has built under the spruce tree is extinguished, he
   a. starts it again with very little effort
   b. huddles with his dog to warm his hands and feet
   c. realizes he may have just been given a death sentence
   d. panics and immediately begins running toward the camp

_____ **15.** The man is unable to run all the way to the camp because
   a. he lacks the endurance to run that far
   b. he is afraid of getting his feet wet again
   c. his legs are frozen and he can't run
   d. he can't follow the trail while running

COLLECTIONS 9–10

Expanded Response *(30 points)*

16. Complete the following diagram by filling in the circles with some of the details Jack London uses to describe the Yukon in "To Build a Fire." One of the circles has been filled in, as an example. *(15 points)*

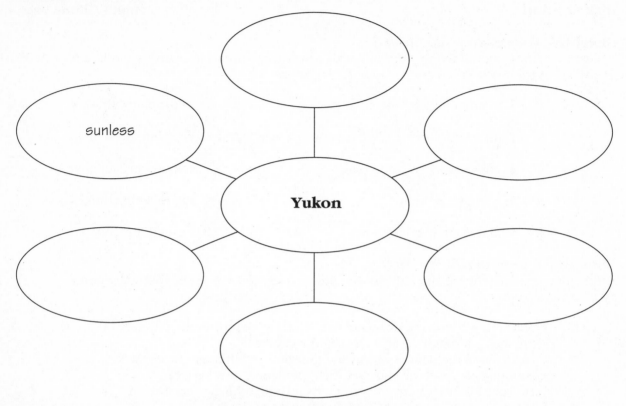

17. Which of the following statements do you think *best* reflects naturalist theories of human existence? On the lines provided, write the letter of the answer you choose and briefly defend your choice. There is more than one possible answer. Use at least one example from the selection to support your ideas. *(15 points)*

  a. The man dies because he is not smart enough to survive the bitter cold.
  b. The odds against the man's survival—factors over which he has no control—are too great.
  c. The dog is better suited to the Yukon environment than the man is.
  d. Even with a human companion, it still would have been a dangerous day for the man to travel.

_____

_____

_____

_____

_____

Written Response *(25 points)*

18. On a separate sheet of paper, write one paragraph that describes how the man's fate is foreshadowed in "To Build a Fire." Support your description with at least three examples from the selection.

THE AMERICAN LANGUAGE

American Dialects

On the line provided, write the letter of the *best* answer to each of the following items.
(10 points each)

_____ 1. In the 1820s, James Fenimore Cooper said that there were no American dialects because
   a. there were no class or occupational distinctions in the United States
   b. American unity and mobility discouraged the establishment of dialects
   c. not even regional variations could be detected in the country
   d. there had never been dialects in America

_____ 2. Cooper's attitude toward dialects was shared by
   a. Mark Twain
   b. James Russell Lowell
   c. John Steinbeck
   d. Noah Webster

_____ 3. Mark Twain saw local speech as
   a. a way of describing the inhabitants of a region
   b. harmful to a national literature
   c. a rebuke to national unity
   d. a way to poke fun at his characters

_____ 4. Two nineteenth-century views of American speech contrasted
   a. standard usage and informal usage
   b. the unity of American speech and the existence of regional distinctions
   c. British usage and American usage
   d. nationally accepted usage and slang

_____ 5. A dialect can be defined as the characteristic language habits of a specific
   a. occupation
   b. age group
   c. speech community
   d. state

_____ 6. Dialects differ *least* from standard English in their
   a. pronunciation
   b. vocabulary
   c. use of slang
   d. grammar

_____ 7. Dialects differ *most* from standard English in their
   a. pronunciation
   b. vocabulary
   c. use of slang
   d. grammar

COLLECTIONS 9–10

_____ **8.** In the United States, the greatest number of dialects is still found in the
    a. South
    b. North
    c. West
    d. East

_____ **9.** Scholars divide American speech into three basic types: Northern, Southern, and
    a. Eastern
    b. Western
    c. Midland
    d. standard

_____ **10.** Dialect is an important element of literature because
    a. speech patterns are essential aspects of character and setting
    b. different speech patterns create humorous effects
    c. every region has its own speech pattern
    d. regional literature is the most influential school of American writing

COLLECTION 10 TEST

From Innocence to Experience

Responding to Literature *(70 points)*

1. In "An Occurrence at Owl Creek Bridge" and "A Mystery of Heroism" we learn about a character's beliefs or expectations about warfare, and we see how each character acts upon them. Use the chart below to show the character's beliefs or expectations and the resulting actions. *(10 points)*

Character: _____

Belief(s) About Warfare	Action(s) That Result from the Beliefs

2. Some of the characters in Collection 10 are offered advice by more-experienced people. Complete the chart below to show what advice was provided and by whom, whether or not it was heeded, and what the outcome was. *(10 points)*

Character Who Offers Advice: _____

Character Who Receives Advice: _____

Advice Offered	Heeded? Yes / No *(circle one)* Outcome

COLLECTIONS 9–10

Respond to each of the questions below. Attach an extra sheet of paper if necessary.
(25 points each)

3. Write a paragraph that explains why learning based on experience can sometimes be more effective than learning acquired through textbooks and lectures. Support your opinions with examples from at least two of the selections in Collection 10.

_____

_____

_____

_____

_____

_____

_____

_____

_____

_____

4. The vantage point from which a story is told is called the *point of view*. The most common points of view are the omniscient, the third-person limited, and the first person. Choose two selections from Collection 10 and write a paragraph explaining which points of view are used in each of the two selections. Use at least one specific example from each of the two selections to demonstrate the effectiveness of the point of view used.

_____

_____

_____

_____

_____

_____

_____

_____

_____

_____

Vocabulary Review *(10 points)*
In the space provided, write the letter of the word that *best* completes the sentence.
(2 points each)

_____ **5.** Something that is *lifeless* is said to be
     a. energetic   **b.** inanimate   **c.** complacent   **d.** somber

_____ **6.** To *extend* means to
     a. rescind   **b.** expel   **c.** protract   **d.** pretend

_____ **7.** To treat someone with *respect* means to show him or her
     a. deference   **b.** scorn   **c.** resignation   **d.** compassion

_____ **8.** Someone who is *lazy* is said to be
     a. diligent   **b.** exhausted   **c.** prostrate   **d.** indolent

_____ **9.** Something that is *not easily perceived* is considered
     a. excruciating   **b.** imperceptible   **c.** evident   **d.** impervious

Language Workshop Review: Inserting Adverb and Adjective Clauses *(20 points)*
Combine each pair of the following simple sentences into a single complex sentence by using an adjective clause or an adverb clause. *(5 points each)*

    EXAMPLE: Mark Twain wrote about life on the Mississippi River.
               He spent his boyhood in Hannibal, Missouri.

               Mark Twain, who spent his boyhood in Hannibal, Missouri, wrote about life on the
               Mississippi River. [joined by an *adjective clause*]

10. Twain had gained mastery of the language of the river. For him, the river had lost its grace and poetry forever.

_____

_____

11. The Federal scout rode past the plantation again. He was heading northward.

_____

_____

12. The officer could not be heard above the noise of battle. He was mortally wounded.

_____

_____

13. The fire was burning intensely. Snow falling from the spruce tree extinguished it.

_____

_____

COLLECTIONS 9–10

LITERARY PERIOD TEST

The Rise of Realism: The Civil War and Postwar Period

Reading an Excerpt

The following selection comes from the early part of Mark Twain's novel *Adventures of Huckleberry Finn*. At this point in the novel (Chapter 5), Huck has been taken away from his irresponsible, drunken father and placed with a pious widow who is attempting to "civilize" him. Huck's father has heard that Huck has received some money, and the old man comes creeping into Huck's room one night in search of it. When Huck goes to his room and lights his candle, "there sat Pap—his own self!" Read the selection carefully, and then answer the questions that follow.

Pap Starts in on a New Life
by Mark Twain

I had shut the door to. Then I turned around, and there he was. I used to be scared of him all the time, he tanned[1] me so much. I reckoned I was scared now, too; but in a minute I see I was mistaken—that is, after the first jolt, as you may say, when my breath sort of hitched, he being so unexpected; but right away after I see I warn't scared of him worth bothring about.

He was most fifty, and he looked it. His hair was long and tangled and greasy, and hung down, and you could see his eyes shining through like he was behind vines. It was all black, no gray; so was his long, mixed-up whiskers. There warn't no color in his face, where his face showed; it was white; not like another man's white, but a white to make a body sick, a white to make a body's flesh crawl—a tree-toad white, a fish-belly white. As for his clothes—just rags, that was all. He had one ankle resting on t'other knee; the boot on that foot was busted, and two of his toes stuck through, and he worked them now and then. His hat was laying on the floor—an old black slouch with the top caved in, like a lid.

I stood a-looking at him; he set there a-looking at me, with his chair tilted back a little. I set the candle down. I noticed the window was up; so he had clumb in by the shed. He kept a-looking me all over. By and by he says:

"Starchy clothes—very. You think you're a good deal of a big-bug, *don't* you?"

"Maybe I am, maybe I ain't," I says.

"Don't you give me none o' your lip," says he. "You've put on considerable many frills since I been away. I'll take you down a peg before I get done with you. You're educated, too, they say—can read and write. You think you're better'n your father, now, don't you, because he can't? *I'll* take it out of you. Who told you you might meddle with such hi-falut'n foolishness, hey?—who told you you could?"

"The widow. She told me."

"The widow, hey?—and who told the widow she could put in her shovel about a thing that ain't none of her business?"

"Nobody never told her."

"Well, I'll learn her how to meddle. And looky here—you drop that school, you hear? I'll learn people to bring up a boy to put on airs over his own father and let on to be better'n what *he* is. You lemme catch you fooling around that school again, you hear? Your mother couldn't read, and she couldn't write, nuther, bother she died. None of the family couldn't before *they* died. I can't, and here you're a-swelling yourself up like this. I ain't the man to stand it—you hear? Say, lemme hear you read."

I took up a book and begun something about General Washington and the wars. When I'd read about a half a minute, he fetched the book a whack with his hand and knocked it across the house. He says:

"It's so. You can do it. I had my doubts when you told me. Now looky here; you

[1] **tanned:** whipped.

stop that putting on frills. I won't have it. I'll lay for you, my smarty; and if I catch you about that school I'll tan you good. First you know you'll get religion, too. I never see such a son."

He took up a little blue and yaller picture of some cows and a boy, and says: "What's this?"

"It's something they give me for learning my lessons good."

He tore it up, and says:

"I'll give you something better—I'll give you a cowhide."

He set there a-mumbling and a-growling a minute, and then he says:

"*Ain't* you a sweet-scented <u>dandy</u>, though? A bed; and bed-clothes; and a look'n'-glass; and a piece of carpet on the floor—and your own father got to sleep with the hogs in the tanyard. I never see such a son. I bet I'll take some o' these frills out o' you before I'm done with you. Why, there ain't no end to your airs—they say you're rich. Hey?—how's that?"

"They lie—that's how."

"Looky here—mind how you talk to me; I'm a-standing about all I can stand now—so don't gimme no sass. I've been in town two days, and I hain't heard nothing but about you bein' rich. I heard about it away down the river, too. That's why I come. You git me that money tomorrow—I want it."

"I hain't got no money."

"It's a lie. Judge Thatcher's got it. You git it. I want it."

"I hain't got no money, I tell you. You ask Judge Thatcher; he'll tell you the same."

"All right. I'll ask him; and I'll make him pungle,[2] too, or I'll know the reason why. Say, how much you got in your pocket? I want it."

"I hain't got only a dollar, and I want that to—"

"It don't make no difference what you want it for—you just shell it out."

He took it and bit it to see if it was good, and then he said he was going downtown to get some whiskey, said he hadn't had a drink all day. When he had got out on the shed he put his head in again, and cussed me for putting on frills and trying to do better than him; and when I reckoned he was gone he came back and put his head in again, and told me to mind about that school, because he was going to lay for me and lick me if I didn't drop that.

Next day he was drunk, and he went to Judge Thatcher's and bullyragged him, and tried to make him give up the money; but he couldn't, and then he swore he'd make the law force him.

The judge and the widow went to law to get the court to take me away from him and let one of them be my <u>guardian</u>; but it was a new judge that had just come, and he didn't know the old man; so he said courts mustn't interfere and separate families if they could help it; said he'd druther not take a child away from its father. So Judge Thatcher and the widow had to quit on the business.

That pleased the old man till he couldn't rest. He said he'd cowhide me till I was black and blue if I didn't raise some money for him. I borrowed three dollars from Judge Thatcher, and Pap took it and got drunk, and went a-blowing around and cussing and whooping and carrying on; and he kept it up all over town, with a tin pan, till most midnight; then they jailed him, and the next day they had him before court, and jailed him again for a week. But he said *he* was satisfied; said he was boss of his son, and he'd make it warm for *him*.

When he got out the new judge said he was a-going to make a man of him. So he took him to his own house, and dressed him up clean and nice, and had him to breakfast and dinner and supper with the family, and was just old pie to him, so to speak. And after supper he talked to him about <u>temperance</u> and such things till the old man cried, and said he'd been a fool, and fooled away his life; but now he was a-going to turn over a new leaf and be a man nobody wouldn't be ashamed of, and he hoped

---

[2] **pungle:** pay the money.

COLLECTIONS 9–10

the judge would help him and not look down on him. The judge said he could hug him for them words; so *he* cried, and his wife she cried again; Pap said he'd been a man that had always been misunderstood before, and the judge said he believed it. The old man said that what a man wanted that was down was <u>sympathy</u>, and the judge said it was so; so they cried again. And when it was bedtime the old man rose up and held out his hand, and says:

"Look at it, gentlemen and ladies all; take a-hold of it; shake it. There's a hand that was the hand of a hog; but it ain't so no more; it's the hand of a man that's started in on a new life, and'll die before he'll go back. You mark them words—don't forget I said them. It's a clean hand now; shake it—don't be afeared."

So they shook it, one after the other, all around, and cried. The judge's wife she kissed it. Then the old man he signed a pledge—made his mark. The judge said it was the holiest time on record, or something like that. Then they tucked the old man into a beautiful room, which was the spare room, and in the night some time he got powerful thirsty and clumb out on to the porch roof and slid down a stanchion and traded his new coat for a jug of forty-rod, and clumb back again and had a good old time; and toward daylight he crawled out again, drunk as a fiddler, and rolled off the porch and broke his left arm in two places, and was most froze to death when some-body found him after sun-up. And when they come to look at that spare room they had to take soundings before they could <u>navigate</u> it.

The judge he felt kind of sore. He said he reckoned a body could reform the old man with a shotgun, maybe, but he didn't know no other way.

Understanding Vocabulary *(20 points)*
Each of the underlined words below has also been underlined in the selection. Re-read those passages and use context clues to help you select an answer. Write the letter of the word(s) that *best* completes each sentence. *(4 points each)*

1. A <u>dandy</u> is a man who pays too much attention to his _____ .
   a. education   **b.** appearance   **c.** diet

2. If you serve as a minor's <u>guardian</u>, you are his or her _____ .
   a. guide   **b.** legal caretaker   **c.** captor

3. A person who believes in <u>temperance</u> practices _____ in the consumption of alcoholic beverages.
   a. abstinence   **b.** inebriation   **c.** recklessness

4. Someone who yearns for <u>sympathy</u> typically wants _____ .
   a. discipline   **b.** congruity   **c.** compassion

5. To <u>navigate</u> is to _____ a course.
   a. divert   **b.** mobilize   **c.** steer

Thoughtful Reading *(35 points)*
On the line provided, write the letter of the *best* answer to each of the following items. *(7 points each)*

_____ 6. Which of these events happens first in the excerpt?
   a. Pap falls and breaks his arm.
   b. The widow and Judge Thatcher go to court.
   c. Pap is waiting in Huck's room.
   d. Pap demands money from Judge Thatcher.

_____ 7. The primary reason Pap has come to see his son is that he
    a. is concerned about Huck's well-being
    b. has heard that Huck is rich
    c. wants to warn Huck about becoming a dandy
    d. wants to give Huck a tanning for attending school

_____ 8. What does Pap think about Huck's ability to read?
    a. He is proud of his son and wants Huck to teach him how to read.
    b. He accuses Huck of trying to better himself.
    c. He tries to prove that Huck cannot really read.
    d. He says he'll approve of it if Huck will give him money.

_____ 9. Which of the following statements about Pap's conversion is **not** true?
    a. Pap cries openly and proclaims that he is going to change.
    b. Pap signs a temperance pledge.
    c. Pap trades his new coat for a jug of whiskey.
    d. Pap becomes a church member and gets a job.

_____ 10. What happens last in the excerpt?
    a. The judge realizes he has been bamboozled.
    b. The judge and his wife invite Pap to work for them and live in their house.
    c. Pap falls off the porch and breaks his left arm in two places.
    d. Huck runs away to avoid getting a tanning from Pap.

Expanded Response (15 points)

11. Based on the description of Pap and Huck's relationship in the excerpt, what do you think will happen next between father and son? On the lines provided, write the letter of the answer you choose and briefly defend your choice. There is more than one possible answer. Use at least one example from the selection to support your ideas.
    a. Huck and Pap will reconcile their differences and will live together as a family again.
    b. Huck will attempt to avoid his father.
    c. Huck will see the futility of the situation and will run away in order to avoid his father entirely.
    d. Other: _____

_____

_____

_____

_____

_____

_____

_____

_____

_____

_____

COLLECTIONS 9–10

Written Response *(30 points)*

12. Like some of the characters in the Collection 10 selections, Huck takes a step from innocence to experience. On the lines provided, compare Huck in this excerpt from *Adventures of Huckleberry Finn* with a character from one of the Collection 10 selections who also gains valuable insight through experience. Discuss at least one similarity between the characters and at least one difference. Provide at least two examples from each story to illustrate your points.

_____

_____

_____

_____

_____

_____

_____

_____

_____

_____

_____

_____

_____

_____

_____

_____

_____

_____

_____

_____

_____

_____

Elements of Literature

LITERARY PERIOD INTRODUCTION TEST

The Moderns

On the line provided, write the letter of the *best* answer to each of the following items.
(10 points each)

_____ 1. Until the beginning of the twentieth century, all of the following were part of the American dream **except** a
   a. respect for the mysterious workings of the subconscious mind
   b. belief that the country's abundance and bounty were limitless
   c. trust in the ultimate triumph of any self-reliant individual
   d. faith in America's progress toward prosperity

_____ 2. After World War I, American writers began to
   a. try to tighten their connections with the past
   b. grow cynical about traditional authority and values
   c. urge the country to build economic opportunities
   d. abandon their art and find new ways of making a living

_____ 3. The modernist movement challenged American writers to
   a. adopt Marxism as a philosophical basis for their work
   b. set their stories and poems in the South or Midwest
   c. find new themes, subjects, and styles for their work
   d. avoid the influences and ideas of European writers

_____ 4. A growing interest in psychoanalysis led writers to
   a. doubt the value and sincerity of their work
   b. rely on doctors to help them find meaning in life
   c. criticize works that described characters' feelings
   d. try to capture their characters' thought processes

_____ 5. During the Jazz Age, many American writers and artists
   a. supported Prohibition in their work
   b. openly criticized the music of the period
   c. lived as expatriates in France
   d. embraced the idea of America as Eden

_____ 6. Ernest Hemingway created major characters who
   a. express themselves in flamboyant ways
   b. avoid the challenges of day-to-day life
   c. are willing to do anything to achieve their goals
   d. behave honorably in a world without purpose

_____ 7. Some American poets were inspired by modernist European painting and began to use its imagery and symbolism, while others looked to
   a. American painters for style and subjects
   b. traditional forms and ordinary speech
   c. ancient Greek and Roman myths for themes
   d. forms they admired in modern British drama

_____ **8.** Poets of the Harlem Renaissance wrote American poetry that involved
   a. metrically regular and rhymed verse
   b. ghetto speech and rhythms from jazz and blues
   c. references to ancient African forms of poetry
   d. discussions of the decline of American cities

_____ **9.** Many American modernist writers
   a. maintained a vision of America as Eden
   b. embraced the boundless optimism of earlier times
   c. believed nature had outlived its usefulness
   d. focused on obscure questions and issues

_____ **10.** American modernist writers managed to
   a. avoid fundamental questions asked by writers of the past
   b. destroy our illusions about American dreams and ideals
   c. create literature that reflected many American voices
   d. focus only on the positive aspects of American culture

SELECTION TEST

A Wagner Matinée
Willa Cather

Pupil's Edition page 539

Checking Vocabulary *(20 points)*

Match each word in the left-hand column with its meaning in the right-hand column. Place the letter of the correct meaning in the space provided. *(2 points each)*

_____ **1.** deluge	**a.** at a slant	
_____ **2.** eluding	**b.** escaping	
_____ **3.** grotesque	**c.** dull; slow	
_____ **4.** inert	**d.** anxious uncertainty	
_____ **5.** legacy	**e.** countless	
_____ **6.** myriad	**f.** strange; absurd	
_____ **7.** obliquely	**g.** deeply respectful	
_____ **8.** pious	**h.** inheritance	
_____ **9.** reverential	**i.** rush; flood	
_____ **10.** trepidation	**j.** devoted to one's religion	

Thoughtful Reading *(25 points)*

On the line provided, write the letter of the *best* answer to each of the following items. *(5 points each)*

_____ **11.** On greeting his aunt, Clark is struck by how
   a. eager she is to attend concerts again
   b. unfriendly and distant she acts
   c. easily she adapts to life in Boston
   d. shabby she looks and how exhausted she seems

_____ **12.** Which sentence *best* describes Clark's view of his Uncle Howard?
   a. He is a cruel man who treats Georgiana badly.
   b. He is unable to give Georgiana a comfortable life.
   c. He is a cultured man who misses the cities of the East.
   d. He is an ambitious and prosperous farmer.

_____ **13.** In the descriptions of the two settings—Nebraska and Boston—the narrator
   a. explains his aunt's reasons for permanently returning to the city
   b. contrasts the purity of one with the decadence of the other
   c. contrasts the bleakness of one with the liveliness of the other
   d. explains major reasons for the Westward Expansion movement

_____ **14.** Which statement *best* summarizes why Georgiana cries during the concert?
   a. She is suddenly homesick for Nebraska and her family.
   b. She realizes anew how important music is to her.
   c. She dislikes being exposed to a snobbish atmosphere.
   d. She is satisfied that she gave up her career as a pianist.

_____ **15.** Clark sympathizes with his aunt because
   a. long ago she shared her love of music with him
   b. he remembers his own difficulties in returning to Boston
   c. he, too, has few opportunities to attend cultural events
   d. Howard has written to him about Georgiana's decline

Expanded Response *(30 points)*

16. What is the major impression Clark has as he leaves the matinée? On the lines provided, write the letter of the answer you choose and briefly defend your choice. There is more than one possible answer. Use at least one example from the selection to support your ideas.
(15 points)
   a. Going to the concert has been a mixed blessing for Georgiana.
   b. It is a huge mistake to pressure people into new experiences.
   c. Georgiana has never completely adjusted to life in Nebraska.
   d. A joyful experience influences the rest of one's life.

_____

_____

_____

_____

17. Georgiana has lost one of the major pleasures in her life. What is that loss? Write the name of this loss in the middle section of the following graphic. In what way is Georgiana a victim of circumstance in this loss? In what way has the loss arisen from her own choice? Note your answers to these questions in the side panels of the graphic. *(15 points)*

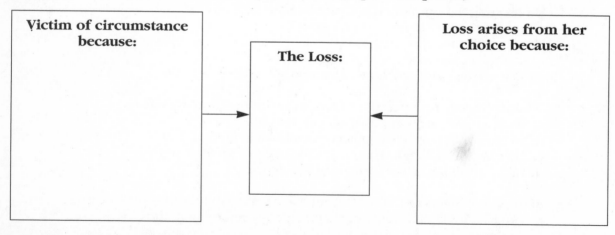

Written Response *(25 points)*

18. "A Wagner Matinée" is written from the point of view of Clark, and we see Georgiana's reactions to the concert through his eyes. On a separate sheet of paper, describe the concert from Georgiana's point of view. Focus on the feelings and thoughts that cause her to react as she does. Make at least two references to specific details in the selection to support your ideas.

SELECTION TEST

His Father's Earth
Thomas Wolfe

Pupil's Edition page 549

Checking Vocabulary *(20 points)*
Match each Word to Own in the left-hand column with its meaning in the right-hand column.
Place the letter of the correct meaning in the space provided. *(2 points each)*

____ **1.** exulted

____ **2.** frugal

____ **3.** garnished

____ **4.** intermittent

____ **5.** languid

____ **6.** nominal

____ **7.** opulent

____ **8.** prodigal

____ **9.** surmise

____ **10.** vistas

a. abundant; plentiful

b. topped

c. guess

d. rejoiced greatly

e. weak, as from exhaustion

f. views

g. very small

h. pausing occasionally

i. extremely abundant

j. thrifty; economical

Thoughtful Reading *(25 points)*
On the line provided, write the letter of the *best* answer to each of the following items.
(5 points each)

____ **11.** In his imaginary experience of circus life, the boy sees himself as
   a. escaping from an unhappy family life
   b. suffering from the unkind treatment of circus workers
   c. taking care of the circus workers
   d. learning to be a circus performer

____ **12.** The descriptions of food convey
   a. admiration for the father's skills as a farmer
   b. a picture of the poverty and hunger in America
   c. the idea that the abundance of American resources cannot last long
   d. a sense of personal nourishment and fulfillment

____ **13.** The vision of exciting travel contrasts with
   a. the ease of the circus's routine
   b. dangers in the outside world
   c. an image of returning home eagerly
   d. the hardships of urban life

____ **14.** Birdsong is described in a way that makes it seem
   a. like the plaintive cries of animals
   b. as exciting as the sensations of circus life
   c. ordinary compared with life on the road
   d. like an ominous foreshadowing of tragedy

____ **15.** The father reacts to the boy's homecoming with
   a. joy and acceptance
   b. rebukes and criticism
   c. questions and concerns
   d. lack of attention or interest

Expanded Response *(30 points)*

16. Choose the option that *best* completes the following statement. On the lines provided, write the letter of the answer you choose and briefly defend your choice. There is more than one possible answer. Use at least one example from the selection to support your ideas. *(15 points)*
The boy's vision enables him to
   a. experience a feeling of what home is
   b. understand his parents' problems
   c. see himself as a useful and nurturing person
   d. experience the adventure of running away with the circus

_____

_____

_____

_____

_____

_____

17. Like most daydreams and visions, the young boy's imaginings have both realistic and fantastic aspects to them. In the following chart, list at least two ideas or details from the story that fall into each category. *(15 points)*

Realistic Aspects	Fantastic Aspects

Written Response *(25 points)*

18. Consider the titles of two of Wolfe's novels: *Look Homeward, Angel* and *You Can't Go Home Again*. On a separate sheet of paper, describe how "His Father's Earth" is also about an idea of home. Make at least two references to specific details or events in the story to support your ideas.

NAME _____ CLASS _____ DATE _____ SCORE _____

SELECTION TEST

Design / Nothing Gold Can Stay / Once by the Pacific
Neither Out Far Nor In Deep / Birches / The Death of the Hired Man

Robert Frost   Pupil's Edition pages 560–569

Thoughtful Reading (*40 points*)
On the line provided, write the letter of the *best* answer to each of the following items.
(*5 points each*)

_____ 1. In "Design," the overall imagery suggests that
    a. the moth is not actually dead
    b. evil may masquerade as innocence
    c. the spider is aware of the speaker
    d. all of nature is beautiful

_____ 2. The gold in "Nothing Gold Can Stay" is a symbol of
    a. the magnificence of autumn leaves
    b. sunrise in the Garden of Eden
    c. human greed and selfishness
    d. fleeting beauty and perfection

_____ 3. In "Neither Out Far Nor In Deep," people look at the ocean rather than at the land because they are
    a. intrigued by mystery   **c.** fascinated by a sinking ship
    b. disgusted by worldly events   **d.** longing for an ocean voyage

_____ 4. Which poem expresses pessimism about our ability to grasp the calamity that awaits humankind?
    a. "Nothing Gold Can Stay"   **c.** "Once by the Pacific"
    b. "Neither Out Far Nor In Deep"   **d.** "The Death of the Hired Man"

_____ 5. According to Frost, the boy who swings on birch trees experiences
    a. a frightening near-death vision
    b. the pleasures of both heaven and earth
    c. the wrath of an indignant landowner
    d. a variety of minor injuries

_____ 6. In "Once by the Pacific," the speaker's attitude toward the ocean is best described as
    a. reverent   **c.** fearful
    b. loving   **d.** optimistic

_____ 7. Which pair of lines that follows is an example of blank verse?
    a. "He's worn out. He's asleep beside the stove. / When I came up from Rowe's I found him here . . ."
    b. "The people along the sand / All turn and look one way."
    c. "There would be more than ocean-water broken / Before God's last *Put out the Light* was spoken."
    d. "So dawn goes down to day. / Nothing gold can stay."

_____ 8. In "The Death of the Hired Man," the feelings of the characters are revealed by
    a. how the characters react to death
    b. the characters' different definitions of home
    c. the observations of the third-person narrator
    d. what the characters say to one another

Expanded Response (30 points)

9. Worn-out and ill, Silas comes back to Warren and Mary's farm to die. What does this decision reveal about Silas's character? On the lines provided, write the letter of the answer you choose and briefly defend your choice. There is more than one possible answer. Use at least one example from the selection to support your ideas. *(15 points)*

a. Silas knows he has worked hard laboring on Warren and Mary's farm.

b. Silas has always been independent, making his own choices about where he wishes to be.

c. Silas has always been a reliable and loyal member of Mary and Warren's family.

d. Silas is manipulative, and knows that the kindhearted Mary—unlike his own brother—will take him in.

_____

_____

_____

_____

_____

10. It is easy to imagine "The Death of the Hired Man" as a short story or play, for the poem vividly develops each character. In the chart below, show how "The Death of the Hired Man" might be viewed as a short story or play by identifying each character and describing each one's values and the conflicts that each faces. *(15 points)*

Characters	Their Values	Conflicts They Face
1.	1.	1.
2.	2.	2.
3.	3.	3.

Written Response (30 points)

11. Some readers view Frost's poems as *pessimistic*—that is, as dwelling on the downside of life. Other readers view the poems as *realistic*—that is, as balancing negative and positive aspects. Which of these two views is closest to your own opinion of Frost's work? On a separate sheet of paper, respond to this question. Make at least two references to specific details in Frost's poems to support your ideas.

SELECTION TEST

Bells for John Whiteside's Daughter
John Crowe Ransom

Pupil's Edition page 577

Shine, Perishing Republic
Robinson Jeffers

Pupil's Edition page 580

Thoughtful Reading *(40 points)*
On the line provided, write the letter of the *best* answer to each of the following items.
(5 points each)

_____ 1. In "Bells for John Whiteside's Daughter," the two contrasting tones are
  a. amusement and solemnity
  b. pessimism and optimism
  c. sarcasm and sorrow
  d. amazement and disillusionment

_____ 2. In "Shine, Perishing Republic," Robinson Jeffers combines the tones of
  a. humor and irritation
  b. hope and wonder
  c. cynicism and anguish
  d. optimism and pessimism

_____ 3. In "Bells for John Whiteside's Daughter," Ransom seeks to convey
  a. the relief the geese feel when their tormentor dies
  b. the contrast between a still corpse and an active child
  c. the reasons that justify the death of a young person
  d. the futility of mourning those who have passed away

_____ 4. The speaker remembers John Whiteside's daughter mostly for her
  a. quiet obedience to her elders
  b. deep insights into the meaning of life
  c. beauty and grace
  d. mischievous ways

_____ 5. In her coffin, John Whiteside's daughter seems to be in a "brown study," which is
  a. a seriousness unlike the lively way she acted in life
  b. a dark and somber room that reflects the family's sorrow
  c. an apt comment on the unhappiness of her youth
  d. symbolic of the way she studied the geese

_____ 6. In "Shine, Perishing Republic," Jeffers views America as
  a. full of powerful instincts for change and renewal
  b. a place where democratic ideals have been realized
  c. a thickening, decaying, and rotting empire
  d. fighting off onslaughts from foreign forces

_____ 7. Jeffers seems to feel that his children
  a. are willing and complacent victims of technology
  b. may hate him for his love of the natural world
  c. can escape destruction by opting for a rural life
  d. have discovered a way of life that is better than his

From "Bells for John Whiteside's Daughter" from *Selected Poems* by John Crowe Ransom. Copyright 1924 by **Alfred A. Knopf, Inc.;** copyright renewed 1952 by John Crowe Ransom. Reprinted by permission of the publisher.

_____ **8.** Which sentence below *best* states a similar theme for both "Bells for John Whiteside's Daughter" and "Shine, Perishing Republic"?
  a. In the light of eternity, human life has no real purpose.
  b. Humankind is corrupt and is causing its own destruction.
  c. Immortality is guaranteed to those who live exemplary lives.
  d. The finest lives are those lived in accordance with nature.

Expanded Response *(30 points)*

9. Choose the option that *best* completes the following statement. On the lines provided, write the letter of the answer you choose and briefly defend your choice. There is more than one possible answer. Use at least one example from the selection to support your ideas. *(15 points)*
  In "Shine, Perishing Republic," we can strongly sense the speaker's
  a. total dismay about the development of urban America
  b. reverence and respect for the patterns of nature
  c. feeling that human beings have not managed the earth well
  d. determination to fight in defense of his country

_____

_____

_____

_____

10. Death is a theme in both "Bells for John Whiteside's Daughter" and "Shine, Perishing Republic." In the chart below, note who or what dies, and what unique thing is lost as a consequence. *(15 points)*

Who or What Dies?	What Unique Thing Is Lost Forever?
"Bells for John Whiteside's Daughter"	
"Shine, Perishing Republic"	

Written Response *(30 points)*

11. Though both Ransom and Jeffers deal with the subject of loss and death, the tones they use are different. On a separate sheet of paper, contrast the tones in "Bells for John Whiteside's Daughter" and "Shine, Perishing Republic." Make at least one reference to a specific image in each poem to support your ideas.

COLLECTION 11 TEST

Loss and Redemption

Responding to Literature *(80 points)*

1. Loss, endings, and finality are themes in many of the selections you've read in Collection 11. Choose two of the selections listed below and enter their titles in the rows provided. In the left-hand column, note what has come to an end in each selection. In the right-hand column, note what the speaker in each selection seems to feel about this ending. *(15 points)*

"Nothing Gold Can Stay"   "The Death of the Hired Man"
"Bells for John Whiteside's Daughter"   "Shine, Perishing Republic"
"Once by the Pacific"

What Has Ended	Speaker's Feelings About This Ending
Selection:	
Selection:	

2. Redemption, or the regaining of something almost lost, is also a theme in many of the selections you've read. Choose one of the titles below and enter it in the space provided. Then, describe what has been redeemed or recovered. *(15 points)*

"A Wagner Matinée"   "His Father's Earth"
"Birches"   "The Death of the Hired Man"

Selection Title:
What Has Been Redeemed or Recovered:

Respond to each of the following questions. Attach an extra sheet of paper if necessary.

3. Write a paragraph that compares Frost's "Once by the Pacific" and Jeffers's "Shine, Perishing Republic." In your paragraph, identify and discuss the theme common to both of these poems. Support your ideas with at least one example from each poem. *(25 points)*

_____

_____

_____

_____

_____

_____

_____

_____

_____

_____

_____

_____

_____

_____

_____

_____

_____

_____

_____

_____

_____

_____

_____

4. Descriptions of settings and of human feelings figure heavily in all the selections in Collection 11. From the titles that follow, choose the selection that impresses you most in its descriptive passages and write a paragraph about it. In your paragraph, quote or restate at least one of the passages or lines and tell why it moves or impresses you. *(25 points)*

"Neither Out Far Nor In Deep"   "Birches"
"Design"   "His Father's Earth"
"A Wagner Matinée"

_____

_____

_____

_____

_____

_____

_____

_____

_____

_____

_____

_____

_____

_____

_____

_____

_____

_____

_____

_____

_____

Vocabulary Review (20 points)

In the space provided, write the letter of the word that correctly completes the sentence.
(*4 points each*)

5. Rain showers that start and end suddenly could best be described as _____.
   a. frugal
   b. grotesque
   c. intermittent
   d. inert

6. A dress that is _____ is made of expensive material.
   a. opulent
   b. garnished
   c. nominal
   d. pious

7. To leave a person a _____ is to make him or her part of your inheritance.
   a. deluge
   b. myriad
   c. surmise
   d. legacy

8. When you see a(n) _____ person, you might infer that she or he is weak or tired.
   a. languid
   b. reverential
   c. prodigal
   d. exultant

9. A detective's _____ might lead her to approach a criminal with great caution.
   a. vistas
   b. trepidation
   c. refrain
   d. eluding

SELECTION TEST

Winter Dreams
F. Scott Fitzgerald

Pupil's Edition page 586

Checking Vocabulary *(20 points)*

Match each word in the left-hand column with its meaning in the right-hand column. Place the letter of the correct meaning in the space provided. *(2 points each)*

_____ 1. reserve   **a.** joyfulness

_____ 2. turbulence   **b.** variance; difference

_____ 3. malicious   **c.** irregular behavior

_____ 4. plaintive   **d.** celebration

_____ 5. petulance   **e.** feeling of alarm or agitation

_____ 6. elation   **f.** intentionally hurtful

_____ 7. ludicrous   **g.** expressing sadness

_____ 8. divergence   **h.** self-restraint

_____ 9. mirth   **i.** irritability; impatience

_____ 10. perturbation   **j.** laughable; absurd

Thoughtful Reading *(25 points)*

On the line provided, write the letter of the *best* answer to each of the following items. *(5 points each)*

_____ 11. What is Dexter Green's motivation for pursuing Judy Jones?
   a. He wants to work for her father.
   b. He sees her as a symbol of "the best."
   c. He is the only man she is interested in.
   d. She seems shy and lonely.

_____ 12. Dexter Green can *best* be described as
   a. ambitious and full of desires
   b. judgmental and comical
   c. courageous and helpful
   d. honest and trustworthy

_____ 13. What is Dexter's eventual attitude toward Judy Jones's flirtations with men?
   a. Dexter is outraged that Judy flirts with many men.
   b. Dexter often criticizes Judy for flirting with numerous men.
   c. Dexter enjoys watching Judy flirt with numerous men.
   d. Dexter does not condemn Judy for flirting with numerous men.

_____ **14.** What happens to Dexter and Judy's engagement?
     a. Dexter breaks off the engagement.
     b. Dexter and Judy are never engaged.
     c. Judy breaks off the engagement.
     d. Judy finds out that Dexter is married.

_____ **15.** At the end of the story, Devlin tells Dexter that
     a. Judy's husband does not treat her well
     b. Judy and her husband are divorced
     c. Judy still dates a number of men
     d. Judy cannot stand her husband

Expanded Response *(30 points)*
16. Choose the statement that you think most accurately describes Judy Jones. On the lines provided, write the letter of the answer you choose and briefly defend your choice. There is more than one possible answer. Use at least one example from the selection to support your ideas. *(15 points)*
     a. Judy Jones pursues men who are slipping away from her.
     b. Judy Jones is confident and condescending.
     c. Judy Jones does not take love seriously.
     d. Other: _____

_____

_____

_____

17. In the following chart, briefly describe one of Dexter's decisions. Then, write down what you think might have motivated Dexter's decision based on what you know about him from the story. *(15 points)*

Dexter's Decision	Possible Motivation

Written Response *(25 points)*
18. On a separate sheet of paper, complete the following statement. Then give at least three examples or ideas from the story to support the statement.

At the end of the story, tears stream down Dexter's face because . . .

SELECTION TEST

The Leader of the People
John Steinbeck   **Pupil's Edition page 607**

Checking Vocabulary *(20 points)*
Match each word in the left-hand column with its meaning in the right-hand column. Place the letter of the correct meaning in the space provided. *(2 points each)*

_____ **1.** immune   **a.** improper

_____ **2.** rancor   **b.** proud and overly confident

_____ **3.** arrogant   **c.** assembled

_____ **4.** marshaling   **d.** unhappily

_____ **5.** unseemly   **e.** protected

_____ **6.** cleft   **f.** opening

_____ **7.** disconsolately **g.** anger

_____ **8.** contemptuously **h.** leading; guiding

_____ **9.** humoring   **i.** scornfully

_____ **10.** convened   **j.** indulging

Thoughtful Reading *(25 points)*
On the line provided, write the letter of the *best* answer to each of the following items.
(5 points each)

_____ **11.** Grandfather's reaction to Carl's statement that nobody wants to hear his stories anymore is an example of
   a. dramatic irony
   b. parody
   c. conflict
   d. satire

_____ **12.** Which of the following statements is true about Jody's father?
   a. He insists that Jody ask his permission before doing anything on the ranch.
   b. He never gives in during a confrontation with anyone, including his wife.
   c. He will not allow Jody to kill mice despite Jody's constant pleading.
   d. He is rather carefree, which annoys his family when there is work to be done.

_____ **13.** Jody's father feels conflict in relation to Grandfather because
   a. Grandfather insists upon putting iron plates in the wagon wheels
   b. Grandfather constantly changes the ending of his story
   c. Grandfather continues to tell the same stories over and over again
   d. Grandfather insists upon taking over the farm whenever he comes to visit

____ **14.** At the end of Steinbeck's story, Grandfather says that if he had not been the
leader of the people
a. the whole group would have died of disease
b. another person would have been the leader
c. the American Indians would have been treated more fairly
d. the horses would have been stolen

____ **15.** According to Grandfather, some men hate the ocean because in the past
a. the ocean did not provide sufficient drinking water
b. the men realized that they had lost their way
c. the men were afraid of the unpredictability of the ocean
d. the ocean prevented them from continuing westward

Expanded Response *(30 points)*
16. What do you think is the main conflict in the story? On the lines provided, write the letter
of the answer you choose and briefly defend your choice. Use at least one example from the
selection to support your choice. There is more than one possible answer. *(15 points)*
a. the mice versus the dogs
b. Jody's father versus Jody's grandfather
c. dreams versus reality
d. other: _____

_____

_____

_____

_____

17. Jody, his mother, and his father have different opinions about Grandfather's stories. In
the boxes below, briefly describe the attitude each character has toward Grandfather's
storytelling. *(15 points)*

Jody:
Jody's mother:
Jody's father:

Written Response *(25 points)*
18. On a separate sheet of paper, describe two conflicts that occur in "The Leader of the
People." Mention the personality of the characters involved. Do you think that the conflicts
are resolved peacefully, angrily, or not at all? Use at least two examples from the story to
support your opinions.

SELECTION TEST

The Secret Life of Walter Mitty
James Thurber   Pupil's Edition page 624

Checking Vocabulary (20 points)

Match each word in the left-hand column with its meaning in the right-hand column. Place the letter of the correct meaning in the space provided. (2 points each)

_____ 1. craven   **a.** arrogant

_____ 2. bedlam   **b.** troubled

_____ 3. rakishly   **c.** wild confusion

_____ 4. haggard   **d.** place or condition of noise or confusion

_____ 5. distraught   **e.** violent ripping apart

_____ 6. insolent   **f.** suggestively

_____ 7. cannonading   **g.** very fearful; cowardly

_____ 8. insinuatingly   **h.** artillery fire

_____ 9. rending   **i.** wasted or worn in appearance

_____ 10. pandemonium   **j.** dashingly; jauntily

Thoughtful Reading (25 points)

On the line provided, write the letter of the *best* answer to each of the following items. (5 points each)

_____ 11. James Thurber's descriptions of Walter Mitty's fantasies can be seen
as parodies because they
   a. humorously imitate real life
   b. humorously imitate action-adventure stories
   c. seriously imitate twentieth-century drama
   d. seriously imitate mystery novels

_____ 12. Which of the following statements *best* describes Mrs. Mitty?
   a. She does all the shopping for the household.
   b. She cannot make decisions.
   c. She is always working.
   d. She constantly tells Walter what to do.

_____ 13. When Walter imagines that he is on the witness stand, he
   a. brilliantly argues for his innocence in the murder of Gregory Fitzhurst
   b. proudly admits that he could have killed Gregory Fitzhurst with his left hand
   c. successfully demonstrates that the district attorney murdered Gregory Fitzhurst
   d. acts as his own lawyer in the trial for the murder of Gregory Fitzhurst

_____ **14.** Walter imagines that he fixes an anesthetizer machine in the operating room using
  a. a fountain pen   **c.** a puppy biscuit
  b. a glove   **d.** a pencil

_____ **15.** In all of his fantasies, Walter Mitty imagines that he is
  a. an outlaw narrowly escaping from the authorities
  b. a man who shows control in difficult situations
  c. a person who knows exactly how to follow orders
  d. a hero who saves lives

Expanded Response *(30 points)*
16. In the boxes below, give a brief description of two of the characters that Walter Mitty creates in his fantasies. First, name the character's profession or area of expertise. Then describe some of the character's traits. *(15 points)*

	Character's Expertise or Profession	**Character's Traits**
1.		
2.		

17. In reality, what kind of person is Walter Mitty? On the lines provided, write the letter of the answer you choose and briefly defend your choice. There is more than one possible answer. Use at least one example from the selection to support your ideas. *(15 points)*
  a. passive   **b.** uneducated   **c.** imaginative   **d.** other

_____

_____

_____

_____

Written Response *(25 points)*
18. Do you think that Walter Mitty is trying to escape from reality? If so, what reality is he trying to escape from? Explain your opinion on a separate sheet of paper. Give at least two examples from the story to support your response.

SELECTION TEST

A Worn Path
Eudora Welty

Checking Vocabulary *(20 points)*

Match each word in the left-hand column with its meaning in the right-hand column. Place the letter of the correct meaning in the space provided. *(2 points each)*

_____ **1.** intent   **a.** continuing

_____ **2.** radiation   **b.** groove in the land made by a plow

_____ **3.** solemn   **c.** purposeful

_____ **4.** persistent   **d.** serious

_____ **5.** meditative   **e.** lighted up

_____ **6.** appointed   **f.** pattern; arrangement

_____ **7.** pendulum   **g.** deeply thoughtful

_____ **8.** illumined   **h.** formal

_____ **9.** furrow   **i.** assigned

_____ **10.** ceremonial   **j.** freely swinging weight suspended from a fixed point to regulate a clock's movement

Thoughtful Reading *(25 points)*

On the line provided, write the letter of the *best* answer to each of the following items. *(5 points each)*

_____ **11.** The main theme of "A Worn Path" can best be described as the
     a. persistent temptation to steal as a test of faith
     b. incredible physical strength that comes as a result of age and wisdom
     c. overwhelming presence of nature that threatens the lives of human beings
     d. strong devotion that helps someone to continue on a long journey

_____ **12.** On her journey, Phoenix encounters
     a. an old woman with a cane
     b. a hunter and his dog
     c. a young girl with a piece of cake
     d. an alligator under a log

_____ **13.** How is Phoenix able to remember the way to the doctor's office?
     a. After many trips to the doctor, her feet remember where to take her.
     b. She asks many helpful people for directions.
     c. She is able to find her way with the help of some schoolchildren.
     d. She is able to find her way with the help of a large black dog.

____ **14.** When Phoenix arrives at the doctor's office, what does the attendant think?
 a. She thinks that Phoenix is in the wrong building.
 b. She thinks that Phoenix is insane.
 c. She supposes that Phoenix is from the country.
 d. She supposes that Phoenix is a "charity case."

____ **15.** Phoenix is going to use her two nickels to buy
 a. a paper windmill
 c. a new dress
 b. some throat medicine
 d. a new cane

Expanded Response *(30 points)*
16. Why did Phoenix make her journey? On the lines provided, write the letter of the answer you choose and briefly defend your choice. Use at least one example from the selection to support your ideas. *(15 points)*
 a. She made her journey to get medicine for her grandson.
 b. She made her journey to raise money for her hometown.
 c. Her journey was an act of love.
 d. Other: _____

_____

_____

_____

_____

17. In the chart below, describe three events that occur during Phoenix's journey to the doctor. Include only events that occur *before* Phoenix reaches the building where the doctor is located. *(15 points)*

Event #1	Event #2	Event #3

Written Response *(25 points)*
18. On a separate sheet of paper, write an essay describing Phoenix's character. What kind of person is she? Use at least three examples from the story to support your descriptions.

COLLECTION 12 TEST

The Dream and the Reality

Responding to Literature *(90 points)*

For each activity below, choose a different character from the following list and apply the activity to that character. *(15 points each)*

Dexter Green   Jody's grandfather   Walter Mitty   Phoenix Jackson

1. In each of the selections in Collection 12, a character dreams or fantasizes. Using the following chart, explain the character's dream or fantasy and tell how it relates to the character's personality.

Character:	
Dream or Fantasy	**How the Dream or Fantasy Relates to Character's Personality**

2. Some of the characters in Collection 12 possess a specific purpose or goal. In the chart below, choose a character and describe the character's purpose or goal. Then explain what you think motivates the character toward that goal. Also, tell whether the character succeeds or fails.

Character:		
Character's Purpose or Goal	**Character's Motivation**	**How Does the Character Succeed or Fail?**

Respond to each of the questions below. Attach an extra sheet of paper if necessary. *(30 points each)*

3. Discuss examples of the American dream and disillusionment in either "The Leader of the People" or "Winter Dreams." Use at least two examples from the story in your essay.

_____

_____

_____

_____

_____

_____

4. Which do you think is more important: ordinary, daily triumphs or spectacular, extraordinary adventures? Support your opinions with examples from either "A Worn Path" or "The Secret Life of Walter Mitty."

_____

_____

_____

_____

_____

_____

_____

Vocabulary Review *(10 points)*

In the space provided, write the letter of the word or words that have the same meaning as the word in boldface type. *(2 points each)*

____ 5. Something that is **ludicrous** is
    a. destructive   **b.** creative   **c.** absurd   **d.** unknown

____ 6. Someone who is **arrogant** is
    a. cleverly deceptive   **b.** foolish   **c.** ignorant   **d.** overly proud

____ 7. To speak **insinuatingly** is to speak
    a. suggestively   **b.** unintelligibly   **c.** softly   **d.** aggressively

____ 8. A place described as **bedlam** is filled with
    a. sleepiness   **b.** confusion   **c.** idealism   **d.** solitude

____ 9. A **ceremonial** gesture is one that is
    a. formal   **b.** hurried   **c.** sarcastic   **d.** hidden

SELECTION TEST

Richard Cory
Miniver Cheevy
Edwin Arlington Robinson

Pupil's Edition page 645

Pupil's Edition page 646

Thoughtful Reading *(40 points)*
On the line provided, write the letter of the *best* answer to each of the following items.
(5 points each)

_____ 1. The basic irony in "Richard Cory" is that a wealthy, enviable gentleman
    a. is detested by ordinary people
    b. doesn't understand human suffering
    c. finds nothing to live for
    d. won't talk to his neighbors

_____ 2. Richard Cory's eventual fate
    a. results from business failures
    b. shows his underlying villainy
    c. was predictable, given his everyday behavior
    d. comes as a surprise to the townspeople

_____ 3. "Richard Cory" contains strong visual images of
    a. life in a small New England town
    b. impoverished people living on the street
    c. fashions and customs of a bygone era
    d. the darkness of a midsummer night

_____ 4. The final mystery of Richard Cory's life revolves around
    a. what unspeakable sadness he kept hidden
    b. why he took frequent strolls into town
    c. how he managed to impress other people
    d. what kind of treasures he had

_____ 5. The irony of Miniver Cheevy's story is that he
    a. enjoys thinking about ancient times
    b. dreams of great deeds while failing to act
    c. has a thorough knowledge of medieval history
    d. fails to use his wealth wisely

_____ 6. Miniver Cheevy can *best* be characterized as the type of person who
    a. blames his parents for the woes he suffers
    b. likes to discuss his goals with friends
    c. feels he is out of place and misunderstood
    d. strikes out violently when he is criticized

_____ 7. To comfort himself, Cheevy
    a. writes about knighthood
    b. dresses in regal clothing
    c. teaches Greek history
    d. relies on alcohol

_____ **8.** Richard Cory and Miniver Cheevy are most alike in that they both have
   a. secret miseries
   b. antisocial attitudes
   c. slim physiques
   d. comfortable homes

Expanded Response *(30 points)*

9. Which of the following statements do you think *best* applies to Richard Cory? On the lines provided, write the letter of the answer you choose and briefly defend your choice. There is more than one possible answer. Use at least one example from the poem to support your ideas. *(15 points)*
   a. Many people hide deep sadness under a veneer of politeness.
   b. Rich and elegant people are impressive to those who are less fortunate.
   c. Beneath a friendly countenance there may lie terrible sins against humanity.
   d. A person with great material wealth may have a harder life than does an ordinary wage earner.

_____

_____

_____

_____

10. In "Miniver Cheevy," the speaker describes several things that Cheevy longs for that can be seen both positively and negatively. Choose an object, person, or place from the poem and identify it on the line provided. Then, in the double-edged sword below, describe the positive and negative aspects of this image. *(15 points)*

Object, person, or place: _____

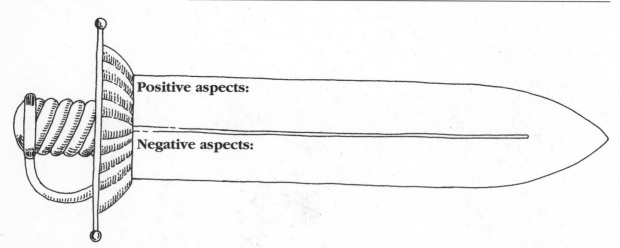

Positive aspects:

Negative aspects:

Written Response *(30 points)*

11. In both "Richard Cory" and "Miniver Cheevy," the characters seem to yearn for things they feel they lack in life. On a separate sheet of paper, describe what you think the characters long for. Support your ideas with at least one example from each poem.

SELECTION TEST

Soldier's Home
Ernest Hemingway

Checking Vocabulary *(20 points)*
Match each word in the left-hand column with its meaning in the right-hand column. Place the letter of the correct meaning in the space provided. *(2 points each)*

____ **1.** alliances

____ **2.** apocryphal

____ **3.** atrocity

____ **4.** consequences

____ **5.** elaborately

____ **6.** engagements

____ **7.** exaggeration

____ **8.** hysteria

____ **9.** intrigue

____ **10.** nauseated

a. feeling sickness or discomfort in the stomach

b. close associations for common objectives

c. of questionable authority; false

d. with great care

e. battles

f. scheming

g. uncontrolled excitement

h. horrible; brutal

i. results of an action

j. overstatement

Thoughtful Reading *(25 points)*
On the line provided, write the letter of the *best* answer to each of the following items. *(5 points each)*

____ **11.** Which sentence below *best* states the theme of "Soldier's Home"?
   a. Family and friends want returning soldiers to find good jobs.
   b. Most civilians never appreciate the heroism of soldiers.
   c. Wartime combat is so devastating that it changes one completely.
   d. Soldiers return home with little respect for their neighbors.

____ **12.** Krebs can *best* be described as a person who
   a. deeply distrusts everyone around him
   b. looks forward to taking up peacetime activities
   c. has lost his goals and the energy to pursue them
   d. has suffered injuries that leave him physically weak

____ **13.** Krebs has returned home too late to
   a. find a comfortable place to live
   b. feel any interest about wartime events
   c. receive news of the whereabouts of his fellow soldiers
   d. receive an elaborate welcome from the town

_____ **14.** Krebs's sister Helen seems to
    a. need his love and approval
    b. grow embarrassed by his behavior
    c. resent his long absence from home
    d. be jealous of the attention he gets

_____ **15.** After the conversation with his mother, Krebs decides to go away because he
    a. wants to avoid any kind of conflict
    b. hears of a job opportunity in Kansas City
    c. realizes that his parents no longer love him
    d. yearns to find a rural area and settle down

Expanded Response (30 points)

16. What does Krebs seem to need most when he returns home? On the lines provided, write the letter of the answer you choose and briefly defend your choice. There is more than one possible answer. Use at least one example from the selection to support your ideas. *(15 points)*
    a. to share his feelings with compassionate listeners
    b. to rest and unwind from his perilous wartime experiences
    c. to drive a car and date women
    d. other: _____

_____

_____

_____

_____

17. As shown in the following chart, the word *home* in "Soldier's Home" may have two meanings. In the chart, note two ideas from the story that enable you to see Krebs's home in two different ways. *(15 points)*

The Battlefield as Krebs's Home	Krebs's Hometown as his Home

Written Response (25 points)

18. Krebs thinks a great deal about lies. On a separate sheet of paper, explain why Krebs feels that he is lying. Make at least two references to specific details in the selection to support your ideas.

SELECTION TEST

The Love Song of J. Alfred Prufrock
T. S. Eliot

Pupil's Edition page 663

Thoughtful Reading *(60 points)*
On the line provided, write the letter of the *best* answer to each of the following items.
(10 points each)

_____ 1. Prufrock's dramatic monologue enables the reader to
    a. see logical, sequential connections between ideas
    b. understand the lives of many other people
    c. glimpse the defining events in Prufrock's childhood
    d. follow the stream of Prufrock's rambling thoughts

_____ 2. Which sentence *best* reflects Prufrock's view of himself?
    a. I am a victim of bad luck and poor choices.
    b. I am unable to take risks.
    c. Women have always admired me.
    d. My youth was adventurous, but my old age is dull.

_____ 3. Prufrock thinks of the frolicking mermaids as creatures who
    a. live in a world of freedom and immortality
    b. lure him toward death and destruction
    c. laugh at the peculiarities of the Romantic age
    d. know that the ocean is safer than the land

_____ 4. Prufrock seems to be a man who has
    a. suffered a hard life in a London suburb
    b. experienced a pleasant home and family life
    c. avoided opportunities for heroism and change
    d. treated other people with malice

_____ 5. Which sentence *best* states the theme of the poem?
    a. The modern world has no need of intellectual people.
    b. Modern life is spiritually bankrupt.
    c. In modern times, heroes are not needed.
    d. Modern people are generous and kind.

_____ 6. "The Love Song of J. Alfred Prufrock" is considered to be a challenging poem by many readers because it
    a. makes several literary references and allusions
    b. presents a conversation between many characters
    c. suggests that animals experience complex feelings
    d. uses a formal rhyme scheme and iambic pentameter

Written Response *(40 points)*
7. Prufrock expresses a general sense of despair. On a separate sheet of paper, identify the passage or image in the poem that you think most vividly communicates this feeling of despair. Give at least one reason why this passage or image impresses you.

SELECTION TEST

The Life You Save May Be Your Own
Flannery O'Connor   **Pupil's Edition page 673**

Checking Vocabulary *(20 points)*
Match each word in the left-hand column with its meaning in the right-hand column. Place the letter of the correct meaning in the space provided. *(2 points each)*

_____ **1.** amble

a. regretted

_____ **2.** gaunt

b. very eager

_____ **3.** guffawing

c. like a loud burst of laughter

_____ **4.** irked

d. leisurely pace

_____ **5.** listed

e. firing of many shots at once

_____ **6.** morose

f. very thin

_____ **7.** ravenous

g. humid and still

_____ **8.** rued

h. annoyed; irritated

_____ **9.** sultry

i. tilted

_____ **10.** volley

j. gloomy

Thoughtful Reading *(25 points)*
On the line provided, write the letter of the *best* answer to each of the following items. *(5 points each)*

_____ **11.** The elder Lucynell allows Shiftlet to live with them because she wants him to
  a. repair the car
  b. fix a fence
  c. marry her daughter
  d. pay the mortgage

_____ **12.** The mother and Shiftlet are similar because they both
  a. exploit other people
  b. have a sense of humor
  c. protect animals
  d. understand Shiftlet's goal

_____ **13.** The climax of the story occurs when Shiftlet
  a. leaves Lucynell in The Hot Spot
  b. gets the ancient car to start
  c. tells the hitchhiker about his mother
  d. notices a highway warning sign

_____ **14.** Near the beginning of the story, Shiftlet suggests to the mother that he may be a liar. This is an example of foreshadowing because it
   a. shows that Shiftlet knows himself well
   b. hints at a deception to come
   c. reveals the mother's goals
   d. indicates that Shiftlet likes the daughter

_____ **15.** Mr. Shiftlet's dissatisfaction with his marriage ceremony is probably a result of the fact that
   a. he would prefer to marry the elder Lucynell
   b. he is already married and is breaking the law by marrying again
   c. the elder Lucynell has made fun of his physical disabilities
   d. he only married the younger Lucynell in order to get the car

Expanded Response *(30 points)*

16. Which of the following statements do you think *best* describes the younger Lucynell? On the lines provided, write the letter of the answer you choose and briefly defend your choice. There is more than one possible answer. Use at least one example from the selection to support your ideas. *(15 points)*
   a. She likes Shiftlet and shows it.
   b. She knows more about life than she is willing to reveal.
   c. She is a pawn in a contest between Shiftlet and her mother.
   d. She is a trusting soul who is content with her life on the farm.

_____

_____

_____

_____

17. Complete the diagram below to show how Shiftlet and the elder Lucynell are alike and how they are different. *(15 points)*

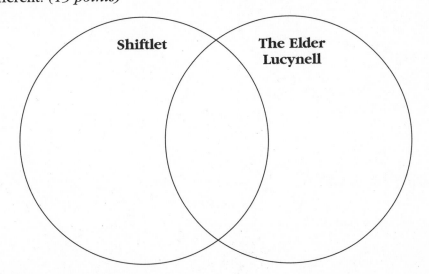

Shiftlet   The Elder Lucynell

Written Response *(25 points)*

18. The end of the story describes a violent storm filled with strange clouds, crashing thunder, and pelting rain. On a separate sheet of paper, explain what this storm may symbolize. Make at least two references to specific details in the selection to support your ideas.

COLLECTION 13 TEST

No Time for Heroes

Responding to Literature *(70 points)*

1. Although J. Alfred Prufrock and Miniver Cheevy are different in many ways, they seem to share similar feelings about modern life and their place in it. In the first column of the chart, describe how each character feels about modern life. In the second column of the chart, note whether you sympathize with each character, and briefly tell why or why not. *(10 points)*

	Character's Attitudes Toward Modern Life	Your Reactions to the Character's Attitudes
Prufrock		
Cheevy		

2. Richard Cory, Krebs, and Shiftlet all have secrets that they can't or won't share with others. In the chart, note your ideas about the secrets each man harbors. In the column on the right, note what results from this unwillingness or inability to tell the truth. *(10 points)*

Characters	Secret	Result of Not Telling the Truth
Richard Cory		
Krebs		
Shiftlet		

Elements of Literature

Respond to each of the questions below. Attach an extra sheet of paper if necessary. *(25 points each)*

3. Write a paragraph explaining why some people feel that heroes are non-existent or hard to find in today's world. Support your opinions with examples from at least two selections in Collection 13.

_____

_____

_____

_____

_____

_____

_____

_____

_____

_____

4. "The Love Song of J. Alfred Prufrock" uses *dramatic monologue.* Discuss how this technique reveals Prufrock's character. Then explain the technique by which we come to know one of these characters: Shiftlet, in "The Life You Save May Be Your Own"; *or* Krebs, in "Soldier's Home."

_____

_____

_____

_____

_____

_____

_____

_____

_____

_____

_____

Vocabulary Review *(10 points)*

In the space provided, write the letter of the word that correctly completes each sentence. *(2 points each)*

5. A (An) _____ story is one which may or may not be true.
    a. apocryphal   **b.** ravenous   **c.** sultry   **d.** atrocity

6. A speaker's humorous tale may result in a lot of _____ from the audience.
    a. exaggeration   **b.** intrigue   **c.** engagements   **d.** guffawing

7. _____ are (is) formed among people who have common goals.
    a. Alliances   **b.** Consequences   **c.** Engagements   **d.** Hysteria

8. The building was declared unsafe to enter, because it _____ .
    a. rued   **b.** listed   **c.** irked   **d.** nauseated

9. _____ over failing the test, the man came home with a dejected attitude.
    a. Amble   **b.** Elaborately   **c.** Morose   **d.** Gaunt

Language Workshop Review: Using Subordinating Conjunctions *(20 points)*

Each of the following sentences contains two clauses joined by the simple conjunction *and*. Rewrite each sentence, replacing *and* with a subordinating conjunction that more precisely explains the relationship between the two clauses. *(4 points each)*

    EXAMPLE: I request quiet and I need time to study.

          I request quiet whenever I need time to study.

10. Heroes need public support *and* they can't work alone in a vacuum.

_____

_____

11. Prufrock acted timidly *and* he expected people to treat him roughly.

_____

_____

12. Krebs didn't do much *and* a discussion with his mother caused him to take action.

_____

_____

13. Perhaps Richard Cory would not have shot himself *and* he had shared his problems with someone.

_____

_____

14. Heroic people sometimes act on impulse, *and* their own personal welfare doesn't matter.

_____

_____

SELECTION TEST

Richard Bone
Lucinda Matlock
Edgar Lee Masters

Pupil's Edition page 692

Recuerdo
Edna St. Vincent Millay

Pupil's Edition page 698

Thoughtful Reading *(40 points)*
On the line provided, write the letter of the *best* answer to each of the following items.
(5 points each)

_____ 1. At the end of the poem Richard Bone compares himself to the
   a. undertaker
   b. historian
   c. preacher
   d. newspaper editor

_____ 2. Conscience-stricken Richard Bone describes himself as a hypocrite because he continued working at a job that required him to
   a. report history
   b. praise the rich
   c. support war
   d. write lies

_____ 3. Lucinda Matlock's story is a proud account of
   a. arrogance and prejudice
   b. pleasure and hardship
   c. crime and punishment
   d. faith, hope, and charity

_____ 4. Lucinda Matlock suggests that a well-lived life depends upon
   a. adequate money
   b. strength of character
   c. good health
   d. a loving marriage

_____ 5. Lucinda Matlock's chief comment about the younger generation focuses on young people's
   a. lack of spirit
   b. rebelliousness
   c. hopefulness
   d. independence

_____ 6. Midway through each poem, both "Lucinda Matlock" and "Richard Bone" change from one tone to another. Which phrase below *best* describes the change of tone in both poems?
   a. from bitter cynicism to acceptance
   b. from interest in life to nonchalance about it
   c. from serious thoughts to humorous observations
   d. from memories of innocence to pessimistic realizations

_____ **7.** The main setting of "Recuerdo" is
  a. an endurance contest
  b. an elopement celebration
  c. a trip on a ferryboat
  d. a salon in Greenwich Village

_____ **8.** In "Recuerdo," the speaker's tone can *best* be described as
  a. excited about a new romance
  b. nostalgic about a past experience
  c. bitter about a missed opportunity
  d. skeptical about the meaning of life

Expanded Response *(30 points)*

9. Choose the option that *best* completes the following statement. On the lines provided, write the letter of the answer you choose and briefly defend your choice. There is more than one possible answer. Use at least one example from the selection to support your ideas. *(15 points)*

Richard Bone compares himself to historians because
a. historians don't always know the ultimate truth
b. Bone uses old reports and records to find factual data
c. like some scholars, Bone learns the truth about people by living among them
d. historians are often pressured to rewrite the past

_____

_____

_____

_____

10. According to some interpretations, the speaker in "Recuerdo" simply relishes the past, while Lucinda Matlock is telling about her past in a style that seems boastful. In the following chart, explain what elements of the poems convey these different impressions. *(15 points)*

Speaker in "Recuerdo": Relishing the past	Lucinda Matlock: Boasting about her past

Written Response *(30 points)*

11. A common theme in literature is how people or characters react to their past. On a separate sheet of paper, describe how this theme applies to Richard Bone, Lucinda Matlock, and the speaker in "Recuerdo." Use at least one idea or image from each of the three poems to support your conclusions.

SELECTION TEST

The Jilting of Granny Weatherall
Katherine Anne Porter

Pupil's Edition page 703

Checking Vocabulary (20 points)

Match each word in the left-hand column with its meaning in the right-hand column.
Place the letter of the correct meaning in the space provided. (2 points each)

____ 1. clammy	**a.** something showy, frivolous, or unnecessary
____ 2. disputed	**b.** cold and damp
____ 3. dwindled	**c.** rejected after being previously accepted
____ 4. frippery	**d.** annoy
____ 5. jilted	**e.** diminished
____ 6. margin	**f.** skilled in saying the right thing
____ 7. nimbus	**g.** aura; halo
____ 8. plague	**h.** extra amount
____ 9. tactful	**i.** contested
____ 10. vanity	**j.** excessive pride

Thoughtful Reading (25 points)

On the line provided, write the letter of the *best* answer to each of the following items.
(5 points each)

____ 11. Granny Weatherall's attitude can *best* be described as
   a. resolute and determined
   b. sweetly nostalgic
   c. sarcastic
   d. humorous

____ 12. The story is told from the point of view of
   a. Doctor Harry
   b. Cornelia
   c. Ellen Weatherall
   d. George

____ 13. Porter chose to use the stream-of-consciousness style of narration in order to
   a. express the thoughts of people gathered around a deathbed
   b. point out the injustices Granny Weatherall has suffered
   c. vividly describe the hard life of a pioneer
   d. allow the reader to get inside Granny's mind

_____ **14.** Granny Weatherall's marriage to John was evidently
     a. filled with conflict   **c.** disappointing and dreary
     b. long and successful   **d.** a source of material wealth

_____ **15.** Which of the following would be the most accurate subtitle for the story?
     a. "A Dutiful Child"   **c.** "An Incurable Wound"
     b. "A Doctor's Success"   **d.** "The Fear of Life"

Expanded Response *(30 points)*

16. What is the basic irony in the story? On the lines provided, write the letter of the answer you choose and briefly defend your choice. There is more than one possible answer. Use at least one example from the selection to support your ideas. *(15 points)*
     a. One sad event can shape a life that is otherwise productive and happy.
     b. The momentous occasion of death may be accompanied by trivial concerns and observations.
     c. In spite of determination and willpower, death is inevitable.
     d. What is most important and memorable to one person may never be conveyed to others.

_____

_____

_____

_____

_____

17. As she lies dying, Granny experiences in her own mind things that are quite different from what those around her perceive. In the chart, note two instances in the story where this occurs. *(15 points)*

Granny Weatherall experiences . . .	Others perceive . . .
1.	1.
2.	2.

Written Response *(25 points)*

18. At the end of the story, the dying Granny Weatherall asks God to give her a "sign." On a separate sheet of paper, explain what kind of sign Granny is looking for, what the response is, and how this response reflects the central event in Granny Weatherall's past.

SELECTION TEST

A Rose for Emily
William Faulkner

Pupil's Edition page 715

Checking Vocabulary (20 points)
Match each word in the left-hand column with its meaning in the right-hand column.
Place the letter of the correct meaning in the space provided. *(2 points each)*

_____ 1. acrid

_____ 2. archaic

_____ 3. circumvent

_____ 4. doddering

_____ 5. pauper

_____ 6. perpetuity

_____ 7. tranquil

_____ 8. valance

_____ 9. vindicated

_____ 10. virulent

a. shaky; trembling from old age

b. extremely poor person

c. short decorative drapery

d. eternity

e. full of hate; venomous

f. bitter; irritating

g. old-fashioned

h. proved correct

i. to get the better of by craft or ingenuity

j. calm; quiet

Thoughtful Reading (25 points)
On the line provided, write the letter of the *best* answer to each of the following items.
(5 points each)

_____ 11. The emotions a reader might be expected to feel toward Miss Emily include
    a. amusement and gratitude
    b. pity and horror
    c. contempt and disappointment
    d. approval and satisfaction

_____ 12. After her father dies, Miss Emily
    a. moves to another town
    b. sees many suitors
    c. becomes a supporter of the arts
    d. refuses to acknowledge his death

_____ 13. The last time the townspeople see Homer Barron alive, he is
    a. buying a suit of clothes
    b. drinking with other men
    c. proposing marriage to Emily
    d. entering Miss Emily's house

_____ **14.** The strand of gray hair discovered at the end of the story signifies that
    a. Miss Emily has apparently lain beside the skeleton
    b. Miss Emily has forgotten about her family
    c. Homer Barron kept a lock of Emily's hair
    d. Emily was much older than Homer Barron

_____ **15.** The social environment described in the story is
    a. an idealized view of Southern society
    b. an inconsequential backdrop to the main action
    c. a reflection of indifference to one's neighbors
    d. a crucial part of the story's setting

Expanded Response *(30 points)*

16. What is the importance of Tobe's role in the story? On the lines provided, write the letter of the answer you choose and briefly defend your choice. There is more than one possible answer. Use at least one example from the selection to support your ideas. *(15 points)*
    a. Tobe's role emphasizes the position of African Americans in the South during this period.
    b. Tobe's appearances enable Miss Emily's neighbors and the reader to sense the passage of many years.
    c. As a plot device, Tobe makes it realistically possible for Miss Emily to stay sequestered in her home.
    d. Other: _____

_____

_____

_____

_____

17. Various male characters influence the course of Miss Emily's life. In the following chart, note how each character affects Miss Emily. *(15 points)*

Character	Effect on Miss Emily
Emily's father	
Colonel Sartoris	
Homer Barron	

Written Response *(25 points)*

18. How different would "A Rose for Emily" have been if the events had taken place in a large city or in the North? On a separate sheet of paper, explain the importance of the story's setting, noting whether you think changing the setting would make a significant difference. Make at least two references to specific details in the selection to support your ideas.

Elements of Literature

COLLECTION 14 TEST

Shadows of the Past

Responding to Literature *(90 points)*

1. All the characters listed in the following chart can recall unhappy events in their pasts. In the center column, identify the unhappy events. In the right-hand column, compare the characters to show how they are alike and different in their reactions to past adversity or tragedy. *(20 points)*

Characters	Unhappy Events	Similarities and Differences
Granny Weatherall		
Miss Emily		
Lucinda Matlock		

2. The characters in the selections in Collection 14 reveal a range of attitudes toward events in their pasts. In the center column of the following chart, note a character whose feeling toward his or her past matches the attitude listed in the first column. Then, in the right-hand column, briefly describe how this attitude is revealed in the selection. *(20 points)*

Attitude Toward Past	Character	How Attitude is Revealed in the Selection
regret		
nostalgia		
pride		

Respond to each of the following questions.
(25 points each)

3. Each of the selections in Collection 14 reflects elements of modernism in its subject matter, themes, and/or techniques. Choose one of the selections and describe how it is modernist, keeping in mind some of the following characteristics of modernism: a sense of disillusionment; an interest in the inner workings of the human mind; the use of new narrative techniques; and rejection of traditional themes and subjects. Support your ideas with at least two examples from the poem or story.

_____

_____

_____

_____

_____

_____

_____

_____

_____

_____

_____

_____

_____

_____

_____

_____

_____

_____

_____

_____

_____

4. Compare and contrast the settings of two selections from Collection 14. Include at least two details from each selection about the people as well as the places that make up the settings, and explain how the settings are important to the events in the selections.

_____

_____

_____

_____

_____

_____

_____

_____

_____

_____

_____

_____

_____

_____

_____

_____

_____

_____

_____

_____

_____

_____

_____

_____

Vocabulary Review (10 points)

In the space provided, write the letter of the word that correctly completes the sentence.
(2 points each)

___ 5. A person known for her or his _____ probably indulges in things that are showy.
   a. valance
   b. frippery
   c. perpetuity
   d. plague

___ 6. People who are naturally _____ make good diplomats.
   a. acrid
   b. archaic
   c. clammy
   d. tactful

___ 7. If you are _____ in a legal verdict, you are likely to feel considerable satisfaction.
   a. disputed
   b. dwindled
   c. vindicated
   d. jilted

___ 8. A(n) _____ phrase is likely to provoke anger or shame.
   a. archaic
   b. doddering
   c. virulent
   d. tranquil

___ 9. An individual's _____ may lead to exaggerated statements about his or her accomplishments and talents.
   a. nimbus
   b. vanity
   c. margin
   d. perpetuity

SELECTION TEST

Go Down, Death James Weldon Johnson
America Claude McKay

Pupil's Edition page 737
Pupil's Edition page 744

Thoughtful Reading *(40 points)*

On the line provided, write the letter of the *best* answer to each of the following items.
(5 points each)

_____ 1. In Johnson's poem, the figure of Death is personified as a
    a. preacher in heaven
    b. cruel and devious angel
    c. rescuer on horseback
    d. huge comet in the sky

_____ 2. The speaker in "Go Down, Death" comforts Sister Caroline's family by explaining
that Sister Caroline is
    a. resting with Jesus
    b. joining the natural world
    c. bound to recover
    d. being reunited with departed friends

_____ 3. Death responds to God's urgent command with
    a. a brief argument
    b. swift and silent obedience
    c. a long-winded agreement
    d. a humorous delay

_____ 4. The speaker in Johnson's poem characterizes Jesus as a
    a. weeping friend
    b. beautiful child
    c. stern judge
    d. loving parent

_____ 5. The theme of McKay's poem "America" concerns the speaker's mixed feelings about
    a. the Russian revolution
    b. Southern Gothic literature
    c. the Harlem Renaissance
    d. life in the United States

_____ 6. The central conflict in McKay's poem takes place between
    a. the speaker's contradictory observations and feelings
    b. the king of the state and the leader of a group of rebels
    c. the speaker's past dreams and present reality
    d. a rich man and a poor man

_____ 7. The speaker in "America" draws strength from
    a. the beauty found in nature
    b. the support of established writers
    c. America's vastness and energy
    d. the belief that things will get better

_____ **8.** The speaker in McKay's poem envisions America's future as
    a. a sad and unnecessary decline
    b. the rise of a world superpower
    c. a vastly improved and just nation
    d. a disastrous social experiment

Expanded Response *(30 points)*

9. In the following chart, evaluate "Go Down, Death: A Funeral Sermon" by checking whether you find it comforting, somewhat comforting, or not comforting. Then give the reasons for your response. Support your response with at least one example from the poem. *(15 points)*

Evaluation of "Go Down, Death: A Funeral Sermon"		
Comforting _____	Somewhat Comforting _____	Not Comforting _____
Reasons for your choice:		

10. What is the attitude of the speaker in "America" toward his country? On the lines provided, write the letter of the answer you choose and briefly defend your choice. Use at least one example from the selection to support your ideas. There is more than one possible answer. *(15 points)*
    a. He is angered by his country's injustices.
    b. He imagines that one day his country will fall.
    c. He stands in awe of the greatness of his country.
    d. He does not care about his country.

_____

_____

_____

_____

_____

Written Response *(30 points)*

11. In both "Go Down, Death" and "America," the poets use personification to give their subjects human qualities. On a separate sheet of paper, describe how personification is used in the two poems. Make at least two references to specific details in each poem to support your ideas.

SELECTION TEST

Tableau
Incident
Countee Cullen

Pupil's Edition page 747

Pupil's Edition page 748

Thoughtful Reading *(40 points)*
On the line provided, write the letter of the *best* answer to each of the following items.
(5 points each)

_____ 1. In "Tableau," the boys are walking together because they
    a. are trying to cause trouble
    b. hope to provoke social change
    c. are following local custom
    d. enjoy each other's company

_____ 2. How do other people react to the behavior of the two boys in "Tableau"?
    a. They cheer the two boys on.
    b. They are upset by the display.
    c. They ignore the boys' presence.
    d. They quietly approve of the friendship.

_____ 3. In the last stanza of "Tableau," the boys
    a. angrily confront the adults of the town
    b. happily continue walking
    c. sadly go their separate ways
    d. speak to each other loudly

_____ 4. "Tableau" seems to present a simple picture, but a larger focus of the poem is the
    a. boys' friendship
    b. reaction of other children
    c. state of race relations
    d. poet's childhood dreams

_____ 5. There is irony in the apparently simple title "Incident," because the poem describes
    a. an event with serious consequences
    b. more than one personal event
    c. a series of historical events
    d. the poet's experience

_____ 6. While riding through Baltimore, the speaker in "Incident" at first feels
    a. frightened, yet fascinated
    b. eager, yet timid
    c. puzzled and homesick
    d. happy and optimistic

_____ 7. Upon seeing another boy, the speaker in "Incident"
    a. attempts to scare him
    b. is reminded of his brother
    c. tries to be friendly
    d. strikes up a conversation

_____ **8.** The encounter with the boy in Baltimore
   a. leaves a strong impression on the speaker
   b. has no particular effect on the speaker
   c. provokes the speaker to lash out in anger
   d. is remembered fondly by the speaker

Expanded Response *(30 points)*

9. In the following chart, identify two images or metaphors from "Tableau." Then note what each image or metaphor conveys. *(15 points)*

Image or Metaphor	Ideas Conveyed

10. What is the theme of "Incident"? On the lines provided, write the letter of the answer you choose and briefly defend your choice. Use at least one example from the selection to support your ideas. There is more than one possible answer. *(15 points)*
   a. Children can be as mean as adults.
   b. A cruel word can leave a lasting impression.
   c. Public transportation is dangerous.
   d. Other: _____

   _____

   _____

   _____

   _____

   _____

   _____

Written Response *(30 points)*

11. How are interactions between people of different races portrayed in the two Cullen poems you have read? On a separate sheet of paper, compare and contrast the two portrayals. Make at least two references to examples from each of the poems to support your ideas.

SELECTION TEST

from Dust Tracks on a Road
Zora Neale Hurston

Pupil's Edition page 751

Checking Vocabulary *(20 points)*

Match each word in the left-hand column with its meaning in the right-hand column. Place the letter of the correct meaning in the space provided. *(2 points each)*

____ **1.** hail   **a.** think; imagine

____ **2.** brazenness   **b.** deeply

____ **3.** caper   **c.** stepping

____ **4.** exalted   **d.** greet

____ **5.** realm   **e.** foolish prank

____ **6.** avarice   **f.** greed

____ **7.** tread   **g.** kingdom

____ **8.** profoundly   **h.** boldness

____ **9.** resolved   **i.** lifted up

____ **10.** conceive   **j.** made a decision; determined

Thoughtful Reading *(25 points)*

On the line provided, write the letter of the *best* answer to each of the following items. *(5 points each)*

____ **11.** Which of the following quotations from *Dust Tracks on a Road* demonstrates the use of slang?
     a. "I used to take a seat on top of the gatepost and watch the world go by."
     b. "Not only was I barefooted, but my feet and legs were dusty."
     c. "She would cut her eyes and give us a glare that meant trouble . . ."
     d. "They came and went, came and went."

____ **12.** Upon seeing cars and carriages pass by her house, Zora Neale would
     a. ask the travelers for a ride
     b. follow them with her bike
     c. run to inform her parents
     d. try to race the cars on foot

____ **13.** Zora Neale's grandmother feared her granddaughter's boldness would
     a. cause her to fall off the gatepost
     b. make her unpopular at school
     c. provoke white people to harm her
     d. one day cause a traffic accident

____ **14.** The students' good behavior in school is most influenced by
   a. their wish to impress their teachers
   b. the threat of Mrs. Calhoun's palmetto switch
   c. the absence of visitors in the classroom
   d. the hope that visitors will recognize them

____ **15.** What is Zora Neale's reaction to the gifts given to her by the visitors from Minnesota?
   a. She is grateful but disappointed because she'd hoped for more.
   b. She is embarrassed that the women singled her out.
   c. It is one of the most joyful experiences of her life.
   d. She is suspicious of the women's generosity.

Expanded Response *(30 points)*

16. Why do Mrs. Johnstone and Miss Hurd give gifts to Zora Neale? On the lines provided, write the letter of the answer you choose and briefly defend your choice. Use at least one example from the selection to support your ideas. There is more than one possible answer. *(15 points)*
   a. They recognize her talent.
   b. They wish to adopt her.
   c. They believe she will benefit from their gifts.
   d. Other: _____

_____

_____

_____

_____

17. Which of Zora Neale's actions reveal the *most* about her character? In the following chart, describe two of Zora Neale's actions, and then explain what each action says about her character. *(15 points)*

Zora Neale's Actions	What Is Revealed About Her Character

Written Response *(25 points)*

18. Sometimes a person's heroes or heroines tell you a lot about that person. On a separate sheet of paper, describe the kind of literary characters that attract Zora Neale. Then explain why you think she is drawn to these characters. Make at least two references to details in the selection to support your ideas.

SELECTION TEST

The Weary Blues
Harlem
Langston Hughes

Pupil's Edition page 761

Pupil's Edition page 764

Thoughtful Reading *(40 points)*
On the line provided, write the letter of the *best* answer to each of the following items.
(5 points each)

_____ 1. The song performed in "The Weary Blues" addresses
    a. all people who are unhappy
    b. the plight of underpaid musicians
    c. the musician's poor health
    d. men without children

_____ 2. The musician in "The Weary Blues" feels tired because he
    a. works all night
    b. receives low wages
    c. can't find satisfaction
    d. suffers from lack of sleep

_____ 3. At the end of "The Weary Blues," the musician
    a. sleeps like the dead
    b. meets the poet
    c. smiles at the audience
    d. passes around a hat

_____ 4. Rhythms in "The Weary Blues"
    a. are highly regular
    b. reflect the rhythms of blues music
    c. require piano in the background
    d. echo the traditional sonnet form

_____ 5. The tone of a poem refers to
    a. the emotion felt by the writer
    b. the attitude of the writer
    c. the emotion felt by the reader
    d. the attitude of the reader

_____ 6. According to the speaker in "Harlem," conditions for people living in Harlem
    a. improved after the birth of the blues
    b. deteriorated since they moved there
    c. have not changed much over the years
    d. promised to get better in time

_____ 7. The speaker in "Harlem" uses "we" to refer to
    a. residents of Manhattan
    b. people selling bread in Harlem
    c. people who remember the Depression
    d. African Americans in Harlem

____ **8.** In the final stanza of "Harlem," people
    a. thoughtfully observe the outside world
    b. recall World War II
    c. begin to organize the civil rights movement
    d. decide to leave the neighborhood

Expanded Response *(30 points)*

9. The speaker in "Harlem" remembers the past while expressing his concern for the future. In the chart below, briefly describe at least two of Harlem residents' past and present experiences. *(15 points)*

Past	Present

10. Choose the statement that you believe *best* describes the musician in "The Weary Blues." On the lines provided, write the letter of the answer you choose and briefly defend your choice. Use at least one example from the selection to support your choice. There is more than one possible answer. *(15 points)*
    a. The musician creates melancholy sounds and words.
    b. The musician wishes he were someone else.
    c. The musician's songs seem to ease his mind.
    d. Other: _____

_____

_____

_____

_____

_____

_____

Written Response *(30 points)*

11. Are the situations described in the two Langston Hughes poems similar or different? On a separate sheet of paper, compare and contrast the hardship(s) described by the speaker in "Harlem" with the musician's experience(s) in "The Weary Blues." Make at least two references to examples from both poems to support your ideas.

COLLECTION 15 TEST

I, Too, Sing America

Responding to Literature *(90 points)*

For each activity below, choose a poem from the following list and apply the activity to that poem.

"Go Down, Death"   "Tableau"   "Incident"   "The Weary Blues"   "America"   "Harlem"

1. Choose two poems and list their titles in the following chart. In the left-hand column, give an example of a figure of speech from each poem and briefly describe it. In the right-hand column, describe how each figure of speech adds to the meaning of the poem. *(20 points)*

Figure of Speech	How It Adds to the Poem's Meaning
Poem Title:	
Poem Title:	

2. Choose two poems and list their titles in the following chart. In the left-hand column, briefly describe the main characters and the other characters or situations that they are in conflict with. In the right-hand column, explain why you think each conflict arises. *(20 points)*

Character or Situations in Conflict	Why the Conflict Arises
Poem Title:	
Poem Title:	

Respond to each of the following questions. Attach an extra sheet of paper if necessary.
(25 points each)

3. Like much of the other literature produced during the Harlem Renaissance, the selections in Collection 15 address issues of race, either directly or indirectly, by focusing on subjects such as racism, the interactions between people of different races, and the experiences within different aspects of African American heritage. Choose two selections and compare and contrast how these works address issues of race. Support your ideas with at least two specific examples from each selection.

_____

_____

_____

_____

_____

_____

_____

_____

_____

_____

_____

_____

_____

_____

_____

_____

_____

_____

_____

_____

_____

4. Compare and contrast the speaker's tone in two of the following selections: "Go Down, Death," "America," or the excerpt from *Dust Tracks on a Road*. Provide examples from the selections to support your opinions.

_____

_____

_____

_____

_____

_____

_____

_____

_____

_____

_____

_____

_____

_____

_____

_____

_____

_____

_____

_____

_____

_____

_____

_____

_____

Vocabulary Review *(10 points)*

For each item below, write on the line provided the letter of the word that has the same meaning as the italicized word. *(2 points each)*

_____ 5. To *hail* means to
    a. fall upon
    b. direct
    c. greet
    d. change

_____ 6. A person who shows *brazenness* exhibits
    a. boldness
    b. strength
    c. passion
    d. cheerfulness

_____ 7. A person's *realm* is his or her
    a. weakness
    b. secret
    c. wish
    d. kingdom

_____ 8. When you *tread*, you are
    a. commanding
    b. deceiving
    c. craving
    d. stepping

_____ 9. To act with *avarice* is to behave
    a. viciously
    b. greedily
    c. thoughtlessly
    d. cautiously

SELECTION TEST

The River-Merchant's Wife: A Letter
Ezra Pound

Pupil's Edition page 774

Thoughtful Reading *(40 points)*
On the line provided, write the letter of the *best* answer to each of the following items.
(10 points each)

_____ 1. In "The River-Merchant's Wife: A Letter," the speaker recalls how she first met her husband
    a. when they were children   **c.** during courtship
    b. on their wedding day   **d.** five months ago

_____ 2. The speaker describes her behavior during the early days of the marriage as
    a. coy and flirtatious   **c.** shy and somber
    b. joyful and lighthearted   **d.** reckless and nervous

_____ 3. The couple became separated when the husband
    a. fell ill and went to a hospital   **c.** died unexpectedly
    b. left home on business   **d.** was kidnapped

_____ 4. In her loneliness, the speaker finds it painful even to watch
    a. a pair of butterflies   **c.** the swirling river
    b. purple plums   **d.** chattering monkeys

Expanded Response *(30 points)*
5. The left column of the following chart lists images found in the poem. In the right column, explain what each image communicates. The first row has been completed as an example.

Image	What the Image Communicates
Hair cut straight across her forehead	She is a young girl.
As a child, the wife pulls flowers.	
Shortly after getting married, the wife looks at a wall and doesn't answer her husband.	
The wife desires her dust to be mingled with her husband's.	
Before her husband leaves, the wife stops climbing the lookout.	
The monkeys make sorrowful sounds.	

Written Response *(30 points)*
6. Various images in "The River-Merchant's Wife: A Letter" contribute to the overall mood of the poem. On a separate sheet of paper, describe what you think the mood of the poem is and how two images help create that mood.

SELECTION TEST

The Red Wheelbarrow
The Great Figure
William Carlos Williams

Pupil's Edition page 779

Thoughtful Reading (40 points)
On the line provided, write the letter of the *best* answer to each of the following items.
(5 points each)

_____ 1. "The Red Wheelbarrow" contains all of the following except
    a. green grass
    b. white chickens
    c. a red wheelbarrow
    d. rain water

_____ 2. "The Red Wheelbarrow" depicts a
    a. realistic scene
    b. series of fantastic images
    c. character's sorrow
    d. historically important moment

_____ 3. The speaker in "The Red Wheelbarrow"
    a. makes allusions to musical compositions
    b. emphasizes the importance of trust
    c. regrets past actions
    d. offers an opinion about life

_____ 4. To describe the images in "The Red Wheelbarrow," Williams uses
    a. colors and simple language
    b. references to Imagist theory
    c. elaborate figures of speech
    d. sounds and rhythms

_____ 5. What does the title of "The Great Figure" literally refer to?
    a. vast size
    b. the figure 5
    c. a famous person
    d. a Greek statue

_____ 6. The scene of "The Great Figure" is a
    a. dense forest in New Jersey
    b. beautiful but deserted town
    c. rainy night on a city street
    d. busy day in a large city

_____ 7. Williams uses all of the following images in "The Great Figure" **except**
    a. clanging gongs
    b. tolling bells
    c. howling sirens
    d. rumbling wheels

_____ **8.** The poem "The Great Figure" creates an overall impression of
  a. dramatic action
  b. peace and quiet
  c. dangerous menace
  d. an ordinary workday

Expanded Response *(30 points)*

9. In the following chart, list two images from each of Williams's poems and indicate which sense (sight, touch, hearing, smell, taste) each image primarily appeals to. *(15 points)*

	Image	Sense
"The Red Wheelbarrow"		
"The Great Figure"		

10. Which of the following statements provides the *best* description of Williams's poetry? On the lines provided, write the letter of the answer you choose and briefly defend your choice. There is more than one possible answer. Use at least one example from each poem to support your answer. *(15 points)*
  a. Williams's poems involve complex language and symbols.
  b. Williams uses details that present objects or scenes just as they are.
  c. Williams's poems are deceptively simple.
  d. Other: _____

_____

_____

_____

_____

Written Response *(30 points)*

11. "The Red Wheelbarrow" and "The Great Figure" share an ability to surprise the reader by creating a sense of expectation early in the poems. On a separate sheet of paper, describe how the two poems by Williams foster an element of surprise. Make references to at least one example in each poem to support your ideas.

SELECTION TEST

Anecdote of the Jar
Wallace Stevens

Pupil's Edition page 784

Poetry
Marianne Moore

Pupil's Edition page 787

Thoughtful Reading *(40 points)*
On the line provided, write the letter of the *best* answer to each of the following items.
(5 points each)

_____ 1. Which word *best* describes the effect that the jar's placement has on the wilderness in Stevens's poem?
   a. spoiling   **c.** uplifting
   b. taming   **d.** distracting

_____ 2. What is described as "slovenly" in Stevens's poem?
   a. the jar   **c.** the hill
   b. Tennessee   **d.** the wilderness

_____ 3. The jar in Stevens's poem is generally described
   a. as a beautiful, fragile object
   b. with long, descriptive adjectives
   c. as a piece of scientific equipment
   d. in terms of its physical appearance

_____ 4. One theme of "Anecdote of the Jar" addresses how
   a. art is controlled by science
   b. human civilization dominates nature
   c. the state of Tennessee remains independent
   d. jars are extremely durable

_____ 5. In "Poetry," the speaker claims that grasping hands, dilating eyes, and rising hair are important because
   a. a sophisticated interpretation can be applied to them
   b. they are derivative
   c. they are useful
   d. they are new and exotic

_____ 6. What is "all this fiddle" that the speaker refers to in Moore's poem?
   a. poetry   **c.** interpretations
   b. adjectives   **d.** contempt

_____ 7. The rhythm of Moore's poem can be described as
   a. mimicking the sonnet form   **c.** free but somewhat regular
   b. resembling a blues song   **d.** nonexistent

_____ 8. According to "Poetry," a good poet would
   a. symbolize love as a heart
   b. read Homer for inspiration
   c. dismiss the importance of textbooks and papers
   d. present imaginary places with real details

Expanded Response (30 points)

9. Which of the following statements *best* describes the message of Moore's "Poetry"? On the lines provided, write the letter of the answer you choose and briefly defend your choice. There is more than one possible answer. Use at least one example from the poem to support your ideas. *(15 points)*

 a. All poetry should focus on the natural world.
 b. If you say you dislike poetry, you probably just dislike certain kinds of poetry.
 c. Poets should write with imagination about topics that are useful.
 d. Other: _____

 _____

 _____

 _____

 _____

 _____

10. Both "Anecdote of the Jar" and "Poetry" address the subjects of art or human creative endeavor. In the following chart, briefly express what you believe each poem says about art. Then compare and contrast the messages of the two poems by citing one significant similarity and one significant difference between them. *(15 points)*

	"Anecdote of the Jar"	"Poetry"
What the poem says about art		
Similarity:		
Difference:		

Written Response (30 points)

11. Based on your understanding of Moore's ideas in "Poetry," would she like or dislike Stevens's poem? Support your opinion with at least one reference to each poem. Write your essay on a separate sheet of paper.

SELECTION TEST

Chicago
Carl Sandburg   **Pupil's Edition page 792**

what if a much of a which of a wind
E. E. Cummings   **Pupil's Edition page 797**

Thoughtful Reading *(40 points)*
On the line provided, write the letter of the *best* answer to each of the following items.
(5 points each)

_____ 1. "Chicago" opens with a description of the city's reputation as a center for
  a. computer software and other high tech industries
  b. railroads, manufacturing, and stockyards
  c. music, theater, and cultural activities
  d. immorality and political corruption

_____ 2. In Sandburg's poem, the speaker compares Chicago to
  a. a hog that refuses to be slaughtered
  b. a painted woman under a gas lamp
  c. a fighter who has never lost a battle
  d. a mighty steam-driven locomotive

_____ 3. "Chicago" makes use of apostrophe in that
  a. the speaker addresses the city as if it were a person
  b. the poem contains inflated language and imagery
  c. the poem contains experimental use of punctuation
  d. the speaker expresses that he does not like Chicago

_____ 4. The speaker's attitude toward Chicago is
  a. admiring and affectionate
  b. indifferent and nonchalant
  c. sad and repulsed
  d. ambivalent and wary

_____ 5. In "what if a much of a which of a wind," the images describe
  a. a tornado in the Midwest
  b. the destruction of the universe
  c. a gravitational problem
  d. global weather changes

_____ 6. Cummings's poem expresses the speaker's confidence in
  a. natural phenomena
  b. poetry
  c. humanity
  d. the rational mind

_____ 7. In each stanza of Cummings's poem, the speaker describes
  a. disaster and the human response to it
  b. daytime disturbances followed by evening peace
  c. arguments between fierce opponents
  d. Earth's collision with other planets

_____ **8.** In Cummings's poem, the word *blow* may be interpreted as meaning
    a. knocking down to the ground
    b. leaving a place behind
    c. a sound made by a musical instrument
    d. transforming through force

Expanded Response *(30 points)*

9. Both "Chicago" and "what if . . ." contain powerful language and imagery even though they are about very different topics. In the following chart, match each image with the poem that it comes from by placing a checkmark in the appropriate box. *(15 points)*

Image	"Chicago"	"what if . . ."
a. A powerful wind bloodies the sun.		
b. A lifted head sings with pride at being alive.		
c. A fierce dog laps its tongue in anticipation.		
d. Screaming hills get flayed with sleet and snow.		
e. A young man laughs under the burden of destiny.		

10. Which of the following statements do you think *best* describes the effect of apostrophe in "Chicago"? On the lines provided, write the letter of the answer you choose and briefly defend your choice. There is more than one possible answer. Use at least one example from the selection to support your ideas. *(15 points)*
    a. The use of apostrophe produces a heightened dramatic effect.
    b. The use of apostrophe gives the speaker's voice more authority.
    c. Apostrophe is used to point out the city's connections with other cities.
    d. Other: _____

_____
_____
_____
_____
_____
_____
_____

Written Response *(30 points)*

11. Despite their differences, "Chicago" and "what if . . ." are similar in several ways. On a separate sheet of paper, write a paragraph in which you compare the two poems. You should be able to find at least two ways that the poems are similar. Make references to at least one example in each poem to support your ideas.

THE AMERICAN LANGUAGE

American Slang   Pupil's Edition page 801

On the line provided, write the letter of the *best* answer to each of the following items.
(10 points each)

_____ **1.** Slang or its equivalent
    a. is a product of laziness and silliness
    b. flourishes only among the uneducated
    c. is as ancient as language itself
    d. is easier to understand than standard English

_____ **2.** One of the early words for slang—*argot*—referred to the specialized vocabulary of
    a. formal studies
    b. kinship
    c. age groups
    d. occupations

_____ **3.** According to anthropologists, the main function of slang is to
    a. simplify language use
    b. define members of a group
    c. communicate meaning
    d. develop more colorful language

_____ **4.** Another explanation for the popularity of slang is that
    a. slang always refers to concrete objects
    b. people enjoy inventing informal, playful language
    c. slang generally derives from musical concepts
    d. using slang is a sign of economic success

_____ **5.** Most slang words and expressions
    a. disappear quickly
    b. are adopted by most people
    c. become a permanent part of the language
    d. communicate effectively

_____ **6.** For those who do not use it, the response to slang is often
    a. approval
    b. indifference
    c. fascination
    d. highly critical

_____ **7.** Why has the United States been a particularly fertile ground for slang since the 1830s?
    a. Americans have developed a keen interest in language.
    b. Americans have found standard English difficult.
    c. The informality of slang is associated with democratic ideals.
    d. Slang has been taught in American schools.

_____ 8. Slang words and phrases develop
    a. at the suggestion of professional linguists
    b. in exactly the same way as other additions to the language
    c. only when used by a particular occupational group
    d. because they are colorful rather than useful

_____ 9. Backwoodsmen of the nineteenth century were responsible for introducing slang words that were
    a. variations of existing words
    b. standard words clipped to form shortened words
    c. borrowed from another language
    d. imaginative and wild inventions

_____ 10. Certain words are considered slang for generations because they
    a. are confined to a small group
    b. fulfill only general purposes
    c. seem so informal
    d. make poetry out of the commonplace

NAME _____ CLASS _____ DATE_____ SCORE _____

Make It New!

Responding to Literature *(90 points)*
For each activity that follows, choose appropriate poems from the following list and apply the
activity to those poems. *(20 points each)*

"The River-Merchant's Wife: A Letter"   "The Red Wheelbarrow"   "The Great Figure"
"Anecdote of the Jar"   "Poetry"   "Chicago"
"what if a much of a which of a wind"

1. In several poems in Collection 16, the poet presents negative or bleak descriptions but then
   presents a positive message. Choose two poems and, using the chart below, describe what is
   presented negatively and positively in each poem.

What Is Negative	What Is Positive
Poem:	
Poem:	

2. Several of the poems in Collection 16 present an image or an action that may at first seem
   trivial, but that becomes significant in its implications or symbolic meaning. In the chart
   below, list two poems, identify an apparently trivial image or action in each poem, and then
   explain how it takes on greater significance.

Trivial Image or Action	How the Image or Action Is Significant
Poem:	
Poem:	

Elements of Literature

Respond to each of the following questions. Attach an extra sheet of paper if necessary.
(25 points each)

3. Most of the poets in Collection 16 followed the tenets of Imagism and maintained definite ideas about what the purpose and conventions of poetry should be. Choose two poets and briefly describe their ideas about poetry. Then explain how a poem by each poet illustrates his or her ideas about poetry. Make references to at least one specific example in each poem to support your ideas.

_____

_____

_____

_____

_____

_____

_____

_____

_____

4. Collection 16 begins with a poem by Ezra Pound and covers an era of American literature dominated by Pound's ideas, which stress the importance of clear, precise images. Which images from Collection 16 stick out most in your mind? Identify two poems whose images you recall vividly, describe the images, and explain why you think these images make an impact on you.

_____

_____

_____

_____

_____

_____

_____

_____

_____

Language Workshop Review: Using the Literary Present (10 points)

On the lines provided, rewrite each of the following sentences using the literary present. (2 points each)

EXAMPLE: The speaker in Moore's poem defended poetry as a place where important ideas may be expressed.

The speaker in Moore's poem defends poetry as a place where important ideas may be
expressed.

5. Cummings's poem described a very destructive force.

_____

6. A firetruck barreled through the town in Williams's poem.

_____

7. In "Poetry," the speaker said that the subject matter of poetry should be raw and genuine.

_____

8. The jar in Stevens's poem may have symbolized human consciousness.

_____

9. Sandburg called Chicago the city of the big shoulders in the poem titled "Chicago."

_____

LITERARY PERIOD TEST

The Moderns

Reading Poetry
Read the following poems carefully, and then answer the questions that follow.

Daybreak in Alabama
by Langston Hughes

When I get to be a composer
I'm gonna write me some music about
Daybreak in Alabama
And I'm gonna put the purtiest songs in it
5   Rising out of the ground like a swamp mist
And falling out of heaven like soft dew.
I'm gonna put some tall tall trees in it
And the scent of pine needles
And the smell of red clay after rain
10   And long red necks
And poppy colored faces
And big brown eyes
Of black and white black white black people
And I'm gonna put white hands
15   And black hands and brown hands and yellow
hands
And red clay earth hands in it
Touching everybody with kind fingers
And touching each other natural as dew
In that dawn of music when I
20   Get to be a composer
And write about daybreak
In Alabama.

The Planet on the Table
by Wallace Stevens

Ariel was glad he had written his poems.
They were of a remembered time
Or of something seen that he liked.

Other makings of the sun
5   Were waste and welter
And the ripe shrub writhed.

His self and the sun were one
And his poems, although makings of his self,
Were no less makings of the sun.

10   It was not important that they survive.
What mattered was that they should bear
Some lineament or character,

Some <u>affluence</u>, if only half-perceived
In the poverty of their words,
15   Of the planet of which they were part.

Understanding Vocabulary (20 points)

Each of the following underlined words has also been underlined in the preceding poems. Re-read those lines and use context clues to help you select an answer. On the lines provided, write the letter of the word or phrase that *best* completes each sentence. *(4 points each)*

_____ **1.** A <u>composer</u> is a
    a. trumpet player
    b. painter
    c. songwriter
    d. collector

_____ **2.** <u>Welter</u> could be
    a. a disordered jumble
    b. rich growth
    c. brightly colored paper
    d. useful products

_____ **3.** A snake that <u>writhed</u> probably
    a. became stronger
    b. twisted and turned
    c. grew heartily
    d. stood out

_____ **4.** <u>Lineament</u> is best described as a
    a. type of cloth
    b. muscle pain
    c. healing balm
    d. distinctive feature

_____ **5.** <u>Affluence</u> refers to the planet's
    a. abundance
    b. rivers
    c. land mass
    d. size

Thoughtful Reading (35 points)

On the line provided, write the letter of the *best* answer to each of the following items. *(7 points each)*

_____ **6.** In Hughes's poem which of the following things is **not** something the composer says he is going to put into his music?
    a. tall trees
    b. swamp mist
    c. the smell of red clay after rain
    d. the scent of pine needles

_____ **7.** To what does Hughes compare the color of people's faces?
    a. daybreak
    b. music
    c. clay
    d. poppies

_____ **8.** In Hughes's poem, what could "daybreak in Alabama" refer to?
    a. a beautiful sunset
    b. westward migration
    c. a natural disaster
    d. change for the better

_____ **9.** The subject of Stevens's poem is the
    a. writing of poetry
    b. solar system
    c. speaker's disillusionment
    d. richness of language

_____ **10.** In "The Planet on the Table" which of the following statements is **not** true about the poems that Ariel writes?
    a. It is not essential that they survive.
    b. They were of a forgotten time.
    c. Ariel is happy that he wrote them.
    d. They were creations of the sun.

Expanded Response *(15 points)*

11. In the chart below, list three images from "Daybreak in Alabama" that appeal to three different senses and note which sense each image appeals to. Then offer an interpretation of what you think these images add up to in the poem.

Image	Sense It Appeals To

Interpretation:

Written Response *(30 points)*

12. Like several poems in Collection 16, "The Planet on the Table" makes a statement about poetry itself. On the lines below, write a paragraph in which you first explain what this poem says about poetry. Then compare and contrast the poem's message with that of a poem in Collection 16. Point out at least one significant similarity and one significant difference between the poems.

_____

_____

_____

_____

_____

_____

_____

_____

_____

_____

_____

_____

_____

_____

_____

_____

_____

_____

_____

LITERARY PERIOD INTRODUCTION TEST

American Drama

On the line provided, write the letter of the *best* answer to each of the following items.
(10 points each)

_____ 1. Unlike a poem or novel, a play is never finished because
  a. it must have a definite beginning, middle, and end
  b. it must take into consideration the emotions of the audience
  c. after it is written, it still needs to be brought to life on stage
  d. after it is written, the playwright must find more funding

_____ 2. The protagonist of a play is the
  a. major character who usually drives the action forward
  b. character that the audience always finds the most appealing
  c. most interesting and memorable character in the drama
  d. character who eventually gets what she or he strives for

_____ 3. Exposition gives the audience
  a. the physical setting of the play
  b. background information
  c. the play's conclusion
  d. the play's psychological realism

_____ 4. Most of the plays produced in the United States today are
  a. produced with the hope that they will make money
  b. put on with the intention of shocking the public
  c. written by either Thornton Wilder or Arthur Miller
  d. written by the play's producer and given to the director

_____ 5. Playwrights must usually find an agent who
  a. directs the play and screens the actors and actresses
  b. ensures that the play is suitable for Broadway
  c. submits a play to producers who are likely to consider it
  d. takes charge of set design, costume design, and music

_____ 6. The first important figure in American drama is generally considered to be
  a. Samuel Beckett
  b. Edward Albee
  c. Eugene O'Neill
  d. William Inge

_____ 7. Ibsen, Strindberg, and Chekhov were
  a. European playwrights who realistically presented characters and situations
  b. American playwrights who presented the psychological complexities of
     their characters
  c. producers in the New York Absurdist group who produced new European plays
  d. European playwrights who were heavily influenced by the plays of
     Edward Albee and Clifford Odets

COLLECTION 17

_____ **8.** The Provincetown Players and the Washington Square Players
    a. founded the Theater of the Absurd in the latter part of the nineteenth century
    b. placed themselves in opposition to the established commercial theater
    c. were famous for their goal of participating only in one-act plays
    d. collaborated to present an electrifying performance of *The Bald Soprano*

_____ **9.** Some of the plays of Arthur Miller and most of the plays of Tennessee Williams
    a. focus primarily on social responsibility
    b. combine realism with imaginative elements
    c. usually feature female protagonists
    d. involve colorful, visually dramatic sets

_____ **10.** Expressionist drama aims to
    a. shock the audience by portraying characters with unrealistic conflicts
    b. make people in the audience focus on themselves, not on the stage
    c. keep drama within the confines of a "beginning, middle, end" pattern
    d. reveal the inner consciousness of characters

SELECTION TEST

A Raisin in the Sun, Act Two
Lorraine Hansberry

Pupil's Edition page 851

HRW material copyrighted under notice appearing earlier in this book.

COLLECTION 17

Checking Vocabulary *(20 points)*
Match each word in the left-hand column with its meaning in the right-hand column.
Place the letter of the correct meaning in the space provided. *(2 points each)*

_____ 1. fraternal   **a.** sassily; impertinently

_____ 2. dominant   **b.** pleading; entreating

_____ 3. sobriety   **c.** brotherly; friendly

_____ 4. resignation   **d.** acquiescence; reluctant acceptance

_____ 5. revelation   **e.** tense; rigid

_____ 6. imploring   **f.** intense strength; vitality

_____ 7. vigor   **g.** prevailing; principal

_____ 8. exuberant   **h.** intensely happy; visibly enthusiastic

_____ 9. saucily   **i.** state or quality of being sober

_____ 10. taut   **j.** disclosure; something made known

Thoughtful Reading *(25 points)*
On the line provided, write the letter of the *best* answer to each of the following items.
(5 points each)

_____ 11. What does Mama decide to do with the insurance money?
   a. She puts $3,500 down on a house, gives the rest to Walter to manage, and tells him to set aside $3,000 for Beneatha's medical schooling.
   b. She puts $3,500 down on a house and gives $6,500 to Walter to do with as he pleases.
   c. She puts aside $3,500 for a European vacation and gives the rest to Walter.
   d. She puts aside $3,500 for a European vacation, puts aside $3,500 for Beneatha's medical schooling, and gives the rest to Walter.

_____ 12. What does Walter do with the money that Mama gives him?
   a. He puts $3,000 in the bank and gives the rest to Willy.
   b. He puts $6,500 in the bank and gives the rest to Willy.
   c. He puts it all in the bank.
   d. He gives it all to Willy.

_____ 13. Karl Lindner visits the Youngers in order to
   a. welcome the Youngers to Clybourne Park
   b. ask the Youngers to join the Clybourne Park Improvement Association
   c. make an offer on the house that Mama is buying
   d. ask Walter for suggestions about dealing with community problems

_____ **14.** Mama decides to give Walter part of the insurance money because she realizes that
   a. Walter is dependent on Ruth for money
   b. she has received more money than she expected
   c. she needs to demonstrate her trust in Walter
   d. Walter would have taken the money anyway

_____ **15.** What is Beneatha's attitude toward George Murchison?
   a. She admires his sense of style and his British accent.
   b. She finds him pleasant but somewhat stifling.
   c. She wants to teach him about Chicago's history.
   d. She thinks he is cruel and overly serious.

Expanded Response (30 points)

16. Living "the good life" means different things to different characters in *A Raisin in the Sun*. Choose a character in the play and then the option that you believe *best* describes what living "the good life" means to that character. On the lines provided, write the letter of the answer you choose and briefly defend your choice. There is more than one possible answer. Use at least one example from the selection to support your ideas. *(15 points)*
   a. being your own boss and becoming materially prosperous
   b. having a healthy family and a comfortable home
   c. being married and having many children
   d. being educated and fulfilling intellectual goals

_____

_____

_____

_____

17. Characterization is the process by which the writer reveals the personality of a character. Choose a character from the play and, using the chart below, explain how Hansberry characterizes him or her. First, write down what you think is a dominant characteristic of the character (for example, shyness, intelligence, or athletic ability). Then, in the other boxes, support your opinion with examples of what the character says and does. *(15 points)*

Character	
Characteristic	
What the Character Says	
What the Character Does	

Written Response (25 points)

18. On a separate sheet of paper, write a paragraph explaining how what Walter does with the money affects the dreams of the other characters. Can any of their dreams be salvaged? Make at least two references to examples in the play to support your ideas.

SELECTION TEST

A Raisin in the Sun, Act Three
Lorraine Hansberry

Pupil's Edition page 876

Checking Vocabulary *(20 points)*
Match each word in the left-hand column with its meaning in the right-hand column.
Place the letter of the correct meaning in the space provided. *(2 points each)*

_____ **1.** flippancy   **a.** anxious; frantic

_____ **2.** wrought   **b.** way of walking; stride

_____ **3.** monologue   **c.** busyness; energetic activity

_____ **4.** gait   **d.** created; made

_____ **5.** agitated   **e.** speech given by one person

_____ **6.** epitaph   **f.** impertinence; glibness

_____ **7.** negotiate   **g.** make a bargain; come to an agreement

_____ **8.** groping   **h.** memorable or descriptive phrase written on a tombstone or in memory of the dead

_____ **9.** reverie   **i.** thought; musing

_____ **10.** bustling   **j.** searching; fumbling

Thoughtful Reading *(25 points)*
On the line provided, write the letter of the *best* answer to each of the following items.
(5 points each)

_____ **11.** What inspired Beneatha to try to become a doctor?
    a. She met a famous surgeon who befriended her.
    b. She wanted never to have to worry about money.
    c. She saw a boy split his face open on an icy sidewalk.
    d. She watched a doctor perform minor surgery on Travis.

_____ **12.** Asagai's dream is to
    a. be a leader in Nigeria's fight for independence
    b. marry Beneatha and start a family in Chicago
    c. become a professor of political philosophy
    d. open a liquor store with Walter and Willy

_____ **13.** What makes Mama decide to continue with the move to the house?
    a. She finds out that Walter has saved some money.
    b. She learns of Walter's plan to sell out to Karl Lindner.
    c. She sees Travis cry.
    d. She opens the present of gardening tools.

COLLECTION 17

_____ **14.** At the end of the play, Beneatha
  a. decides to marry George Murchison   **c.** argues with Walter about her plans
  b. refuses to help the family move   **d.** tells Mama she wants to live by herself

_____ **15.** Walter can be considered a dynamic character because he
  a. declares that he will never become wealthy
  b. learns that human dignity is more important than money
  c. gets angry over making mistakes
  d. thinks Beneatha's dream is more important than his own

Expanded Response *(30 points)*

16. Several characters in *A Raisin in the Sun* can be considered dynamic characters. In the first column of the following chart, list the names of two dynamic characters. In the second column, briefly explain why these characters can be considered dynamic. Then, in the last column, note an action by each character that shows how he or she has changed during the course of the play. *(15 points)*

Character	Why the Character Is Dynamic	Action That Shows Change

17. Several characters are faced with hard decisions in the course of the play. Choose the decision you believe is the hardest to make. On the lines provided, write the letter of the answer you choose and briefly defend your choice. There is more than one possible answer. Use at least one example from the play to support your ideas. *(15 points)*
  a. Mama's decision to move the family to Clybourne Park
  b. Walter's decision to turn down Karl Lindner's money
  c. Mama's decision to entrust $6,500 to Walter
  d. other: _____

_____

_____

_____

Written Response *(25 points)*

18. The Langston Hughes poem that serves as the play's opening quotation asks what happens to dreams that are deferred or thwarted. On a separate sheet of paper, write a paragraph in which you explain how *A Raisin in the Sun* answers the question that Hughes's poem asks. Make at least two references to examples in the play to support your ideas.

THE AMERICAN LANGUAGE

Euphemisms

Pupil's Edition page 892

On the line provided, write the letter of the *best* answer to each of the following items.
(10 points each)

_____ **1.** The Victorian Age was known for its
    a. many new English words
    b. extreme concern with respectability
    c. excessive preoccupation with money
    d. glorification of the Dutch monarchy

_____ **2.** A euphemism is a word or phrase that
    a. has a pleasant musical sound
    b. is derived from Greek or Latin
    c. is substituted for one considered offensive
    d. expresses strong emotion

_____ **3.** Words become offensive when
    a. people consider them so
    b. their inherent nature is revealed
    c. they are derived from a foreign language
    d. they are associated with certain foods

_____ **4.** The Puritans created a favorable environment for euphemisms by
    a. wiping out profanity completely
    b. creating a society that was hostile to vulgar speech
    c. trying to create a distinctly American form of English
    d. penalizing nonconformity in language

_____ **5.** A mixture of profane and overly delicate language was prevalent in communities of
    a. Puritans
    b. Victorians
    c. pioneers
    d. political activists

_____ **6.** "The language of anticipation" reflects an outlook characterized by
    a. religiosity
    b. realism
    c. pessimism
    d. optimism

_____ **7.** Early American euphemisms reflected democratic ideals in their
    a. titles for people and occupations
    b. terms for geographical areas
    c. striving for national uniformity
    d. concern for using words coined in this country

COLLECTION 17

____ **8.** The English language is composed mostly of
  a. Anglo-Saxon and Greek words
  b. Anglo-Saxon and Latin-based words
  c. Anglo-Saxon and German words
  d. Latin and Greek words

____ **9.** Latinate words tend to
  a. sound educated and sophisticated
  b. metamorphose into slang words
  c. be difficult to understand
  d. be shorter than French words

____ **10.** Euphemisms are often used to
  a. make language simpler
  b. obscure meaning
  c. provoke argument
  d. evoke emotion

LITERARY PERIOD TEST

American Drama

Reading a Play

The following scene is taken from Tennessee Williams's play *The Glass Menagerie*. The characters appearing in this scene are: Amanda Wingfield; her daughter, Laura Wingfield, who survived a childhood illness which left one of her legs shorter than the other; and her son, Tom Wingfield, who narrates the play. After carefully reading the passage, answer the questions that follow.

FROM *The Glass Menagerie*
by Tennessee Williams

Scene 1

The Wingfield apartment is in the rear of the building, one of those vast hive-like conglomerations of cellular living-units that flower as warty growths in overcrowded urban centers of lower middle-class population and are symptomatic of the impulse of this largest and fundamentally enslaved section of American society to avoid fluidity and differentiation and to exist and function as one interfused mass of <u>automatism</u>.

The apartment faces an alley and is entered by a fire escape, a structure whose name is a touch of accidental poetic truth, for all of these huge buildings are always burning with the slow and implacable fires of human desperation. The fire escape is part of what we see—that is, the landing of it and steps descending from it.

The scene is memory and is therefore nonrealistic. Memory takes a lot of poetic license. It omits some details; others are exaggerated, according to the emotional value of the articles it touches, for memory is seated predominantly in the heart. The interior is therefore rather dim and poetic.

At the rise of the curtain, the audience is faced with the dark, grim rear wall of the Wingfield tenement. This building is flanked on both sides by dark, narrow alleys which run into murky canyons of tangled clotheslines, garbage cans, and the sinister latticework of neighboring fire escapes. It is up and down these side alleys that exterior entrances and exits are made during the play. At the end of TOM's *opening commentary, the dark tenement wall slowly becomes transparent and reveals the interior of the ground floor Wingfield apartment.*

Nearest the audience is the living room, which also serves as a sleeping room for LAURA, *the sofa unfolding to make her bed. Just beyond, separated by a wide arch or second proscenium with transparent faded portieres[1] (or second curtain), is the dining room. In an old-fashioned whatnot[2] in the living room are seen scores of transparent glass animals. A blown-up photograph of the father hangs on the wall of the living room, to the left of the archway. It is the face of a very handsome young man in a doughboy's First World War cap. He is gallantly smiling, ineluctably smiling, as if to say "I will be smiling forever."*

Also hanging on the wall, near the photograph, are a typewriter keyboard chart and a Gregg shorthand diagram. An upright typewriter on a small table stands beneath the charts.

The audience hears and sees the opening scene in the dining room through both the transparent fourth wall of the building and the transparent gauze portieres of the dining-room arch. It is during this revealing scene that the fourth wall slowly ascends, out of sight. This transparent exterior wall is not brought down again until the very end of the play, during TOM's *final speech.*

1. **portieres** (pôr•tyerz´): curtains covering a doorway, used instead of a door.
2. **whatnot:** open shelves for holding small objects ("whatnots").

COLLECTION 17

The narrator is an undisguised convention of the play. He takes whatever license with dramatic convention is convenient to his purposes.

[TOM *enters, dressed as a merchant sailor, and strolls across to the fire escape. There he stops and lights a cigarette. He addresses the audience.*]

Tom. Yes, I have tricks in my pocket, I have things up my sleeve. But I am the opposite of a stage magician. He gives you illusion that has the appearance of truth. I give you truth in the pleasant disguise of illusion. To begin with, I turn back time. I reverse it to that quaint period, the thirties, when the huge middle class of America was matriculating in a school for the blind. Their eyes had failed them, or they had failed their eyes, and so they were having their fingers pressed forcibly down on the fiery Braille alphabet of a dissolving economy. In Spain there was revolution. Here there was only shouting and confusion. In Spain there was Guernica. Here there were disturbances of labor, sometimes pretty violent, in otherwise peaceful cities such as Chicago, Cleveland, Saint Louis . . . This is the social background of the play.

[*Music begins to play.*]

The play is memory. Being a memory play, it is dimly lighted, it is sentimental, it is not realistic. In memory everything seems to happen to music. That explains the fiddle in the wings. I am the narrator of the play, and also a character in it. The other characters are my mother, Amanda, my sister, Laura, and a gentleman caller who appears in the final scenes. He is the most realistic character in the play, being an emissary from a world of reality that we were somehow set apart from. But since I have a poet's weakness for symbols, I am using this character also as a symbol; he is the long delayed but always expected something that we live for. There is a fifth character in the play who doesn't appear except in this larger-than-life-size photograph over the mantel. This is our father who left us a long time ago. He was a telephone man who fell in love with long distances; he gave up his job with the telephone company and skipped the light fantastic out of town . . . The last we heard of him was a picture postcard from Mazatlán, on the Pacific coast of Mexico, containing a message of two words—"Hello—Goodbye!" and no address. I think the rest of the play will explain itself . . . .

[AMANDA's *voice becomes audible through the portieres.*]

[*Legend on screen:* "Où sont les neiges."[3]]

[TOM *divides the portieres and enters the upstage area.* AMANDA *and* LAURA *are seated at a drop-leaf table. Eating is indicated by gestures without food or utensils.* AMANDA *faces the audience.* TOM *and* LAURA *are seated in profile. The interior has lit up softly and through the screen we see* AMANDA *and* LAURA *seated at the table.*]

Amanda *(calling).* Tom?

Tom. Yes, Mother.

Amanda. We can't say grace until you come to the table!

Tom. Coming, Mother. *(He bows slightly and withdraws, reappearing a few moments later in his place at the table.)*

Amanda *(to her son).* Honey, don't *push* with your *fingers.* If you have to push with something, the thing to push with is a crust of bread. And chew—chew! Animals have secretions in their stomachs which enable them to digest food without mastication, but human beings are supposed to chew their food before they swallow it down. Eat food leisurely, son, and really enjoy it. A well-cooked meal has lots of delicate flavors that have to be held in the mouth for appreciation. So chew your food and give your salivary glands a chance to function!

---

3. **"Où sont les neiges":** French for "Where are the snows?" This is a reference to a famous line by the fifteenth-century French poet, François Villon. The complete line is a sad question about the passing of time: "But where are the snows of yesteryear?"

[TOM *deliberately lays his imaginary fork down and pushes his chair back from the table.*]

Tom. I haven't enjoyed one bite of this dinner because of your constant directions on how to eat it. It's you that make me rush through meals with your hawklike attention to every bite I take. Sickening—spoils my appetite—all this discussion of animals' secretion—salivary glands—mastication!

Amanda *(lightly).* Temperament like a Metropolitan star! [TOM *rises and walks toward the living room.*]

You're not excused from the table.

Tom. I'm getting a cigarette.

Amanda. You smoke too much.

[LAURA *rises.*]

Laura. I'll bring in the blanc mange.[4]

[TOM *remains standing with his cigarette by the portieres.*]

Amanda *(rising).* No, sister—you be the lady this time and I'll be the servant.

Laura. I'm already up.

Amanda. Resume your seat, little sister—I want you to stay fresh and pretty—for gentlemen callers!

Laura *(sitting down).* I'm not expecting any gentlemen callers.

Amanda *(crossing out to the kitchenette, airily)* Sometimes they come when they are least expected! Why, I remember one Sunday afternoon in Blue Mountain—

[*She enters the kitchenette.*]

Tom. I know what's coming!

Laura. Yes. But let her tell it.

Tom. Again?

Laura. She loves to tell it.

[AMANDA *returns with a bowl of dessert.*]

Amanda. One Sunday afternoon in Blue Mountain—your mother received—*seventeen*—gentlemen callers! Why, sometimes there weren't chairs enough to accommodate them all. We had to send the servant over to bring in folding chairs from the parish house.

Tom *(remaining at the portieres).* How did you entertain those gentlemen callers?

Amanda. I understood the art of conversation!

Tom. I bet you could talk.

Amanda. Girls in those days *knew* how to talk, I can tell you.

Tom. Yes?

[*Image on screen:* AMANDA *as a girl on a porch, greeting callers.*]

Amanda. They knew how to entertain their gentlemen callers. It wasn't enough for a girl to be possessed of a pretty face and a graceful figure—although I wasn't slighted in either respect. She also needed to have a nimble wit and a tongue to meet all occasions.

Tom. What did you talk about?

Amanda. Things of importance going on in the world! Never anything coarse or common or vulgar. [*She addresses* TOM *as though he were seated in the vacant chair at the table though he remains by the portieres. He plays this scene as though reading from a script.*] My callers were gentlemen—all! Among my callers were some of the most prominent young planters of the Mississippi Delta—planters and sons of planters!

[TOM *motions for music and a spot of light on* AMANDA. *Her eyes lift, her face glows, her voice becomes rich and elegiac.*]

[*Screen legend:* "Où sont les neiges d'antan?"]

There was young Champ Laughlin who later became vice-president of the Delta Planters Bank. Hadley Stevenson who was drowned in Moon Lake and left his widow

4. **blanc mange** (blə• mänj´): a dessert shaped in a mold.

one hundred and fifty thousand in Government bonds. There were the Cutrere brothers, Wesley and Bates. Bates was one of my bright particular beaux! He got in a quarrel with that wild Wainwright boy. They shot it out on the floor of Moon Lake Casino. Bates was shot through the stomach. Died in the ambulance on his way to Memphis. His widow was also well-provided for, came into eight or ten thousand acres, that's all. She married him on the rebound—never loved her—carried my picture on him the night he died! And there was that boy that every girl in the Delta had set her cap for! That beautiful, brilliant young Fitzhugh boy from Greene County!

Tom. What did he leave his widow?

Amanda. He never married! Gracious, you talk as though all of my old admirers had turned up their toes to the daisies!

Tom. Isn't this the first you've mentioned that still survives?

Amanda. That Fitzhugh boy went North and made a fortune—came to be known as the Wolf of Wall Street! He had the Midas touch, whatever he touched turned to gold! And I could have been Mrs. Duncan J. Fitzhugh, mind you! But—I picked your *father!*

Laura *(rising).* Mother, let me clear the table.

Amanda. No, dear, you go in front and study your typewriter chart. Or practice your shorthand a little. Stay fresh and pretty!—It's almost time for our gentlemen callers to start arriving. [*She flounces girlishly toward the kitchenette.*] How many do you suppose we're going to entertain this afternoon?

[TOM *throws down the paper and jumps up with a groan.*]

Laura *(alone in the dining room).* I don't believe we're going to receive any, Mother.

Amanda *(reappearing, airily).* What? No one—not one? You must be joking!

[LAURA *nervously echoes her laugh. She slips in a fugitive manner through the half-open portieres and draws them gently behind her. A shaft of very clear light is thrown on her face against the faded tapestry of the curtains. Faintly the music of "The Glass Menagerie" is heard as she continues lightly:*]

Not one gentleman caller? It can't be true! There must be a flood, there must have been a tornado!

Laura. It isn't a flood, it's not a tornado, Mother. I'm just not popular like you were in Blue Mountain . . . .[TOM *utters another groan.* LAURA *glances at him with a faint, apologetic smile. Her voice catches a little.*] Mother's afraid I'm going to be an old maid.

[*The scene dims out with "The Glass Menagerie" music.*]

Understanding Vocabulary (20 points)

Each of the underlined words below has also been underlined in the selection. Re-read those passages and use context clues to help you select an answer. Write the letter of the word or phrase that *best* completes each sentence. *(4 points each)*

_____ 1. A society characterized by <u>automatism</u> is
    a. compassionate, or concerned for others
    b. overly proud and arrogant, or egotistical
    c. lacking in creativity, or machine-like

_____ 2. A person who is <u>matriculating</u> is
    a. enrolling
    b. dancing
    c. protesting

_____ 3. An emissary is someone who
   a. has a position in the military
   b. is sent to carry out a purpose or mission
   c. owns a number of large corporations

_____ 4. Mastication is the act of
   a. studying
   b. complaining
   c. chewing

_____ 5. When Amanda flounces, she
   a. struggles with great difficulty
   b. moves with quick, flinging motions
   c. steps forward slowly and cautiously

Thoughtful Reading (35 points)

On the line provided, write the letter of the *best* answer to each of the following items.
(7 points each)

_____ 6. The Wingfield family lives in a
   a. wealthy neighborhood
   b. poverty-stricken community
   c. lower-middle-class urban area
   d. secluded rural area

_____ 7. Amanda does not want Laura to clear the table or get dessert because she
   a. wants Laura to recover from her illness
   b. wants Laura to look fresh for male visitors
   c. thinks Laura is superior to the rest of the family
   d. believes that Laura is an incompetent person

_____ 8. Tom says that he cannot enjoy his dinner because
   a. he is suffering from indigestion
   b. his knife and spoon are only imaginary
   c. his mother's health worries him
   d. his mother criticizes his eating habits

_____ 9. Which of the following statements *best* describes Tom's attitude toward Amanda's account of her seventeen gentlemen callers?
   a. He doesn't want to hear her tell it again, but listens anyway.
   b. He is shocked by Amanda's past behavior, but hides his surprise.
   c. He openly admires his mother's unique gift for storytelling.
   d. He refuses to listen to Amanda's constant lies and exaggerations.

_____ 10. The dialogue involving Tom, Laura, and Amanda suggests that
   a. Amanda's husband will probably reunite with his family
   b. Amanda wants to relive her past through her daughter
   c. Laura has a number of admirers, just like her mother
   d. Laura is withholding a secret from her mother

COLLECTION 17

Expanded Response (15 points)

11. The characters in *The Glass Menagerie,* like the characters in *A Raisin in the Sun,* see a contrast between a glorified ideal and a less glorious reality. For Amanda, her glorious days exist in the past. In the first column of the following chart, describe Amanda's vision of her past. In the second column, describe her present situation. In the third column, note how Amanda's nostalgia affects her relationship with her daughter Laura.

Amanda's Vision of Her Past	Her Present Situation	The Effect of Amanda's Nostalgia on Her Relationship with Laura

Written Response (30 points)

12. Much American drama from the second half of this century combines realistic portrayals with imaginative elements. On the lines provided, write a one-paragraph essay describing how Williams uses both realistic and imaginative techniques in the scene you have read from *The Glass Menagerie.* Make at least two references to details in the play to support your ideas.

_____

_____

_____

_____

_____

_____

_____

_____

_____

LITERARY PERIOD INTRODUCTION TEST

Contemporary Literature

On the line provided, write the letter of the *best* answer to each of the following items.
(10 points each)

_____ 1. Contemporary writers like Kurt Vonnegut and Joseph Heller have described war as
   a. an expression of patriotic loyalty
   b. a reflection of the madness of modern life
   c. the ultimate test of masculinity
   d. a logical response to personal frustration

_____ 2. According to the introduction, the chief drawback of the proliferation
   of technology is
   a. the dehumanization of the individual
   b. decreased life expectancy
   c. the extinction of some animals
   d. sluggish economic activity

_____ 3. U.S. involvement in the Vietnam War
   a. spurred the concept of war as glorious and heroic
   b. lasted for two years
   c. greatly enhanced the United States' image abroad
   d. sharply divided the American public

_____ 4. In general, postmodern literature can be viewed as
   a. closely resembling modernist works of the 1930s
   b. open to multiple interpretations and innovative in form and content
   c. lacking in meaning other than what the reader brings to it
   d. realistic and known for its reliance on the past

_____ 5. Short stories like Donald Barthelme's "Sentence" and novels like Walter Abish's
   Alphabetical Africa are notable for their
   a. conventional viewpoints and detached tones
   b. familiar characters and themes
   c. nontraditional forms and structures
   d. focus on different worlds and cultures

_____ 6. Postmodern fiction is characterized by
   a. linear, chronological plots and standard methods of character development
   b. nontraditional forms that crisscross the boundaries between fiction and nonfiction
   c. themes advancing the idea that life is finite and limited
   d. imitation and the nostalgic pursuit of the past

_____ 7. New Journalists like Truman Capote and Joan Didion attracted attention by
   a. introducing historical characters into purely imaginative stories
   b. using archaic language to describe cultural events
   c. asserting the writer's personal presence in nonfiction pieces
   d. mixing realistic narrative devices with elements of magic and dreams

COLLECTIONS 18–21

_____ **8.** Nonfiction has become as much of an art form as fiction or poetry because
  a. journalists and other nonfiction writers now receive improved training in writing
  b. contemporary nonfiction often incorporates literary elements such as suspense, symbolism, and metaphor
  c. writers care more about accuracy than about providing an entertaining story
  d. critics and the general public have become disillusioned with other forms of entertainment

_____ **9.** Postmodern poetry can be described as
  a. an attempt to follow Ezra Pound's insistence that the image is the core of the poem
  b. a reflection of the conformity and complacency that is seen in society as a whole
  c. a frank and often brutal re-creation of the poet's travel experiences
  d. a rebellion against impersonal, objective poetry that emphasizes intellectual analysis

_____ **10.** Since the 1970s American poetry has
  a. been characterized by diverse voices and styles
  b. experienced a decline in live oral readings
  c. reflected an increasingly elitist perspective
  d. been appreciated for its simplicity and earnestness

SELECTION TEST

Tamar
Mark Helprin   Pupil's Edition page 921

Checking Vocabulary (20 points)
Match each word in the left-hand column with its meaning in the right-hand column. Place the letter of the correct answer in the space provided. (*2 points each*)

_____ **1.** vulnerability   **a.** rumpled; messed up

_____ **2.** superficial   **b.** summary

_____ **3.** précis   **c.** sociability

_____ **4.** disheveled   **d.** scholars of religious doctrine

_____ **5.** hierarchy   **e.** clarity; rationality

_____ **6.** theologians   **f.** innocently or frankly; without slyness

_____ **7.** gregariousness   **g.** interrupted with; inserted

_____ **8.** interjected   **h.** obvious; shallow

_____ **9.** guilelessly   **i.** class system of social ranking

_____ **10.** lucidity   **j.** state of being open for attack

Thoughtful Reading (25 points)
On the line provided, write the letter of the *best* answer to each of the following items.
(*5 points each*)

_____ **11.** The main subjects of "Tamar" are
   a. love and illness
   b. youth and truth
   c. innocence and war
   d. education and money

_____ **12.** The narrator's stories about Palestine are told to
   a. demonstrate his personal courage
   b. entertain his adolescent companions
   c. inspire enthusiasm for a military career
   d. frighten the adults

_____ **13.** The narrator can *best* be characterized as
   a. bitter
   b. power-hungry
   c. selfish
   d. naive

COLLECTIONS 18–21

_____ **14.** The narrator arrives late at Herr Dennis's house because he
    a. gets caught in highway traffic
    b. never wears a watch
    c. sleeps through his alarm
    d. leaves the address behind

_____ **15.** The narrator views the children at the table as
    a. somewhat sheltered but likable
    b. immature for their ages
    c. worldly and hardened to reality
    d. intelligent but cruel

Expanded Response *(30 points)*

16. Which of the following statements *best* describes the narrator's attitude toward Tamar? On the lines provided, write the letter of the answer you choose and briefly defend your choice. Use at least one example from the selection to support your ideas. There is more than one possible answer. *(15 points)*
    a. He admires her intelligence and fearlessness.
    b. He sees her as a symbol of vulnerable beauty.
    c. He finds her behavior bizarre and inexplicable.
    d. He is enchanted by her but maintains his distance.

_____

_____

_____

_____

17. Irony, a discrepancy between expectation and reality, highlights the fact that regardless of how ambitious, talented, or intelligent people may be, they have little control over impersonal fate. In the chart below, describe at least three instances in which Mark Helprin uses irony to depict how war affects the lives of his characters. Then explain why each instance is ironic. *(15 points)*

Uses of Irony	Why It's Ironic

Written Response *(25 points)*

18. In "Tamar," Helprin portrays various characters and groups of people as vulnerable. How do you think Helprin defines the concept of vulnerability? What makes the characters and groups vulnerable? On a separate sheet of paper, write an essay addressing these questions. Support your ideas with at least two examples from the story.

         Elements of Literature

SELECTION TEST

The Death of the Ball Turret Gunner
Randall Jarrell   **Pupil's Edition page 932**

A Noiseless Flash
from **Hiroshima**
John Hersey   **Pupil's Edition page 936**

Checking Vocabulary *(20 points)*
Match each word in the left-hand column with its meaning in the right-hand column. Place the letter of the correct answer in the space provided. *(2 points each)*

____ **1.** rendezvous   **a.** preoccupied; haunted

____ **2.** abstinence   **b.** designed to cause fires

____ **3.** obsessed   **c.** prolonged

____ **4.** philanthropies   **d.** meeting

____ **5.** incendiary   **e.** one who believes in noble, though often impractical, goals; a dreamer

____ **6.** debris   **f.** charitable gifts

____ **7.** hedonistic   **g.** rubble; broken pieces

____ **8.** sustained   **h.** pleasure-loving; self-indulgent

____ **9.** convivial   **i.** staying away

____ **10.** idealist   **j.** jovial; sociable

Thoughtful Reading *(25 points)*
On the line provided, write the letter of the *best* answer to each of the following items. *(5 points each)*

____ **11.** Jarrell's ball turret gunner entered the armed forces
    a. after careful decision
    b. under protest
    c. without much thought
    d. as a fierce patriot

____ **12.** The tone of "The Death of the Ball Turret Gunner" can *best* be described as
    a. humorous
    b. patriotic
    c. condescending
    d. elegiac

____ **13.** A main theme of "A Noiseless Flash" is that
    a. chance alone determined who survived the attack
    b. many individuals anticipated the nuclear holocaust
    c. people respond methodically in emergencies
    d. all people suffer equally in war

COLLECTIONS 18–21

_____ **14.** Examples of objective reporting from Hersey's piece include all of the following **except**

    a. historical data

    b. direct quotations

    c. a variety of statistics

    d. commentary by the author

_____ **15.** The six people Hersey focuses on can *best* be characterized as

    a. exceptional cases   **c.** ordinary people

    b. wealthy civilians   **d.** heroic soldiers

Expanded Response *(30 points)*

16. Which of the following statements *best* explains the significance of the belly images in Randall Jarrell's "The Death of the Ball Turret Gunner"? On the lines provided, write the letter of the answer you choose and briefly defend your choice. There is more than one possible answer. Use at least one example from the selection to support your ideas. *(15 points)*

    a. The comforting, nurturing environment of the womb turns into the metallic, dangerous belly of the airplane.

    b. The images illustrate a conflict between good and evil.

    c. The womb symbolizes innocence while the ball turret symbolizes the loss of innocence.

    d. Other: _____

_____

_____

_____

_____

17. Choose two of the people in John Hersey's account of the bombing of Hiroshima. Show how Hersey develops them as characters by listing at least four details (relating to appearances, actions, thoughts, or feelings) about each one and the conclusions you can draw from these details. *(15 points)*

Character	Details	Conclusions

Written Response *(25 points)*

18. *Hiroshima* has been called a nonfiction novel. On a separate sheet of paper, write a brief essay in which you explain how, based on the excerpt you have read, this book can be categorized as both fiction and nonfiction. Use at least two examples from "A Noiseless Flash" to support your opinion.

SELECTION TEST

For the Union Dead
Robert Lowell

Pupil's Edition page 949

Game
Donald Barthelme

Pupil's Edition page 956

Checking Vocabulary (20 points)

Match each word in the left-hand column with its meaning in the right-hand column. Place the letter of the correct meaning in the space provided. *(2 points each)*

_____ 1. sensors	**a.** order	
_____ 2. nether	**b.** trick; deception	
_____ 3. console	**c.** lower	
_____ 4. precedence	**d.** satisfied	
_____ 5. exemplary	**e.** detecting devices	
_____ 6. sated	**f.** approaches; offers	
_____ 7. acrimoniously	**g.** at the same time	
_____ 8. simultaneously	**h.** desklike control panel	
_____ 9. overtures	**i.** serving as a model	
_____ 10. ruse	**j.** bitterly; harshly	

Thoughtful Reading (25 points)

On the line provided, write the letter of the *best* answer to each of the following items. *(5 points each)*

_____ 11. In "For the Union Dead," the speaker describes the Boston Aquarium as a
   a. useless relic of the past
   b. treasured place of memory
   c. fantasy that never existed
   d. monument from the Revolutionary era

_____ 12. In Lowell's poem, Colonel Shaw is portrayed as
   a. an angry, embittered person
   b. a typical man of his times
   c. the forerunner of a new generation
   d. a stern, remarkable hero

_____ 13. The subject of "Game" can *best* be described as
   a. the survival of the fittest
   b. the dehumanization of individuals
   c. the profound childishness of adults
   d. the need for discipline in the armed forces

COLLECTIONS 18–21

____ **14.** The men in "Game" are distressed by
    a. their opposing religious beliefs
    b. the lack of enough food and water to survive
    c. the realization that relief is not coming
    d. an approaching enemy force

____ **15.** The narrator of "Game" gives the impression that he is
    a. not well
    b. always lying
    c. an accomplished writer
    d. testing Shotwell

Expanded Response *(30 points)*

16. In the following chart, list two images from "For the Union Dead." Then explain the message you think each image conveys to the reader. *(15 points)*

Image	Message

17. Which of the sentences below *best* describes the relationship between the narrator and Shotwell in "Game"? On the lines provided, write the letter of the answer you choose and briefly defend your choice. There is more than one possible answer. Use at least one example from the story to support your ideas. *(15 points)*

    a. They are suspicious of each other.
    b. They communicate rarely although they have a lot in common.
    c. They refuse to help each other.
    d. Other: _____

_____

_____

_____

_____

_____

_____

Written Response *(25 points)*

18. Both the Lowell poem and the Barthelme story critique the conditions of life in the United States during the late twentieth century. On a separate sheet of paper, write an essay discussing how Lowell and Barthelme depict the problems of contemporary life. You should note what each writer specifically criticizes. Support your ideas with at least one example from each selection.

SELECTION TEST

Speaking of Courage
Tim O'Brien

Pupil's Edition page 965

Checking Vocabulary (20 points)

Match each word in the left-hand column with its meaning in the right-hand column. Place the letter of the correct meaning in the space provided. (2 points each)

_____ 1. affluent

_____ 2. tepid

_____ 3. mesmerizing

_____ 4. drone

_____ 5. recede

_____ 6. valor

_____ 7. municipal

_____ 8. mortars

_____ 9. profundity

_____ 10. tactile

a. belonging to a city or town

b. intellectual depth

c. become more distant and indistinct

d. cannons used to fire explosive shells

e. lukewarm

f. monotonous hum

g. perceptible by touch

h. well-to-do

i. great courage

j. hypnotic

Thoughtful Reading (25 points)

On the line provided, write the letter of the *best* answer to each of the following items. (5 points each)

_____ 11. O'Brien's story deals with the subject of
   a. freedom
   b. self-acceptance
   c. greed
   d. boredom

_____ 12. Paul's character can *best* be described as
   a. fearful
   b. lively
   c. reckless
   d. honest

_____ 13. The chilly interior of the air-conditioned car may represent
   a. the Vietnam War
   b. recent United States history
   c. Paul's feelings of isolation
   d. the death of Frenchie Tucker

_____ 14. Paul's repeated circling of the lake is an expression of his
   a. confusion
   b. boredom
   c. sincerity
   d. patriotism

_____ **15.** Images of the stagnant lake and people going about their business as usual suggest
   a. rejection of politics
   b. fear of the unknown
   c. contempt for veterans
   d. indifference to the Vietnam War

Expanded Response *(30 points)*

16. Which of the following statements *best* explains what the resolution of "Speaking of Courage" implies about Paul? On the lines provided, write the letter of the answer you choose and briefly defend your choice. There is more than one possible answer. Use at least one example from the selection to support your ideas. *(15 points)*
   a. Paul will never adjust to civilian life.
   b. Paul will ultimately accept himself for who he is.
   c. Paul will probably reenlist in the Army since it is the only place he can find comfort.
   d. Paul will always dream of winning a Silver Star.

   _____

   _____

   _____

   _____

   _____

17. "Speaking of Courage" focuses on the protagonist's internal conflicts. In the first arrow of the following graphic, briefly describe what Paul desires or wishes he had. Then in the second arrow note the feelings or inner forces that oppose the fulfillment of Paul's desires. *(15 points)*

#1   #2

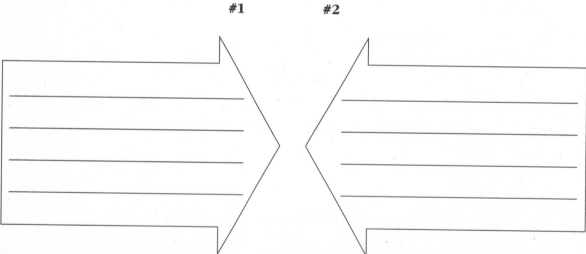

Written Response *(25 points)*

18. In an attempt to justify continued United States involvement in Vietnam, President Richard Nixon said Americans want a peace they can live with, a peace they can be proud of. In what ways do these statements apply to Paul Berlin? On a separate sheet of paper, write an essay in which you explain the kind of peace Paul needs. Support your ideas with at least two examples from the selection.

SELECTION TEST

Monsoon Season
Yusef Komunyakaa

Pupil's Edition page 975

Thoughtful Reading *(40 points)*
On the line provided, write the letter of the *best* answer to each of the following items.
(10 points each)

_____ 1. Yusef Komunyakaa creates images in "Monsoon Season" that are much like those of a painter because he
   a. creates complexity by layering images
   b. uses violent contrasts of color, texture, and perspective
   c. creates arrangements of shapes that invite the reader into the landscape
   d. employs the techniques of the French Impressionists

_____ 2. The frog and the snake in "Monsoon Season" probably represent
   a. the living and the dead
   b. elephant grass and flame trees
   c. American and Vietcong soldiers
   d. the past and the present

_____ 3. The poem is *best* summarized as being about
   a. the discomfort of a tropical climate
   b. the natural beauty and danger of the jungle
   c. a battle between people and nature
   d. troubled memories of death that the weather evokes

_____ 4. The speaker of the poem tries to count
   a. wet leaves   c. raindrops
   b. muddy boots   d. grounded choppers

Expanded Response *(30 points)*
5. Komunyakaa uses sensory language to depict a Vietnam experience. In the following chart, describe at least one image of sight, hearing, and touch from the poem and explain the effect of each.

	Sight	Hearing	Touch
Image			
Effect			

Written Response *(30 points)*
6. Propaganda is defined as "the systematic communication of information that is designed to influence opinion." Whether true or false, this information is always carefully selected for its political effect. Would you say that the purpose of "Monsoon Season" was to deliver a political message or some other message? On a separate sheet of paper, describe what you think Komunyakaa's purpose was in writing the poem. Support your ideas with at least two examples from the poem.

COLLECTION 18 TEST

The Wages of War

Responding to Literature *(80 points)*

1. While the poems by Jarrell, Lowell, and Komunyakaa appear on the surface to have little in common beyond the subject of war, they actually share a number of similarities. Compare the similarities of the three poems using the following chart. In the appropriate columns note the tone, a theme, and an image from each poem. *(15 points)*

Poem	Tone	Theme	Image
"The Death of the Ball Turret Gunner"			
"For the Union Dead"			
"Monsoon Season"			

2. In "A Noiseless Flash," John Hersey subtly blends fiction and nonfiction techniques to convey the horror of the dropping of the atomic bomb and its effect on the lives of six survivors. In the chart below, list one fiction technique and one nonfiction technique from the selection and describe the effects of each. *(15 points)*

	Techniques	Effects
Fiction		
Nonfiction		

Respond to each of the questions below. Attach an extra sheet of paper if necessary.
(25 points each)

3. Throughout history the intensity of the events and emotions that surround war has drawn writers to this subject. Whether they write to commemorate victories, inspire their readers to action, or lament the sadness and horror of the circumstances, these writers help us to understand what we might otherwise know only from newspapers and television. Write a one-paragraph essay discussing which single work from this collection made the biggest impact on you. Be sure to discuss the author's purpose as well as the techniques that he used to stimulate your thoughts and feelings.

_____

_____

_____

_____

_____

4. Irony, the discrepancy between appearance and reality, is one of the techniques writers use to achieve some emotional distance from their subjects. By reversing readers' expectations, writers also can highlight character change (or lack of it), conflict resolution, or theme, in order to communicate a message. Choose one work of poetry and one work of prose from this collection, and discuss how the use of irony reinforces each author's purpose.

_____

_____

_____

_____

_____

Vocabulary Review *(20 points)*
In the space provided, write the letter of the word that correctly completes the sentence.
(2 points each)

5. Even though Eli was new at school, his outgoing personality and natural _____ soon made him the most popular person in the eleventh grade.
   a. vulnerability   **c.** gregariousness
   b. lucidity   **d.** idealism

6. The typical spy movies from the 1930s and 1940s were filled with male characters wearing wide-brimmed hats and long raincoats who arranged secret _____ sites in abandoned buildings or on crowded bridges.
   a. hierarchy   **c.** debris
   b. abstinence   **d.** rendezvous

7. Alan's _____ tendencies are most apparent on weekends when he wants to do nothing but have fun.
   a. hedonistic   **c.** guileless
   b. disheveled   **d.** obsessed

8. Although volunteers are often viewed as _____ because they are out to change the world, they often simply hope to make a small difference in the lives of those who are not as fortunate.
   a. disheveled   **c.** idealistic
   b. vulnerable   **d.** convivial

9. "I don't have time for a long, involved account, Mike. Why don't you just give me a five-minute _____ of what occurred at the meeting," snapped Ms. Unger.
   a. abstinence   **c.** lucidity
   b. précis   **d.** debris

10. Understanding the _____ of a business organization helps employees grasp the interactions of people and departments.
    a. rendezvous   **c.** debris
    b. vulnerability **d.** hierarchy

11. _____ with physical fitness and good health, Cesar runs eighty miles a week and follows a strict vegetarian diet.
    a. Obsessed   **c.** Hedonistic
    b. Disheveled   **d.** Abstinent

12. Kaneesha mistakenly interpreted Earl's shyness as _____ ; she soon learned, however, that he was stubborn and strong willed.
    a. lucidity   **c.** conviviality
    b. vulnerability **d.** obsessed

13. Roberta Peters and Kathleen Battle are two operatic sopranos capable of pure, _____ high notes that often echo for minutes.
    a. sustained   **c.** interjected
    b. incendiary   **d.** obsessed

14. Contrary to their typically _____ appearance, the twins were attired in starched shirts, trim black pants, and highly polished black shoes.
    a. superficial   **c.** disheveled
    b. obsessed   **d.** convivial

SELECTION TEST

The Magic Barrel
Bernard Malamud

Checking Vocabulary (20 points)

Match each word in the left-hand column with its meaning in the right-hand column.
Place the letter of the correct meaning in the space provided. (2 points each)

____ 1. evident

____ 2. clientele

____ 3. traditional

____ 4. meager

____ 5. ascetic

____ 6. dowry

____ 7. suppress

____ 8. upbraided

____ 9. nuptial

____ 10. machinations

a. to restrain; hold back

b. severely criticized

c. poor; inadequate

d. severe; stern

e. customers

f. related to weddings or marriage

g. clear; obvious

h. plots; schemes

i. established; customary

j. money or goods a bride brings with her in a marriage

Thoughtful Reading (25 points)

On the line provided, write the letter of the *best* answer to each of the following items.
(5 points each)

____ 11. The social setting of "The Magic Barrel" is
   a. Jewish and suburban
   b. Christian and rural
   c. Jewish and urban
   d. Christian and suburban

____ 12. The main conflict in the story occurs between
   a. Leo and Lily
   b. Leo and himself
   c. Salzman and himself
   d. Salzman and Stella

____ 13. The main theme of the story concerns
   a. marriage and dating rituals
   b. the rigors of rabbinical studies
   c. the observance of old customs in modern times
   d. a process of self-discovery

COLLECTIONS 18–21

_____ **14.** The woman in the photograph seems familiar to Leo because
   a. Leo has met Stella before
   b. Stella looks like a movie star
   c. Stella resembles her father
   d. Lily reminds Leo of his mother

_____ **15.** Salzman could be described as a
   a. static character
   b. dynamic character
   c. stoic character
   d. stock character

Expanded Response *(30 points)*

16. What is Leo Finkle's attitude toward Pinye Salzman? On the lines provided, write the letter of the answer you choose and briefly defend your choice. There is more than one possible answer. Use at least one example from the selection to support your ideas. *(15 points)*
   a. He sees Salzman as a prosperous and talented matchmaker.
   b. He is wary of Salzman after their first meeting.
   c. He thinks of Salzman as a crafty, somewhat mystical figure.
   d. Other: _____

_____

_____

_____

_____

17. In the following chart, indicate whether you think Leo is a static or a dynamic character. Then briefly explain your response using at least two examples from the story. *(15 points)*

Static or Dynamic Character:
Explanation:

Written Response *(25 points)*

18. On a separate sheet of paper, discuss your reaction to the tradition of matchmaking described in "The Magic Barrel." What are the positive and negative aspects of the process? Support your opinions with at least two examples from the story.

SELECTION TEST

Elegy for Jane
Theodore Roethke   Pupil's Edition page 1002

The Beautiful Changes
Richard Wilbur   Pupil's Edition page 1006

Homework
Allen Ginsberg   Pupil's Edition page 1009

Thoughtful Reading *(40 points)*

On the line provided, write the letter of the *best* answer to each of the following items.
(5 points each)

_____ 1. Which of the following lines from "Elegy for Jane" includes a figure of speech?
   a. "I remember the neckcurls, limp and damp"
   b. "And how, once startled into talk"
   c. "The leaves, their whispers turned to kissing"
   d. "I, with no rights in this matter"

_____ 2. The speaker in Roethke's poem tries to find consolation in
   a. the beauty found in nature   **c.** the presence of his family
   b. great works of literature   **d.** an active social life

_____ 3. In "Elegy for Jane," the speaker compares Jane to
   a. moss under a bed of roses   **c.** a tree branch swaying in the wind
   b. a small stone in a brook   **d.** a bird singing in harmony with nature

_____ 4. The speaker of "The Beautiful Changes" mostly describes examples of beauty and change
   a. created by human endeavor   **c.** that occur in the spring
   b. found in the natural world   **d.** produced by the speaker

_____ 5. "The Beautiful Changes"
   a. records the birth of beautiful insects
   b. celebrates beautiful transformations in nature
   c. argues that beauty does not exist
   d. laments the destruction of beautiful forests

_____ 6. The chameleon and the mantis in Wilbur's poem are described as
   a. endangered species that must be saved   **c.** interacting with natural surroundings
   b. sly predators of smaller creatures   **d.** resembling beautiful, green leaves

_____ 7. "Homework" involves an extended metaphor comparing
   a. a washing machine to time   **c.** world problems to dirty laundry
   b. river pollution to nuclear waste   **d.** the earth to a drier

_____ 8. The speaker of "Homework" refers to all of the following **except**
   a. contamination of the Love Canal   **c.** fallout from nuclear bombs
   b. U.S. involvement in Central America **d.** the presence of smog and acid rain

COLLECTIONS 18–21

Expanded Response *(30 points)*

9. Which of the following phrases best describes Jane's character as she is portrayed in "Elegy for Jane"? On the lines provided, write the letter of the answer you choose and briefly defend your choice. There is more than one possible answer. Use at least one example from the poem to support your choice. *(15 points)*

   a. an eloquent student
   b. a person capable of great sadness
   c. an adventurous young woman
   d. other: _____

   _____

   _____

   _____

   _____

10. An ambiguity is an expression that accidentally or deliberately suggests two or more different, and sometimes conflicting, meanings. Find a line that contains an ambiguity in Wilbur's poem and write it on the line provided. Then in the arrows below, note two possible meanings of the expression. *(15 points)*

    Line: _____

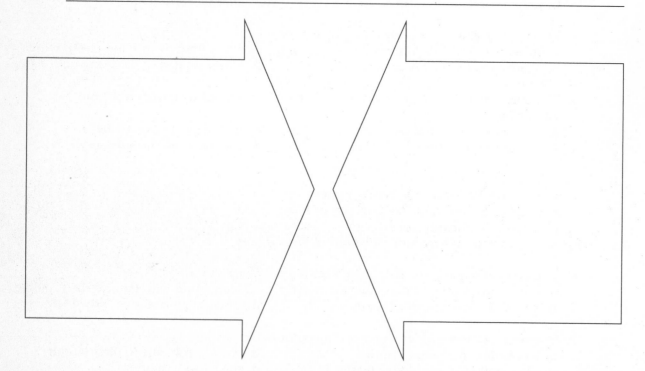

Written Response *(30 points)*

11. Roethke, Wilbur, and Ginsberg use minute details to flesh out the ideas of the three poems you have read. On a separate sheet of paper, discuss the detailed observations or descriptions used in "Elegy for Jane," "The Beautiful Changes," and "Homework." In your essay, note the primary source of the detailed images in each poem and explain why you think the poets used these details to convey their ideas. Include at least one example from each poem to support your ideas.

SELECTION TEST

from Black Boy
Richard Wright

Checking Vocabulary *(20 points)*
Match each word in the left-hand column with its meaning in the right-hand column. Place the letter of the correct meaning in the space provided. *(2 points each)*

_____ **1.** elapse   **a.** fascinated

_____ **2.** dispirited   **b.** useless; pointless

_____ **3.** enthralled   **c.** irritated; angered

_____ **4.** ardently   **d.** to pass by; slip away

_____ **5.** galled   **e.** intensely; eagerly

_____ **6.** withering   **f.** to hide unnoticed

_____ **7.** futile   **g.** frantic behavior; wildness

_____ **8.** clamor   **h.** drying up; weakening

_____ **9.** lurk   **i.** discouraged

_____ **10.** frenzy   **j.** loud noise; uproar

Thoughtful Reading *(25 points)*
On the line provided, write the letter of the *best* answer to each of the following items.
(5 points each)

_____ **11.** Which of the following sentences does **not** accurately describe dialogue?
  a. It quotes two or more people.   **c.** It is only used in drama.
  b. It may reflect an actual conversation.   **d.** It often shows thoughts and feelings.

_____ **12.** In this excerpt from his autobiography, Richard Wright's principal subject is
  a. divorce   **c.** danger
  b. racial prejudice   **d.** poverty

_____ **13.** In Memphis, Wright's mother locks him out of the house because she wants him to learn
  a. the importance of honesty   **c.** obedience to his elders
  b. how to survive   **d.** good manners

_____ **14.** Wright's mother placed him and his brother in an orphanage
  a. in anger   **c.** by order of the court
  b. in desperation   **d.** at their father's insistence

_____ **15.** The emphasis on food and descriptions of hunger underscore the young Wright's
  a. emotional deprivation   **c.** high intelligence
  b. poor health   **d.** rebelliousness

COLLECTIONS 18–21

Expanded Response (30 points)

16. At several points in the selection, Wright recalls being unable to act in complex or challenging childhood situations. In the first column of the following chart, describe two instances in which young Richard Wright finds himself unable to act. Then in the second column, explain what you think causes his ineffectiveness in each situation. *(15 points)*

Instances of Inaction	Causes of Inaction

17. In the excerpt from *Black Boy*, Wright describes a number of childhood awakenings and realizations he made as an adult. Which of the following events do you think provokes the author's most striking realization? On the lines provided, write the letter of the answer you choose and briefly defend your choice. There is more than one possible answer. Use at least one example from the selection to support your ideas. Be sure to describe what Wright learns from the event. *(15 points)*

a. seeing the boat that will take him to Memphis
b. the departure of his father
c. being forced to buy groceries
d. seeing his father twenty-five years later

_____

_____

_____

_____

_____

Written Response (25 points)

18. Wright describes a series of tough situations that he faced as a child. How would you characterize the young Richard Wright? What do you think is the adult writer's attitude toward his childhood? On a separate sheet of paper, write an essay addressing these questions. Make at least two references to examples in the selection to support your ideas.

SELECTION TEST

Everything Stuck to Him
Raymond Carver

Pupil's Edition page 1027

Checking Vocabulary *(10 points)*

Match each word in the left-hand column with its meaning in the right-hand column. Place the letter of the correct meaning in the space provided. *(2 points each)*

_____ **1.** striking   **a.** to occur at the same time

_____ **2.** fitfully   **b.** impressive; attractive

_____ **3.** overcast   **c.** communication by letters

_____ **4.** coincide   **d.** irregularly; in stops and starts

_____ **5.** correspondence   **e.** cloudy; gloomy

Thoughtful Reading *(25 points)*

On the line provided, write the letter of the *best* answer to each of the following items. *(5 points each)*

_____ **6.** Which of the following sentences does **not** describe elements of Carver's style?
  a. There are no quotation marks around dialogue.
  b. Most of his characters aren't given names.
  c. He seems to have deleted all unnecessary words.
  d. He uses the present tense to describe past events.

_____ **7.** The person listening to the story of the teenage couple is probably
  a. a complete stranger to the man speaking
  b. the new wife of the husband in the story
  c. the baby in the story—about twenty years later
  d. the teenage wife in the story—about twenty years later

_____ **8.** The phrase that *best* describes the teenage husband in the story within the story is
  a. ambitious and optimistic about the future
  b. ambitious, yet pessimistic about the future
  c. purposeless, yet hopeful that things will change
  d. purposeless and pessimistic about the future

_____ **9.** The conflict between the boy and the girl involves
  a. the question of the boy's commitment to the family
  b. the girl's feelings toward her new baby
  c. the couple's inability to take care of the baby
  d. the daughter's conflicting feelings about the couple's divorce

_____ **10.** The young couple assure each other that
  a. their baby cannot possibly be sick
  b. their baby will be brilliant
  c. they will soon leave town
  d. they will not fight anymore

COLLECTIONS 18–21

Expanded Response *(40 points)*

11. In "Everything Stuck to Him," a story is told in which the desires of a teenage wife and husband conflict. In the following chart, briefly describe those conflicting desires, and the resolution of the conflict. *(20 points)*

Wife's Desire	Husband's Desire

Resolution of the Conflict:

12. After telling his story, the man in "Everything Stuck to Him" remains by the window, remembering. What do you think he is feeling at this moment? On the lines provided, write the letter of the answer you choose and briefly defend your choice. There is more than one possible answer. Use at least one example from the story to support your ideas. *(20 points)*
   a. regret
   b. nostalgia for the past
   c. helplessness
   d. other: _____

_____

_____

_____

_____

Written Response *(25 points)*

13. On a separate sheet of paper, describe what you think might be the present situation of the family described in the story within the story. Are the boy and girl still married? Why or why not? Give at least two examples from the story to support your opinions.

SELECTION TEST

The Fish
Elizabeth Bishop   **Pupil's Edition page 1035**
Remember
Joy Harjo   **Pupil's Edition page 1040**

Thoughtful Reading *(40 points)*
On the line provided, write the letter of the *best* answer to each of the following items.
(5 points each)

_____ 1. The fish in Bishop's poem is
    a. dangerous and ugly
    b. young and multicolored
    c. smooth and graceful
    d. aged and battered

_____ 2. After catching the fish, the speaker
    a. watches it thrash in the boat
    b. is cut by the fish's gills
    c. closely examines its body
    d. spreads oil on its wounds

_____ 3. The speaker notices that the fish
    a. is not big enough to eat
    b. has escaped from other fish lines
    c. must be the last one in the lake
    d. has eyes that resemble roses

_____ 4. At the end of Bishop's poem, the speaker's attitude toward the fish can best be described as
    a. admiring
    b. disgusted
    c. disappointed
    d. indifferent

_____ 5. What is the refrain in Harjo's poem?
    a. earth
    b. people
    c. remember
    d. you

_____ 6. Lines 1 through 6 in Harjo's poem refer to images of
    a. plants, trees, and animals
    b. motion, language, and dance
    c. tribes, families, and children
    d. the sun, moon, and stars

_____ 7. The speaker of "Remember" requests that the reader
    a. recognize and respect various forms of life
    b. plant a tree for every tree that is cut down
    c. recall events from the Western expansion movement
    d. commemorate Kiowa cultural history

COLLECTIONS 18–21

____ **8.** According to "Remember," every person
    a. must endure a difficult journey through life
    b. is part of the motion and energy of life
    c. should dance to celebrate life's richness
    d. is less important than the moon and stars

Expanded Response *(30 points)*

9. Both Bishop and Harjo use personification in their poems. In the first column of the following chart, note an example of personification from each poem. Then, in the second column, describe the effects of personification for each example you give. *(15 points)*

	Examples of Personification	**Effects of Personification**
"The Fish"		
"Remember"		

10. Choose the option that *best* completes the following statement about "The Fish." On the lines provided, write the letter of the answer you choose and briefly defend your choice. There is more than one possible answer. Use at least one example from the poem to support your ideas. *(15 points)*
The speaker lets the fish go because she or he
    a. discovers something extraordinary about it
    b. takes pity on the fish because it looks weary
    c. respects and admires it
    d. other: _____

_____

_____

_____

_____

Written Response *(30 points)*

11. Both "The Fish" and "Remember" describe the relations between individuals and elements or creatures in the natural world. On a separate sheet of paper, write an essay describing what kinds of relationships between people and other elements or creatures are expressed in each poem. Do the poets seem to convey a message about what the relationships between people and other living beings should be? Give at least one example from each poem to support your interpretations.

SELECTION TEST

The Girl Who Wouldn't Talk
Maxine Hong Kingston   **Pupil's Edition page 1044**

Checking Vocabulary (10 points)
Match each word in the left-hand column with its meaning in the right-hand column. Place the letter of the correct meaning in the space provided. (*2 points each*)

_____ **1.** nape   **a.** usually

_____ **2.** temples   **b.** back of the neck

_____ **3.** loitered   **c.** scornful; mocking

_____ **4.** habitually   **d.** sides of the forehead

_____ **5.** sarcastic   **e.** spent time; hung around

Thoughtful Reading (25 points)
On the line provided, write the letter of the *best* answer to each of the following items. (*5 points each*)

_____ **6.** This story focuses on the subject of
    a. racial injustice
    b. women's rights
    c. youthful cruelty
    d. religious persecution

_____ **7.** The narrator stays late after school because she
    a. wants to play on the playground and in the building
    b. has gotten in trouble with her teachers
    c. is waiting for her parents to pick her up
    d. is trying to hide from her sister and the other girls

_____ **8.** The narrator knows that the quiet girl can talk because she
    a. reads aloud in class
    b. speaks privately with teachers
    c. whispers during recess
    d. sings to herself

_____ **9.** After harrassing the quiet girl, the narrator
    a. becomes ill for eighteen months
    b. begs the girl for forgiveness
    c. buys the girl candy and a comic book
    d. is punished by her parents

_____ **10.** As she grows up, the quiet girl
    a. eventually learns how to speak up
    b. stops spending time with her sister
    c. becomes domineering and mean
    d. remains protected by her parents

COLLECTIONS 18–21

NAME _____ CLASS _____ DATE _____ SCORE _____

Expanded Response *(40 points)*

11. "The Girl Who Wouldn't Talk" presents both external and internal conflicts between opposing forces or characters. In the first column of the following chart, describe an example of external conflict in the story. Then, in the second column, note an example of internal conflict. *(20 points)*

Example of External Conflict	Example of Internal Conflict

12. Why does the narrator hate the quiet girl? On the lines provided, write the letter of the answer you choose and briefly defend your choice. There is more than one possible answer. Use at least one example from the story to support your ideas. *(20 points)*
   a. The girl refuses to do what the narrator tells her to do.
   b. The girl reminds the narrator of what she does not like in herself.
   c. The narrator perceives the girl as weak and unassertive.
   d. The girl is much smaller than the narrator.

_____

_____

_____

_____

Written Response *(25 points)*

13. Why do you think the narrator tries to force the quiet girl to speak? On a separate sheet of paper, explain your point of view. Use at least two examples from the story to support your ideas.

240 *Selection Test: The Girl Who Wouldn't Talk*   *Elements of Literature*

SELECTION TEST

from Blue Highways
William Least Heat-Moon   **Pupil's Edition page 1055**

Checking Vocabulary *(20 points)*
Match each word in the left-hand column with its meaning in the right-hand column. Place the letter of the correct meaning in the space provided. *(2 points each)*

____ **1.** incised   **a.** started

____ **2.** infallible   **b.** guarantee

____ **3.** commenced   **c.** completely soaked

____ **4.** lore   **d.** written down

____ **5.** saturated   **e.** sure; never wrong

____ **6.** recollect   **f.** arranged in order of occurrence

____ **7.** vouch   **g.** allowing light to pass through

____ **8.** transcribed   **h.** deeply marked

____ **9.** translucent   **i.** traditional knowledge or teachings

____ **10.** chronologically   **j.** remember

Thoughtful Reading *(25 points)*
On the line provided, write the letter of the *best* answer to each of the following items.
(5 points each)

____ **11.** Which of the following sentences explains how Heat-Moon uses dialect?
   a. He pokes fun at the beliefs of people he encounters.
   b. He describes the way people speak in particular areas.
   c. He doesn't mention the names of the people he meets.
   d. He exposes the external and internal conflicts of his characters.

____ **12.** The selection from *Blue Highways* mainly describes Heat-Moon's experiences
   a. dining on highways in the U.S.
   b. traveling with a dog
   c. searching for Nameless, Missouri
   d. meeting interesting people

____ **13.** Heat-Moon asks the Wattses
   a. how the town got its name
   b. why so few people live in the area
   c. if he can buy their store
   d. how to get to Cookeville

COLLECTIONS 18–21

____ **14.** Miss Ginny treats Heat-Moon
  a. like a long-lost son
  b. warily but with warm hospitality
  c. with hostility and anger
  d. like a customer in her shop

____ **15.** Most of the humor in this selection can be described as
  a. gentle
  b. biting
  c. irreverent
  d. vengeful

Expanded Response *(30 points)*

16. Heat-Moon says that he is traveling in search of something he calls "harmony." In the first column of the following chart, describe what you think Heat-Moon means when he talks about harmony. In the second column, note an instance or moment from the selection when he may have found harmony. *(15 points)*

What Harmony Is	Moment of Harmony

17. How would you describe the Watts family? On the lines provided, write the letter of the answer you choose and briefly defend your choice. There is more than one possible answer. Use at least one example from the selection to support your ideas. *(15 points)*
  a. generous and talkative
  b. threatening and suspicious
  c. traditional about certain matters
  d. other: _____

_____

_____

_____

Written Response *(25 points)*

18. On a separate sheet of paper, discuss why you think Heat-Moon chooses to take the back roads rather than the main highways. Support your ideas with at least two examples from the selection.

Elements of Literature

COLLECTION 19 TEST

Discoveries and Awakenings

Responding to Literature *(90 points)*
For each item below, choose stories or poems from the following list and apply them to the activity.

"The Magic Barrel"	"The Girl Who Wouldn't Talk"	"Remember"
"Elegy for Jane"	"The Beautiful Changes"	"The Fish"
"Homework"	"Everything Stuck to Him"	from *Black Boy*
		from *Blue Highways*

1. Select two poems from Collection 19 that express a close connection between human beings and nature. In the first column of the following chart, write the titles of those poems. Then, in the second column, describe how the connections between people and nature are portrayed in each poem. *(15 points)*

Title of the Poem	Connections Between Human Beings and Nature

2. Some of the stories in Collection 19 portray people in conflict, while others depict harmonious relationships. In the first column of the following chart, note the titles of two prose selections, either fiction or nonfiction, from this collection. Then, in the second column, indicate whether the relationship between two characters in each selection demonstrates conflict or harmony. In the third column, give at least one example from each selection to support your opinion. *(15 points)*

Title of Selection	Conflict or Harmony	Example from the Selection

COLLECTIONS 18–21

Elements of Literature

Respond to each of the following questions. Use an extra sheet of paper if necessary.
(30 points each)

3. Dialogue represents the directly quoted words of conversation between two or more characters or people. Write an essay discussing the use of dialogue by two of the following authors: Richard Wright, William Least Heat-Moon, Bernard Malamud, Maxine Hong Kingston, or Raymond Carver. Be sure to note how each author's use of dialogue adds meaning to the selection.

_____

_____

_____

_____

_____

_____

_____

_____

_____

_____

_____

4. Write a paragraph in which you explain the process of discovery presented in one of the selections in this collection. Describe the discovery, the situation leading to the discovery, and the characters or elements involved.

_____

_____

_____

_____

_____

_____

_____

_____

_____

_____

Vocabulary Review *(10 points)*
In the space provided, write the letter of the word that *best* completes each sentence.
(2 points each)

5. After walking for miles in the storm, Perry's clothing was _____ with rain water.
   a. vouched
   b. transcribed
   c. commenced
   d. saturated

6. I suspect that this is another of the villain's wily _____ for escaping blame.
   a. machinations
   b. dowries
   c. temples
   d. clientele

7. The group _____ in front of the store for hours without ever buying anything.
   a. coincided
   b. loitered
   c. elapsed
   d. upbraided

8. The couple managed to stay true to their _____ values.
   a. overcast
   b. traditional
   c. galled
   d. enthralled

9. My sister Sue Ellen _____ wishes to become a surgeon.
   a. chronologically
   b. dryly
   c. ardently
   d. meagerly

COLLECTIONS 18–21

SELECTION TEST

Son
John Updike

Pupil's Edition page 1069

Checking Vocabulary (20 points)
Match each word in the left-hand column with its meaning in the right-hand column.
Place the letter of the correct meaning in the space provided. (2 points each)

_____ 1. antagonists

a. complete disorder

_____ 2. siblings

b. joking; comical

_____ 3. irksome

c. in an affectedly dainty manner

_____ 4. jocular

d. school for training ministers, priests, or rabbis

_____ 5. jaunty

e. equally balanced

_____ 6. mincingly

f. adversaries; opponents

_____ 7. symmetrical

g. confident; carefree

_____ 8. seminary

h. irritating

_____ 9. docile

i. sisters or brothers

_____ 10. anarchy

j. passive

Thoughtful Reading (25 points)
On the line provided, write the letter of the *best* answer to each of the following items.
(5 points each)

_____ 11. "Son" portrays the relationship(s) between
   a. the narrator and his son
   b. the narrator and his father
   c. fathers and sons over four generations
   d. husbands and wives over two generations

_____ 12. The first son mentioned in the story is described as
   a. nervous and fragile
   b. exhausting his mother
   c. affectionate and jolly
   d. yearning for perfection

_____ 13. In 1949, the son
   a. dreams of becoming a soccer star
   b. hears his parents arguing
   c. observes his father crying
   d. visits his grandparents

_____ 14. The narrator's grandfather tells the narrator's father that
   a. he is proud of his grandchildren
   b. the narrator's father should become a musician
   c. the Christian ministry is a vocation or a calling
   d. his hometown no longer exists

COLLECTIONS 18–21

_____ **15.** The narrator fails to discipline his son because he admires the boy's
    a. intelligence   **c.** spirit
    b. humor   **d.** verbal ability

Expanded Response *(30 points)*

16. This selection involves conflicts between fathers and sons, between fathers and themselves, and between various other family members. In the right-hand column of the following chart, identify the conflicts that apply to the characters listed in the first column of each row. *(15 points)*

Characters	Conflicts
the narrator's son and his family	
the narrator as a teenager and his parents	
the narrator's grandfather and himself	

17. Which of the following statements *best* expresses the theme of "Son"? On the lines provided, write the letter of the answer you choose and briefly defend your choice. There is more than one possible answer. Use at least one example from the selection to support your ideas. *(15 points)*
    a. Fathers and sons are involved in both internal and external conflicts.
    b. Fathers and sons mystify each other.
    c. Certain traits and behaviors are repeated from generation to generation.
    d. Other: _____

_____

_____

_____

_____

_____

_____

_____

Written Response *(25 points)*

18. On a separate sheet of paper, describe how the unusual format of the story adds to its theme or message. Support your ideas with at least two examples from the selection.

SELECTION TEST

Daughter of Invention
Julia Alvarez

Pupil's Edition page 1077

Checking Vocabulary (20 points)

Match each word in the left-hand column with its meaning in the right-hand column.
Place the letter of the correct meaning in the space provided. (2 points each)

____	**1.** labyrinth	**a.**	wrong terms or names
____	**2.** misnomers	**b.**	intent on revenge
____	**3.** ultimatum	**c.**	place full of intricate passageways; maze
____	**4.** disclaimer	**d.**	separated from the body
____	**5.** disembodied	**e.**	to make peace
____	**6.** reconcile	**f.**	last offer; final proposition
____	**7.** eulogy	**g.**	showy
____	**8.** communal	**h.**	public speech of praise
____	**9.** florid	**i.**	a giving up of a claim or connection
____	**10.** vengeful	**j.**	belonging to an entire group

Thoughtful Reading (25 points)

On the line provided, write the letter of the *best* answer to each of the following items.
(5 points each)

____ **11.** Besides the narrator herself, a central character in the story is the
   a. narrator's sister
   b. narrator's mother
   c. narrator's teacher
   d. head nun

____ **12.** The family in the story has come to the United States to
   a. expand the father's medical practice
   b. get the narrator and her sisters into a good school
   c. buy a new black car
   d. escape the dictator Trujillo

____ **13.** The phrase below that *best* describes what the adult narrator looking back on her childhood probably feels toward her mother and father is
   a. complete understanding
   b. amusement and affection
   c. emotional indifference
   d. bitter regret

_____ **14.** The narrator thinks her mother's last invention is
   a. suitcase rollers
   b. a ticking key chain
   c. Cukita's speech
   d. her daughter's poems

_____ **15.** Cukita's argument with her mother over the way she and her sisters are treated
   in school is an example of
   a. motivation
   b. denouement
   c. internal conflict
   d. external conflict

Expanded Response *(30 points)*

16. Age and experience can create a generation gap that leads two people to see the same situation differently. In the chart below, give both the father's and the daughter's versions of the conflict over the speech she writes. *(15 points)*

Father's Side	Daughter's Side

17. What do you think is the most important factor affecting the conflict between the father and Cukita? On the lines provided, write the letter of the answer you choose and briefly defend your choice. There is more than one possible answer. Use at least one example from the selection to support your ideas. *(15 points)*
   a. Cukita's exposure to new ideas and experiences
   b. the father's experience living under a dictatorship
   c. the mother's obsession with inventing
   d. other: _____

_____

_____

_____

_____

Written Response *(25 points)*

18. In what ways are Cukita and her mother similar? On a separate sheet of paper, write a paragraph in which you compare Cukita and her mother. Support your ideas with at least two examples from the selection.

SELECTION TEST

The Bells
Anne Sexton   **Pupil's Edition page 1089**

from **The Way to Rainy Mountain**
N. Scott Momaday   **Pupil's Edition page 1093**

Checking Vocabulary *(20 points)*
Match each word in the left-hand column with its meaning in the right-hand column.
Place the letter of the correct meaning in the space provided. *(2 points each)*

____ **1.** tenuous   **a.** above all else

____ **2.** opaque   **b.** filled with life

____ **3.** preeminently   **c.** humor; please; satisfy

____ **4.** indulge   **d.** abundant; rich

____ **5.** infirm   **e.** hatreds

____ **6.** vital   **f.** to scatter

____ **7.** luxuriant   **g.** not transparent; not letting light pass through

____ **8.** enmities   **h.** carefulness; caution

____ **9.** disperse   **i.** physically weak

____ **10.** wariness   **j.** not firm; insubstantial; slight

Thoughtful Reading *(25 points)*
On the line provided, write the letter of the *best* answer to each of the following items.
(5 points each)

____ **11.** Which of the following lines from Sexton's poem provides the *best* example
of visual imagery?
a. "and the children have forgotten / if they knew at all."
b. "This was the sound where it began"
c. "Today the circus poster / is scabbing off the concrete wall"
d. "the distant thump of the good elephants"

____ **12.** In "The Bells," the speaker recalls
a. being scared by lions at the circus   **c.** getting lost in a crowd
b. feeling protected by her or his father   **d.** eating cotton candy at the circus

____ **13.** The setting described in the excerpt from *The Way to Rainy Mountain* is
a. the border between Texas and Mexico
b. the plains of Oklahoma
c. southern New England
d. the Northern Pacific coast

____ **14.** The narrator travels to Rainy Mountain to
  a. meet his nephew   **c.** go camping at the base of the mountain
  b. visit his grandmother's grave   **d.** forget about his troubles

____ **15.** According to Momaday's piece, the Kiowas
  a. settled and prospered in Yellowstone
  b. fought with the Crows
  c. had reverence for the sun
  d. were peaceful farmers

Expanded Response *(30 points)*

16. The following chart lists images from "The Bells." In the right-hand column, identify the senses that each image appeals to. An image may appeal to more than one sense. The senses are sight, touch, hearing, taste, and smell. *(15 points)*

Image	Sense(s)
the thump of elephants	
trembling bells	
strangers' rough legs	
pounding breath	

17. The excerpt from *The Way to Rainy Mountain* spans about three hundred years. It encompasses the history of the Kiowas, the life of the author's grandmother, and descriptions of the land on which they lived. Which of these do you think experienced the most change? On the lines provided, write the letter of the answer you choose and briefly defend your choice. There is more than one possible answer. Use at least one example from the selection to support your ideas. *(15 points)*
  a. the Kiowas
  b. the author's grandmother
  c. the land
  d. other: _____

_____

_____

_____

_____

_____

_____

Written Response *(25 points)*

18. Both "The Bells" and the excerpt from *The Way to Rainy Mountain* focus on someone in the present remembering the past. On a separate sheet of paper, compare and contrast the attitudes of the speaker or narrator in the selections toward the past. Support your ideas with at least one example from each selection.

SELECTION TEST

from In Search of Our Mothers' Gardens
Alice Walker

Checking Vocabulary (20 points)

Match each word in the left-hand column with its meaning in the right-hand column.
Place the letter of the correct meaning in the space provided. (4 points each)

_____ 1. profusely

_____ 2. ingenious

_____ 3. vibrant

_____ 4. conception

_____ 5. medium

a. mental formation of ideas

b. full of energy

c. clever

d. material for an artist

e. in great quantities

Thoughtful Reading (25 points)

On the line provided, write the letter of the best answer to each of the following items.
(5 points each)

_____ 6. This selection is considered a personal essay because
   a. the author reveals intimate details about a person
   b. it is a work of fiction with a subjective focus
   c. it is a short work of nonfiction prose with a personal slant
   d. the author feels free to ramble with little focus

_____ 7. The quilt depicting the Crucifixion that hangs in the Smithsonian Institution
   was made by
   a. an anonymous African American woman
   b. Alice Walker's mother
   c. Virginia Woolf
   d. Robert Burns

_____ 8. The author and her mother share a talent for
   a. writing poems
   b. growing flowers
   c. quilt making
   d. storytelling

_____ 9. The author **not** mentioned in this selection is
   a. Virginia Woolf
   b. James Baldwin
   c. Phillis Wheatley
   d. Richard Wright

_____ 10. Walker believes that from her mother and previous generations of African American
   women she has inherited
   a. the ability to grow different varieties of plants
   b. a disdain for cooking and domestic chores
   c. a respect for strength and love of beauty
   d. an appreciation for the importance of relaxation

COLLECTIONS 18–21

NAME _____ CLASS _____ DATE _____ SCORE _____

Expanded Response *(30 points)*

11. What examples of creativity does Walker describe in this selection? In the chart below, list three people whom Walker mentions and identify the kinds of creative work they produce. *(15 points)*

Person	Creative Work

12. How is Walker's mother portrayed in the selection? On the lines provided, write the letter of the answer you choose and briefly defend your choice. There is more than one possible answer. Use at least one example from the selection to support your ideas. *(15 points)*
   a. as a hard-working and resourceful person
   b. as a kind and protective parent
   c. as someone who values creative work
   d. other: _____

_____

_____

_____

_____

_____

_____

_____

Written Response *(25 points)*

13. Why do you think Walker searched for her mother's garden? What did she discover in the process? On a separate sheet of paper, write an essay addressing these questions. Support your ideas with at least two examples from the selection.

Elements of Literature

SELECTION TEST

from Rules of the Game
Amy Tan   **Pupil's Edition page 1110**

What For
Garrett Hongo   **Pupil's Edition page 1122**

Checking Vocabulary *(20 points)*

Match each word in the left-hand column with its meaning in the right-hand column.
Place the letter of the correct meaning in the space provided. *(2 points each)*

____	**1.** ancestral	**a.**	quick answer
____	**2.** touted	**b.**	highly praised
____	**3.** concessions	**c.**	concealed
____	**4.** successive	**d.**	extremely gifted person
____	**5.** retort	**e.**	inherited
____	**6.** malodorous	**f.**	bad-smelling
____	**7.** intricate	**g.**	complicated
____	**8.** obscured	**h.**	lurched sideways
____	**9.** prodigy	**i.**	consecutive
____	**10.** careened	**j.**	acts of giving in

Thoughtful Reading *(25 points)*

On the line provided, write the letter of the *best* answer to each of the following items.
(5 points each)

____ **11.** In "Rules of the Game," the gift that Waverly receives for Christmas is
   a. a chess set
   b. a twelve-pack of candy
   c. a glass vial of lavender toilet water
   d. a coin bank in the shape of the world

____ **12.** Which of the following statements *best* explains Waverly's motivation for striving
   to excel in chess?
   a. She realizes that her talent is a source of power and pride.
   b. Chess allows her to skip math classes.
   c. Chess represents rebellion against authority.
   d. Her ability makes her the most popular child at school.

____ **13.** Waverly's family makes many concessions to allow her to practice chess.
   Which of the following concessions is **not** one that they make?
   a. She gets a room to herself.
   b. She doesn't have to wash dishes.
   c. She no longer has to practice the piano.
   d. She doesn't have to finish her meals.

_____ **14.** What two refrains occur in "What For"?
    a. "he told me" and "he trusted"   **c.** "his pains" and "his deafness"
    b. "I knew that" and "he knew that"   **d.** "I lived for" and "I wanted to"

_____ **15.** In Hongo's poem, the speaker mentions his or her
    a. mother and father   **c.** father and uncles
    b. brothers and sisters   **d.** grandparents and father

Expanded Response *(30 points)*

16. How would you describe Mrs. Jong's attitude toward Waverly in "Rules of the Game"? On the lines provided, write the letter of the answer you choose and briefly defend your choice. There is more than one possible answer. Use at least one example from the selection to support your ideas. *(15 points)*
    a. She wants her daughter to succeed in life.
    b. She is proud of Waverly and encourages her talent.
    c. She is jealous of the attention that Waverly receives.
    d. Other: _____

_____

_____

_____

_____

_____

_____

17. "What For" is a poem about the power of spoken words. It contains several examples of words that are spoken or heard. In the following web, list three such examples from the poem. Then offer your interpretation of what these spoken words have the power to do. *(15 points)*

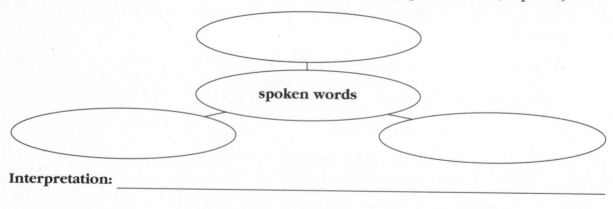

Interpretation: _____

_____

_____

Written Response *(25 points)*

18. Both "Rules of the Game" and "What For" portray relationships between children and their parents. On a separate sheet of paper, compare and contrast the two parent-child relationships. Support your ideas with at least one example from each selection.

COLLECTION 20 TEST

From Generation to Generation

Responding to Literature *(90 points)*
For each activity below, choose titles from the following list and apply the activity to those selections. *(20 points each)*

"Son"   "Daughter of Invention"   *from* "Rules of the Game"
"The Bells"   *from* The Way to Rainy Mountain   *from* "In Search of Our Mothers'
"What For"   Gardens"

1. Several selections in Collection 20 involve characters who look back to events in the past. In the chart below, identify two such selections, describe the event or situation that is recalled, and tell what the character's attitude is toward the past.

Selection	Recalled Event or Situation	Character's Attitude Toward the Past

2. Most of the selections in this collection portray relationships between children and their parents. In some selections the two generations are in conflict, but other selections convey harmony between parents and children. In the chart below, identify three selections, who the parents and children are, and whether the nature of the relationship is one of conflict or harmony.

Selection	Characters	Nature of Relationship

COLLECTIONS 18–21

Respond to each of the following questions. Attach an extra sheet of paper if necessary.
(25 points each)

3. In many of the selections in Collection 20, parents and grandparents give their children and grandchildren gifts of knowledge, encouragement, or inspiration. Choose two selections and write an essay describing the intangible gifts that older family members give their children or grandchildren. Support your ideas with at least one example from each selection.

_____

_____

_____

_____

_____

_____

_____

_____

_____

_____

4. Write an essay comparing and contrasting the conflicts in two selections from this collection. Be sure to identify who is involved, what each conflict is about, and the possible reasons for each conflict. Support your ideas with at least one example from each selection.

_____

_____

_____

_____

_____

_____

_____

_____

_____

_____

Vocabulary Review *(10 points)*

For each item below, write in the space provided the letter of the word or words that have the same meaning as the italicized word. *(2 points each)*

_____ 5. When you give someone an *ultimatum* you are giving them a
    a. written document
    b. detailed plan
    c. final offer
    d. precious gift

_____ 6. If something is *opaque* it
    a. doesn't allow light to pass through
    b. is crusty and old
    c. consists of several pieces
    d. refers to dreams

_____ 7. Someone who is *docile* is
    a. often angry
    b. passive
    c. funny
    d. seldom obedient

_____ 8. If something is *malodorous* it
    a. feels sticky
    b. smells bad
    c. has musical qualities
    d. is inexpensive

_____ 9. Flowers that bloom *profusely* are blooming
    a. unwanted
    b. with little aid
    c. in small patches
    d. in great quantities

COLLECTIONS 18–21

SELECTION TEST

New African
Andrea Lee

Pupil's Edition page 1129

Checking Vocabulary *(20 points)*
Match each word in the left-hand column with its meaning in the right-hand column. Place the letter of the correct meaning in the space provided. *(2 points each)*

____ **1.** sacrilege

____ **2.** sedate

____ **3.** defiantly

____ **4.** affected

____ **5.** wistfulness

____ **6.** ambiguousness

____ **7.** mortal

____ **8.** discreet

____ **9.** dispelling

____ **10.** omniscient

a. life-threatening; extreme

b. strongly and openly resisting

c. all-knowing

d. wisely cautious

e. lack of clarity; uncertainty

f. calm and composed

g. put on for show

h. violation of something sacred

i. vague longing

j. driving away

Thoughtful Reading *(25 points)*
On the lines provided, write the letter of the *best* answer to each of the following items.
(5 points each)

____ **11.** "New African" focuses primarily on
  a. community spirit
  b. the rules of writing
  c. the civil rights movement
  d. childhood memories

____ **12.** During the church service, Sarah feels restless because she
  a. is bored and would rather be playing
  b. has not eaten anything all day
  c. plans to be baptized soon and is impatient
  d. quarreled with her brother earlier

____ **13.** Which of the following statements *best* describes an internal conflict that Sarah experiences?
  a. She argues with Aunt Bessie over proper behavior.
  b. She challenges her father's insistence that she should go to church.
  c. She considers whether she should get baptized.
  d. She struggles with the decision to go to a private school.

COLLECTIONS 18–21

_____ **14.** After the struggle with Aunt Bessie, Sarah's parents
      a. scold Sarah and tell her that she must be baptized
      b. endlessly question Sarah about her motivations
      c. do not pressure Sarah to be baptized
      d. tell members of the congregation to leave Sarah alone

_____ **15.** As an adult, Sarah remembers her father as a
      a. stern and disapproving parent   **c.** charismatic and affectionate person
      b. shy and retiring figure   **d.** brilliant Biblical scholar

Expanded Response (30 points)

16. Which of the following statements *best* characterizes Reverend Phillips, Sarah's father? On the lines provided, write the letter of the answer you choose and briefly defend your choice. There is more than one possible answer. Use at least one example from the selection to support your ideas. *(15 points)*
    a. He cares more about his church than he does about his children.
    b. He is a strong leader and a civil rights activist.
    c. He is a wise and compassionate parent.
    d. Other: _____

_____

_____

_____

_____

17. The young protagonist of the story is in the process of forging her own identity as an individual. At times her concerns are those of a child, and at other times her concerns are those of an adult. In the chart below, list two examples in each column of ways in which Sarah is like a child and how she is like an adult. *(15 points)*

Child	Adult

Written Response (25 points)

18. At the end of "New African," Sarah says that her father gave her a gift of freedom through his silence. What do you think she means by this statement? Why was this freedom important to Sarah? On a separate sheet of paper, write an essay that answers these questions. Support your ideas with at least two examples from the story.

SELECTION TEST

Autobiographical Notes
James Baldwin

Pupil's Edition page 1142

Checking Vocabulary *(20 points)*
Match each word in the left-hand column with its meaning in the right-hand column. Place the letter of the correct meaning in the space provided. *(2 points each)*

_____ **1.** censored

a. crushed; destroyed

_____ **2.** explicit

b. to take over

_____ **3.** assess

c. cheerless

_____ **4.** interloper

d. riddle

_____ **5.** bleak

e. clear, logical, and consistent

_____ **6.** pulverized

f. cut or changed to remove material deemed objectionable

_____ **7.** coherent

g. clear; definite

_____ **8.** conundrum

h. intruder or meddler

_____ **9.** appropriate

i. critical; decisive

_____ **10.** crucial

j. to evaluate; judge the value of

Thoughtful Reading *(25 points)*
On the lines provided, write the letter of the *best* answer to each of the following items.
(5 points each)

_____ **11.** In the first part of "Autobiographical Notes" Baldwin describes his
  a. theories about the purpose of life
  c. adventures in the French countryside
  b. fondness and aptitude for poetry
  d. early development as a writer

_____ **12.** Baldwin states that it is a writer's duty to
  a. write about patriotic or familial subjects
  b. examine attitudes in a nonsuperficial manner
  c. fight against governmental conspiracies
  d. focus on a single important image in all writings

_____ **13.** Baldwin says that as an African American writer he faces difficulties that
  a. derive from the demands and dangers of his social situation
  b. are far more harmful than those of other writers
  c. are based on general lack of interest in his subject matter
  d. arise whenever he tries to publish plays in mainstream publications

_____ **14.** Baldwin's interests include all of the following **except**
  a. arguing
  c. making movies
  b. eating and drinking
  d. lecturing

COLLECTIONS 18–21

_____ **15.** Baldwin insists on perpetually criticizing America because he
   a. loves America more than any other country
   b. has been exiled for political activism
   c. wants America to be more like France
   d. thinks America needs to have a monarchy

Expanded Response *(30 points)*

16. Which of the following words *best* describes the tone of "Autobiographical Notes"? On the lines provided, write the letter of the answer you choose and briefly defend your choice. There is more than one possible answer. Use at least one example from the selection to support your ideas. *(15 points)*

   a. reflective   **b.** humorous   **c.** angry   **d.** other: _____

_____

_____

_____

_____

_____

17. At several points in the selection, Baldwin expresses his opinions on writing and life and then supports his statements with examples from his personal experience. In the chart below, note two of Baldwin's opinions and the experiences he uses to back up his opinions. *(15 points)*

Baldwin's Opinions	Baldwin's Experiences

Written Response *(25 points)*

18. It has been more than forty years since Baldwin wrote his *Notes of a Native Son,* the book in which "Autobiographical Notes" appears. If Baldwin were writing this essay today, what do you think would be different? What would be the same? On a separate sheet of paper, write an essay that answers these questions. Support your ideas with at least two examples from the selection.

SELECTION TEST

Mirror
Sylvia Plath   **Pupil's Edition page 1149**

The Fifteenth Summer
James Merrill   **Pupil's Edition page 1156**

Thoughtful Reading *(40 points)*
On the lines provided, write the letter of the *best* answer to each of the following items.
(5 points each)

_____ 1. Which of the following claims does the mirror in Plath's poem make about itself?
   a. It is not cruel, only truthful.
   b. It can allow people to see what they want to see.
   c. It is something that people don't really see.
   d. It is lonely and neglected.

_____ 2. When the woman in "Mirror" sees her reflection she
   a. realizes that she must forget the past
   b. is reminded of her maternal grandmother
   c. decides to polish the mirror's surface
   d. becomes agitated and upset

_____ 3. At the end of "Mirror," the woman sees
   a. a goldfish in a tank   **c.** the person she wanted to become
   b. herself aging   **d.** a young girl playing

_____ 4. Which of the following descriptions from Plath's poem is an example of personification?
   a. The mirror is silver and exact.
   b. The candles and the moon are liars.
   c. The opposite wall is pink with speckles.
   d. A woman's face replaces the darkness.

_____ 5. In Merrill's poem, when the boy climbs the tree, he takes along
   a. a scale   **c.** a book
   b. a rope   **d.** a necklace

_____ 6. While he was in the tree, the boy in Merrill's poem
   a. dreamed about becoming a dancer
   b. counted birds that flew overhead
   c. thought about life's questions
   d. hid treasures in a hole in the tree

_____ 7. The adult speaker in Merrill's poem seems to regard the boy's actions as
   a. dangerous and silly   **c.** immature but harmless
   b. important and admirable   **d.** kind and generous

_____ 8. The rhyme scheme of the first stanza of "The Fifteenth Summer" can be described as
   a. nonexistent   **c.** following a definite pattern
   b. inconsistent and random   **d.** dependent on slant rhyme

Expanded Response (30 points)

9. There are many examples of personification in "Mirror." Identify two such examples in the following chart. In the left-hand column, write what is being personified. Then in the right-hand column indicate how Plath personifies it. (15 points)

What Is Personified	How It Is Personified

10. What does the boy in "The Fifteenth Summer" accomplish by climbing the tree? On the lines provided, write the letter of the answer you choose and briefly defend your choice. There is more than one possible answer. Use at least one example from the selection to support your ideas. (15 points)
    a. He begins to learn the value of things and his place in the world.
    b. He finishes all his homework every day while he is in the tree.
    c. He gives himself time to contemplate things that he might not think about while on the ground.
    d. Other: _____

    _____

    _____

    _____

    _____

    _____

Written Response (30 points)

11. On a separate sheet of paper, write an essay in which you compare the function of the mirror in "Mirror" with that of the tree in "The Fifteenth Summer." How do Plath and Merrill make use of these subjects? What things do they allow people to do? Support your ideas with at least two examples from each poem.

Elements of Literature

SELECTION TEST

Straw into Gold: The Metamorphosis of the Everyday
Sandra Cisneros   Pupil's Edition page 1159

Checking Vocabulary *(20 points)*
Match each word in the left-hand column with its meaning in the right-hand column. Place the letter of the correct meaning in the space provided. *(2 points each)*

____ 1. subsisting   **a.** wandering

____ 2. edible   **b.** take all of one's attention

____ 3. taboo   **c.** impressive; having distinction

____ 4. obsess   **d.** staying alive

____ 5. prestigious   **e.** capable of being eaten

____ 6. flourished   **f.** did well; blossomed

____ 7. nostalgia   **g.** without conscious reasoning

____ 8. ventured   **h.** something that is forbidden

____ 9. nomadic   **i.** longing

____ 10. intuitively   **j.** dared or risked going

Thoughtful Reading *(25 points)*
On the lines provided, write the letter of the *best* answer to each of the following items.
(5 points each)

____ **11.** At the beginning of the essay, Cisneros recalls being
    a. instructed by her grandfather in the art of making tortillas
    b. locked in a room and ordered to spin straw into gold
    c. invited to dinner while living in France
    d. asked to make a gourmet meal for twenty people

____ **12.** Cisneros compares the difficulty of making tortillas to
    a. writing a critical essay   **c.** living in a house with six brothers
    b. living abroad for a year   **d.** writing a poem in the fifth grade

____ **13.** When her family moved into a permanent home in Chicago, Cisneros
    a. met people who would become characters in her stories
    b. overcame her shyness among strangers
    c. became homesick for the other places she had lived
    d. acquired her own room where she could write

____ **14.** Which of the following statements is **not** true about Cisneros's life?
    a. She taught herself to garden.
    b. She left home before her older brothers did.
    c. She has traveled throughout Europe.
    d. She moved to Texas.

COLLECTIONS 18–21

_____ **15.** The folk tale that the title of this essay alludes to is
  a. Cinderella   **c.** Snow White
  b. Rumpelstiltskin   **d.** The Grasshopper and the Ant

Expanded Response *(30 points)*

16. According to the selection, which of the following sources has had the most significant impact on Cisneros's writing? On the lines provided, write the letter of the answer you choose and briefly defend your choice. There is more than one possible answer. Use at least one example from the selection to support your ideas. *(15 points)*
  a. her experiences at an artists' colony in upstate New York
  b. her interactions with her brothers and her other familial memories
  c. growing up as a person of Mexican descent
  d. other: _____

_____

_____

_____

_____

_____

17. At one point in the essay, Cisneros says that she sees herself as the eleven-year-old girl she once was. Complete the following web, by noting three characteristics or behaviors that Cisneros attributes to herself as a young girl. Then answer the question that follows. *(15 points)*

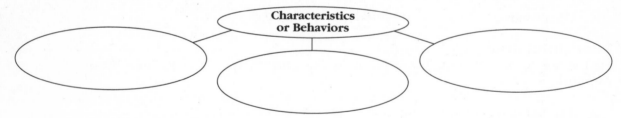

Do you find it surprising that Cisneros became a writer? Briefly explain your answer.

_____

_____

_____

_____

_____

Written Response *(25 points)*

18. In "Straw into Gold," Cisneros mentions many of the things that she draws upon as subjects for her writing. What do these things have in common? Why do you think she chooses these things over others? On a separate sheet of paper, write an essay that describes what Cisneros considers the appropriate subjects for her writing. Support your ideas with at least two examples from the selection.

SELECTION TEST

The Latin Deli: An Ars Poetica
Judith Ortiz Cofer   Pupil's Edition page 1167
The Satisfaction Coal Company
Rita Dove   Pupil's Edition page 1171

Thoughtful Reading *(40 points)*
On the lines provided, write the letter of the *best* answer to each of the following items.
(5 points each)

_____ 1. The central character in "The Latin Deli" is
   a. the ghost of the speaker's lost love
   b. a woman who runs a store
   c. a poet who writes in Latin
   d. the speaker's sister

_____ 2. Most of the descriptions in "The Latin Deli" refer to
   a. pharmaceutical items   **c.** food and language
   b. money and work   **d.** toys and gifts

_____ 3. All the customers in "The Latin Deli" seek
   a. fame and fortune   **c.** *jamón y queso* sandwiches
   b. the comfort of spoken Spanish   **d.** news of events in their countries of origin

_____ 4. The quotation from Ortiz Cofer's poem that provides the *best* example of concrete
   language is
   a. "as they speak to her and each other / of their dreams and their disillusions"
   b. "the others, / whose needs she must divine, conjuring up products"
   c. "the heady mix of smells from the open bins / of dried codfish, the green plantains"
   d. "she is the Patroness of Exiles, / a woman of no-age who was never pretty"

_____ 5. The man in "The Satisfaction Coal Company" remembers cleaning the offices of a
   coal company
   a. for fifty years   **c.** every day of the week
   b. as a child   **d.** during the 1930s

_____ 6. In the first part of "The Satisfaction Coal Company," the man
   a. steps outside on a cold, snowy day   **c.** sees a dog running down the street
   b. walks past a gorge filled with trees **d.** converses with his new neighbor

_____ 7. The man in Dove's poem preferred working on Saturdays at the coal company because
   a. he could sing songs while he worked
   b. he and a friend worked together on Saturdays
   c. no one would bother him and he enjoyed the solitude
   d. his children would help him and play

_____ 8. In the last part of Dove's poem, the man seems to remember his past experiences with
   a. bitterness and regret   **c.** thoughtful nostalgia
   b. joy and laughter   **d.** casual indifference

From "The Latin Deli: An Ars Poetica" by Judith Ortiz Cofer from *The Americas Review,* vol. 19, no. 1. Published by Arte Público Press–University of Houston, 1991. Reprinted by permission of *Arte Público Press.*

COLLECTIONS 18–21

Expanded Response *(30 points)*

9. "The Latin Deli" contains several descriptions of Spanish being spoken. In the top part of the following chart, list three examples of spoken language from the poem. Then answer the question in the bottom part of the chart. *(15 points)*

Examples of Spoken Language		
What messages beyond the literal meanings of their words do the customers convey to each other in each of the examples above?		

10. If the man in "The Satisfaction Coal Company" were to voice what he feels about his days working at the coal company, what would he say? On the lines provided, write the letter of the answer you choose and briefly defend your choice. There is more than one possible answer. Use at least one example from the selection to support your ideas. *(15 points)*
   a. "I wouldn't have thought so at the time, but that job gave me a lot of satisfaction."
   b. "Although times were hard, I felt a sense of purpose in my life."
   c. "That was a demeaning job and the work was truly unpleasant."
   d. Other: _____

   _____

   _____

   _____

   _____

   _____

   _____

Written Response *(30 points)*

11. On a separate sheet of paper, write an essay comparing and contrasting the woman in "The Latin Deli" with the man in "The Satisfaction Coal Company." In your essay, you should describe the characters' attitudes toward their work and toward memories of past experiences and the social roles they occupy. Support your ideas with at least two examples from each poem.

THE AMERICAN LANGUAGE

High Tech's Influence

Pupil's Edition page 1178

On the line provided, write the letter of the *best* answer to each of the following items.
(10 points each)

_____ **1.** The word *technology* as it is used today refers to
   a. simple practical arts
   b. applied science
   c. pure science
   d. advances in physics

_____ **2.** The technology of the early nineteenth century that had the greatest effect on language was
   a. fossil fuels
   b. electronics
   c. aeronautics
   d. steam

_____ **3.** New railroad words came from
   a. inventions
   b. combinations of existing words
   c. borrowing from other forms of transportation
   d. all of the above

_____ **4.** The words *telegraph* and *photograph* derive from
   a. Greek root words
   b. German technological terms
   c. Latin phrases
   d. French idioms

_____ **5.** An acronym is
   a. an alphabetical designation of a person
   b. a word formed from the combination of the first letters of a phrase
   c. an abbreviation of a long word
   d. a coined word that means "high technology"

_____ **6.** Examples of acronyms include
   a. lingo, jargon, and argot
   b. telly, TV, and television
   c. radar, snafu, and WAC
   d. cabin, steward, and rudder

_____ **7.** The twentieth-century invention that has had an effect on American culture similar to that of the railroad in the nineteenth century is
   a. the airplane
   b. television
   c. the space shuttle
   d. radio

COLLECTIONS 18–21

_____ **8.** Many words used in aeronautics are borrowed from
     a. running
     b. sailing
     c. automotives
     d. communications

_____ **9.** Standard English words whose meanings have been altered by their technical usage in the computer industry include
     a. adjectives that are used as nouns
     b. pronouns that refer to computer parts
     c. nouns that have been changed to verbs
     d. adverbs that are no longer in use

_____ **10.** RAM and ROM are
     a. words referring to 1930s technology
     b. examples of aeronautical clichés
     c. terms associated with computers
     d. the names of two Greek gods

COLLECTION 21 TEST

The Created Self

Responding to Literature *(70 points)*

For each activity below, choose a different title from the following list and apply the activity to that title. *(10 points each)*

"New African"　　　"Autobiographical Notes"　　"The Satisfaction Coal Company"　　"Mirror"
"The Latin Deli"　　"Straw into Gold"　　　　　"The Fifteenth Summer"

1. Many of the selections in Collection 21 describe a moment of awareness in a character's life. They become aware that they have changed, are in the process of changing, or that there has been a change in their situations. In the following chart, identify two selections and the characters who come into awareness. Then describe the changes that each character experiences.

Selection:	Selection:
Character:	Character:
Change:	Change:

2. Using the chart below, describe the internal conflicts experienced by characters from two of the selections in Collection 21. At least one of the selections should differ from those that you used in Question 1.

Selection:	Character:
Conflict:	
Selection:	Character:
Conflict:	

COLLECTIONS 18–21

Respond to each of the following questions. Attach an extra sheet of paper if necessary.
(25 points each)

3. The title of this collection is "The Created Self." Write a paragraph in which you explain what the created self is, as conveyed in these selections. How do the writers and characters create themselves? What events or issues does the process of creation involve? Support your ideas with at least one example from each selection.

_____

_____

_____

_____

_____

_____

_____

_____

4. In most of the selections in this collection, the author or the main character recalls her or his experiences as a child or much younger person. How do the writers or protagonists seem to regard their younger selves? What similarities or differences do you see between the younger and older versions of the same character or person? Choose two selections and write an essay addressing these questions. Support your ideas with at least one example from each selection.

_____

_____

_____

_____

_____

_____

_____

_____

Vocabulary Review *(10 points)*

In the space provided, write the letter of the word or words that have the same meaning as the word in boldface type. *(2 points each)*

_____ **5.** Someone who experiences **wistfulness** feels a
   a. sudden pain   **b.** vague longing   **c.** rising anger   **d.** quick regret

_____ **6.** Writing that is **explicit** is
   a. stilted   **b.** literary   **c.** humorous   **d.** clear

_____ **7.** A person who is **convulsing** is
   a. shaking   **b.** choking   **c.** bending   **d.** perspiring

_____ **8.** **Nomadic** animals tend to
   a. gather food   **b.** hunt   **c.** wander   **d.** be aggressive

_____ **9.** An award that is **prestigious**
   a. carries a monetary reward   **c.** is presented annually
   b. has an excellent reputation   **d.** is decided by committee

Language Workshop Review: Using Effective Diction *(20 points)*

Rewrite each of the following sentences according to the directions indicated in the brackets following each sentence. You may add or delete words, and change the writing as necessary. *(4 points each)*

10. Nigel said he ain't sure you didn't never call him. *[Change colloquial diction into formal diction.]* _____

_____

11. A bear stood up, sniffed the air, and roared. *[Change plain diction into poetic diction.]*

_____

_____

12. Arturo, this is my mom. *[Change informal diction into formal diction.]* _____

_____

13. A pallid cloud drowsily expanded over the knife-like peaks and monstrous crags of the tremendous beast of a mountain. *[Change ornate diction into plain diction.]*

_____

_____

14. I request politely that you engage your brain before speaking your mind. *[Change lofty diction into simple diction.]*

_____

_____

COLLECTIONS 18–21

LITERARY PERIOD TEST

Contemporary Literature

Reading Fiction

The following selection is an excerpt from the novel *Bone*. Read the selection carefully, and then answer the questions that follow.

FROM *Bone*
by Fae Myenne Ng

Everything had an alert quality. Brisk wind, white light. I turned down Sacramento and walked down the hill at a snap-quick pace toward Mah's Baby Store.

Mason was the one who started calling it the Baby Store, and the name just stuck. The old sign with the characters for "Herb Shop" still hangs precariously above the door. I've offered to take it down for Mah, but she's said No every time. Mason thinks she wants to hide.

An old carousel pony with a gouged eye and chipped tail stands in front of the store like a guard looking out onto Grant Avenue. I tapped it as I walked past, my quick good-luck stroke. A string of bells jingled as I pushed through the double doors.

A bitter ginseng odor and a honeysuckle balminess greeted me. Younger, more Americanized mothers complain that the baby clothes have absorbed these old world odors. They must complain about how old the place looks, too, with the custom-made drawers that line the wall from floor to ceiling, the factory lighting. Leon wanted to tear down the wall of mahogany drawers and build a new storage unit. But Mah doesn't want him touching anything in her store, and I was glad, too, because I love the tuck-perfect fit of the drawers, and the *tock!* sound the brass handles make against the hard wood.

Mah was showing off her newest stock of jackets to a woman and her child. I gave a quick nod and went straight to the back, where the boxes were stacked two-high. The fluorescent lights glowed, commercial bright.

The woman tried to bargain the price down but Mah wouldn't budge; she changed the subject. "Your girl is very pretty. How about I don't charge tax?"

Hearing that gave me courage. Mah was in a generous, no-tax mood, and that gave me high hopes for some kind of big discount, too. I knew I'd be tongue-tied soon, so I tried to press my worry down by telling myself what Grandpa Leong used to tell me, that the best way to conquer fear is to act.

Open the mouth and tell.

As soon as the woman and her child walked out the door, I went up to Mah and started out in Chinese, "I want to tell you something."

Mah looked up, wide-eyed, expectant.

I switched to English, "Time was right, so Mason and I just went to City Hall. We got married there."

Mah's expression didn't change.

"In New York," I said.

No answer.

"You know I never liked banquets, all that noise and trouble. And such a waste of so much money.

She still didn't say anything. Suddenly I realized how quiet it was, and that we were completely alone in the store. I heard the hum of the lights.

"Mah?" I said. "Say something."

She didn't even look at me, she just walked away. She went to the back of the store and ripped open a box. I followed and watched her bend the flaps back and pull out armfuls of baby clothes. I waited. She started stacking little mounds. She smoothed out sleeves on top of sleeves, zipped zippers, and cupped the colored hoods, one into another. All around our feet were tangles of white hangers.

"Nina was my witness." My voice was whispery, strange.

Mah grunted, a huumph sound that came out like a curse. My translation was: Disgust, anger. There's power behind her sounds. Over the years I've listened and rendered her Chinese grunts into English words.

She threw the empty box on the floor and gave it a quick kick.

"Just like that.
Did it and didn't tell.
Mother Who Raised You.
Years of work, years of worry.
Didn't! Even! Tell!"

What could I say? Using Chinese was my undoing. She had a world of words that were beyond me.

Mah reached down and picked up a tangle of hangers. She poked them into the baby down coats, baby overalls, baby sleepers. Her wrists whipped back and forth in a way that reminded me of how she used to butcher birds on Salmon Alley. Chickens, pheasants, and pigeons, once a frog. The time with the frog was terrible. Mah skinned it and then stopped. She held the twitching muscle out toward us; she wanted us to see its pink heart. Her voice was spooky, breathless: "Look how the heart keeps beating!" Then the frog sprang out of her hand, still vigorous.

Now I said in English, "It was no big deal."

"It is!"

Mah was using her sewing-factory voice, and I remembered her impatience whenever I tried to talk to her while she was sewing on a deadline.

She rapped a hanger on the counter. "Marriage is for a lifetime, and it should be celebrated! Why sneak around, why act like a thief in the dark?"

I wanted to say: I didn't marry in shame. I didn't marry like you. Your marriages are not my fault. Don't blame me.

Just then the bells jingled and I looked up and saw two sewing ladies coming through the door. I recognized the round hair, the hawk eyes.

"What?" I was too upset to stop. "What?" I demanded again. "You don't like Mason, is that it?"

"Mason," Mah spoke his name soft, "I love."

For love, she used a Chinese word: to embrace, to hug.

I stepped around the boxes, opened my arms and hugged Mah. I held her and took a deep breath and smelled the dried honeysuckle stems, the bitter ginseng root. Above us, the lights beamed bright.

I heard the bells jingle, the latch click, and looked up to see the broad backs of the ladies going out the door toward Grant Avenue. They were going to Portsmouth Square, and I knew they were talking up everything they heard, not stopping when they passed their husbands by the chess tables, not stopping until they found their sewing-lady friends on the benches of the lower level. And that's when they'd tell, tell their long-stitched version of the story, from beginning to end.

Let them make it up, I thought. Let them talk.

COLLECTIONS 18–21

Understanding Vocabulary *(20 points)*

Each of the underlined words below has also been underlined in the selection. Re-read those passages and use context clues to help you determine the meaning of each word. Then, in the space provided, write the letter of the word that best completes each sentence. *(4 points each)*

_____ **1.** A plate that is placed <u>precariously</u> on a table
  a. looks elegant and stylish **b.** is in danger of falling **c.** doesn't draw attention

_____ **2.** A <u>gouged</u> piece of wood probably displays
  a. grooves or holes **b.** new decoration **c.** the color green

_____ **3.** A scent that gives off <u>balminess</u> is
  a. soothing **b.** unfamiliar **c.** addictive

_____ **4.** <u>Mahogany</u> is a type of
  a. paper **b.** pasteboard **c.** wood

_____ **5.** Words that have been <u>rendered</u> have been
  a. mocked **b.** confronted **c.** changed

Thoughtful Reading *(35 points)*

On the line provided, write the letter of the *best* answer to each of the following items. *(7 points each)*

_____ **6.** What significant action has taken place before the excerpt begins?
  a. Two women walk into the store. **c.** The mother has had another baby.
  b. The mother has sold the store. **d.** The daughter has gotten married.

_____ **7.** Which of the following facts about Mah **cannot** be known from this selection?
  a. She used to butcher animals and birds.
  b. She eloped when she was her daughter's age.
  c. She normally does not bargain with customers.
  d. She has been married more than once.

_____ **8.** What seems to reconcile the mother and daughter?
  a. The daughter helps her mother fold baby clothes.
  b. The daughter reminds her mother of past problems.
  c. The mother says that she adores Mason.
  d. The mother gives her daughter advice.

_____ **9.** What do the two sewing ladies do at the end of the selection?
  a. They demand that Mah help them choose baby clothes.
  b. They quarrel with each other over a gift.
  c. They leave the store to gossip with their friends.
  d. They look for their husbands who are playing chess.

_____ **10.** How does the narrator's mood at the end of the selection differ from her mood at its beginning?
  a. She has become preoccupied. **c.** She seems depressed.
  b. She is more relaxed. **d.** She regrets her action.

Expanded Response *(15 points)*

11. Why do you think Mah becomes angry when she hears the narrator's news? On the lines provided, write the letter of the answer you choose and briefly defend your choice. There is more than one possible answer. Use at least one example from the selection to support your ideas.
    a. She feels betrayed by her daughter's secretiveness.
    b. She doesn't like the narrator's husband.
    c. She is reminded of her own marriage problems.
    d. Other: _____

    _____

    _____

    _____

    _____

    _____

    _____

    _____

Written Response *(30 points)*

12. The idea of "the created self" is a common theme within contemporary literature. In what way does the excerpt from *Bone* contribute to your understanding of the created self? On the lines below, relate this theme to the selection. Your answer should make at least one comparison and one contrast between the selection and two selections from Collections 18 through 21.

    _____

    _____

    _____

    _____

    _____

    _____

    _____

    _____

    _____

    _____

    _____

    _____

COLLECTIONS 18–21

STANDARDIZED TEST PREPARATION

What Is a Standardized Test?

A standardized test is one in which your score is evaluated according to a "standard" or "norm" established by compiling the scores of other students who have taken the same test. Some standardized tests may be developed by a school district or state. The best-known tests of this type are those given to students across the entire United States.

- the *Preliminary Scholastic Aptitude Test (PSAT)*
- the *National Merit Scholars Qualifying Test (NMSQT)*
- the *Scholastic Aptitude Test (SAT-I Reasoning Test)*
- the *Scholastic Aptitude Test (SAT-II Subject Test)*
- the *American College Testing Program (ACT)*

There are two basic types of standardized tests: those testing aptitude and those testing achievement.

Aptitude (or Reasoning) Tests	• are intended to evaluate basic skills or reasoning abilities needed in various general areas of study • often cover material you have learned during many years of study (such as verbal expression skills and critical thinking ability)
Achievement (or Academic Subject) Tests	• are intended to measure knowledge of specific subjects (such as history, literature, sciences, mathematics, or foreign languages)

HOW TO PREPARE FOR STANDARDIZED TESTS
1. *Learn what specific abilities will be tested.* Information booklets may be provided. Practice with these or with published study guides.
2. *Know what materials you will need.* On the day of the test, you may need to bring specific materials, such as your official test registration card, number 2 pencils, or lined paper for writing essay answers.
3. *Determine how the test is evaluated.* If there is no penalty for wrong answers, make your best guess on all questions possible. However, if wrong answers are penalized, make guesses only if you are fairly sure of the correct answer.

Taking Standardized Tests

One purpose of standardized tests is to predict how well you may perform in the college environment. These tests examine your ability to identify and correct problems with verbal expression, and to analyze and interpret the meaning, purpose, and organization of reading passages.

Kinds of Test Questions

Most test questions are either limited-response questions or open-response questions.

Limited-Response Questions. Limited-response questions give you a limited number of choices from which you select the most appropriate answer. Questions of this type include multiple-choice questions, true/false questions, and matching questions.

Open-Response Questions. Open-response questions require you to provide a written response to a specific prompt. The responses may vary widely in length; questions may be fill-in-the-blank, short-answer, or essay questions.

TEST PREPARATION

STANDARDIZED TEST PREPARATION

Tests of Verbal Expression

Standardized tests often contain limited-response questions that measure your understanding of written expression. The following chart outlines the language skills covered in most verbal expression tests.

MATERIAL COVERED ON VERBAL EXPRESSION TESTS	
Grammar Questions	You identify the most correct answer, using standard grammar and usage rules. These test items often cover the correct use of • subject-verb agreement • principal parts of verbs • pronouns
Punctuation Questions	You identify the correct use of punctuation. These test items often cover the correct use of • end marks and commas • dashes, semicolons, and colons • quotation marks and hyphens
Sentence Structure Questions	You demonstrate knowledge of what is (and what is not) a complete sentence. These test items often cover • fragments and run-on sentences • sentence combining • modifiers • verb tense • parallel structure • transitional words
Revision-in-Context Questions	You show an appropriate revision of either a part of a composition or a whole composition. These test items often cover the correct use of • composition structure • unity and coherence • diction or word choice • arrangement of ideas
Rhetorical Strategies Questions	You show an understanding of strategies used by writers to express ideas and opinions. These test items often cover • strategies of development • sequence of ideas • diction or word choice

In the best-known national tests, multiple-choice, verbal expression questions are asked in a variety of forms. Typically, you are given a sample passage with several words and phrases underlined and numbered. Then you are given a series of test items related to the passage. You are expected to pick the choice that best expresses the meaning, is most grammatically correct, or is most consistent with the style and tone of the passage. Following is a sample test passage with sample questions. Read the passage and study the questions and responses. The correct responses have been filled in.

Sample Verbal Expression Test Passage

[A] In an Age of Science—and among all the periods of history, <u>none of them merits</u> that name better than our own—trained scientists are fortunate people. [B]
              1
Their training is of national <u>concern, because</u> our nation badly needs more scientists
                              2
than it has. [C] They can often advance quickly. [D] They can climb as far as their ambitions and talents permit. <u>Most important is that they stand</u> at the very center of
                                                                                    3
the forces that are conquering and remaking the world around us. [E] Their futures are bright. [F] No wonder so many young people dream about entering the scientific professions. Yet many students do not pursue this dream to its realization.

SAMPLE VERBAL EXPRESSION TEST PASSAGE QUESTIONS	
1. Which of the following is the best revision of the portion of the passage indicated by number 1? Ⓐ No change Ⓑ none of them are meriting Ⓒ none of them meriting Ⓓ none of them merit	This is a question about grammar; it requires you to know the correct subject-verb agreement.
2. Which of the following is the best revision of the portion of the passage indicated by number 2? Ⓐ No change Ⓒ concern. Because Ⓑ concern; because Ⓓ concern because	This is a question about punctuation; it requires you to know which punctuation mark is appropriate here.
3. How should sentences C and D be combined? Ⓐ In science, because they can often advance quickly, they can climb as far as their ambitions permit. Ⓑ They can often advance as fast and as far in science as their ambitions and talents permit. Ⓒ They can often advance quickly and far in science, because of their ambitions and talents. Ⓓ As quickly and as far in science as their ambitions will permit them, they can advance. Ⓔ Talented and ambitious, they can often advance far quickly.	This is a question about sentence structure; it requires you to know how to combine sentences effectively.

SAMPLE VERBAL EXPRESSION TEST PASSAGE QUESTIONS

4. Which is the best revision of the portion of the passage indicated by number 3? Ⓐ Most important, they stand Ⓑ It is most important that they stand Ⓒ It is most important; they stand Ⓓ Most importantly that they stand Ⓔ More importantly, they stand	This is a revision-in-context question; it requires you to use revision skills to best express the ideas in the passage.
5. This passage might next discuss Ⓐ organizations that provide grants for scientific research Ⓑ why science is not respected in other nations Ⓒ specific occupations for young people in the sciences Ⓓ why there are not enough scientists Ⓔ why our time is called the Age of Science	This is a question about rhetorical strategies; it requires you to use your knowledge of writing strategy, organization, and style in order to draw conclusions about the passage.

In other typical verbal expression test formats, you will see individual sentences. In one of these types of tests, several words or phrases in each sentence will be underlined and lettered. You will be asked to identify the one underlined word or phrase, if there is one, that needs to be corrected. In another sentence-type verbal expression test, a part of one sentence will be underlined. You will be asked to identify the choice that presents the most effective revision of the underlined text.

SAMPLE SENTENCE QUESTIONS / VERBAL EXPRESSION

1. Because variation's in the sun's warming pattern cause Ⓐ Ⓑ Ⓒ wind, wind power is actually considered a kind of solar Ⓓ energy. No error Ⓔ	This question is about mechanics. It requires you to know that an apostrophe is not necessary to form the plural of a noun.
2. Of all the poems that Emily Dickinson wrote, perhaps Ⓐ none isn't more curious than "I'm Nobody!" is. No error Ⓑ Ⓒ Ⓓ Ⓔ	This question is about standard usage. It requires you to recognize the use of a double negative as being incorrect.
3. During a job interview, the interviewee should answer questions succinctly, maintain eye contact, and to sit up straight. Ⓐ the interviewee should answering questions succinctly, maintaining eye contact, and to sit up straight Ⓑ some things that the interviewee should do are answering questions succinctly, maintaining eye contact, and to sit up straight Ⓒ the interviewee should answer questions succinctly, maintain eye contact, and sit up straight Ⓓ some things that should be done by the interviewee are answer questions succinctly, maintaining eye contact, and sitting up straight Ⓔ in which the interviewee should answer questions succinctly, maintain eye contact, and to sit up straight	This question addresses effective style. It requires you to realize that three phrases separated by commas should be parallel.

Elements of Literature

As you can see, there are only a few basic types of questions used to test verbal expression on the most current, best-known national tests.

MOST COMMON TYPES OF VERBAL EXPRESSION TEST ITEMS	
Passages	
"No Change" Items	• give a list of suggested revisions of underlined, numbered portions of the passage • always contain one "No change" choice (these words are often printed in capital letters) among the list of choices, to be selected if the indicated part is correct as is
Critical Thinking Items	• ask you to analyze and evaluate the passage as a whole • ask you to make inferences about parts of a passage as related to the whole
Sentences	
"No Error" Items	• give you individual sentences with certain words and phrases • always include one "No error" choice to be selected if none of the underlined parts of the sentence is an error
Sentence Revision Items	• give you individual sentences, each containing one group of underlined words • repeat the underlined text in choice A, which should be selected if no revision is required

TEST PREPARATION

STANDARDIZED TEST PREPARATION

Verbal Expression: Test Passages

Directions. Read the following passages carefully, noting any errors in grammar, punctuation, structure, or style. Using the rules of standard written English, answer the questions that follow, referring back to each passage when necessary. Identify your response by shading in the circle around the letter of your choice.

Passage I

When Americans are asked to describe the Doppler <u>effect, you usually give</u> the
1

classic example of a stationary listener standing next to a railroad track. As a train

approaches, the tone emitted by its whistle sounds higher and higher to the observer.

This phenomenon occurs because as the locomotive approaches, the rate of sound

waves reaching the observer's ears <u>increase, and this increase raises</u> the pitch of the
2

locomotive's whistle. Conversely, as the train moves away from the listener, <u>they</u>
3

<u>receive less waves</u> per unit of time, and so the pitch decreases.

    However, it is important to note that the Doppler effect occurs not only with

sound waves, but with all forms of waves. In fact, Christian Johann Doppler is famous

for predicting that light, which has wavelike properties, would experience the same

shift in its frequency <u>that sound does.</u> Doppler's theory could be proven by observ-
4

ing the light coming from celestial bodies such as stars and galaxies. Although most

people consider these objects to be immobile, they are actually moving at tremen-

dous speeds. <u>As the locomotive's case,</u> this velocity changes the frequency of the
5

light waves produced by the celestial objects. Since a shift in frequency can influence

the visible color of light created, the Doppler effect <u>changes a moving star and its</u>
6

<u>color of light produced.</u>

    [A] Therefore, stars moving at tremendous speeds toward Earth increase the fre-

quency of light produced, creating a "blue shift" in the light created by that celestial

body. [B] <u>As a consequence,</u> a star moving away from Earth at high velocities—such
7

as 27,000 miles per second—exhibits a decrease in frequency that is similar to the decrease in pitch of the locomotive's whistle. [C] By using the Doppler effect, astronomers can determine the speed and distance of an unknown celestial object.

[D] This leads to a "red shift" in the visible light produced by the receding star.

Questions 1–7 correspond to the numbered and underscored portions of the text.

For each item below, choose the letter that is the best revision of the portion of the passage indicated by the number of the test question.

1. Ⓐ No change
   Ⓑ effect, they usually give
   Ⓒ effect usually, you give
   Ⓓ effect, a person will usually give

2. Ⓐ No change
   Ⓑ increase, and this rises
   Ⓒ increases, and this raises
   Ⓓ increase, which rises

3. Ⓐ No change
   Ⓑ a person receives waves that are less
   Ⓒ you receive fewer waves
   Ⓓ fewer waves are received

4. Ⓐ No change
   Ⓑ which does sound. Doppler's
   Ⓒ that sounds do; Doppler's
   Ⓓ that sound does. Dopplers'

5. Ⓐ No change
   Ⓑ With the locomotive's case
   Ⓒ Such is the case of the locomotive
   Ⓓ As is the case with the locomotive

6. Ⓐ No change
   Ⓑ changes the color of light and movement produced
   Ⓒ changes the color of light produced by a moving star
   Ⓓ produces a change in the light's color and the star's motion

7. Ⓐ No change   Ⓑ In contrast   Ⓒ Ultimately   Ⓓ As a result of this phenomenon

Questions 8–10 refer to the passage as a whole.

8. Which of the following sequences of sentences will make the last paragraph more logical?
   Ⓐ No change   Ⓑ C, A, B, D   Ⓒ B, A, C, D   Ⓓ A, B, D, C

9. Are the phrases *blue shift* and *red shift* used appropriately in this essay?
   Ⓐ No, because the explanation of their meaning is never clearly stated.
   Ⓑ No, because they are irrelevant to the topics discussed in the essay.
   Ⓒ Yes, because they clarify a point made earlier.
   Ⓓ Yes, because they provide an example of a situation.

10. Which of the following sentences would most effectively summarize the whole essay?
    Ⓐ All forms of waves are susceptible to the Doppler effect.
    Ⓑ The Doppler effect has proven very useful to astronomers.
    Ⓒ The frequency of a wave is similar for both light and sound.
    Ⓓ Many changes in frequency are attributable to the Doppler effect.

Passage II

[A] Our student council recently considered a proposal that would lengthen the time spent in homeroom from thirty minutes to fifty-five minutes, the same time as our regular classes. [B] Some students strongly objected to this idea. [C] Claiming that it served no relevant purpose at all, staying an extra twenty-five minutes at school each day held no appeal for them. [D] This faction stated that homeroom was already too long, since few people studied during it anyway. [E] Also, since some students go to work immediately after school, this would adversely affect their work schedules.

TEST PREPARATION

[F] However, many other students liked the idea. [G] It would allow the people who used homeroom properly to finish most of their homework while at school. [H] Furthermore, since homeroom would now last the same amount of time as a regular class; certain electives could be offered at that time, such as art and jazz band, and it would give to the students a more interesting curriculum. [I] They argued that it could even help the students who work. [J] Those students could be allowed to take their last-period class during homeroom, and then be permitted to leave for work at the start of last period. [K] This would mean that the students who worked would get out even earlier than before.

1. In context, which of the following is the *best* revision of the parts of the passage underlined below?

   Some students strongly objected to this idea. Claiming that it served no relevant purpose at all, staying an extra twenty-five minutes at school each day held no appeal for them.
   Ⓐ No change
   Ⓑ idea, claiming that it served no relevant purpose at all. Staying
   Ⓒ idea; claiming that it served no relevant purpose at all, and that staying
   Ⓓ idea, and they claimed that it served no relevant purpose at all, and to stay
   Ⓔ idea, and were claiming that it served no relevant purpose at all, so staying

2. In context, which of the following is the best version of the part of the passage underlined below?

   Furthermore, since homeroom would now last the same amount of time as a regular class; certain electives could be offered at that time, such as art and jazz band, and it would give to the students a more interesting curriculum.
   Ⓐ No change
   Ⓑ class; certain electives could be offered at that time, art and jazz band, to give to the students a more interesting curriculum
   Ⓒ class, certain electives could be offered at that time; art, jazz band, and it would give to the students a more interesting curriculum
   Ⓓ class, so that certain electives could be offered at that time, such as art and jazz band, giving the students a more interesting curriculum
   Ⓔ class, certain electives, such as art and jazz band, could be offered at that time, giving the students a more interesting curriculum

3. Which of the following *best* replaces the word *They* in Sentence I?
   Ⓐ The plan   Ⓓ The student council
   Ⓑ The students against the plan   Ⓔ The students who work
   Ⓒ The students for the plan

4. Which of the following sentences could *best* be inserted between Sentences H and I?
   Ⓐ They would have to obtain a waiver from their parents and their employers, of course.
   Ⓑ The idea of staying longer just doesn't matter to some students.
   Ⓒ Clubs could also meet during this period, and they would have more time to organize.
   Ⓓ Art has always been an interesting topic to me.
   Ⓔ Students who aren't doing their homework have no right to complain about the issue.

5. Suppose the plan is passed and a student who works follows the ideas stated in Sentences J and K. If nothing else changes, in contrast with the old schedule this student should now arrive at work
   Ⓐ fifty-five minutes later   Ⓓ thirty minutes earlier
   Ⓑ twenty-five minutes later   Ⓔ fifty-five minutes earlier
   Ⓒ twenty-five minutes earlier

STANDARDIZED TEST PREPARATION

Verbal Expression: Identifying Sentence Errors   Test 1

Directions. In this section, each question contains an individual sentence with several words or phrases underlined and lettered. Determine the underlined word or phrase that needs to be corrected and shade in the circle around your choice. If there is no error, choose *E*.

1. Accustomed to acting before sellout crowds, the cast of the play were disappointed when few
   Ⓐ   Ⓑ   Ⓒ   Ⓓ
   people showed up for the final performance. No error
                                               Ⓔ

2. Accept for her inability to get to school on time, Ancida had always been a model student
   Ⓐ   Ⓑ   Ⓒ
   who was liked by all her teachers. No error
   Ⓓ   Ⓔ

3. With hardly no provocation whatsoever, the committee chairperson lashed out at her financial
   Ⓐ   Ⓑ   Ⓒ
   officer and accused him of trying to undermine her authority. No error
               Ⓓ   Ⓔ

4. The experimental medical treatment, slowly and painstakingly administered to the grievously
                              Ⓐ   Ⓑ   Ⓒ
   ill man, was fortunately very successful. No error
   Ⓓ   Ⓔ

5. While Plekhanov's theories outraged the public and created an uproar, there was actually very
               Ⓐ   Ⓑ
   little data available to support its claims. No error
        Ⓒ   Ⓓ   Ⓔ

6. The kind man who you knew as your employer has just admitted to living under a false name.
       Ⓐ   Ⓑ   Ⓒ   Ⓓ
   No error
   Ⓔ

7. It seemed like an impossible task: Winning the state volleyball championship required
                                                                       Ⓐ
   tall, agile players as well as powerful servers, and Harris's team had neither. No error
   Ⓑ   Ⓒ   Ⓓ   Ⓔ

8. After Hurricane Amy devastated the coastal town, the inhabitants learned a valuable lesson,
                                                          Ⓐ   Ⓑ
   and so less houses were built directly on the shore. No error
       Ⓒ   Ⓓ   Ⓔ

9. Compared by the other cars in its class, such as the Brazen or the Lotalus, the Kestrel
            Ⓐ   Ⓑ   Ⓒ
   fares well in the fuel efficiency and safety categories. No error
   Ⓓ   Ⓔ

10. Leaving most of his possessions behind, David boarded the bus, and hoped that his quest
            Ⓐ   Ⓑ   Ⓒ
    would turn out to be successful. No error
         Ⓓ   Ⓔ

STANDARDIZED TEST PREPARATION

Verbal Expression: Identifying Sentence Errors
Test 2

Directions. In this section, each question contains an individual sentence with several words or phrases underlined and lettered. Determine the underlined word or phrase that needs to be corrected and shade in the circle around your choice. If there is no error, choose *E*.

1. Our father was unable to install the new pantry door, and even after Dad called a specialist,
   Ⓐ
   he too was unable to set their hinges correctly. No error
   Ⓑ   Ⓒ   Ⓓ   Ⓔ

2. To be the starting pitcher in a big league baseball game, that is a dream I have had since I was
   Ⓐ   Ⓑ   Ⓒ
   a youth. No error
   Ⓓ   Ⓔ

3. Although she could not lie while on the stand, the defendant distorted the facts, and manipu-
                          Ⓐ   Ⓑ
   lated the events of her story so much that the judge reprimanded her. No error
   Ⓒ   Ⓓ   Ⓔ

4. The guest speaker had been asked by the staff to be ready to speak to the delegates at
                                                Ⓐ
   8:00, but the delegate's schedules listed the speech as starting at 9:00. No error
   Ⓑ   Ⓒ   Ⓓ   Ⓔ

5. Unable to determine the exact age of the artifact, yet certain their find was exceptional, the
                                         Ⓐ   Ⓑ
   three archaeologists resigned themselves to calling in a fourth party for assistance. No error
                         Ⓒ   Ⓓ   Ⓔ

6. The proud, determined cyclist, wearied by the endless hours of biking in the sun, finally
          Ⓐ
   accepted the fact that she could ride no further that day. No error
   Ⓑ   Ⓒ   Ⓓ   Ⓔ

7. The skills required to become certified as a captain in the merchant marine are not
                       Ⓐ   Ⓑ
   as stringent as the navy. No error
   Ⓒ   Ⓓ   Ⓔ

8. No matter what anyone else has to say, I will not go back to that restaurant again, ever in my
   Ⓐ   Ⓑ   Ⓒ   Ⓓ
   whole life. No error
              Ⓔ

9. Thomas always carried a small pocket knife with him when he went fishing, as a consequence
                                                      Ⓐ   Ⓑ
   he needed to cut something. No error
   Ⓒ   Ⓓ   Ⓔ

10. Since the animal had mottled skin, shaggy hooves, and a gray, bushy mane, none of us had any
                    Ⓐ   Ⓑ
    idea exactly what kind of a horse it was. No error
                    Ⓒ   Ⓓ   Ⓔ

STANDARDIZED TEST PREPARATION

Verbal Expression: Identifying Sentence Errors   Test 3

Directions. In this section, each question contains an individual sentence with several words or phrases underlined and lettered. Determine the underlined word or phrase that needs to be corrected and shade in the circle around your choice. If there is no error, choose *E*.

1. After she broke her leg in the skiing accident, Courtney found that it was difficult to adopt to
   Ⓐ   Ⓑ
   a more sedentary lifestyle. No error
   Ⓒ   Ⓓ   Ⓔ

2. The necklace had been missing for over two weeks, and the family had almost decided to give
   Ⓐ   Ⓑ
   up on its recovery, when suddenly it was found in the garden. No error
   Ⓒ   Ⓓ   Ⓔ

3. At least once in their lives, most every American has had a near accident while driving. No error
   Ⓐ   Ⓑ   Ⓒ   Ⓓ   Ⓔ

4. Faced to the consequences, the explorers knew that there was only one solution: They had to
   Ⓐ   Ⓑ   Ⓒ
   keep going, since there was no way back. No error
   Ⓓ   Ⓔ

5. One of the best ideas about the proper way to realign the districts are to hold a series of meet-
   Ⓐ   Ⓑ   Ⓒ   Ⓓ
   ings with various community leaders. No error
   Ⓔ

6. Ladies and gentlemen, please be sure to return the chairs to its proper places when you have
   Ⓐ   Ⓑ   Ⓒ   Ⓓ
   finished dancing. No error
   Ⓔ

7. The elegant woman who seemed to be quite shy, suddenly jumped onto the stage and began
   Ⓐ   Ⓑ   Ⓒ
   to sing with the band. No error
   Ⓓ   Ⓔ

8. On nights when it is cold, our cat likes to lay down at the foot of our bed while we are sleep-
   Ⓐ   Ⓑ   Ⓒ   Ⓓ
   ing. No error
   Ⓔ

9. With an election as close as this year's mayoral race, it is impossible to predict whose going to
   Ⓐ   Ⓑ   Ⓒ   Ⓓ
   win. No error
   Ⓔ

10. The Andersons' garden yielded a bumper crop of tomatoes; unfortunately, we had no such
    Ⓐ   Ⓑ   Ⓒ
    luck with our garden. No error
    Ⓓ   Ⓔ

TEST PREPARATION

STANDARDIZED TEST PREPARATION

Verbal Expression: Sentence Revision

Test 1

Directions. In this section, a part of each of the following sentences is underlined. Using the rules of standard written English, determine the answer choice that represents the most effective revision of the underlined text. Identify your response by shading in the circle around the letter of your choice. If there is no error, choose *A*.

1. Having soundly defeated the marauders, the colonel, leading his troops back to the city, and greeted by cheering crowds.

   Ⓐ marauders, the colonel, leading his troops back to the city, and greeted
   Ⓑ marauders, the colonel, leads his troops back to the city, and is greeted
   Ⓒ marauders with his troops, the colonel led them to the city, and to greet
   Ⓓ marauders, the colonel led them back to the city, and they were greeted
   Ⓔ marauders, the colonel led his troops back to the city to be greeted

2. That dog, which for weeks now has been mauling my roses, he is again back in my garden.

   Ⓐ That dog, which for weeks now has been mauling my roses, he is again back in my garden.
   Ⓑ That dog, which has been mauling my roses for weeks, is back in my garden.
   Ⓒ That dog is back in my garden, which has been mauling my roses for weeks.
   Ⓓ Back in my garden again is that dog who has been mauling my roses for weeks now.
   Ⓔ For weeks now, that dog has been mauling my roses, and again, he is back in my garden.

3. While many thought that giving Juliet two puppies for her birthday was a bad idea, to herself, the dog's gift was a wonderful present.

   Ⓐ to herself, the dog's gift was
   Ⓑ to her, the dog's gift was
   Ⓒ to her, the dogs were
   Ⓓ but to her, the gift of the dogs, were
   Ⓔ to herself the dogs were

4. By maintaining a good, consistent speed throughout the trip, the border of Montana was reached by the travelers at noon.

   Ⓐ the border of Montana was reached by the travelers at noon
   Ⓑ the border of Montana was reached at noon by the travelers
   Ⓒ the border of Montana was reached by noon by the travelers
   Ⓓ the travelers reached the border of Montana at noon
   Ⓔ Montana's border was reached at noon by the travelers

5. Those not wanting to go to the museum will now report to study hall.

   Ⓐ Those not wanting to go to the museum will now report
   Ⓑ Anyone not wanting to go to the museum, you are now reporting
   Ⓒ Those, who do not want to go to the museum, are reporting
   Ⓓ Those not wanting the museum trip have been now reported
   Ⓔ Those which did not want to go to the museum, they will now be reported

STANDARDIZED TEST PREPARATION

Verbal Expression: Sentence Revision

Test 2

Directions. In this section, a part of each of the following sentences is underlined. Using the rules of standard written English, determine the answer choice that represents the most effective revision of the underlined text. Identify your response by shading in the circle around the letter of your choice. If there is no error, choose *A*.

1. Barely making the deadline, <u>Nathan went to him to give to his boss his summary.</u>
   - Ⓐ Nathan went to him to give to his boss his summary
   - Ⓑ Nathan went to give his summary to his boss
   - Ⓒ Nathan gave his boss's summary to him
   - Ⓓ Nathan's summary was given to his boss
   - Ⓔ his boss was given Nathan's summary

2. Since the last time <u>Rasmussen was reprimanded for sleeping in the employee lunchroom, a great transformation has occurred</u> in his attitude.
   - Ⓐ Rasmussen was reprimanded for sleeping in the employee lunchroom, a great transformation has occurred
   - Ⓑ Rasmussen had been reprimanded for sleeping in the employee lunchroom, a great transformation was occurring
   - Ⓒ Rasmussen, reprimanded for sleeping in the employee lunchroom, a great transformation has occurred
   - Ⓓ the reprimand of Rasmussen, asleep in the employee lunchroom, a great transformation has been occurring
   - Ⓔ Rasmussen had been reprimanded for sleeping in the employee lunchroom, a great transformation occurred

3. <u>The treacherous mountain, it was climbed, using only her hands and feet, by Nhu.</u>
   - Ⓐ The treacherous mountain, it was climbed, using only her hands and feet, by Nhu.
   - Ⓑ The treacherous mountain, it was climbed by Nhu, using only her hands and feet.
   - Ⓒ Nhu climbed the treacherous mountain, using only her hands, and her feet.
   - Ⓓ Nhu, using only her hands and feet, she climbed the treacherous mountain.
   - Ⓔ Using only her hands and feet, Nhu climbed the treacherous mountain.

4. Griselda knew that she would not win the <u>triathlon, on the contrary, which</u> did not stop her from competing anyway.
   - Ⓐ triathlon, on the contrary, which
   - Ⓑ triathlon; On the contrary, it
   - Ⓒ triathlon, yet this knowledge
   - Ⓓ triathlon but it
   - Ⓔ triathlon. Which

5. <u>The plan was not executed properly, he had hoped it would.</u>
   - Ⓐ The plan was not executed properly, he had hoped it would.
   - Ⓑ He had been hoping that the plan will be executed properly.
   - Ⓒ He had hoped that it, the plan, would be executed, properly.
   - Ⓓ The plan was not executed properly, as he had hoped it would be.
   - Ⓔ While the plan was not executed properly, he had hoped it would.

STANDARDIZED TEST PREPARATION

Verbal Expression: Sentence Revision   Test 3

Directions. In this section, a part of each of the following sentences is underlined. Using the rules of standard written English, determine the answer choice that represents the most effective revision of the underlined text. Identify your response by shading in the circle around the letter of your choice. If there is no error, choose *A*.

1. Thinking all their guests had arrived, <u>Angela surprised the Pattersons by arriving</u> at midnight.
   - Ⓐ Angela surprised the Pattersons by arriving
   - Ⓑ at midnight Angela surprised the Pattersons by arriving
   - Ⓒ the Pattersons were surprised when Angela arrived
   - Ⓓ the Pattersons surprised Angela when she arrived
   - Ⓔ Angela surprised the Pattersons when she arrived

2. Everyone who signed up for the blood drive may now go to the auditorium, <u>while they who</u> did not should report to their homerooms.
   - Ⓐ while they who
   - Ⓑ when anyone that
   - Ⓒ when everyone who
   - Ⓓ while those who
   - Ⓔ while you that

3. <u>To take everything for granted may be Andy's idea of good business, but it is not Maria's.</u>
   - Ⓐ To take everything for granted may be Andy's idea of good business, but it is not Maria's.
   - Ⓑ Taking everything for granted may be Andy's idea of good business, it was not Maria's.
   - Ⓒ Andy's, not Maria, idea of good business was to just taking everything for granted.
   - Ⓓ Andy's idea of good business may be taking everything for granted, not Maria's.
   - Ⓔ Andy, not Maria, had an idea to take everything for granted, that was good business.

4. Regarded as a <u>brilliant singer, Gwyn Jones, a local favorite, she was returning</u> to her hometown for a series of performances.
   - Ⓐ brilliant singer, Gwyn Jones, a local favorite, she was returning
   - Ⓑ local favorite, and brilliant singer, Gwyn Jones returned
   - Ⓒ brilliant singer, Gwyn Jones, local favorite, finally she returned
   - Ⓓ local favorite Gwyn Jones, a brilliant singer, was returning
   - Ⓔ brilliant singer, local favorite Gwyn Jones was returning

5. <u>Heading toward the river, for water, and rushing out of its den, was the badger.</u>
   - Ⓐ Heading toward the river, for water, and rushing out of its den, was the badger.
   - Ⓑ Heading for water toward the river and rushing out of its den, was the badger.
   - Ⓒ Rushing out its den, then heading toward the river for water, the badger.
   - Ⓓ The badger, heading toward the river for water, and rushing out of its den.
   - Ⓔ The badger rushed out of its den and headed toward the river for water.

STANDARDIZED TEST PREPARATION

Tests of Critical Reading

Standardized tests may contain a number of limited-response questions that measure your ability to analyze and interpret a piece of writing. These questions require you to look critically at a particular piece of writing to find the meaning, purpose, and organization of the selection. In addition, these questions require you to evaluate the effectiveness of the passage in conveying the writer's intended meaning.

MATERIAL COVERED ON CRITICAL READING TESTS	
Organization Questions	You identify the organizational techniques used by the writer of a passage. These test items often cover the identification of • the author's use of particular writing strategies • the main idea of a passage • the arrangement of supporting details • the transitional devices that make the passage coherent • the techniques used to conclude the passage
Evaluation Questions	You judge the effectiveness of the techniques used by the author of a passage. These test items often cover the identification of • the author's opinion • the author's intended audience • the author's tone or point of view • the author's purpose
Interpretation Questions	You draw conclusions or make inferences about the meaning of the information presented in a passage. These test items often cover the identification of • ambiguous information • conclusions or inferences based on given material • the specific conclusions or inferences that can be drawn about the author or the topic of a passage
Synthesis Questions	You demonstrate your knowledge of how parts of a passage fit together into a whole. These test items often cover the interpretation of • the techniques used to unify details • the cumulative meaning of details in a passage
Vocabulary-in-Context Questions	You infer the meaning of an unfamiliar word by an analysis of its context. These test items often cover the determination of • the meaning of a passage to learn the meaning of a word • the meaning of an unfamiliar word by using context clues
Style Questions	You analyze a passage to evaluate the author's use of style. These test items often cover the identification of • the author's style • the author's voice and tone • the author's intended audience

TEST PREPARATION

Here is a sample reading passage with sample questions.

Sample Reading Passage

By the end of 1855, Walt Whitman was seeing his "wonderful and ponderous book," *Leaves of Grass,* through its final stages. He read the typeset pages by candlelight. When the poet Hart Crane began working on *The Bridge* some sixty years later, he worked under an electric light. Before 1920, few major American cities had been electrified. By the 1930s, nearly every American city was illuminated by electricity.

Henry Adams saw his first electric generator, or dynamo, in Paris at the Great Exposition of 1900. Because they could produce cheap electricity, these dynamos had commercial use. In time they were used to generate the brilliant lights of San Francisco, New York, and Philadelphia, thus replacing the gas street lamps that had been the hallmark of American cities in the nineteenth century.

Yet arc lights were simply unsuitable for home use because of their intense brightness. Credit for the discovery and promotion of the incandescent light used in household light bulbs must go to Thomas Alva Edison. Financed by a group of wealthy backers, Edison and his team designed an entire system to provide electricity comprised of filaments, wiring, efficient dynamos, safety features, and even the sockets themselves. In 1881, Edison unveiled his famous Pearl Street Station in New York City. Edison's men laid the wires to the square mile around 257 Pearl Street, and they wired individual households and installed meters to measure electricity use. Edison's stations would eventually supply power to over 400,000 lamps in places such as Chicago, Milan, New Orleans, and Berlin.

At the outset, electricity for the home was an expensive luxury for the elite. In 1907, for example, only 8 percent of American homes had electricity. However, large-scale generators and greater consumption gradually allowed the costs to drop. By 1920, 34 percent of American homes had electricity, and by 1941 that figure had grown to nearly 80 percent. Today, we simply take electricity for granted.

By candlelight, Whitman handwrote his poetry. By fluorescent light, a modern poet keystrokes poetry into a computer. Electrification, communication, urbanization—all are processes and systems that affect our lives. Only by understanding the history of these technological developments can we truly understand their importance.

SAMPLE CRITICAL READING QUESTIONS

1. According to the passage, what is the chronological order of the following events?
   I. Eight percent of American homes have electricity.
   II. Walt Whitman writes *Leaves of Grass.*
   III. Henry Adams sees the dynamo at the Great Exposition.
   IV. Edison begins operation of Pearl Street Station in New York.

   (A) II, IV, III, I   (D) II, IV, I, III
   (B) II, III, IV, I   (E) I, II, III, IV
   (C) II, I, III, IV

[This is an organization question; it requires you to identify the time sequence of these events and to arrange them in the correct historical order.]

2. Readers of this passage are likely to describe it as
   (A) informal   (D) biographical
   (B) historical   (E) ludicrous
   (C) inspirational

[This is a question of style; it requires you to analyze the way the passage is written to determine the category or type of writing it represents.]

SAMPLE CRITICAL READING QUESTIONS (continued)

3. The word *elite* in the fourth paragraph may be defined as
Ⓐ a variety of type found on a typewriter
Ⓑ a group of arrogant, stubborn people
Ⓒ the last people to agree to a new idea
Ⓓ the wealthiest members of a social group
Ⓔ proponents of electrification

[This is a vocabulary-in-context question; it requires you to examine the context in which the word appears in the passage in order to determine the appropriate definition.]

4. Imagine that after reading the passage your classmate wrote the following paragraph.

In the home, women were thought to be the beneficiaries of electrification. Irons, vacuum cleaners, hot water heaters, clothes washers, and refrigerators—all were hailed as inventions that would make women's lives easier. Though they were indeed labor-saving devices, describing them as being beneficial to women in particular reinforced the idea that the woman's place was in the home. For a variety of reasons, some people have recently begun to question whether these so-called technological advances were advantages at all.

You could assume that your classmate is critical of the idea that technological advances
Ⓐ are often invisible   Ⓓ exist independently of each other
Ⓑ are inexpensive   Ⓔ benefit only women
Ⓒ are beneficial to everyone

[This is an evaluation question; it requires you to identify the main points of the original passage and to recognize which of these points your classmate disputed.]

5. The phrase "keystrokes poetry into a computer" is best taken to mean that electrification is a form of progress that
Ⓐ jeopardizes our historical awareness
Ⓑ influences our daily lives
Ⓒ improves our ability to compose poetry
Ⓓ most affects students
Ⓔ has few real-world applications

[This is an interpretation question; you are asked to examine the context of the words noted in order to explain their meaning in the passage.]

6. It can be inferred from the description of Thomas Alva Edison that he was
Ⓐ a man who represented the nineteenth century
Ⓑ a man who changed his ideas frequently
Ⓒ an organized, driven man
Ⓓ a capitalist concerned only for his own welfare
Ⓔ a backward-looking romantic

[This is a synthesis question; it requires you to infer from the passage as a whole that Edison, the project director, was a driven man with great organizational powers.]

The following tips can help you on critical reading tests:

- Look over the questions before you read the passage. By looking over the questions, you can figure out what kind of information you will be expected to obtain from the passage.
- The directions for most standardized tests say to choose the *best* answer from all of the alternatives given. Sometimes more than one answer is partially correct. Remember to read all of the answers before choosing one.

TEST PREPARATION

STANDARDIZED TEST PREPARATION

Critical Reading Test

Directions. In this section, read the following passage carefully, then choose the *best* possible answer to each of the questions that follow, referring back to the passage when necessary. Identify your response by shading in the circle around the letter of your choice.

In 1895, German physicist Wilhelm Roentgen was experimenting with releasing high-voltage electrical discharges in a vacuum tube when he noticed an unusual occurrence. In the corner of the laboratory was a fluorescent screen, a device that lit up whenever electromagnetic energy hit it. This piece of equipment was not meant to be part of his experiment, but Roentgen noticed that whenever he discharged electrons in the vacuum tube, the fluorescent screen started to glow. This unexpected phenomenon certainly demanded further inspection. Roentgen covered the vacuum tube with thin metal sheets, and then discharged electrons again. When the screen glowed even though the tube was shielded, Roentgen correctly conjectured
10　　that a previously unknown form of radiation, or energy, had been produced by the discharged electrons in the vacuum tube. Since the scientific symbol for the unknown was the letter x, Roentgen called this new energy "X-ray" radiation.

Once discovered, the importance of this new energy soon became apparent. Scientists quickly learned that X-rays, like visible light, are a form of electromagnetic radiation, a term that applies to any energy that travels in the form of a wave and has electric and magnetic attributes. However, the X-ray's wavelength—the distance between successive crests of a wave—is at least forty times shorter than the wavelength of visible light. The shorter wavelengths of X-rays create higher levels of energy, allowing X-rays more force to penetrate and pass through objects. This is why X-rays
20　　were able to pass through the thin metal sheets in Roentgen's experiment; visible light, with its longer wavelength and lower energy, is easily stopped by such obstacles.

These distinctive properties explain why X-rays have so many practical uses. Within months of Roentgen's discovery, doctors were using X-rays to examine patients for broken bones. This process, known as radiography, a procedure undergone by most Americans at least once in their lives, involves firing X-rays through a person's body and onto a piece of photographic film. Bones absorb more energy than muscle or soft tissue and partially block the X-rays that pass easily through the rest of the body and onto the film. Thus, a clear, white outline of the skeletal struc-
30　　ture is created.

Doctors are not the only people to make use of this powerful form of energy. X-rays are used in a wide variety of fields, ranging from art history to astronomy. As early as 1896, for example, art historians were exposing paintings to X-rays in order to learn more about artists' techniques and creative processes. Without harming a painting, the X-ray test can tell an art historian what type of pigment was used, what condition the canvas is in, and whether or not any earlier artwork has been painted over.

Astronomers have used their knowledge about how X-rays are formed to help them locate "black holes," collapsed stars with huge gravitational fields.
40　　Theoretically, in a star system containing another star that is very close to a black hole, the gravitational force exerted by the black hole pulls in matter from the other star. This onrushing matter eventually groups together and collides, creating an electron discharge that emits X-rays. Astronomers have found a star system, Cygnus X-1, where just such a phenomenon is occurring, convincing many that Cygnus X-1 is a star system with a black hole.

Even today, X-rays are still an integral part of modern technology. For example, engineers are now implementing highly sophisticated computer scanning equipment that uses microscopic X-ray beams. Roentgen's providential discovery of X-rays earned him the first Nobel Prize ever awarded in physics.

Questions

1. Which of the following would be the *best* title for this passage?
   Ⓐ "The History and Applications of X-Rays"
   Ⓑ "The Accomplishments of Wilhelm Roentgen"
   Ⓒ "X-Ray Radiography and Its Benefits"
   Ⓓ "Characteristics of Electromagnetic Radiation"
   Ⓔ "Modern Uses for X-Rays"

2. The author's purpose is
   Ⓐ to analyze a problem
   Ⓑ to describe a conflict
   Ⓒ to predict an outcome
   Ⓓ to discuss a topic
   Ⓔ to list a resource

3. The author's tone can best be described as
   Ⓐ uninterested
   Ⓑ instructional
   Ⓒ calculating
   Ⓓ informal
   Ⓔ mathematical

4. The property of the X-ray that allows it to pass through dense objects is
   Ⓐ its electric attributes
   Ⓑ its magnetic attributes
   Ⓒ its invisibility
   Ⓓ its low energy
   Ⓔ its short wavelength

5. Which of the following *best* describes the organization of the third paragraph?
   Ⓐ A mysterious event is described, and a hypothesis is made.
   Ⓑ Two ideas are presented, and one is chosen.
   Ⓒ A phenomenon is explained, and an illustration is given.
   Ⓓ An example is mentioned, and then explained.
   Ⓔ A previous statement is proven, and a conclusion is provided.

6. According to the passage, compared with the energy of X-rays, the energy level of visible light is
   Ⓐ fifty times greater
   Ⓑ greater
   Ⓒ less
   Ⓓ fifty times less
   Ⓔ The passage does not say.

TEST PREPARATION

7. X-rays have all the following properties **except**
  Ⓐ an electrical component
  Ⓑ a magnetic component
  Ⓒ a wavelike form
  Ⓓ gravity
  Ⓔ the ability to pass through all people

8. In line 48, the word *providential* most nearly means
  Ⓐ mysterious
  Ⓑ fortunate
  Ⓒ trivial
  Ⓓ random
  Ⓔ monumental

9. It may be inferred from the passage that electromagnetic radiation with a wavelength shorter than that of X-rays
  Ⓐ has not yet been discovered
  Ⓑ would be visible to the human eye
  Ⓒ is impossible
  Ⓓ would have less energy
  Ⓔ would have more energy

10. This passage would most likely appear in
  Ⓐ a book on scientific discoveries
  Ⓑ an essay on black holes
  Ⓒ an encyclopedia article on Roentgen
  Ⓓ a technical article on electromagnetism
  Ⓔ a speech given at a medical convention

STANDARDIZED TEST PREPARATION

Tests of Critical Analysis

Standardized tests may contain a number of limited-response questions that measure your ability to recognize specific kinds of relationships.

Analogy Questions
These ask you to analyze the relationship between a pair of words and to use reasoning skills to identify a second pair of words that have the same relationship.

> EXAMPLE: CATCH : BASEBALL :: _____
>
> Ⓐ paint : brush
> Ⓑ willow : tree
> Ⓒ plaster : break
> Ⓓ wind : moan
> Ⓔ dribble : basketball

The key to doing well on an analogy question is to define the relationship between the first two words in the clearest way possible. Then look for that same relationship in the answer choices. In this case, the analogous relationship *CATCH : BASEBALL* can be stated in a sentence as, "You catch a baseball." The correct answer choice for this analogy will have an identical format, "You _____ a _____ ." This is because the two sets of words express the same relationship. The correct answer to the analogy item above is *e, dribble : basketball,* because you dribble a basketball, just as you catch a baseball. Both pairs of words express an "Action and Object" relationship. Most analogy questions fall into the following categories.

ANALOGY CHART		
TYPE	**EXAMPLE**	**SOLUTION**
Synonyms	ROUND : CIRCULAR :: strong : muscular	*Round* is similar in meaning to *circular,* just as *strong* is like *muscular.*
Antonyms	PATRIOT : TRAITOR :: loyal : unfaithful	A *patriot* is the opposite of a *traitor,* just as *loyal* means the opposite of *unfaithful.*
Cause	VIRUS : SICKNESS :: water : dampness	A *virus* causes *sickness,* just as *water* causes *dampness.*
Effect	TEARS : SORROW :: smile : joy	*Tears* are the effect of *sorrow,* just as *a smile* is the effect of *joy.*
Whole to Part	WALL : BRICKS :: deck : cards	A *wall* contains *bricks,* just as a *deck* contains *cards.*
Classification	BAGEL : BREAD :: pork : meat	A *bagel* is a type of *bread,* just as *pork* is a type of *meat.*
Characteristics	PUPPIES : FURRY :: fish : slippery	*Puppies* feel *furry,* just as *fish* feel *slippery.*

TEST PREPARATION

ANALOGY CHART *(continued)*		
TYPE	**EXAMPLE**	**SOLUTION**
Degree	COLOSSAL : LARGE :: microscopic : small	*Colossal* means *very large,* just as *microscopic* means *very small.*
Use	DESK : STUDY :: bed : sleep	A *desk* is used for *study,* just as a *bed* is used for *sleep.*
Action and Object	BOIL : EGG :: throw : ball	You *boil* an *egg,* just as you *throw* a *ball.*
Performer and Action	AUTHOR : WRITE :: chef : cook	An *author's* profession is to *write,* just as a *chef's* profession is to *cook.*
Performer and Object	SURGEON : SCALPEL :: plumber : wrench	A *surgeon* works with a *scalpel,* just as a *plumber* works with a *wrench.*

Logic Questions

These ask you to analyze a sentence or a brief passage in order to fill in one or more blanks with the most appropriate word or words given.

EXAMPLE: Because electrification began to gain _____ at the turn of the century, this era signals an important _____ in American History.

    Ⓐ mediocrity . . . collapse
    Ⓑ momentum . . . juncture
    Ⓒ patents . . . tragedy
    Ⓓ popularity . . . rendezvous
    Ⓔ enthusiasm . . . pattern

The key to correctly answering logic questions is to use context clues to make sure that words in your choices appropriately fit the blanks in the sentence. In the example given above, the correct answer is *b.* The words *momentum* and *juncture* both make sense in the sample sentence. In some of the other choices in this problem one word in the pair may make sense, but the other one does not. Be sure that you read both words carefully before making your choice.

STANDARDIZED TEST PREPARATION

Critical Analysis: Analogies

Test 1

Directions. In the following section, analyze the relationship between the initial pair of words. Using your skills of reasoning, determine which pair of words from the answer choices shows the same relationship. Identify your response by shading in the circle around the letter of your choice.

1. DISTRACTION : ATTENTION ::
   Ⓐ change : continuity
   Ⓑ insertion : interruption
   Ⓒ glare : blindness
   Ⓓ relaxation : meditation
   Ⓔ appeal : resolve

2. ADVERSARY : DUEL ::
   Ⓐ rebel : chaos
   Ⓑ diplomat : negotiation
   Ⓒ savior : desperation
   Ⓓ student : measurement
   Ⓔ counselor : friendship

3. ASSAILANT : ATTACK ::
   Ⓐ orator : run
   Ⓑ kidnapper : rescue
   Ⓒ scientist : experiment
   Ⓓ soldier : victory
   Ⓔ captor : conquest

4. CONSTITUTION : BODY ::
   Ⓐ religion : congregation
   Ⓑ spirit : soul
   Ⓒ mentality : mind
   Ⓓ secular : parochial
   Ⓔ president : corporation

5. SEIZE : PLUNDER ::
   Ⓐ compensate : withdrawal
   Ⓑ extract : splinter
   Ⓒ lend : bank
   Ⓓ operate : surgeon
   Ⓔ promote : resignation

6. CONFISCATE : PROPERTY ::
   Ⓐ reject : support
   Ⓑ abolish : protestation
   Ⓒ upheaval : government
   Ⓓ demote : rank
   Ⓔ petition : approval

7. POPULOUS : DESERTED ::
   Ⓐ diffuse : scattered
   Ⓑ chastened : humbled
   Ⓒ stingy : wealthy
   Ⓓ mortal : grave
   Ⓔ elfin : burly

8. GROVELER : SUPPLICATE ::
   Ⓐ alien : apply
   Ⓑ mentor : undermine
   Ⓒ juror : acquit
   Ⓓ liar : deceive
   Ⓔ merchant : support

9. ABHOR : LOATHE ::
   Ⓐ revere : denounce
   Ⓑ suspend : invigorate
   Ⓒ falter : relapse
   Ⓓ shimmy : vibrate
   Ⓔ negotiate : compete

10. SOVEREIGN : DOMINION ::
   Ⓐ boundary : territory
   Ⓑ athlete : agility
   Ⓒ force : superiority
   Ⓓ monarch : regicide
   Ⓔ fertility : acreage

11. OBSEQUIOUS : IMPUDENT ::
   Ⓐ mulish : docile
   Ⓑ tacit : private
   Ⓒ careless : rash
   Ⓓ sordid : scandalous
   Ⓔ petulant : rude

12. EXECRATION : SHAME ::
   Ⓐ praise : pride
   Ⓑ guillotine : edge
   Ⓒ beautification : ruin
   Ⓓ denouement : plot
   Ⓔ lamentation : envy

TEST PREPARATION

STANDARDIZED TEST PREPARATION

Critical Analysis: Analogies

Test 2

Directions. In the following section, analyze the relationship between the initial pair of words. Using your skills of reasoning, determine which pair of words from the answer choices shows the same relationship. Identify your response by shading in the circle around the letter of your choice.

1. POSTERITY : FUTURE ::
  A offspring : children
  B eternity : end
  C patience : time
  D prediction : fortune
  E ancestry : past

2. ENCUMBRANCE : DELAY ::
  A bribery : greed
  B faction : harmony
  C justice : loyalty
  D ambivalence : hesitation
  E vaccination : sickness

3. AVERSION : DISLIKE ::
  A coercion : expulsion
  B punishment : severity
  C fascination : interest
  D bravery : duty
  E tension : rebuke

4. MANIFEST : OBVIOUS ::
  A radiant : opaque
  B archaic : mysterious
  C florid : odorous
  D perpetual : enduring
  E magnetic : repellent

5. SLOUGH : SNAKE ::
  A rind : orange
  B bruise : skin
  C gill : amphibian
  D fin : shark
  E acorn : elm

6. TACIT : STATED ::
  A static : fixed
  B lavish : spare
  C morose : abrupt
  D clandestine : secret
  E obscure : confusing

7. REJOINDER : QUESTION ::
  A eulogy : sermon
  B evasion : capture
  C applause : finale
  D rebuttal : argument
  E jest : humor

8. ERUDITE : SCHOLAR ::
  A flaccid : muscle
  B guilty : suspect
  C amiable : friend
  D dour : patriarch
  E ambitious : royalty

9. UBIQUITOUS : SCARCE ::
  A expensive : rare
  B rotund : stout
  C malleable : stiff
  D terminal : final
  E indigenous : endangered

10. INIQUITY : VILLAIN ::
  A scandal : slanderer
  B camaraderie : ally
  C appreciation : investment
  D trial : advocate
  E honesty : mountebank

11. INTEGRATE : AMALGAMATE ::
  A approve : endorse
  B calculate : incorporate
  C energize : conserve
  D throng : disperse
  E multiply : offend

12. OSTENTATION : FOP ::
  A stoicism : squire
  B humility : wag
  C concern : ruffian
  D uniqueness : courtier
  E continence : monk

STANDARDIZED TEST PREPARATION

Critical Analysis: Analogies

Test 3

Directions. In the following section, analyze the relationship between the initial pair of words. Using your skills of reasoning, determine which pair of words from the answer choices shows the same relationship. Identify your response by shading in the circle around the letter of your choice.

1. DELUGE : WATER ::
   Ⓐ sky : cloud
   Ⓑ gale : wind
   Ⓒ bank : ocean
   Ⓓ river : stream
   Ⓔ mountain : valley

2. MORTAR : BOMBARD ::
   Ⓐ shovel : dig
   Ⓑ cannon : load
   Ⓒ stethoscope : wear
   Ⓓ war : pacify
   Ⓔ odor : smell

3. SPARK : CONFLAGRATION ::
   Ⓐ bypass : highway
   Ⓑ fire : kindling
   Ⓒ yawn : boredom
   Ⓓ gap : chasm
   Ⓔ riot : coup

4. PIOUS : IRRELIGIOUS ::
   Ⓐ extreme : successful
   Ⓑ holy : ancient
   Ⓒ invincible : stalwart
   Ⓓ stern : devout
   Ⓔ poignant : numbing

5. LEGACY : HEIR ::
   Ⓐ property : lawyer
   Ⓑ clan : war
   Ⓒ gratuity : waiter
   Ⓓ estate : will
   Ⓔ pate : scalp

6. EXTREMITY : BODY ::
   Ⓐ knuckle : hand
   Ⓑ fanatic : cause
   Ⓒ limb : tree
   Ⓓ pedals : bicycle
   Ⓔ brakes : automobile

7. COMPLACENCY : CONTENTMENT ::
   Ⓐ vitality : commitment
   Ⓑ rewarding : business
   Ⓒ harmony : concordance
   Ⓓ dissonance : ineptitude
   Ⓔ restitution : loss

8. ABRASION : GOUGE ::
   Ⓐ trickle : torrent
   Ⓑ fallacy : argument
   Ⓒ scar : wound
   Ⓓ aspiration : intellect
   Ⓔ paper : cut

9. MYRIAD : MANIFOLD ::
   Ⓐ glacial : sultry
   Ⓑ wealthy : famous
   Ⓒ gifted : destined
   Ⓓ modest : coy
   Ⓔ complex : articulate

10. FASTIDIOUS : PERFECTIONIST ::
   Ⓐ deliberate : philosopher
   Ⓑ indolent : layabout
   Ⓒ mistaken : identity
   Ⓓ fleet : messenger
   Ⓔ ideal : scenario

11. OPULENT : SPARTAN ::
   Ⓐ obtuse : antediluvian
   Ⓑ imbecilic : asinine
   Ⓒ honored : venerable
   Ⓓ standard : novel
   Ⓔ dominant : aggressive

12. SENTINEL : PROTECT ::
   Ⓐ hostler : improve
   Ⓑ poet : embody
   Ⓒ tinker : create
   Ⓓ banker : purchase
   Ⓔ quisling : betray

TEST PREPARATION

STANDARDIZED TEST PREPARATION

Critical Analysis: Analogies

Test 4

Directions. In the following section, analyze the relationship between the initial pair of words. Using your skills of reasoning, determine which pair of words from the answer choices shows the same relationship. Identify your response by shading in the circle around the letter of your choice.

1. HYSTERIA : EXCITEMENT ::
- Ⓐ breeze : cold
- Ⓑ hope : sadness
- Ⓒ fury : anger
- Ⓓ wood : stiffness
- Ⓔ whistle : stop

2. MARGIN : PAGE ::
- Ⓐ headline : article
- Ⓑ border : territory
- Ⓒ petal : flower
- Ⓓ epilogue : book
- Ⓔ desertion : army

3. CONSEQUENCE : ACTION ::
- Ⓐ harmony : reconciliation
- Ⓑ progress : delay
- Ⓒ climax : play
- Ⓓ test : results
- Ⓔ brevity : wit

4. EXAGGERATION : TRUTH ::
- Ⓐ ambivalence : introduction
- Ⓑ courtesy : falsehood
- Ⓒ deception : guide
- Ⓓ caricature : portrait
- Ⓔ manipulation : events

5. CHOP : CLEFT ::
- Ⓐ transform : matter
- Ⓑ intensify : flux
- Ⓒ amplify : address
- Ⓓ dissolve : solution
- Ⓔ collapse : rock

6. DIVERGENCE : VARIANCE ::
- Ⓐ modernization : abstractions
- Ⓑ hostility : concessions
- Ⓒ multiplication : division
- Ⓓ terror : omens
- Ⓔ solidarity : unity

7. FRENZY : BEHAVIOR ::
- Ⓐ irrigation : productivity
- Ⓑ craze : fad
- Ⓒ annulment : marriage
- Ⓓ senselessness : destruction
- Ⓔ gyration : movement

8. ARCHAIC : CURRENT ::
- Ⓐ precise : relative
- Ⓑ electrical : forceful
- Ⓒ eclectic : reprehensible
- Ⓓ licentious : immoral
- Ⓔ rounded : buttressed

9. CANNONADE : SHOT ::
- Ⓐ bombardment : artillery
- Ⓑ volley : bullet
- Ⓒ refrain : melody
- Ⓓ moat : castle
- Ⓔ siege : engine

10. VALANCE : DRAPERY ::
- Ⓐ shell : atom
- Ⓑ twig : branch
- Ⓒ chair : armrest
- Ⓓ bed : river
- Ⓔ sofa : cushion

11. DESTITUTION : PAUPER ::
- Ⓐ expertise : connoisseur
- Ⓑ solemnity : vicar
- Ⓒ uncertainty : beggar
- Ⓓ strength : fencer
- Ⓔ adumbration : sculptor

12. PLAINTIVE : DOLEFUL ::
- Ⓐ enterprising : vibrant
- Ⓑ exotic : amazing
- Ⓒ tranquil : pacific
- Ⓓ commonplace : abstruse
- Ⓔ simplistic : elaborate

Elements of Literature

STANDARDIZED TEST PREPARATION

Critical Analysis: Analogies
Test 5

Directions. In the following section, analyze the relationship between the initial pair of words. Using your skills of reasoning, determine which pair of words from the answer choices shows the same relationship. Identify your response by shading in the circle around the letter of your choice.

1. BOUNDARY : REALM ::
   - Ⓐ engine : automobile
   - Ⓑ division : empire
   - Ⓒ outline : shape
   - Ⓓ distance : solitude
   - Ⓔ caution : safety

2. SENSOR : DETECT ::
   - Ⓐ argument : destroy
   - Ⓑ citation : revoke
   - Ⓒ prisoner : punish
   - Ⓓ rudder : steer
   - Ⓔ hero : rescue

3. ALLY : CONFLICT ::
   - Ⓐ peasant : farming
   - Ⓑ benefactor : wealth
   - Ⓒ supporter : debate
   - Ⓓ clique : popularity
   - Ⓔ community : morals

4. AVARICE : GENEROSITY ::
   - Ⓐ philanthropy : benevolence
   - Ⓑ candor : guile
   - Ⓒ malice : pomposity
   - Ⓓ sympathy : irony
   - Ⓔ style : flair

5. DIPLOMAT : NEGOTIATE ::
   - Ⓐ turbine : heat
   - Ⓑ inspector : scrutinize
   - Ⓒ brigand : apprehend
   - Ⓓ conspirator : revile
   - Ⓔ maxim : memorize

6. PROFOUND : TREMENDOUS ::
   - Ⓐ lush : opulent
   - Ⓑ tawdry : bright
   - Ⓒ prescient : conscious
   - Ⓓ abhorrent : severe
   - Ⓔ volatile : static

7. DEVASTATION : DEBRIS ::
   - Ⓐ upheaval : government
   - Ⓑ confiscation : destitution
   - Ⓒ dawn : time
   - Ⓓ dissent : factions
   - Ⓔ construction : lumber

8. GREGARIOUS : RETIRING ::
   - Ⓐ mobile : itinerant
   - Ⓑ austere : bashful
   - Ⓒ gorgeous : pristine
   - Ⓓ torrid : humid
   - Ⓔ relevant : digressive

9. EPITAPH : TOMBSTONE ::
   - Ⓐ anagram : initials
   - Ⓑ synonym : meaning
   - Ⓒ embroidery : decoration
   - Ⓓ appendix : chapter
   - Ⓔ caption : photograph

10. ABSTINENCE : TEETOTALER ::
    - Ⓐ lassitude : truant
    - Ⓑ obsession : fanatic
    - Ⓒ obedience : child
    - Ⓓ pomp : ceremony
    - Ⓔ vanity : debutante

11. HEDONIST : PLEASURE ::
    - Ⓐ gourmand : food
    - Ⓑ spy : adventure
    - Ⓒ patient : illness
    - Ⓓ arbiter : opinion
    - Ⓔ extrovert : entertainment

12. PRÉCIS : TEXT ::
    - Ⓐ evaluation : performance
    - Ⓑ mastery : thesis
    - Ⓒ foreword : epic
    - Ⓓ ballad : music
    - Ⓔ article : abstract

TEST PREPARATION

STANDARDIZED TEST PREPARATION

Critical Analysis: Analogies   Test 6

Directions. In the following section, analyze the relationship between the initial pair of words. Using your skills of reasoning, determine which pair of words from the answer choices shows the same relationship. Identify your response by shading in the circle around the letter of your choice.

1. WITHERING : DROUGHT ::
- Ⓐ cultivation : crop
- Ⓑ water : canal
- Ⓒ dryness : soil
- Ⓓ refinery : fuel
- Ⓔ death : plague

2. STALKER : LURK ::
- Ⓐ vanguard : lead
- Ⓑ grocer : purchase
- Ⓒ thief : wreck
- Ⓓ tracker : hide
- Ⓔ detective : defend

3. NAPE : NECK ::
- Ⓐ pump : carburetor
- Ⓑ whiskers : chin
- Ⓒ bridge : nose
- Ⓓ grate : fireplace
- Ⓔ stern : ship

4. INTERLOPER : MEDDLES ::
- Ⓐ groom : weds
- Ⓑ diplomat : invades
- Ⓒ trapper : hazards
- Ⓓ guest : invites
- Ⓔ contestant : prizes

5. MINCING : COARSE ::
- Ⓐ choppy : treacherous
- Ⓑ muggy : arid
- Ⓒ believable : inevitable
- Ⓓ durable : constant
- Ⓔ humorous : gross

6. CLAMOR : WHISPER ::
- Ⓐ promontory : canyon
- Ⓑ shout : mystery
- Ⓒ mountain : knoll
- Ⓓ railing : embankment
- Ⓔ reprimand : honor

7. VENTURE : EXPLORER ::
- Ⓐ mutate : insect
- Ⓑ color : potter
- Ⓒ legislate : judge
- Ⓓ forge : smith
- Ⓔ raid : vagabond

8. OPAQUE : TRANSLUCENT ::
- Ⓐ noxious : odious
- Ⓑ potent : weak
- Ⓒ lucid : transparent
- Ⓓ crass : blunt
- Ⓔ ordained : approved

9. SEMINARY : PRIEST ::
- Ⓐ boot camp : soldier
- Ⓑ industry : executive
- Ⓒ courthouse : lawyer
- Ⓓ theater : audience
- Ⓔ congregation : minister

10. TENUOUS : SLIGHT ::
- Ⓐ covetous : generous
- Ⓑ obstinate : stubborn
- Ⓒ spurious : aggressive
- Ⓓ sensuous : delicate
- Ⓔ recalcitrant : docile

11. LABYRINTHINE : MAZE ::
- Ⓐ stoic : expression
- Ⓑ baroque : era
- Ⓒ melodramatic : behavior
- Ⓓ cryptic : code
- Ⓔ dank : catacombs

12. ULTIMATUM : PROPOSAL ::
- Ⓐ oration : appeal
- Ⓑ apologia : justification
- Ⓒ terminus : destination
- Ⓓ rebus : riddle
- Ⓔ summit : plateau

STANDARDIZED TEST PREPARATION

Critical Analysis: Logic

Test 1

Directions. In the following section, each sentence contains one or more blanks to indicate where a word or phrase has been omitted. Analyze the sentence, then choose the answer that most appropriately completes the sentence. Identify your response by shading in the circle around the letter of your choice.

1. The jury's unanimous decision was based on the _____ accuracy of the ten eyewitnesses.
   Ⓐ querulous   Ⓑ arbitrary   Ⓒ indubitable   Ⓓ grudging   Ⓔ shocking

2. Despite the _____ of her objections, Illyena was still grounded for breaking the curfew.
   Ⓐ speciousness   Ⓑ vapidity   Ⓒ coordination   Ⓓ eloquence   Ⓔ tragedy

3. Ali followed the directions on the pesticide can exactly, but he was still unable to _____ all the hornets from their nest in the garage.
   Ⓐ vilify   Ⓑ pervade   Ⓒ expunge   Ⓓ locate   Ⓔ compress

4. Since everybody in town was out Christmas shopping, our brief _____ at the mall was transformed into a _____ ordeal.
   Ⓐ errand . . . tumultuous
   Ⓑ festival . . . social
   Ⓒ spree . . . drab
   Ⓓ sojourn . . . cantankerous
   Ⓔ apparition . . . bewitching

5. The large crowd, angered by the _____ taxes placed upon them, marched to the palace and demanded the _____ of the king.
   Ⓐ copious . . . compassion
   Ⓑ sparse . . . apology
   Ⓒ absurd . . . edict
   Ⓓ exorbitant . . . abdication
   Ⓔ comprehensive . . perseverance

6. The _____ man continued to talk to his date throughout the entire movie, earning the _____ of the people around him.
   Ⓐ flashy . . . respect
   Ⓑ odious . . . imprecations
   Ⓒ contemptible . . . congratulations
   Ⓓ wearisome . . . melancholy
   Ⓔ considerate . . . threats

7. Normally an easygoing person, Clarice objected to my plan so _____ that I decided never to bring it up again.
   Ⓐ thoroughly   Ⓑ expertly   Ⓒ impiously   Ⓓ adroitly   Ⓔ vehemently

8. The baffled physician was unable to _____ my odd symptoms to any known disease.
   Ⓐ inoculate   Ⓑ ascribe   Ⓒ cure   Ⓓ facilitate   Ⓔ pertain

9. The _____ nature of the child could easily be seen in his huge collection of World War II books and _____.
   Ⓐ martial . . . memorabilia
   Ⓑ benevolent . . . paraphernalia
   Ⓒ tyrannical . . . manifests
   Ⓓ innovative . . . gadgets
   Ⓔ caustic . . . novels

10. For the most part, the _____ nature of the professor's lectures promoted a certain _____ in her students that others on campus envied.
    Ⓐ esoteric . . . stupor
    Ⓑ slovenly . . . lethargy
    Ⓒ ostentatious . . . confusion
    Ⓓ rapacious . . . happiness
    Ⓔ erudite . . . alacrity

TEST PREPARATION

STANDARDIZED TEST PREPARATION

Critical Analysis: Logic   Test 2

Directions. In the following section, each sentence contains one or more blanks to indicate where a word or phrase has been omitted. Analyze the sentence, then choose the answer that most appropriately completes the sentence. Identify your response by shading in the circle around the letter of your choice.

1. It is shocking to think that some people in the audience actually believed the _____ statements made by that fanatic.
   Ⓐ judicious   Ⓑ emotional   Ⓒ callow   Ⓓ preposterous   Ⓔ logical

2. The streetlight, situated directly behind the huge sycamore in our front yard, gave the tree a faint _____ when we looked out the front window at night.
   Ⓐ solemnity   Ⓑ impression   Ⓒ inclination   Ⓓ vista   Ⓔ nimbus

3. In his attempt to _____ favor, Kendall was willing to run any errand his boss asked of him.
   Ⓐ eradicate   Ⓑ delay   Ⓒ curry   Ⓓ appease   Ⓔ garnish

4. The chairwoman, who held the _____ vote on the relocation issue, asked for additional time in order to _____ the facts.
   Ⓐ inconsequential . . . reiterate   Ⓓ deciding . . . realign
   Ⓑ pivotal . . . reexamine   Ⓔ key . . . distort
   Ⓒ divergent . . . allay

5. The fact that he was a _____ individual did not stop Iago from engaging in _____.
   Ⓐ craven . . . intrigue   Ⓓ verbose . . . debate
   Ⓑ lenient . . . proposals   Ⓔ base . . . consequences
   Ⓒ clammy . . . plots

6. Unable to _____ the house's alarm system, the burglar _____ decided to smash the patio window.
   Ⓐ decipher . . . impishly   Ⓓ comprehend . . . sagely
   Ⓑ circumvent . . . foolishly   Ⓔ compel . . . abruptly
   Ⓒ control . . . rakishly

7. The gale was so powerful that long after it died down, the windmill continued to _____ wildly.
   Ⓐ broach   Ⓑ blanch   Ⓒ break   Ⓓ gyrate   Ⓔ rupture

8. Although I suspected the ragged treasure map was _____, I was tempted to mount an expedition at once.
   Ⓐ voluminous   Ⓑ sketchy   Ⓒ meditative   Ⓓ apocryphal   Ⓔ anachronistic

9. As if she had been wearing a mask, Danielle never changed her _____ expression, despite the _____ nature of the dental procedure.
   Ⓐ sophisticated . . . complicated   Ⓓ demure . . . morose
   Ⓑ plastic . . . unobtrusive   Ⓔ malleable . . . painful
   Ⓒ stoic . . . excruciating

10. The threat from Sanderson was so _____ that Fulton's _____ was unshaken.
    Ⓐ outright . . . approbation   Ⓓ hysterical . . . frippery
    Ⓑ egregious . . . demeanor   Ⓔ oblique . . . complacency
    Ⓒ truculent . . . composure

STANDARDIZED TEST PREPARATION

Critical Analysis: Logic   Test 3

Directions. In the following section, each sentence contains one or more blanks to indicate where a word or phrase has been omitted. Analyze the sentence, then choose the answer that most appropriately completes the sentence. Identify your response by shading in the circle around the letter of your choice.

1. The high, choppy waves created by the storm caused our dinghy to _____ tremendously.
   Ⓐ rotate   Ⓑ career   Ⓒ float   Ⓓ recede   Ⓔ navigate

2. According to Norse legends, trolls inhabit the _____ regions of the world, coming to the surface only to terrorize humans.
   Ⓐ rocky   Ⓑ populated   Ⓒ nether   Ⓓ inhabited   Ⓔ withering

3. Once he found the only all-you-can-eat sushi restaurant in the city, Darryl was able to _____ his appetite.
   Ⓐ tempt   Ⓑ hunger   Ⓒ sate   Ⓓ expand   Ⓔ comply

4. The _____ of the conversation was _____ to the petulant child, and so he began to scream.
   Ⓐ profundity . . . irksome   Ⓓ topic . . . amusing
   Ⓑ precedence . . . lucid   Ⓔ dialogue . . . entertaining
   Ⓒ shallowness . . . confusing

5. Devastated by riots and internal conflicts, the once _____ nation collapsed into _____.
   Ⓐ haughty . . . democracy   Ⓓ staunch . . . anarchy
   Ⓑ proud . . . stability   Ⓔ reflective . . . tragedy
   Ⓒ imbalanced . . . difficulty

6. As _____ as he loved his girlfriend, Jonathan was unable to stop watching the Super Bowl and answer her phone call.
   Ⓐ wretchedly   Ⓑ equivocally   Ⓒ detachedly   Ⓓ mincingly   Ⓔ ardently

7. Despite all the attempts to decipher it, the enemy's coded message was a _____.
   Ⓐ declaration   Ⓓ transcription
   Ⓑ distraction   Ⓔ conundrum
   Ⓒ correspondence

8. The _____ atmosphere of his apartment contrasted sharply with his _____ stereo system.
   Ⓐ bleak . . . ancient   Ⓓ ascetic . . . extensive
   Ⓑ luxuriant . . . intricate   Ⓔ furnished . . . modern
   Ⓒ spacious . . . electronic

9. Our physics teacher would constantly _____ us with stories from the 1950s, as she thought of that decade with great _____.
   Ⓐ regale . . . nostalgia   Ⓓ frighten . . . compassion
   Ⓑ entertain . . . derision   Ⓔ indulge . . . wariness
   Ⓒ amuse . . . contempt

10. _____ for his tactical error during the skirmish with the rebels, General Darius, unable to accept the _____ of a demotion, resigned his command in the army.
    Ⓐ Pulverized . . . taboo   Ⓓ Spurred . . . hopelessness
    Ⓑ Upbraided . . . humiliation   Ⓔ Lauded . . . possibility
    Ⓒ Coerced . . . indignity

TEST PREPARATION

STANDARDIZED TEST PREPARATION

Essay Tests

Essay tests require you to think about and express your understanding of selected material in an organized way. You can prepare for essay tests by becoming familiar with the key terms and the kinds of information called for.

ESSAY TEST QUESTIONS		
KEY VERB	**TASK**	**SAMPLE QUESTION**
analyze	take something apart to see how each part works	Analyze the main character in Nathaniel Hawthorne's "The Minister's Black Veil."
argue	take a viewpoint on an issue and support it	Argue whether or not your school should forbid students to work on weekday evenings.
compare	point out similarities and differences	Compare the British Parliament with the U.S. Congress as lawmaking bodies.
define	give specific details that make something unique	Define the term *osmosis* as it relates to the permeability of membranes.
demonstrate	provide examples to support a point	Demonstrate that metal conducts electrical charges.
describe	give a picture in words	Describe a tragic event in *Othello*.
discuss	examine in detail	Discuss the term *Romanticism*.
explain	give reasons	Explain why Beneatha is angry.
interpret	give the meaning or significance of something	Interpret the importance of the dismantling of the Berlin Wall.
summarize	give a brief overview of the main points	Summarize the plot of F. Scott Fitzgerald's *The Great Gatsby*.

Follow these guidelines in preparing to answer an essay question.

Read the question carefully, paying attention to important terms. There may be several parts to the question. Find the key verbs, then identify tasks you must accomplish in your essay.

Take a moment to use prewriting strategies. On scratch paper, make notes or a rough outline.

Evaluate and revise as you write. You will not be able to rewrite your whole essay, but you can edit to strengthen specific parts.

QUALITIES OF A GOOD ESSAY
• Good organization
• Clear main ideas and supporting points
• Complete and well-written sentences
• No distracting errors in spelling, punctuation, or grammar

17. *(Responses will vary. A sample response follows.)*

	Image	How It Is Used
Fire	fiery pit of hell	Edwards evokes this image to show what terrible punishment awaits "sinners."
Water	dammed waters ready to burst forth	Edwards compares God's ever-increasing wrath to rising waters.

Written Response

18. Responses will vary. In a model response, students should fulfill the following criteria:
- demonstrate understanding of the prompt
- clearly describe two major ideas expressed by Edwards in his sermon, for example:
  - God is angry with most human beings for being wicked and for not accepting Christ as their savior.
  - God has prepared excruciating torments for those who are not "born again" in Christ.
- support their ideas with at least two references to specific details in the selection, for example:
  - Edwards refers to the fiery pit of hell that awaits all "sinners" and vividly describes people hanging over this place of torture.
  - Edwards emphasizes God's wrath, which seems to be directed toward almost all human beings. Edwards illustrates the potency of this anger by comparing it to a pit of flames, a potential flood, and a bow and arrow ready to pierce the flesh.

from *The Autobiography*

SELECTION TEST, page 19

Checking Vocabulary

1. j	**2.** g	**3.** b	**4.** d	**5.** f
6. i	**7.** c	**8.** h	**9.** a	**10.** e

Thoughtful Reading

11. d   **12.** a   **13.** c   **14.** b   **15.** c

Expanded Response

16. Responses will vary, but students should use at least one example from the selection to support their ideas. The only supportable answers are **a, c,** and **d.** A sample response to each choice follows.
  - **a.** Franklin's belief that one can improve oneself is shown in his methodical "little book," in which he intends to keep track of how he becomes more virtuous week by week.
  - **b.** *(This is not a supportable response.)*
  - **c.** Franklin is not terribly discouraged by the Boston experience. He subsequently acts

with determination to get what he wants, by deciding to find work in other cities.
  - **d.** In his travels, Franklin finds people to facilitate his journey and to provide him with lodging. These interactions reveal his skill in dealing with all kinds of people.

17. *(Responses will vary. A sample response follows.)*
Resolution: Franklin lives up to this precept. Franklin resolves to find work in another city and sets out to do so right away.
Humility: Franklin does not fulfill this precept because he doesn't show much humility in the excerpt. In fact, he seems to be proud of, rather than humble about, his accomplishments. For example, Franklin's belief that within one year he can "master" thirteen virtues is proof of excessive pride.

Written Response

18. Responses will vary. In a model response, students should fulfill the following criteria:
- demonstrate understanding of the prompt
- explain why they chose the virtue as the most difficult for Franklin to master
- support their ideas with at least two references to specific details in the selection, for example:
  - Franklin's tendency to speak with anyone at length supports the choice that "silence" is the virtue most difficult for him to maintain. Franklin seems to enjoy speaking with a variety of people, such as Dr. Brown and the woman who gives him lodging in Burlington.
  - Franklin's apparent pride supports the choice of humility. Franklin displays pride in his accomplishments and takes care to show himself in the best light throughout the selection. For example, he notes his courage when he saves the drunken passenger who fell overboard into the sea and his generosity in giving away rolls.

COLLECTION 2 TEST, page 21

Responding to Literature

1. *(Responses will vary. A sample response follows.)*

Author	View of Earthly Life	View of Afterlife
Bradstreet	misses possessions but finds it just that they were taken by God; looks to God for strength in distress	believes that God's house is permanent and hers is temporary
Taylor	thinks all actions should be for the purpose of glorifying God	sees it as the only true and glorious life

2. *(Responses will vary. A sample response follows.)*

Author	Virtue	Agreement with Franklin	Disagreement with Franklin
Edwards	cleanliness	none (in selection)	Cleanliness alone is relatively unimportant, since simply maintaining good physical condition will not spare you from God's wrath.
Taylor	industry	You should work hard to serve God at all times.	Franklin seems eager to accumulate wealth through his industry. Taylor would probably disapprove of wealth as a goal of industry, since he seems to believe that serving God should be the goal of all endeavor.

3. Responses will vary. In a model response, students should fulfill the following criteria:
- demonstrate understanding of the prompt
- compare and contrast the views of two authors from the collection on one of the universal questions listed in the prompt
- support their ideas with at least two references to the selections, for example:
  - Taylor emphasizes serving God completely as his answer to the question "What is my purpose in life?"
  - Franklin details how one can influence the course of one's life in the section of his autobiography called "Arriving at Moral Perfection."

- Bradstreet and Taylor believe that a glorious afterlife awaits those who serve God.
- Edwards preaches that "sinners" will be severely punished by God after they die.

4. Responses will vary. In a model response, students should fulfill the following criteria:
- demonstrate understanding of the prompt
- discuss the metaphors used in two selections, for example:
  - In "Huswifery," Taylor draws an analogy between a Puritan's ideal life and the process of making cloth.
  - In "Here Follow Some Verses upon the Burning of Our House," Bradstreet describes the home of God as a house.
- discuss the effects of the metaphors, for example:
  - Taylor's metaphor is a conceit that startles the reader by showing correspondence between two seemingly dissimilar things.
- support their ideas with at least two references to the selections, for example:
  - Edwards uses several metaphors in his sermon comparing God's wrath to rising waters and a fiery pit. These figures of speech help instill fear in the audience and give Edwards's message a sense of urgency.
  - Bradstreet's house metaphor contrasts with her description of her actual house, which was destroyed in a fire. Her use of this metaphor emphasizes the difference between the impermanence of her earthly life and the durability of the spiritual life she seeks.

Vocabulary Review

5. c   **6.** b   **7.** a   **8.** b   **9.** d

Collection 3: The American Dream

Speech to the Virginia Convention

SELECTION TEST, page 25
Checking Vocabulary

1. a   **2.** d   **3.** j   **4.** i   **5.** g
6. b   **7.** e   **8.** h   **9.** f   **10.** c

Thoughtful Reading

11. a   **12.** a   **13.** d   **14.** c   **15.** a

Expanded Response

16. Responses will vary. A sample response to each choice follows.

a. The image of a lamp symbolizes enlighten-
ment and knowledge. This image urges the
delegates to look clearly at past experiences
as a guide to their behavior.

b. Henry uses effective imagery to emphasize
his point about the need for action. The
image of someone lying on his or her back
brings to mind a picture of a person who is
defeated; hugging a phantom is like hugging
something that isn't really there.

c. Henry emphasizes the deceitful nature of the
British by comparing them to sirens luring
sailors to their deaths by enchanting them
with sweet songs. He implies that the British
are lying about their intentions.

d. *(Credit may be given for an original
response that is supported by evidence
from the selection.)*

17. *(Responses will vary. Sample responses follow.)*

In balloon 2: This is true! The British are
increasing their forces
every day.

In balloon 3: American lives will be wasted in
this battle. Let's explore other
peaceful solutions before we
fight.

Written Response

18. Responses will vary. In a model response, students should fulfill the following criteria:
- demonstrate understanding of the prompt
- write a paragraph describing Henry's main
point, two of his supporting ideas, and the
different possible reactions of the delegates,
and include details from the selection, for
example:
  - Henry's main point is to persuade the
delegates to fight the British, rather than to
pursue a peaceful means of resolution.
  - Henry supports his point of view by noting
past failed attempts at peaceful reconciliation with the British.
  - He emphasizes that this is the time to act
and that waiting will only make the situation more difficult to combat.
  - Students may describe different reactions of
the delegates both as supportive of Henry's
viewpoint and as detracting from it.

from *The Crisis, No. 1*

SELECTION TEST, page 27

Checking Vocabulary

1. g	**2.** d	**3.** j	**4.** a	**5.** i
6. c	**7.** f	**8.** h	**9.** b	**10.** e

Thoughtful Response

11. c	**12.** c	**13.** d	**14.** c	**15.** a

Expanded Response

16. Responses will vary, but students should use at
least one example from the selection to support
their ideas. The only supportable answers are
a, b, and **d.** A sample response to each choice
follows.

a. Paine frequently refers to American retreats.
He's trying to convince American troops not
to be discouraged by these setbacks.

b. Much of the speech focuses on the futility of
each state trying to defend itself as a separate
entity. Paine asks every state to join the
cause.

c. *(This is not a supportable response.)*

d. Paine describes how British peace offers and
American acceptance of them in the past
have not brought about a cessation
of abuses.

17. *(Responses will vary. A sample response
follows.)*
Paine is referring to a hope that the British will
be merciful if they win the war. Paine suggests
that it is foolish to believe England's promises
that it will be generous with the Americans if
they surrender. The quotation reflects Paine's
eclectic style, because Paine includes a figure of
speech, simple language, and a sophisticated
rhetorical phrase.

Written Response

18. Responses will vary. In a model response, students should fulfill the following criteria:
- demonstrate understanding of the prompt
- respond to the quotation by explaining how
it reflects a theme in the selection, for
example:
  - Paine is appealing to the states to cease
thinking of themselves as separate entities
and instead to think of themselves as a
united force fighting for a common cause.
  - "Lay your shoulder to the wheel" means
work together arduously and in unity to
gain independence.
  - The "object" to which Paine refers is freedom and independence from Britain.

from *The Autobiography: The Declaration of Independence*

SELECTION TEST, page 29

Checking Vocabulary

1. a	**2.** i	**3.** f	**4.** g	**5.** b
6. d	**7.** j	**8.** e	**9.** h	**10.** c

Thoughtful Reading

11. d   **12.** a   **13.** c   **14.** c   **15.** b

Expanded Response

16. Responses will vary, but students should use at least one example from the selection to support their ideas. The only supportable answers are **a, c,** and **d.** A sample response to each choice follows.

  a. Jefferson and the other authors of the Declaration describe the offenses of the British in great detail, stating that these offenses have forced the colonists to declare independence. The list of offenses includes the assertion that the king has refused to pass laws that would benefit the Colonies.

  b. *(This is not a supportable response.)*

  c. The first part of the Declaration of Independence clearly outlines the philosophical justification for democratic government. Jefferson asserts that all people have an intrinsic right to ". . . life, liberty, and the pursuit of happiness . . ." and that the role of government is to guarantee these rights, not to infringe upon them. He emphasizes that governmental power should derive from the consent of the people governed.

  d. Jefferson's precise, eloquent language and his use of parallel constructions make the Declaration memorable and quotable. For example, his use of parallelism in listing grievances against the king gives the essay an air of authority.

17. *(Responses will vary. Sample responses follow.)*

  a. A democratic government was apparently a novelty. Jefferson's description of government under the English king contrasts sharply with his outline of the type of government the colonists desire.

  b. Congress had the power to amend and change documents that affected the nation. Congress seems to have had the final word in drafting the Declaration.

  c. Slavery was prevalent and was important to the economy of the United States. The fact that the abolition of slavery was not included in the Declaration reveals how entrenched slavery was in Colonial society.

18. Responses will vary. In a model response, students should fulfill the following criteria:
- demonstrate understanding of the prompt
- describe two ways that the Declaration displays the hallmarks of good writing, for example:
  - Jefferson is able to carefully develop each of his main ideas.
  - Jefferson uses stylistic devices, such as parallelism.
  - Jefferson is able to persuade using both intellectual and emotional appeals.

THE AMERICAN LANGUAGE, page 31

1. d   **2.** c   **3.** d   **4.** d   **5.** a
6. b   **7.** c   **8.** d   **9.** c   **10.** a

COLLECTION 3 TEST, page 33
Responding to Literature

1. *(Responses will vary. A sample response follows.)*

Selection	Phrase or Image	Emotional Overtones	Message
from *The Crisis, No. 1*	summer soldier and sunshine patriot	The statement derides those who fight only during the best or most comfortable times—those who waver or are uncommitted to the cause.	Paine attempts to persuade the audience that the country needs dedicated soldiers who will face the conflict, even during hard times.
"Speech to the Virginia Convention"	the clanking of chains being "heard on the plains of Boston!"	The statement implies that people have been submissive slaves for too long, but are now prepared to cast off their chains and fight.	Henry attempts to persuade his audience to join the cause of fighting for freedom from British tyrrany.

2. *(Responses will vary. A sample response follows.)*

Writer: Patrick Henry

Colonists' Actions	British Reactions
made efforts to gain liberty from England	offered gracious words but made warlike preparations to frighten colonists into submission
tried arguments, supplication, petitions, remonstrations	refused to meet colonists' demands

3. Responses will vary. In a model response, students should fulfill the following criteria:
- demonstrate understanding of the prompt
- choose two writers and discuss how each one has contributed ideas to a definition of the American dream, for example:
  - Patrick Henry speaks of how natural it is for people to indulge in illusions of hope, peace, and reconciliation. He advocates fighting for the cause of liberty.
  - Thomas Paine appeals to his compatriots' resentment of British atrocities, urges pity for the oppressed, and paints a picture of the glories that are possible if the Colonies strive for complete independence.
- support their ideas with at least two specific examples from the selections, for example:
  - Jefferson's inclusion of the "pursuit of hap-

piness" as an intrinsic right is a concept of the American Dream. His emphasis on the right to be happy and not merely free from oppression is an idea that many people associate with the American dream.

- Paine's anecdote about providing your children with a better life than the one you have is a part of the American dream for many parents. Many immigrants are motivated to come to the United States by the hope of fulfilling this aspect of the dream.

4. Responses will vary. In a model response, students should fulfill the following criteria:
   - demonstrate understanding of the prompt
   - state whether they think the writer they choose would be considered a Rationalist or not
   - support their ideas with at least two specific examples from the selections, for example:
     - The writers in the collection argue their positions logically. They use a forceful style that is designed to be easily understood.
     - The writers in the collection make their pleas emotionally appealing, and they use devices such as anecdote, imagery, metaphor, and analogy.

Vocabulary Review
5. b   **6.** d   **7.** a   **8.** d   **9.** c

Language Workshop Review
(Responses will vary. Sample responses follow.)

10. Thomas Jefferson would rise to eminence in America and become one of the country's most celebrated persons.
11. His beginnings were humble, but Thomas Paine wrote some of the most memorable words in support of American independence.
12. Jefferson founded the University of Virginia, for he believed that education was essential to democracy.
13. John Dickinson opposed the Declaration of Independence, but the rest of the delegates signed it.
14. The colonists protested the "Intolerable Acts" and supported Patrick Henry's call to take up arms against the British.

LITERARY PERIOD TEST, page 36
Understanding Vocabulary
1. a   **2.** c   **3.** b   **4.** a   **5.** c

Thoughtful Reading
6. b   **7.** c   **8.** d   **9.** b   **10.** b

Expanded Response
11. Responses will vary, but students should use at least one example from the selection to support their ideas. The only supportable answers are **b, c,** and **d.** A sample response to each choice follows.
    a. *(This is not a supportable response.)*
    b. Crèvecoeur expresses great hopes for the new country of America. He describes its inhabitants as industrious and capable of creating a better society than those in Europe. He describes the unexplored land as offering unlimited opportunities.
    c. Crèvecoeur expresses throughout the essay great admiration for the people of America. He contrasts the newly established society with European societies and emphasizes the more democratic, less oppressive structure of the American government. He admires the industry and individuality of America's settlers.
    d. *(Accept any response that is supported by the selection.)*

Written Response
12. Responses will vary. In a model response, students should fulfill the following criteria:
    - demonstrate understanding of the prompt
    - compare Crèvecoeur's and Jefferson's points of view
    - support their ideas with at least two references to specific details in the selection, for example:
      - Crèvecoeur wrote about living simply in a natural environment. He saw a land in which every person might find a life full of opportunity for self-development, unhampered by the restrictions of the Old World.
      - Thomas Jefferson writes about how the ties to England and restrictions imposed by the king have interfered with the colonists' opportunities for self-development.
      - Crèvecoeur observes people united by the support of a fair government—people who respect laws rather than fear them, because the laws are equitable.
      - Jefferson advocates similar principles when he says that people have the right to life, liberty, and the pursuit of happiness, and that any government that interferes with these rights should be abolished.
      - Crèvecoeur expresses delight regarding the lack of aristocratic families, kings, and ecclesiastical dominion in the American Colonies.
      - Jefferson emphasizes the need to establish a government by the people after the British king is overthrown.

1. a   **2.** c   **3.** b   **4.** a   **5.** d
6. c   **7.** d   **8.** b   **9.** a   **10.** a

Collection 4: The Transforming Imagination

Rip Van Winkle

SELECTION TEST, page 41

Checking Vocabulary

1. d   **2.** i   **3.** b (or c)   **4.** g   **5.** a
6. c (or b)   **7.** j   **8.** h   **9.** e   **10.** f

Thoughtful Reading

11. d   **12.** d   **13.** b   **14.** c   **15.** a

Expanded Response

16. Responses will vary, but students should use at least one example from the selection to support their ideas. The best answers are **a, b,** and **d.** A sample response to each choice follows.
    a. For Rip, the story ends happily; he does not have to work for a living or live with his wife anymore.
    b. The story provides a useful historical perspective on the American Revolution and describes its effects on one village.
    c. *(Partial credit can be given if students cite the disturbing laziness and self-centeredness of both Rip and his son.)*
    d. The story uses supernatural events to humorously relate Rip's adventure.

17. *(Responses will vary. A sample response follows.)*

Before Rip's Sleep	After Rip's Sleep
picturesque, sleepy, rural, small village inn, farms, children playing, latticed windows	more populous, bustling, people not as friendly, hotel, flagpole, people more concerned with politics

Written Response

18. Responses will vary. In a model response, students should fulfill the following criteria:
    • demonstrate understanding of the prompt
    • describe what Rip escapes from
    • make at least two references to specific incidents in the story, for example:
      • His abusive wife dies while he is away.
      • He has avoided the responsibilities of being a father, since his children have grown up.
      • He has been relieved of financial burdens.
      • He has not experienced the tyranny of British rule.

    • explain why the story is appealing or unappealing as a wish-fulfillment fantasy, for example:
      • The story is unappealing because Rip doesn't do anything to achieve his freedom.
      • The story is appealing because Rip is able to escape his responsibilities without suffering adverse consequences.

Thanatopsis

SELECTION TEST, page 43

Thoughtful Reading

1. b   **2.** a   **3.** c   **4.** a

Expanded Response

5. *(Responses will vary. A sample response follows.)*

Feeling	Reason
Gloom	Bryant vividly describes what it feels like to be dead. He also points out the insignificance of each individual to the world as a whole.
Reassurance	Bryant reminds us that we are not alone in death. Patriarchs and kings have preceded us and others will follow.
Joy	Bryant describes the glorious cycles of life and nature, and makes the reader realize what a magnificent system she or he is a part of.

Written Response

6. Responses will vary. In a model response, students should fulfill the following criteria:
    • demonstrate understanding of the prompt
    • describe Bryant's views on the nature of individual lives
    • choose at least two examples from the selection to support their ideas, for example:
      • The poem suggests that everyone experiences both happiness and sadness. The poem's speaker refers to both "gayer hours" and "darker musings."
      • The speaker emphasizes the transient, fleeting quality of human lives. He or she states "each one as before will chase / His favorite phantom" in life, stressing the futility and impermanence of worldly pursuits.

- The poem places more importance on the process and cycle of life than on individual lives.

The Ropewalk
The Cross of Snow

SELECTION TEST, page 44
Thoughtful Reading

1. a   2. d   3. b   4. d
5. c   6. c   7. c   8. d

Expanded Response

9. *(Responses will vary. A sample response follows.)*

Poem	Sentimental	Realistic
"The Ropewalk"	The descriptions of the maidens on the swing are flowery.	The speaker describes everyday scenes. He or she contrasts pleasant scenes with unpleasant ones. He or she describes the drudgery of the workers.
"The Cross of Snow"	The speaker compares the woman to an angel by using words like "halo" and "martyrdom."	The speaker's tone is mournful as he describes his sorrow over the woman's death. He also describes realistic reactions to death, such as sleepless nights.

10. Responses will vary, but students should use at least two examples from the selections to support their ideas. The best answers are **a, b,** and **c.** A sample response to each choice follows.
   a. In "The Ropewalk" the speaker balances the drudgery experienced by the workers with beautiful descriptions of girls swinging and of a woman drawing water from a well. In "The Cross of Snow" the speaker's fond memories are described along with his sorrow.
   b. In "The Cross of Snow" the speaker describes his reaction to the death of a woman he loved. In "The Ropewalk" the speaker expresses his feelings about a work situation he observes.
   c. In "The Cross of Snow" the speaker dwells on the sadness of losing a loved one. In "The Ropewalk" the speaker reminds the reader of how everyday life can be dull and dreary.
   d. *(Partial credit can be given if students point out that the speaker in "The Cross of Snow" appears to draw inspiration from nature.)*

Written Response

11. Responses will vary. In a model response, students should fulfill the following criteria:
- demonstrate understanding of the prompt
- identify Longfellow's view of life as either optimistic or pessimistic and select at least two examples from the poems to support their ideas, for example:
  - The fact that "The Cross of Snow" is a love poem shows that Longfellow is optimistic.
  - Longfellow's optimism is expressed in his loving descriptions of his wife, such as "legend of a life more benedight."
  - Longfellow uses positive images of life in "The Ropewalk," such as "Squares of sunshine" and "Two fair maidens in a swing."
  - The deep melancholy in "The Cross of Snow" and the fact that his grief is everlasting show Longfellow is pessimistic.
  - Longfellow's pessimism is reflected by the bleak and threatening images from "The Ropewalk," such as "the gallows tree" and the coiled serpent.

from *Snow-Bound:*
A Winter Idyll

SELECTION TEST, page 46
Thoughtful Reading

1. b   2. d   3. a   4. d

Expanded Response

5. Responses will vary. Students should **(1)** identify the lines as appealing mostly to the sense of hearing; **(2)** list some of these words: "shrieking," "moaning," "swaying," "beat," "fingertips"; **(3)** note that the imagery makes the storm seem eerie, forlorn, or like a ghost.

Written Response

6. Responses will vary. In a model response, students should fulfill the following criteria:
- demonstrate understanding of the prompt
- present clear descriptions of the transformations, for example:
  - The outdoor landscape is transformed by both the snow and the moonlight.
  - The indoor environment is transformed by the fire and the sense of coziness and warmth.
- provide clear explanations of Whittier's use of imagery, for example:
  - Exotic images, including "strange domes and towers," and "Transfigured in the silver flood," convey a sense of amazement at the outdoor landscape's transformation.
  - Phrases such as, "Burst, flowerlike, into rosy bloom" describe the transformation of the home after building a fire.

ANSWER KEY

The Chambered Nautilus
Old Ironsides

SELECTION TEST, page 47
Thoughtful Reading
1. a   2. c   3. d   4. b
5. b   6. a   7. a   8. a

Expanded Response
9. Responses will vary, but students should use at least one example from the selection to support their ideas. The best answers are **b** and **c**. A sample response to each choice follows.
   a. *(Partial credit can be given if students point out that in "Old Ironsides" the speaker attempts to convince the reader to help save the old ship.)*
   b. The subject of "Old Ironsides" is the U.S.S. *Constitution.* The subject of "The Chambered Nautilus" is a chambered shell, which the speaker refers to as a ship.
   c. In "Old Ironsides" the speaker expresses respect for the past glories of the U.S. naval fleet. In "The Chambered Nautilus" the speaker expresses the opinion that past experience helps people to move on to better things in the future.
   d. *(Partial credit can be given if students point out that the speaker in "The Chambered Nautilus" refers to her or his spiritual outlook.)*
10. *(Responses will vary. A sample response follows.)*
    Poem title: "The Chambered Nautilus"
    Major metaphor: the shell
    How the poem's message relates to life today: in the same way that it related to life in Holmes's time. The message of the poem is that each event in a life should give us the tools with which to build a richer life in the future.

Written Response
11. Responses will vary. In a model response, students should fulfill the following criteria:
    • demonstrate understanding of the prompt
    • identify characteristics of American Romanticism found in Holmes's poems
    • make at least two references to specific details from the poems to support their ideas, for example:
      • In "The Chambered Nautilus" the focus is on the beauty and truth found in nature.
      • "Old Ironsides" emphasizes the value of the past over the benefits of progress.

THE AMERICAN LANGUAGE, page 49
1. b   2. c   3. a   4. d   5. b
6. c   7. b   8. b   9. c   10. a

COLLECTION 4 TEST, page 51
Responding to Literature
1. *(Responses will vary. A sample response follows.)*

Selection Title	Symbol or Metaphor	Literal Description	Implication
"The Ropewalk"	factory workers as spiders	human spiders constantly spinning	By describing the workers as spiders, the poet implies that the work is dehumanizing.
"Old Ironsides"	the ship	a large sailing vessel	The poet uses the ship to convey the importance of preserving the past.
"The Chambered Nautilus"	the chambered nautilus	a sea creature that lives in a shell with many compartments	The nautilus is an extended metaphor for the ideal progression of a human life.

2. *(Responses will vary. A sample response follows.)*

Characteristics of the American Romantic Hero	Rip Van Winkle's Heroic Characteristics	Rip Van Winkle's Stereotypically American Characteristics
intuitive	possesses youthful qualities	lazy
resourceful	innocent	unsophisticated
close to nature	loves nature and avoids society	uncivilized

3. Responses will vary. In a model response, students should fulfill the following criteria:
   • demonstrate understanding of the prompt
   • choose two selections that illustrate the theme of looking to the wisdom of the past and distrusting progress, such as "The Ropewalk," *Snow-Bound,* and "Old Ironsides"
   • identify similarities and differences between the selections, for example:
     • The tone of "The Ropewalk" is political, while that of *Snow-Bound* is nostalgic.
   • support their ideas with at least two examples from each selection, for example:
     • "The Ropewalk" gives a disturbing portrayal of factory work and the price of industrial progress.
     • *Snow-Bound* offers an idealized picture of a fading way of life.
4. Responses will vary. In a model response, students should fulfill the following criteria:
   • demonstrate understanding of the prompt
   • describe a selection from the collection that represents the spirit of American Romanticism

- use at least two examples from the poem or short story to support their ideas, for example:
  - In "Rip Van Winkle," Irving provides detailed descriptions of nature.
  - Irving also emphasizes the innocence of the central character.

Vocabulary Review
5. b **6.** d **7.** a **8.** d **9.** c

Language Workshop Review
(Responses will vary. Sample responses follow.)

10. Henry Wadsworth Longfellow, the first American poet to earn a living solely by writing poems, was also the first American poet to be honored with a bust in the Poet's Corner of Westminster Abbey.

11. A devout Quaker, John Greenleaf Whittier dedicated just as much of his life to the antislavery movement as he did to his poetry, sometimes risking his life for the cause.

12. An idyll is a brief pastoral poem describing the picturesque in country life.

13. Applied to sentimental writing, the multi-faceted word *romantic* may take on negative connotations.

14. In most Italian sonnets, the first eight lines describe a situation, and the last six lines describe a change in that situation.

LITERARY PERIOD TEST, page 54

Understanding Vocabulary
1. F **2.** T **3.** F **4.** T **5.** T

Thoughtful Reading
6. b **7.** d **8.** c **9.** d **10.** d

Expanded Response
11. Responses will vary, but students should use at least one example from the selection to support their ideas. The only supportable answer is **c.** A sample response follows.
  - **c.** The speaker seems to regard the wood as a place of consolation and rejuvenation. By using words and phrases such as "kindred calm," "gladness," "merrily," "contentment," and "tranquillity," the poet creates a calm and contented tone.

Written Response
12. Responses will vary. In a model response, students should fulfill the following criteria:
  - demonstrate understanding of the prompt
  - discuss how the poem addresses the theme of the imagination's power to transform experience, for example:
    - The poem focuses on how one's inner state can change for the better through imaginative interactions with the natural world.
  - use at least two examples from the poem to support their ideas, for example:
    - The speaker imagines that various natural elements are enjoying their existence, as in lines 22–23 and lines 33–34. This interpretation of nature enables the speaker to find comfort rather than grief in life.

THE AMERICAN RENAISSANCE: A LITERARY COMING OF AGE

LITERARY PERIOD INTRODUCTION TEST, page 57
1. a **2.** c **3.** d **4.** a **5.** b
6. c **7.** d **8.** b **9.** a **10.** a

Collection 5: The Life Worth Living

from *Nature*

SELECTION TEST, page 59
Checking Vocabulary
1. sublime
2. blithe
3. perennial
4. slough
5. integrate
6. admonishing
7. occult
8. indubitably
9. perpetual
10. manifold

Thoughtful Reading
11. b **12.** d **13.** d **14.** a **15.** c

Expanded Response
16. Responses will vary. A sample response to each choice follows.
  - **a.** This quotation shows how much Emerson values nature over society. He says that when he contemplates nature, human concerns seem trivial. Nature is so glorious that, by comparison, our usual concerns are of little importance.

ANSWER KEY

b. This quotation shows that Emerson thinks solitude—being away from people—is something to be desired. It is not only society that keeps a person from experiencing true solitude, however. Even when a person is physically isolated from others, if nature is remote, he or she will not experience the benefits of solitude.

c. This quotation refers to the light that comes from observing nature. This light will cause "him" to lose interest in the trappings of society. This quotation shows that Emerson values nature highly and has some contempt for society.

17. *(Responses will vary. A sample response follows.)*

```
┌─────────────────────────────┐  ┌─────────────────────────────┐
│  Land for Sale              │  │  Land for Sale              │
│  Emersonian Dream           │  │  Great Investment           │
│                             │  │  Opportunity                │
│  • The lake is so clear that│  │                             │
│    it reflects your inner   │  │  • The lake is full of      │
│    soul.                    │  │    popular varieties of fish.│
│  • The forest of tall pines │  │  • There are acres of pine  │
│    points straight to the   │  │    trees, many ready for    │
│    stars.                   │  │    cutting.                 │
│  • The sublime location     │  │  • This valuable property   │
│    will allow you to        │  │    will allow you to see    │
│    experience all the       │  │    your assets grow.        │
│    grandeur of nature.      │  │                             │
└─────────────────────────────┘  └─────────────────────────────┘
```

Written Response

18. Responses will vary. In a model response, students should fulfill the following criteria:
- demonstrate understanding of the prompt
- explain how the quotation exemplifies Emerson's intuitive or emotional style of thinking, for example:
  - Emerson is saying that nature is so glorious it should not be examined rationally. This is an example of his belief that relying on intuition rather than rational thought is the correct way to look at nature.
- write a possible response to the quotation by Benjamin Franklin, for example:
  - A rational thinker like Benjamin Franklin would say that nature's glory can best be understood and appreciated through scientific examination and inquiry. He would probably say that a person's curiosity about nature can never be satisfied. In fact, the more one learns, the more one wants to know.
- demonstrate an understanding of the difference between intuitive thinking and rational thinking

from *Self-Reliance*

SELECTION TEST, page 61
Checking Vocabulary

1. conspiracy	**6.** imparted
2. transcendent	**7.** integrity
3. conviction	**8.** manifest
4. predominating	**9.** aversion
5. proportionate	**10.** benefactors

Thoughtful Reading
11. a   **12.** c   **13.** d   **14.** b   **15.** d

Expanded Response
16. Responses will vary. A sample response to each choice follows.
  a. This is the best expression of Emerson's theme because it emphasizes a person's uniqueness. You must trust yourself, since no one else can know what is inside you. The last part of the sentence takes the idea further, encouraging the reader to act upon his or her own trust of self to gain self-knowledge.
  b. This is the best expression of Emerson's theme because it sums up his message in two simple words: "Trust thyself." The fact that so much can be said in two words is what makes it memorable. The metaphor that follows the two words is resonant and stirring.
  c. This is the best expression of Emerson's theme because it states an absolute rule: The most important thing is to obey your own conscience. As long as you are being true to yourself, what you do and think will be "sacred"—this reflects Emerson's idea that God is in every person.
  d. *(Credit may be given for an original response that is supported by evidence from the selection.)*

17. *(Responses will vary. A sample response follows.)*

Image	What Image Is Compared To	Qualities That Are Being Compared
planting corn	being self-reliant	Both actions require qualities of independence, humility, and self-acceptance.
joint-stock company	society	Members of both give up freedom to get what they want. Both require conformity to obtain dividends.
iron string	one's true self	Both are strong yet flexible.

Written Response

18. Responses will vary. In a model response, students should fulfill the following criteria:
    - demonstrate understanding of the prompt
    - state the theme of Emerson's essay, for example:
        - Individuals should trust themselves and nurture their special gifts, and should not concern themselves with society's insistence on conformity and consistency.
    - state whether or not the quotation contradicts Emerson's theme
    - support their ideas with at least two examples from the selection, for example:
        - Students arguing that the quotation contradicts Emerson's theme may cite the following examples: that belonging to society leads to conformity and consistency; that toil can make a person great.
        - Students arguing that the quotation does not contradict the theme may cite the following examples: that everyone must take himself or herself "for better, for worse"; that everyone must accept his or her destiny.

from *Walden, or Life in the Woods*

SELECTION TEST, page 63
Checking Vocabulary

1. incessantly
2. impervious
3. ethereal
4. superfluous
5. derision
6. effete
7. pertinent
8. encumbrance
9. temporal
10. tumultuous

Thoughtful Reading

11. d   12. b   13. c   14. d   15. a

Expanded Response

16. Responses will vary, but students should use at least one example from the selection to support their ideas. A sample response to each choice follows.
    a. It takes time for beans to grow. One way this experience illustrates the value of simplicity is that, except for hoeing, there is little to do but be patient.
    b. A person who has the time and patience to watch a drama on such a minute scale must be living a life of simplicity.
    c. Thoreau built a small but adequate house using minimal labor and supplies. His intent was to build a simple shelter with little fuss or expense.
    d. *(Credit may be given for an original response that is supported by evidence from the selection.)*

17. *(Responses will vary. A sample response follows.)*

Thoreau's Goals	Goal 1: To Live Deeply	Goal 2: To Live Simply
How Well Accomplished	1 10	1 10
How Accomplished or Not Accomplished	By his own definition, Thoreau lived deeply. Building his house, growing beans, and watching nature were all fulfilling to him. The fact that he left after two years may indicate that he didn't totally fulfill this goal.	In some ways, Thoreau lived a complex life. It is simpler in a way to buy a house than to build one, for example. However, he did achieve simplicity through his solitude— except for buying supplies and selling his beans, he didn't participate in society.

Written Response

18. Responses will vary. In a model response, students should fulfill the following criteria:
    - demonstrate understanding of the prompt
    - identify the meaning of the quotation, for example:
        - Thoreau did not wish to spend his life engaged in what he considered to be useless pursuits required by society, and he felt that most people fritter away their lives with meaningless activities.
    - support their ideas with three examples from the selection of what Thoreau considered "not life," such as
        - luxury
        - needless expense
        - needless complexity
        - eating too many meals or types of food
        - a life of conformity
        - lack of planning
        - lack of a worthy aim
        - commerce (business, industry)
        - being around crowds of people
        - exporting ice
        - talking by telegraph
        - traveling thirty miles an hour

from *Resistance to Civil Government*

SELECTION TEST, page 65
Checking Vocabulary

1. inherent
2. obstruction
3. insurrection
4. perverted
5. impetuous
6. posterity
7. effectual
8. alacrity
9. penitent
10. expedient

Thoughtful Reading

11. c   **12.** b   **13.** d   **14.** a   **15.** c

Expanded Response

16. Responses will vary, but students should use at least one example from the selection to support their ideas. The only supportable answers are **a, b,** and **d.** A sample response to each choice follows.

  a. This principle is probably the least feasible today, because if everyone adopted it, there would be anarchy. Our society is very complex and depends on cooperation so that everyone may receive its benefits.

  b. This principle is not feasible because our society depends upon everyone contributing a comparable amount to keep society running. If everyone adopted this adversarial attitude toward government, there would be anarchy.

  c. *(This is not a supportable response.)*

  d. *(Credit may be given for an original response that is supported by evidence from the selection.)*

17. *(Responses will vary. A sample response follows.)*

Ideal Government	Ideal Individual
1. does not govern at all	1. uses conscience to decide right and wrong
2. has true respect for the individual	2. peacefully leaves others to their own pursuits and contemplations
3. is just to all people	3. refuses to let free spirit be constrained or dictated to by government

Written Response

18. Responses will vary. In a model response, students should fulfill the following criteria:
  • describe Thoreau's purpose, for example:
    • Thoreau wrote this essay to persuade readers to accept his point of view about government and civil disobedience.
  • summarize four other major points of the essay, for example:
    • Thoreau states that the government is apt to be "perverted" by the interests of a few and thus apt to act immorally. The fact that the current government supported slavery and was at war with Mexico to extend slavery further was proof of that corruption.
    • He states that a person's conscience should take precedence over the law or the government.
    • He says that a person is not morally obligated to devote himself or herself to eradicating wrongs but *is* obligated not to support wrongdoing.
    • He criticizes the hypocrisy of those who say they are against slavery and the war in Mexico, yet give their allegiance to the government and pay their taxes. He says that if all who claim to abhor slavery would refuse to pay their taxes and be locked in jail, slavery would be abolished.
    • He describes his night in jail, first describing the "foolishness" of his jailers who did not understand that he considered himself free (free of needing to obey the government, he seems to be implying).
    • He makes other observations about his jail experience, including how he saw his town and its people differently when he came out the next day. He faults his townspeople for choosing lives of subservient conformity.

COLLECTION 5 TEST, page 67

Responding to Literature

1. *(Responses will vary. A sample response follows.)*

Emerson	Thoreau
Nature can repair any disgrace or calamity—the harmony of humanity and nature is an ideal state.	The nation is being ruined by luxury and needless expense; the only cure is rigid economy, stern simplicity of life, and elevation of purpose.
When people trust themselves, they become guides, redeemers, and benefactors, generating faith in goodness and inevitable progress.	Government loses integrity by maintaining its traditions; it is individuals who have kept the country free, settled the West, and educated others—government has tried only to stand in the way.
Society breeds conformity. People should trust the integrity of their own minds above all else.	The only obligation people have is to do what they think is right and not to support what they think is wrong.

2. *(Responses will vary. A sample response follows.)*

	Emerson	Thoreau
Nature	source of goodness; image in which people can perceive divinity	simplicity and divine unity of nature; love of one place as epitome of universe
The Individual	individual intuition as guide to universal truth; abiding faith in boundless resources of human spirit and imagination; affirms self-reliance over conformity and the individual over society	people no longer free and creative, enslaved by division of labor; urges readers to find and pursue their own way
Conformity	means by which free persons are forced into slavery by society	mechanized, standardized, conformist society destroys simplicity and natural qualities of life

3. Responses will vary. In a model response, students should fulfill the following criteria:
   - demonstrate understanding of the prompt
   - respond to whether Thoreau followed his own criteria
   - formulate a clear generalization about the presence or absence of common sense, truth, and beauty in Thoreau's writings
   - support their analyses with specific examples from the selections, for example:
     - Thoreau makes insightful observations such as, "life is frittered away by detail," "how deep the ruts of tradition and conformity," and "the only obligation which I have a right to assume, is to do at any time what I think right."
   - His use of figures of speech enhances the beauty of his prose. For example, he invokes the metaphor of living deeply and sucking out the marrow of life, the extended comparison between weeding beans and the Trojan War, and the comparison between pursuing a loon and playing checkers.

4. Responses will vary. In a model response, students should fulfill the following criteria:
   - demonstrate understanding of the prompt
   - choose either Emerson or Thoreau as the focus of the response
   - explain *why* the writer's philosophy can best be applied to their experience, for example:
     - Emerson's advice of trusting oneself and being a nonconformist is appealing because conformity is a pernicious product of society.
   - explain *how* the writer's philosophy can best be applied to their experience, for example:
     - Thoreau's ideas about observing nature can teach a person a lot about human interactions with the natural world and the lessons we can draw from it.

Vocabulary Review

5. d **6.** b **7.** c **8.** a **9.** d

Collection 6: The Realms of Darkness

The Fall of the House of Usher

SELECTION TEST, page 71

Checking Vocabulary

1. b **2.** e **3.** h **4.** a **5.** g
6. j **7.** d **8.** c **9.** i **10.** f

Thoughtful Reading

11. b **12.** a **13.** b **14.** d **15.** c

Expanded Response

16. Responses will vary, but students should use at least one example from the selection to support their ideas. The only supportable answer is **c.** A sample response follows.
    c. Roderick hears strange sounds from the basement vault, and he seems to know that they are made by Madeline as she seeks to get out of her tomb.

17. *(Responses will vary. A sample response follows.)*

The madman is Roderick because: He has buried his sister alive. He did not rescue her when he first began to suspect the truth.
The madman is the narrator because: He has been unable or unwilling to accept what is happening in the House of Usher.

Written Response

18. Responses will vary. In a model response, students should fulfill the following criteria:
    - demonstrate understanding of the prompt
    - suggest at least two reasons why the narrator stays on at the house
    - support their ideas with at least two references to specific details in the selection, for example:
    - The narrator may stay on because of concern for Roderick. The narrator has come to help his friend; he decides to stay even when he can't cheer up Roderick.
    - The narrator is fascinated by the events at the house of Usher. He describes them in great detail; he is curious about the mysterious Madeline.

• The narrator himself is going insane. His own senses begin to become abnormally acute; he, too, wonders whether Madeline has been buried alive.

The Raven

SELECTION TEST, page 73

Thoughtful Reading

1. c   2. d   3. b   4. a   5. c

Expanded Response

6. Responses will vary, but students should give at least one example from the selection to support their ideas. A sample response to each choice follows.
   a. He learns there is no "balm in Gilead"—that even in death, his experience will be bleak and solitary.
   b. In the second half of the poem, he begins to refer to the raven as if it were diabolical and had come to taunt him.
   c. The raven's repetition of "Nevermore" confirms the speaker's dread that he will not meet Lenore again, even after death.
   d. The speaker starts off as merely blue and distracted, but he soon is wallowing in grief and despair.

7. (Responses will vary. A sample response follows.)

   Realistic: The physical description fits that of an ordinary raven. It acts like a trained pet, like a parrot that has been taught a word and repeats it.
   Unrealistic: The bird-as-demon exists only in the speaker's imagination. It is unrealistic to expect a bird to comprehend what "nevermore" means.

Written Response

8. Responses will vary. In a model response, students should fulfill the following criteria:
   • demonstrate understanding of the prompt
   • explore Poe's purpose in combining the symbols of the raven and Pallas Athena, for example:
     • The raven represents the obsessive, emotional part of the speaker's mind that can't forget past misery. Pallas Athena represents the logical, rational part of the mind with which the speaker, who is probably a student, identifies. By pairing these two symbols, Poe is pointing out the conflict between the emotional self and the rational one.
     • By using these symbols, Poe may also be illustrating the futility of trying to combat wild emotions and irrationality with knowledge and rational argument. The raven maintains a higher position than the bust of Athena and the speaker's fear clearly gets the better of him in the end.

The Minister's Black Veil

SELECTION TEST, page 75

Checking Vocabulary

1. b   2. a   3. i   4. f   5. h
6. j   7. e   8. c   9. d   10. g

Thoughtful Reading

11. b   12. d   13. c   14. a   15. c

Expanded Response

16. Responses will vary, but students should use at least one example from the selection to support their ideas. The only supportable answers are **a, b,** and **d.** A sample response to each choice follows.
    a. People get nervous when they think about Hooper's veil, and they wonder how it applies to them.
    b. Hooper says more than once that we present a false front to others (as if we were wearing a veil to cover our "real" selves).
    c. (This is not a supportable response.)
    d. Early on, we get the feeling that Hooper may have been responsible, or may feel responsible, for the death of the young girl he goes to mourn.

17. (Responses will vary. A sample response follows.)

Positive Effects	Negative Effects
• The parson's veil attracts converts to the congregation. • Hooper feels that the veil is a symbol and an example to his congregation. • Hooper believes that wearing it will bring him peace in the next life.	• The veil causes dread in Hooper's parishioners. • The veil costs Hooper his fiancée and the chance to have a normal family life. • By creating fear and suspicion, the veil detracts from Hooper's many good deeds.

Written Response

18. Responses will vary. In a model response, students should fulfill the following criteria:
    • demonstrate understanding of the prompt
    • explain what Hooper means by his anguished cry
    • support their opinions with at least two references to specific details in the selection, for example:
      • Hooper is trying to remind the congregation that they too have sinned. The sermon Hooper preached at the beginning of the story made his listeners feel that their own secret sins had been exposed.
      • Hooper is trying to remind his parishioners of their imminent mortality. Hooper refuses to take off the veil even at the moment of his death.

The Quarter-Deck

SELECTION TEST, page 77

Checking Vocabulary

1. c   **2.** d   **3.** e   **4.** a   **5.** b

Thoughtful Reading

6. c   **7.** c   **8.** b   **9.** d   **10.** a

Expanded Response

11. Responses will vary, but students should use at least one example from the selection to support their ideas. The only supportable answers are **a,** and **d.** A sample response to each choice follows.
    a. The gold coin provides incentive for the sailors. Aside from this obvious financial benefit, there is the incentive of glory.
    b. *(This is not a supportable response.)*
    c. Ahab speaks movingly about his tragic encounter with Moby-Dick, making an irresistible emotional plea.
    d. *(Credit may be given for an original response that is supported by evidence from the selection.)*
12. *(Responses will vary. A sample response follows.)*
    Skilled Commander: He rallies a mystified crew; in the past, he has led successful whaling expeditions.
    Single-Minded Zealot: He keeps harping on Moby-Dick; he likens whale-hunting to a baptism; he allows no dissension.

Written Response

13. Responses will vary. In a model response, students should fulfill the following criteria:
    • demonstrate understanding of the prompt
    • provide explanations for Starbuck's comments, for example:
      • By "dumb brute," Starbuck means a creature that cannot speak or reason.
      • By "blindest instinct," he means an innate programming.
      • By "blasphemous," he means that to ascribe human traits to a "lowly" creature is to forget that humans are somehow "closer to God."
    • state whether or not they agree with Starbuck's opinions, and then provide reasons for their answers

from *Moby-Dick*

SELECTION TEST, page 79

Checking Vocabulary

1. d   **2.** a   **3.** b   **4.** c   **5.** e

Thoughtful Reading

6. a   **7.** c   **8.** b   **9.** a   **10.** d

Expanded Response

11. Responses will vary, but students should use at least one example from the selection to support their ideas. The only supportable answers are **a, c,** and **d.** A sample response to each choice follows.
    a. The narrator tells how whales often elude the whaling ships.
    b. *(This is not a supportable response.)*
    c. The narrator implies that the crews both envy and resent the whales' ability to adapt to their environment.
    d. Most of the sailors come to believe the very tales they and their cohorts have spread.
12. *(Responses will vary. A sample response follows.)*

Perceptions of Moby-Dick		
Ishmael	**Sailors**	**Ahab**
• enormous, with a wrinkled forehead • a white hump • appears to be solid white • a deformed lower jaw • turns upon its pursuers	• ubiquitous—appears in different oceans at the same time • immortal—cannot be seriously injured or overcome	• malign, evil • a personal enemy

Written Response

13. Responses will vary. In a model response, students should fulfill the following criteria:
    • demonstrate understanding of the prompt
    • clearly describe three of Ahab's personal characteristics that contribute to his leadership ability, such as
      • perseverance
      • persuasive speaking
      • a clear goal
      • an ability to convince others that what is good for him is good for them too
    • identify a contemporary leader and compare and contrast that figure with Ahab

COLLECTION 6 TEST, page 81

1. *(Responses will vary. A sample response follows.)*

Situation	Character's Reaction
Character Who Copes Best: Elizabeth	
Her fiancée, Mr. Hooper, will not fully explain why he wears a black veil.	Though she loves Hooper, Elizabeth leaves him because she doesn't want to marry a man who keeps secrets from her.
Character Who Copes Worst: The speaker in "The Raven"	
A raven enters the room, repeats the word "nevermore," and refuses to leave.	The speaker turns gloomy, dwells morbidly on his lost love, and finally seems to go mad.

ANSWER KEY

2. *(Responses will vary. A sample response follows.)*

Selection	Character's Secret(s)	Is Your Curiosity Satisfied?
"The Fall of the House of Usher"	Why is Roderick so distressed?	Yes. We find out he has suspected his sister was entombed alive.
"The Raven"	Why does the raven visit the speaker?	No. We are never quite sure.
"The Minister's Black Veil"	Why does Hooper wear the black veil?	No. We don't know if he is atoning for a particular sin.
Moby-Dick	Why is Ahab obsessed with the white whale?	Yes. The whale has injured him.

3. Responses will vary. In a model response, students should fulfill the following criteria:
- demonstrate understanding of the prompt
- clearly state why macabre stories and poems are popular with so many readers
- support their explanations with at least one example from each selection, for example:
- "The Fall of the House of Usher" stirs readers' fascination with extraordinary and bizarre events, such as Madeline's burial and her emergence from the tomb.
- "The Raven" reminds readers of moments when their own imaginations scare them to death.
- Mr. Hooper's black veil may make readers squirm with recollections of their own terrible secrets.
- The way Ahab rants about Moby-Dick makes us wonder whether evil is in fact personified in living things.

4. Responses will vary. In a model response, students should fulfill the following criteria:
- demonstrate understanding of the prompt
- identify the major symbol in the chosen selection
- explain how the symbol functions in the story or poem and what it stands for, for example:
- The raven in Poe's poem is a real bird. Its sudden appearance and its constant repetition of the same word, "nevermore," simply amuse and puzzle the speaker for a while. Then the raven begins to take on a symbolic significance. As the speaker becomes mired in gloomy memories and obsessions about his lost love, the raven comes to symbolize the disturbing permanence of grief and despair.

Vocabulary Review
5. d **6.** d **7.** a **8.** b **9.** c

Language Workshop Review
(Responses will vary. Sample responses follow.)
10. Mr. Hooper's parishioners were bewildered by the black veil and asked each other what it meant.
11. Ignoring what he heard was Roderick's way of denying what he knew was true—that Madeline was still alive.
12. Captain Ahab's crew was enthusiastic about the hunt for Moby-Dick and was eager to kill the white whale.
13. Madeline's body had been put into the vault, and the door had been shut tightly.
14. Captain Ahab's desire for revenge was all-consuming and obsessive.

LITERARY PERIOD TEST, page 84
Understanding Vocabulary
1. a **2.** b **3.** c **4.** a **5.** c

Thoughtful Reading
6. c **7.** b **8.** d **9.** a **10.** b

Expanded Response
11. Responses will vary, but students should use at least one example from the letter to support their ideas. The only supportable answers are **b, c,** and **d.** A sample response to each choice follows.
- **a.** *(This is not a supportable response.)*
- **b.** Melville employs wry humor in describing his and Hawthorne's musings after the world's end and the objectivity in his remarks about trying to satisfy both oneself and one's audience.
- **c.** Melville writes "Dollars damn me" and comments that what he most wants to write "will not pay."
- **d.** Melville expresses fear about his work being a "final hash" and states that "all my books are botches."

Written Response
12. Responses will vary. In a model response, students should fulfill the following criteria:
- demonstrate understanding of the prompt
- organize their ideas using the chart
- write a paragraph comparing Melville's, Thoreau's, and Emerson's attitudes toward nature, for example:
- Melville seems to equate nature with farm work and hard labor.
- Emerson sees nature as being full of symbols of greater, spiritual ideas.
- Thoreau believes that nature in its literal form is something from which to learn.

A New American Poetry: Whitman and Dickinson

1. a   2. a   3. b   4. d   5. c
6. d   7. b   8. b   9. c   10. a

Collection 7: The Large Hearts of Heroes

I Hear America Singing
from *Song of Myself* 10, 33, and 52
A Sight in Camp in the Daybreak Gray and Dim

SELECTION TEST, page 89

Thoughtful Reading

1. b   2. a   3. a   4. a
5. c   6. c   7. d   8. c

9. Responses will vary, but students should use at least one example from the selection to support their ideas. The only supportable answers are **a, b,** and **c.** A sample response to each choice follows.

   a. Whitman portrays ordinary people as workers in "I Hear America Singing" and as heroes in "Song of Myself," Number 33. His poems evoke a sense of empathy for these characters, and this focus gives his poetry democratic appeal.

   b. Whitman's use of free verse in all of the poems in this collection enables him to present ideas in a format that seems natural. His emphasis on rhythm rather than on rhyme, as in his use of cadence in "I Hear America Singing," gives his poetry a musical quality.

   c. Whitman blends keen observation of detail with subjective feeling. This technique is apparent in "Song of Myself," Number 10, in which the speaker acts as both observer and participant in several scenes. His ability to make his speakers play both roles gives his poems an air of authority.

   d. *(This is not a supportable response.)*

10. *(Responses will vary. A sample response follows.)*

Alliteration	Assonance	Imagery	Onomatopoeia	Parallel Structure
*b*reast-bone *b*roken	bur*ie*d *me* in their debr*is*	tumbling walls; heat and smoke; distant click	distant click of their picks	I heard … I heard

Written Response

11. Responses will vary. In a model response, students should fulfill the following criteria:
    * demonstrate understanding of the prompt
    * describe what they think Whitman means by the statement
    * support their ideas with at least two references to specific details in the selection, for example:
      * "Barbaric yawp" refers to the new voice, the new style that Whitman brought to American poetry. The term may also refer to the unbridled emotion and honesty of his expression, or to Whitman's celebration of ordinary people.
      * "Roofs of the world" might refer to audiences in other lands, to established poets, or to future generations.

Collection 8: Tell It Slant

Poetry of Emily Dickinson

SELECTION TEST, page 91

Thoughtful Reading

1. b   2. d   3. b   4. a
5. a   6. c   7. a   8. d

Expanded Response

9. Responses will vary. The only supportable answers are **a, b,** and **c.** A sample response to each choice follows.

   a. The poem expresses the idea that we often don't understand the value of life until it's too late.

   b. The poem expresses the idea that our present life may blend very calmly into a future one, beyond death.

   c. The concept of death in this poem is that we think it's going to be terribly dramatic, but may discover that it's very simple, even trivial.

   d. *(This is not a supportable response.)*

10. (Responses will vary. A sample response follows.)
   "The Soul . . .": It is the soul or spirit that chooses whom to love.
   "Heart! . . .": When it comes to love, it's impossible to make your emotions obey your intellect.
   "If you . . .": Even though you may know your loved one isn't going to return, you may go on fantasizing, hoping, and scheming.

Written Response

11. Responses will vary. In a model response, students should fulfill the following criteria:
   • demonstrate understanding of the prompt
   • answer the question with regard to Dickinson and her poetry
   • support their ideas with at least two references to details in the poems, for example:
     • Dickinson's keen observations about death in poems such as "I heard a Fly buzz—when I died" are evidence that she gained wisdom about life despite her isolation.
     • Dickinson displays detailed knowledge about the natural world as expressed in poems such as "I taste a liquor never brewed."

THE AMERICAN LANGUAGE, page 93

1. b	2. c	3. a	4. d	5. b
6. a	7. d	8. b	9. c	10. b

LITERARY PERIOD TEST, page 95

Understanding Vocabulary

1. b	2. b	3. c	4. c	5. a

Thoughtful Reading

6. a	7. c	8. d	9. c	10. b

Expanded Response

11. Responses will vary. The only supportable answers are **a, c,** and **d.** A sample response to each choice follows.
   a. Dickinson uses the sea as a metaphor for a lover or servant who is constantly obedient. Whitman uses the sea as a metaphor for life itself.
   b. (This is not a supportable response.)
   c. Whitman's words from lines 10 and 11 and Dickinson's words from the last stanza reflect deep emotion.
   d. Whitman uses a ship as a metaphor for the human body and soul, while Dickinson compares two lovers to the central metaphor of the moon and sea.

Written Response

12. Responses will vary. In a model response, students should fulfill the following criteria:
   • demonstrate understanding of the prompt
   • choose the poem they consider more universal
   • explain the universal appeal of the chosen poem, for example:
     • The Dickinson poem is universal because it describes the absolute devotion of the speaker to a loved one.
   • identify another poem by the same writer and tell how it is like the chosen poem, for example:
     • The Dickinson poem is similar to "If you were coming in the Fall," which describes a similar devotion.

THE RISE OF REALISM: THE CIVIL WAR AND POSTWAR PERIOD

LITERARY PERIOD INTRODUCTION TEST, page 99

1. a	2. b	3. d	4. a	5. d
6. b	7. c	8. a	9. b	10. c

Collection 9: Shackles

The Battle with Mr. Covey

SELECTION TEST, page 101

Checking Vocabulary

1. A	2. S	3. A	4. A	5. S
6. S	7. A	8. S	9. A	10. S

Thoughtful Reading

11. c	12. a	13. c	14. d	15. b

Expanded Response

16. (Responses will vary. A sample response follows.)

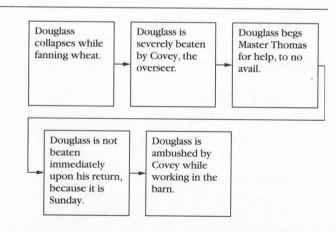

Douglass collapses while fanning wheat. → Douglass is severely beaten by Covey, the overseer. → Douglass begs Master Thomas for help, to no avail.

Douglass is not beaten immediately upon his return, because it is Sunday. → Douglass is ambushed by Covey while working in the barn.

LITERARY PERIOD INTRODUCTION TEST

A New American Poetry
Whitman and Dickinson

Pupil's Edition page 340

On the line provided, write the letter of the *best* answer to each of the following items.
(10 points each)

_____ 1. A major similarity between Whitman and Dickinson is their
   a. willingness to break away from literary conventions
   b. need to support themselves by selling their work
   c. obscurity during their lifetimes
   d. rejection by their intended audience

_____ 2. Dickinson's poems flowed from her
   a. rich internal life and close observation of nature
   b. passionate embrace of democratic ideals
   c. admiration and emulation of great narrative poetry
   d. frustration over the constraints imposed on women

_____ 3. From the beginning, Whitman expected his poetry to be
   a. praised by established American poets
   b. carried like a message into the future
   c. published and admired in Europe
   d. unappreciated by the average reader

_____ 4. Dickinson did not achieve fame during her lifetime because
   a. she hid her poetry from her family and friends
   b. most of her friends discouraged her from becoming a poet
   c. she believed poetry should never be published
   d. most of her poetry was not published until after her death

_____ 5. Whitman's feelings about his own poems are *best* revealed by his
   a. refusal to publish them until they had been approved by writers he admired
   b. dissatisfaction with their wording, and his constant efforts to revise them
   c. belief that they were important enough to publish at his own expense
   d. pursuit of other occupations, while regarding poetry as a part-time activity

_____ 6. Whitman's style and technique are based on cadence, which is the
   a. regular rhythm used in old ballads and epic poems
   b. iambic pentameter used by William Shakespeare
   c. use of exact rhymes and alliteration
   d. rhythm and long sweeps of sound used by great speakers

_____ 7. Dickinson's poetry is noted for its emphasis on
   a. purely emotional appeals to the reader
   b. precise wording and unique poetic forms
   c. ideas that readers can quickly and easily understand
   d. thoughts that are acceptable in polite society

COLLECTIONS 7–8

_____ **8.** Whitman developed a free-verse style, which is
   a. the praise of democratic government and ideals
   b. poetry without predictable end rhyme or meter
   c. an attempt to state old ideas in a new way
   d. verse that uses new techniques from Europe

_____ **9.** To highlight the ideas in her poems, Dickinson
   a. abandons all attempt at rhyme or metaphor
   b. uses the technique of cataloging
   c. uses shifting rhymes and meters
   d. makes references to classical philosophers

_____ **10.** Which of the following statements *best* describes the influence of Dickinson and
   Whitman on later poets?
   a. Their development of vastly different but equally important personal styles has
   inspired generations of poets.
   b. Their poetry has appealed more to European than to American poets.
   c. They both wrote for themselves alone, without worrying about form or structure.
   d. Their poetry suggests that the primary purpose of writing is to move people
   to political action.

LITERARY PERIOD INTRODUCTION TEST

The Rise of Realism
The Civil War and Postwar Period

Pupil's Edition page 406

On the line provided, place the letter of the *best* answer to each of the following items.
(10 points each)

_____ 1. Having seen the horrors of the Civil War firsthand as a Union camp hospital volunteer, Walt Whitman
    a. was still able to retain an optimistic view of the character of Americans
    b. shifted from optimism to pessimism as a result of witnessing the carnage
    c. was overcome with disillusionment after the Battle of Bull Run
    d. was devastated by the death of his wounded brother

_____ 2. Which of the following statements about Herman Melville's response to the Civil War is **not** true?
    a. He believed the fighting during the war to be both heroic and futile.
    b. He wrote a novel about the war based on his visits to battlefields.
    c. His poems about the war reveal his belief in humanity's intrinsic evil.
    d. His poems about the war show respect for the soldiers of both sides.

_____ 3. Because few major American writers experienced the Civil War firsthand,
    a. they were regarded as cowardly and unpatriotic by both North and South
    b. all of the important poetry and fiction created came from newspaper accounts
    c. no realistic accounts of the soldiers' experiences were written
    d. very little important poetry and fiction emerged directly from the war

_____ 4. A great novel of the Civil War was not written until long after the war had ended because
    a. the proper vehicle for such strong material, the realistic novel, had not yet been fully developed in the United States
    b. it was necessary for the intensity of the country's emotions to subside before such a realistic novel would be accepted by the American public
    c. the writers who viewed the war firsthand lacked the skill to adequately describe what was really happening on the battlefields
    d. few American writers of the period were willing to risk visiting the battle sites during the war

_____ 5. The literary form in which heroes and heroines live idealistic lives beyond the level of everyday life is called the
    a. naturalistic novel
    b. psychological novel
    c. realistic novel
    d. romantic novel

_____ 6. After the Civil War, a generation of writers known as realists sought to
    a. use romance not only to entertain readers, but also to reveal truths to them
    b. accurately portray real life without filtering it through Romanticism or idealism
    c. provide an idealistic view of life in order to heal the wounds of the war
    d. accurately portray behavior without seeking explanations for it

COLLECTIONS 9-10

_____ 7. Though regional writers realistically portrayed speech patterns and mannerisms of people in a relatively small geographical area, they
   a. were even more realistic in showing human life as a losing battle
   b. were primarily interested in the impact of social forces on individuals
   c. were often unrealistic in writing about character and social environment
   d. tended to view regional customs with humor and skepticism

_____ 8. The behavior of the characters created by some Naturalist writers
   a. was crude, instinctive, and subject to the natural laws of the universe
   b. may have been foolhardy, but usually resulted in happy endings
   c. was usually much more melodramatic than realistic
   d. demonstrated that humans have control over their own destinies

_____ 9. Which of the following statements *best* describes the psychological novels of Henry James?
   a. They show people driven by animal-like instincts.
   b. They open the inner mind to the techniques of fiction.
   c. They contrast innocent Europeans with sophisticated Americans.
   d. They all take place in the United States.

_____ 10. The principal goal of an ironist is to
   a. examine human behavior under pressure
   b. examine social institutions with the aim of reforming them
   c. juxtapose human pretensions and the indifference of the universe
   d. demonstrate how the universe helps people achieve their desires

17. Responses will vary, but students should use at least one example from the selection to support their ideas. A sample response to each choice follows.
   a. Covey could have pursued and attacked Douglass. Since Douglass was so severely wounded, he could have died in the woods from his untreated injuries.
   b. Covey could have found Douglass and beaten him. Covey had demonstrated that he was determined to attack Douglass.
   c. Douglass was in a very vulnerable position, since it was illegal for a slave to fight back against a white man.
   d. *(Credit may be given for an original response that is supported by evidence from the selection.)*

Written Response

18. Responses will vary. In a model response, students should fulfill the following criteria:
   • demonstrate understanding of the prompt
   • clearly describe the way Douglass is mistreated and his response to this abuse
   • use at least three examples from the selection to support their descriptions, for example:
      • Douglass is beaten when he can no longer work.
      • Covey chases Douglass into a cornfield.
      • Covey attempts to tie Douglass with a rope.
   • analyze how Douglass moves from fear to defiance and self-empowerment

---

A Pair of Silk Stockings

SELECTION TEST, page 103
Checking Vocabulary

1. d	2. b	3. f	4. h	5. e
6. a	7. g	8. j	9. i	10. c

Thoughtful Reading

11. c	12. a	13. c	14. b	15. d

Expanded Response

16. *(Responses will vary. A sample response follows.)*

Once	Now	Future
She had fine clothes and accessories.	Her clothes and accessories are threadbare and simple.	Guilt will cause her to buy clothing for her children first, herself last.
She has no children.	She has the responsibility of children.	Her children grow up and leave home.
She lived an exciting life.	She lives a simple, boring life.	She continues to live a humdrum existence, but wants to escape it.

17. Responses will vary, but students should use at least one example from the selection to support their ideas. A sample response to each choice follows.
   a. She fulfills the desire to enjoy sensuous pleasures as she revels in the feel of her first indulgence, the silk stockings.
   b. Enjoying the music, the food, the wine, and the magazines allows her to fulfill the desire to be part of a society in which people have time for such pleasures and do not have to struggle to survive.
   c. Taking the time to attend the play and to fully enjoy it enables her to fulfill the desire to spend some time focusing on things other than her daily duties and to be among people who have time for such activities.
   d. *(Credit may be given for an original response that is supported by evidence from the selection.)*

Written Response

18. Responses will vary. In a model response, students should fulfill the following criteria:
   • demonstrate understanding of the prompt
   • clearly explain why they think Mrs. Sommers spends the fifteen dollars in the way she does rather than in the way she had originally planned, for example:
      • She had seen "better days" and wants to revisit them.
      • She is overcome by a sudden, unexamined impulse, and once she purchases the silk stockings, the dam of prudence bursts.
      • She wants to escape, if only temporarily, from her everyday existence of scrimping and getting by.
      • She wants to beautify herself, and enhance her physical charms.
   • provide an example from the selection that supports their explanations

ANSWER KEY

Responding to Literature

1. (*Responses will vary. A sample response follows.*)

	Action Taken to Break Free from Bondage	Result(s) of Action
Frederick Douglass	Douglass fights Covey when Covey attempts to tie him with rope.	Douglass regains his self-confidence and gains determination to be free. He eventually achieves his freedom.
Mrs. Sommers	Mrs. Sommers goes on a shopping spree, indulging her need for luxury.	She finds it difficult to return to her dreary and tiring life.

2. (*Responses will vary. A sample response follows.*)

Frederick Douglass: is a slave hired out to a cruel farmer; courageously refuses to accept injustice

Mrs. Sommers: has a large family and very little money; is used to self-sacrifice; secretly desires an easier, more comfortable life

Both: chafe at restrictions; lack independence; feel trapped; have limited options; follow their impulses

3. Responses will vary. In a model response, students should fulfill the following criteria:
   • demonstrate understanding of the prompt
   • clearly explain how they believe a person can be free in a society that relegates him or her to slavery or second-class status, for example:
     • A person can remain free by refusing to be mentally enslaved or oppressed.
   • provide examples from the selections that support their opinions, for example:
     • In "The Battle with Mr. Covey" Douglass describes an incident that awakens his self-confidence and helps him to decide that he will no longer be spiritually enslaved.
     • In "A Pair of Silk Stockings" the main character is able to escape the mentality of second-class status by indulging herself for one day.

4. Responses will vary. In a model response, students should fulfill the following criteria:
   • demonstrate understanding of the prompt
   • clearly explain how they believe the character changed and why, for example:
     • In "The Battle with Mr. Covey" Douglass says that he changes from a slave in "form and fact" to a slave in "form" only.
   • provide at least two events from the selection that could have led to the change, for example:
     • By standing up to Mr. Covey and refusing to be beaten, the narrator regains his self-confidence and determination to be free.

Vocabulary Review

5. b   6. a   7. d   8. c   9. b

Collection 10: From Innocence to Experience

from *Life on the Mississippi*

SELECTION TEST, page 109

Checking Vocabulary

1. c   2. e   3. a   4. j   5. g
6. i   7. d   8. h   9. b   10. f

Thoughtful Reading

11. d   12. b   13. a   14. c   15. b

Expanded Response

16. (*Responses will vary. A sample response follows.*)

Box 1

Twain knows the names of most islands, towns, bars, points, and bends of the river. Bixby tells Twain that he must know the shapes of the riverbanks.

Box 2

Twain learns the shape of the river. Bixby tells Twain that he must remember all of the shoal soundings and marks of every trip.

Box 3

Twain learns to remember the shoal soundings. Bixby gives Twain a lesson on water-reading and tells him that he must be able to read the river intuitively.

Box 4

Twain learns to read the river like a book and becomes a river pilot.

17. Responses will vary, but students should use at least one example from the selection to support their ideas. A sample response to each choice follows.
   a. He is satisfied because he reaches his goal, and he is so familiar with the mighty river that he enjoys reading it like a book.
   b. He is so familiar with the river that it loses its romance and beauty.
   c. He attains his goal of becoming a river pilot, but loses some of his fascination with the river in the process.
   d. *(Credit may be given for an original response that is supported by evidence from the selection.)*

Written Response

18. Responses will vary. In a model response, students should fulfill the following criteria:
   • demonstrate understanding of the prompt
   • clearly show how Twain compares the river to a book
   • support their ideas with at least three examples from the selection, for example:
      • "The face of the water, in time, became a wonderful book . . ."
      • "There never was so wonderful a book written by man; never one whose interest was so absorbing . . ."
      • "Now when I had mastered the language of this water and had come to know every trifling feature that bordered the great river as familiarly as I knew the letters of the alphabet, I had made a valuable acquisition."

An Occurrence at Owl Creek Bridge

SELECTION TEST, page 111

Checking Vocabulary

1. c	**2.** f	**3.** d	**4.** i	**5.** h
6. a	**7.** e	**8.** j	**9.** g	**10.** b

Thoughtful Reading

11. b   **12.** c   **13.** d   **14.** a   **15.** d

Expanded Response

16. Responses will vary, but students should use at least one example from the selection to support their ideas. A sample response to each choice follows.
   a. It seems, at first, that Farquhar has escaped. The rope breaks, and he falls into the river. He is shot at by the Union soldiers, but he manages to swim to safety and return to his home. There are significant hints throughout the story, however, that this escape is merely fantasy.

   b. Farquhar's senses are heightened during his "escape." He sees, hears, and touches extraordinary things. His sense of sight is especially acute: He imagines that he can see the eye color of the man who is shooting at him from a great distance.
   c. Farquhar is entrapped by the federal soldier, who informs the planter that the Owl Creek Bridge is vulnerable to sabotage.
   d. Farquhar's life is very comfortable; at the same time, he is unhappy not to be serving the South as a soldier. Seeing an opportunity to serve the South by blowing up a key bridge under Union control, he risks, and ultimately loses, everything in pursuit of that goal.

17. *(Responses will vary. Sample responses follow.)*

Omniscient	1. the description of Peyton Farquhar's background as a Southern planter
	2. the commentary about the deference and respect with which death should be treated
Objective	1. the description of the bridge and the preparations that have been made for hanging Farquhar
	2. the description of Farquhar's physical characteristics
Third-person Limited	1. the description of Farquhar's fall into the river
	2. the description of Farquhar's journey through the forest

Written Response

18. Responses will vary. In a model response, students should fulfill the following criteria:
   • demonstrate understanding of the prompt
   • clearly show how Bierce hints that Farquhar's escape is a fantasy
   • support their ideas with at least three examples from the selection, for example:
      • When Farquhar came to the surface of the stream after his fall, his physical senses were preternaturally keen and alert, so he saw and heard things as never before.
      • The forest seemed wild and endless to Farquhar, and he thought there was something uncanny in this revelation.
      • Farquhar saw great golden stars grouped in strange constellations that seemed to have a secret and malign significance.

A Mystery of Heroism

SELECTION TEST, page 113

Checking Vocabulary

1. c	**2.** f	**3.** i	**4.** g	**5.** e
6. a	**7.** j	**8.** b	**9.** h	**10.** d

ANSWER KEY

Thoughtful Reading

11. d   **12.** d   **13.** c   **14.** a   **15.** b

Expanded Response

16. *(Responses will vary. Sample responses follow.)*

Left-hand frame:
- Collins angrily reacting to his comrades' mocking remarks
- Collins crossing the meadow as it is being shelled
- Collins filling the canteen in the midst of the gunfire and shelling
- Collins running back to his regiment in fear

Right-hand frame:
- Collins crossing the meadow as it is being shelled
- Collins stopping to give the dying lieutenant a drink
- Collins returning to his regiment with the water

17. Responses will vary, but students should use at least one example from the selection to support their ideas. A sample response to each choice follows.

a. Several times in the selection, Collins clearly states that he is thirsty and wants a drink.

b. Collins's pride is at stake once he angrily tells his jeering comrades that he will go to the well for water. He cannot back down without bringing shame upon himself.

c. Prior to his adventure, Collins is unwilling to retract his decision, even if he could do so without shame. In fact, he is sure of very little at this point.

d. *(Credit may be given for an original response that is supported by evidence from the selection.)*

Written Response

18. Responses will vary. In a model response, students should fulfill the following criteria:
- demonstrate understanding of the prompt
- clearly explain whether they think Collins's act is heroic, foolish, or a combination of both
- Support their explanations with at least two examples from the selection, for example:
  - Collins responds defensively to the goading of his comrades when he speaks of going to the well for water
  - Collins is unwilling to change his mind about going to the well, even though he realizes that he has been goaded into doing so.
  - Collins runs across the meadow amid cannon and rifle fire.
  - Collins is willing to forgo his terror and return to aid the dying lieutenant.
  - Collins gives the water to the captain after he returns to the regiment.

- Collins's run across the meadow is motivated by foolish pride but his return to aid the dying lieutenant is motivated by altruism.

To Build a Fire

SELECTION TEST, page 115

Checking Vocabulary

1. A   **2.** S   **3.** S   **4.** A   **5.** S
6. S   **7.** S   **8.** A   **9.** A   **10.** A

Thoughtful Reading

11. d   **12.** b   **13.** d   **14.** c   **15.** a

Expanded Response

16. *(Responses will vary. Sample responses follow.)*
- cold, gray day
- no clouds
- spruce timberland
- river white with undulations
- hairline trail
- temperature of 75 degrees below zero
- water frozen solid, except at springs

17. Responses will vary, but students should use at least one example from the selection to support their ideas. The only supportable answers are **b, c,** and **d.** A sample response to each choice follows.

a. *(This is not a supportable response.)*

b. This response supports the naturalist theory that human beings are vulnerable to forces of nature beyond their control, which include the bitter cold, the wetness, and the difficulty of building a fire.

c. The dog's instinct indicates that it is too cold to be traveling. The dog is naturally able to survive in exceedingly cold weather. The man can survive only with the aid of heavy, dry clothing and a fire. This supports the naturalist theory that humans are not well adapted to nature.

d. The man has chosen to travel alone, ignoring the advice of those more experienced in traveling the Yukon. Even with companions, it is too cold for anyone to travel. This statement reflects the naturalist theory that no matter how well prepared they seem to be, human beings are subject to forces beyond their control.

Written Response

18. Responses will vary. In a model response, students should fulfill the following criteria:
- demonstrate understanding of the prompt
- describe how the fate of the man is foreshadowed in the selection

- support their descriptions with at least three examples from the selection, for example:
  - This is his first winter in the Yukon, and to him the extremely cold temperatures mean only that he is uncomfortable. He does not consider that people can survive within only a narrow temperature range.
  - The dog's instinct causes it to fear the cold. The animal expects the man to go into camp or to seek shelter and build a fire.
  - For a month no one has come up or down the creek.
  - To get his feet wet in such cold means danger.
  - When the snow falls from the spruce tree and puts out the fire, it is as if he has just been given a death sentence.
  - When his final attempt at starting a fire fails and he cannot use the dog for warmth, he knows it is no longer a matter of frozen feet or toes, but of life and death.

THE AMERICAN LANGUAGE, page 117

1. b	**2.** d	**3.** a	**4.** b	**5.** c
6. d	**7.** a	**8.** d	**9.** c	**10.** a

COLLECTION 10 TEST, page 119

Responding to Literature

1. *(Responses will vary. A sample response follows.)*

Character: Peyton Farquhar

Belief(s) About Warfare	Action(s) That Result from the Beliefs
Serving in the army was an opportunity for distinction. No service was too humble for him to perform. No adventure was too perilous for him to undertake. All is fair in war.	He set out to burn a railroad bridge and was caught and hanged.

2. *(Responses will vary. A sample response follows.)*

Character Who Offers Advice:	old-timer from Sulfur Creek
Character Who Receives Advice:	Klondike traveler
Advice Offered	**Heeded?** Yes / No (circle one) **Outcome**
never travel alone when it is colder than fifty below	traveler dies from exposure

3. Responses will vary. In a model response, students should fulfill the following criteria:
   - demonstrate understanding of the prompt

- clearly explain how learning from experience is sometimes more effective than learning from textbooks and lectures
- provide examples from at least two selections to support their explanations, for example:
  - Twain can learn to navigate the river only by piloting a steamboat.
  - The man in London's story did not have the experience to understand the danger he was in.

4. Responses will vary. In a model response, students should fulfill the following criteria:
   - demonstrate understanding of the prompt
   - clearly explain two selections' points of view and their effectiveness, for example:
     - The excerpt from *Life on the Mississippi* is written in the first-person point of view. This is effective because it emphasizes the narrator's experiences and makes them more real for the reader.
   - use at least one specific example from each of the chosen selections to demonstrate the effectiveness of the point of view used, for example:
     - In the excerpt from *Life on the Mississippi*, the reader can relate to the narrator's fear when he thinks he is going to wreck the boat on a reef.

Vocabulary Review

5. b	**6.** c	**7.** a	**8.** d	**9.** b

Language Workshop Review

(Responses will vary. Sample responses follow.)

10. Although Twain had gained mastery of the language of the river, he then found that, for him, the river had lost its grace and poetry forever.

11. When the Federal scout rode past the plantation again, he was heading northward.

12. The officer who was mortally wounded could not be heard above the noise of battle.

13. The fire was burning intensely until snow falling from the spruce tree extinguished it.

LITERARY PERIOD TEST, page 122

Understanding Vocabulary

1. b	**2.** b	**3.** a	**4.** c	**5.** c

Thoughtful Reading

6. c	**7.** b	**8.** b	**9.** d	**10.** a

Expanded Response

11. Responses will vary, but students should use at least one example from the selection to support their ideas. A sample response to each choice follows.

a. *(This is not a supportable response.)*
b. Huck continues to borrow money from Judge Thatcher to buy Pap's goodwill. Huck knows that when Pap has money he will get drunk. When Pap gets drunk, he will usually land in jail and so be removed from Huck's life for at least a few days.
c. It appears that the judge and the widow will be unable to become Huck's guardians. To avoid the constant meddling of his father, Huck decides to run away.
d. *(Credit may be given for an original response that is supported by evidence from the selection.)*

Written Response
12. Responses will vary. In a model response, students should fulfill the following criteria:
   • demonstrate understanding of the prompt
   • compare Huck with another character from Collection 10

• describe at least one similarity and one difference between the characters
• provide at least two examples from each selection to illustrate their points, for example:
   • Like the young Twain in *Life on the Mississippi,* Huck seems eager to learn new things. Twain works hard to learn how to navigate the river, while Huck has learned how to read.
   • Both Twain and Huck display resilience in the face of adversity. As an apprentice pilot, Twain overcomes discouragement and technical challenges. Huck learns to read despite his father's abusive threats and actions.
   • Unlike Twain and the characters Peyton Farquhar, Collins, and the Yukon traveler, Huck does not voluntarily enter challenging circumstances. He seems to have been born into a difficult situation, which he is trying to get out of.

The Moderns

LITERARY PERIOD INTRODUCTION TEST, page 127
1. a   **2.** b   **3.** c   **4.** d   **5.** c
6. d   **7.** b   **8.** b   **9.** a   **10.** c

Collection 11: Loss and Redemption

A Wagner Matinée

SELECTION TEST, page 129
Checking Vocabulary
1. i   **2.** b   **3.** f   **4.** c   **5.** h
6. e   **7.** a   **8.** j   **9.** g   **10.** d

Thoughtful Reading
11. d   **12.** b   **13.** c   **14.** b   **15.** a

Expanded Response
16. Responses will vary, but students should use at least one example from the selection to support their ideas. The best answers are **a, c,** and **d.** A sample response to each choice follows.
   a. Georgiana enjoys the concert, but she also weeps because she now realizes how much she has missed music.
   b. (Partial credit can be given. Students may feel that Clark regrets being one cause of his aunt's tears.)
   c. Georgiana's sad appearance indicates to Clark that she is still struggling in Nebraska, and her happiness at the concert shows that she misses the cultural opportunities of the East.
   d. From his aunt's behavior at the concert, it is obvious to Clark that music has remained

her greatest joy, even though she has been separated from it for many years.

17. *(Responses will vary. Sample responses follow.)*
   The loss: music
   Victim of circumstance because: She lives in a part of the country where music is not frequently available.
   Loss arises from her choice because: Georgiana fell in love with Howard, married him, and chose to accompany him to an isolated farm, far from the cities where music is readily accessible.

Written Response
18. Responses will vary. In a model response, students should fulfill the following criteria:
   • demonstrate understanding of the prompt
   • describe the concert from Georgiana's point of view, focusing on the thoughts and feelings that cause her to react as she does
   • support their ideas with at least two references to specific details in the selection, for example:
      • Georgiana's initial shyness and fear
      • Clark's kindness and graciousness
      • the beauty of the concert
      • the barrenness of the Nebraska farm

His Father's Earth

Checking Vocabulary

1. d   2. j   3. b   4. h   5. e
6. g   7. a *or* i   8. i *or* a   9. c   10. f

Thoughtful Reading

11. c   12. d   13. c   14. b   15. a

Expanded Response

16. Responses will vary, but students should use at least one example from the selection to support their ideas. The only supportable answers are **a,** **c,** and **d.** A sample response to each choice follows.
    a. The boy has a deeper understanding of what home is after he imagines traveling with the circus and finding his father's home.
    b. *(This is not a supportable response.)*
    c. The boy works to acquire wonderful food for the other circus workers. He seems to gain a sense of fulfillment and acceptance from his role.
    d. The boy is able to have this adventure in his imagination, without actually having to leave home. His dream gives him experiences beyond what he knows from his actual life.

17. *(Responses will vary. A sample response follows.)*

    Realistic Aspects: the hunger and hard work of the circus crew; traveling; gathering crops; buying food
    Fantastic Aspects: young boy being given the responsibility of procuring food for the circus; father holding a ham as he welcomes his son home

Written Response

18. Responses will vary. In a model response, students should fulfill the following criteria:
    • demonstrate understanding of the prompt
    • clearly describe how "His Father's Earth" is linked to the idea of home
    • support their ideas with at least two references to specific details in the selection, for example:
      • the boy's excitement about returning home
      • the portrait of the father as nurturing and welcoming
      • the description of birdsong, which makes home seem nearly as exciting as the circus
      • the fact that the story begins and ends at home

Design
Nothing Gold Can Stay
Once by the Pacific
Neither Out Far Nor In Deep
Birches
The Death of the Hired Man

Thoughtful Reading

1. b   2. d   3. a   4. c
5. b   6. c   7. a   8. d

Expanded Response

9. Responses will vary, but students should use at least one example from the selection to support their ideas. The best answers are **a, b,** and **d.** A sample response to each choice follows.
    a. Silas has worked hard at harvest, applying his skills for stacking and retrieving neat forkfuls of hay and teaching the apprentice about farming.
    b. Silas returns to Warren and Mary's farm after having left for a better offer elsewhere.
    c. (Partial credit can be given.) In some sense, the fact that Silas has come back to die may indicate that he *feels* like a loyal family member.
    d. Mary has not hesitated to let Silas come in. Silas seems to have correctly anticipated this response. Silas has also tried to convince the young farmhand to abandon school, and he may have tried to use the offer of better wages elsewhere to get a raise in pay from Warren.

10. *(Responses will vary. A sample response follows.)*

    Characters: Warren, Mary, Silas
    Their Values: Warren: common sense, earning one's way; **Mary:** concern for others; **Silas:** independence
    Conflicts They Face: Warren and Mary: Should they take Silas in or not?
    Silas: none

Written Response

11. Responses will vary. In a model response, students should fulfill the following criteria:
    • demonstrate understanding of the prompt
    • explain whether they view Frost's poems as pessimistic or realistic
    • support their ideas with at least two references to details in the poems, for example:
      • the pessimistic, angry view of humanity in "Once by the Pacific"
      • the pessimistic view in "Design," with evil lurking even in the most innocent-seeming things

ANSWER KEY

- the realistic view in "Nothing Gold Can Stay," which portrays beauty as rare and transient, but affirms and celebrates its existence
- the realistic view in "Birches," in which the boy (and the speaker) can take time out from chores and responsibilities to experience the joy of playing

Bells for John Whiteside's Daughter
Shine, Perishing Republic

SELECTION TEST, page 135
Thoughtful Reading

1. a	**2.** c	**3.** b	**4.** d
5. a	**6.** c	**7.** c	**8.** d

Expanded Response

9. Responses will vary, but students should use at least one example from the selection to support their ideas. The only supportable answers are **a, b,** and **c.** A sample response to each choice follows.
   a. The poem's descriptions of vulgarity and a hardening mass and thickening center are references to the city and its decay.
   b. Jeffers builds nostalgic, admiring images of flowers, fruits, meteors, and mountains.
   c. The speaker warns his or her sons to be skeptical about human beings, who, though they may be clever, have been hateful masters of the earth.
   d. *(This is not a supportable response.)*

10. *(Responses will vary. Sample responses follow.)*
    "Bells for John Whiteside's Daughter":
    Who Dies: a child
    What Unique Thing Is Lost Forever: her particular mischievousness and the pleasure she brought to others
    "Shine, Perishing Republic":
    What Dies: the American nation
    What Unique Thing Is Lost Forever: the beauty of the American landscape

Written Response

11. Responses will vary. In a model response, students should fulfill the following criteria:
    - demonstrate understanding of the prompt
    - clearly contrast Ransom's sad, fond, and accepting tone with Jeffers's bitter, cynical tone
    - support their ideas with at least one reference to a specific image in each poem, for example:
      - Ransom's cheerful memory of the little girl scaring the geese and of her moving in a swift and graceful manner
      - Jeffers's entirely negative remarks about American cities, industries, and dead ideals

and his images of a natural world destroyed by human corruption

COLLECTION 11 TEST, page 137
Responding to Literature

1. *(Responses will vary. A sample response follows.)*

What Has Ended	Speaker's Feelings About This Ending
Selection: "Nothing Gold Can Stay"	
perfection, youth	sorrow, acceptance
Selection: "Once by the Pacific"	
the world	anger at people

2. *(Responses will vary. A sample response follows.)*

Selection Title: "His Father's Earth"
What Has Been Redeemed or Recovered:
a sense of the warmth and nourishment a home can provide

3. Responses will vary. In a model response, students should fulfill the following criteria:
   - demonstrate understanding of the prompt
   - identify and discuss a common theme in the poems, such as loss of a known world or human failings
   - support their ideas with at least one example from each poem, for example:
     - Frost's image of an angry sea rolling in to devour the land
     - Frost's ominous reference to a light that is put out
     - Jeffers's images of corruption and decay
     - Jeffers's comparison of the United States to a meteor that shines, then disappears

4. Responses will vary. In a model response, students should fulfill the following criteria:
   - demonstrate understanding of the prompt
   - clearly state which of the listed selections most impresses them with its descriptions
   - explain why the passages or lines move or impress them
   - support their ideas with a restatement or quotation of the lines or the passages that have moved or impressed them, for example:
     - Frost's description of the boy swinging high on a birch tree's branches, then returning joyfully to solid land
     - Wolfe's description in "His Father's Earth" of the circus workers hungrily eating their meals
     - Cather's description, at the end of "A Wagner Matinée," of the dreary farm that Georgiana must return to

Vocabulary Review

5. c	**6.** a	**7.** d	**8.** a	**9.** b

Collection 12: The Dream and the Reality

Winter Dreams

SELECTION TEST, page 141

Checking Vocabulary

1. h	**2.** c	**3.** f	**4.** g	**5.** i
6. d *or* a	**7.** j	**8.** b	**9.** a *or* d	**10.** e

Thoughtful Reading

11. b **12.** a **13.** d **14.** c **15.** a

Expanded Response

16. Responses will vary, but students should use at least one example from the selection to support their ideas. A sample response to each choice follows.
   a. Judy asks Dexter to marry her after she learns that he is engaged to Irene. Hence, the reader suspects that Judy pursues men who seem inaccessible or challenging to her.
   b. Judy says that she does not want to return to the "idiotic" dance with her acquaintances, whom she refers to as "children." She also tells Dexter, "of course you could never love anybody but me."
   c. When Judy tells Dexter she loves him, she is not serious. She professes her love to a number of different men.
   d. *(Accept any response that is supported by the selection.)*

17. *(Responses will vary. A sample response follows.)*
   Dexter's Decision: Dexter decides to break off his engagement with Irene.
   Possible Motivation: Dexter wants to achieve what he perceives as the ultimate success by marrying Judy.

Written Response

18. Responses will vary. In a model response, students should fulfill the following criteria:
   • demonstrate understanding of the prompt
   • complete the statement, for example:
      • At the end of the story, tears stream down Dexter's face because he is mourning the loss of a dream or ideal.
   • support their statements with at least three ideas or examples from the story, for example:
      • When Devlin tells him that Judy Jones used to be pretty, Dexter's ideal of Judy as a striking, irresistible beauty is destroyed.
      • When Dexter tries to conjure up the feelings he once had for Judy, he fails. Not only has he lost the glorious image of his ideal, he has also lost touch with his former feelings.
      • Dexter has left behind the world of his youth, where his dreams once flourished.

The Leader of the People

SELECTION TEST, page 143

Checking Vocabulary

1. e	**2.** g	**3.** b	**4.** h	**5.** a
6. f	**7.** d	**8.** i	**9.** j	**10.** c

Thoughtful Reading

11. c **12.** a **13.** c **14.** b **15.** d

Expanded Response

16. Responses will vary, but students should use at least one example from the selection to support their ideas. The only supportable answers are **b, c,** and **d.** A sample response to each choice follows.
   a. *(This is not a supportable response.)*
   b. The conflict between Jody's father and Jody's grandfather creates tension that builds throughout the story and results in the story's climax. The climax of the story occurs when Grandfather overhears Jody's father saying that he doesn't want to hear Grandfather's stories anymore.
   c. The conflict between dreams and reality is the underlying theme of the story. At the end of the story, Grandfather is sad as he contemplates the gulf between his dream of forever moving westward and the reality of having to settle at the continent's edge.
   d. *(Accept any response that is supported by the selection.)*

17. *(Responses will vary. Sample responses follow.)*
   Jody: Jody thinks that Grandfather's stories are thrilling.
   Jody's mother: She says that the stories may be all that Grandfather has left. She wishes that her husband would be more respectful of Grandfather's desire to re-tell his stories.
   Jody's father: He is irritated at having to hear the same stories over and over. However, he indulges Grandfather in order to keep the peace.

Written Response

18. Responses will vary. In a model response, students should fulfill the following criteria:
   • demonstrate understanding of the prompt
   • describe two conflicts in the story, for example:
      • external conflicts between Jody's mother and father over Grandfather's repetitious stories
      • the conflict between Jody and his father about meddling in another's affairs

ANSWER KEY

- the internal conflict Grandfather has between his glorified version of history and historical reality
- explain how the conflicts are resolved, if they are, and use at least two examples from the story to support their opinions

The Secret Life of Walter Mitty

SELECTION TEST, page 145
Checking Vocabulary

1. g	**2.** d *or* c	**3.** j	**4.** i	**5.** b
6. a	**7.** h	**8.** f	**9.** e	**10.** c *or* d

Thoughtful Reading

11. b	**12.** d	**13.** b	**14.** a	**15.** b

Expanded Response

16. *(Responses will vary. Sample responses follow.)*
Character's Expertise or Profession:
1. a surgeon who operates on a millionaire banker
2. the greatest pistol shot in the world
Character's Traits:
1. He is coolheaded, in control, knowledgeable.
2. He is arrogant and fearless.

17. Responses will vary, but students should use at least one example from the selection to support their ideas. The only supportable answers are **a, c,** and **d.** A sample response to each choice follows.
   a. He passively gives in to what his wife wants. For example, he buys the overshoes that she insists he wear even though he does not want them. He also buys puppy biscuits at her request.
   b. *(This is not a supportable response.)*
   c. He has a very active imagination. Any common object can be turned into an interesting one in his imagination. For example, he imagines that his gloves are the gloves of a brilliant, heroic surgeon.
   d. *(Accept any response that is supported by the selection.)*

Written Response

18. Responses will vary. In a model response, students should fulfill the following criteria:
- demonstrate understanding of the prompt
- explain whether they think Mitty is trying to escape from reality and, if so, what that reality is
- support their ideas with at least two examples from the story, for example:
  - Mitty is trying to escape from his passivity in the face of constant directives from his wife. She is always telling him what to do: buy puppy biscuits, wear overshoes, drive more slowly.
  - Mitty is trying to escape from the boredom of his daily life. He daydreams about more exciting and glamorous existences like being a courageous pilot.

A Worn Path

SELECTION TEST, page 147
Checking Vocabulary

1. c	**2.** f	**3.** d	**4.** a	**5.** g
6. i	**7.** j	**8.** e	**9.** b	**10.** h

Thoughtful Reading

11. d	**12.** b	**13.** a	**14.** d	**15.** a

Expanded Response

16. Responses will vary, but students should use at least one example from the selection to support their ideas. The only supportable answers are **a, c,** and **d.** A sample response to each choice follows.
   a. When Phoenix reaches her destination, the doctor's office, she asks the nurse for medicine for her grandson.
   b. *(This is not a supportable response.)*
   c. Phoenix's journey to the doctor to obtain medicine is motivated by love for, concern for, or devotion to her grandson, who is ill.
   d. *(Accept any response that is supported by the selection.)*

17. *(Responses will vary. Sample responses follow.)*
Event #1: Her dress gets caught in a thorn bush.
Event #2: She imagines that she sees a boy with some marble cake.
Event #3: She encounters a hunter, who drops a nickel.

Written Response

18. Responses will vary. In a model response, students should fulfill the following criteria:
- demonstrate understanding of the prompt
- describe Phoenix's character, for example:
  - Phoenix is a devoted grandmother and a persistent person.
- support their descriptions with at least three examples from the story, for example:
  - Phoenix's eyes are bothering her, but she has made that journey so many times that her feet know the way.
  - Although she is wearied by the long journey, she continues along the path to the doctor to get medicine for her grandson.
  - Although the hunter tells her to go home, she remains devoted to her goal.
  - She overcomes a number of obstacles in order to reach the doctor. These obstacles include a barbed-wire fence, a maze of corn stalks, and a thorn bush.

Responding to Literature

1. *(Responses will vary. Sample responses follow.)*
   Character: Walter Mitty
   Dream or Fantasy: Mitty has several fantasies, which include being a famous doctor, a hydroplane commander, and a sharpshooter.
   How the Dream or Fantasy Relates to the Character's Personality: Walter wishes to escape reality. In reality, he bumbles (driving in the wrong lane, muttering "puppy biscuit" aloud to himself). He is controlled by his bossy wife. The flamboyant characters in the fantasies serve as a contrast to Walter's passive, real-life personality.

   Character: Dexter Green
   Dream or Fantasy: Dexter dreams of obtaining glittering things and the privilege that comes with them. He also wants to marry Judy Jones.
   How the Dream or Fantasy Relates to the Character's Personality: Dexter desires wealth and status. Judy Jones, the daughter of a rich man that Dexter once caddied for at a golf course, represents for Dexter material success and ultimate beauty.

2. *(Responses will vary. A sample response follows.)*
   Character: Phoenix Jackson
   Character's Purpose or Goal: Phoenix's goal is to reach the doctor's office in the city. She hopes to obtain medicine for her grandson.
   Character's Motivation: She loves her grandson.
   How does the Character Succeed or Fail? She succeeds in overcoming a series of obstacles along the worn path.

3. Responses will vary. In a model response, students should fulfill the following criteria:
   - demonstrate understanding of the prompt
   - discuss examples of the American Dream and of disillusionment in one of the selections
   - support their ideas with at least two examples from "The Leader of the People" or "Winter Dreams," for example:
     - The dreams of wealth and physical beauty, exemplified by Dexter's wished-for glittering things and a fickle, unobtainable woman whose physical beauty and economic status are more important to Dexter than her character
     - Dexter's disillusionment when Devlin tells him that Judy, no longer beautiful, is married to a man who treats her poorly
     - Grandfather's stories of his own heroic leadership in the journey to the West Coast of the United States
     - Grandfather's disillusionment is expressed by his statement that had he not been the leader, someone else would have replaced him; his statement that he feels the crossing wasn't worth doing; and a description of the people at the shore, angry at the ocean for having stopped their journey.

4. Responses will vary. In a model response, students should fulfill the following criteria:
   - demonstrate understanding of the prompt
   - describe their opinions
   - support their opinions with examples, such as
     - Phoenix's triumph of finding her way to the city despite her diminishing eyesight and memory
     - the bold, assertive characters in Walter Mitty's fantasies who take control of difficult situations (e.g., the doctor in the operating room who calmly repairs the anesthetizer)

Vocabulary Review

5. c   6. d   7. a   8. b   9. a

Collection 13: No Time for Heroes

Richard Cory
Miniver Cheevy

SELECTION TEST, page 151
Thoughtful Reading

1. c   2. d   3. a   4. a
5. b   6. c   7. d   8. a

Expanded Response

9. Responses will vary, but students should use at least one example from the selection to support their ideas. The best answers are **a, b,** and **d.** A sample response to each choice follows.

   a. Richard Cory never revealed to others that he was deeply despondent.
   b. The people were impressed by Cory's fine manners, elegant clothes, and background.
   c. (Partial credit can be given. Some students may feel that Cory kills himself because of guilt over some horrendous deed he has committed.)
   d. The ordinary people in the poem cope philosophically with their daily tasks, while Cory is burdened and depressed by his life.

10. *(Responses will vary. A sample response follows.)*
   Object, person, or place: knight's armor
   Positive aspects: seems glorious and romantic; described in the poem as graceful

Negative aspects: heavy and cumbersome; may not have been as glorious as Cheevy thinks it was

Written Response

11. Responses will vary. In a model response, students should fulfill the following criteria:
    - demonstrate understanding of the prompt
    - clearly describe what the characters yearn for in both poems
    - support their ideas with at least one example from each poem, for example:
      - The townspeople yearn for the riches that Cory possesses.
      - Cory's suicide is evidence of his yearning for contentment that lies beyond his grasp.
      - Miniver Cheevy yearns for the glory of past ages and places, such as King Arthur's court.

Soldier's Home

SELECTION TEST, page 153

Checking Vocabulary

1. b	**2.** c	**3.** h	**4.** i	**5.** d
6. e	**7.** j	**8.** g	**9.** f	**10.** a

Thoughtful Reading

11. c	**12.** c	**13.** d	**14.** a	**15.** a

Expanded Response

16. Responses will vary, but students should use at least one example from the selection to support their ideas. The best answers are **a, b,** and **d.** A sample response to each choice follows.
    a. Krebs has arrived home long after people in his town want to hear about any war stories he might want to share. He feels isolated because he can't talk about his experiences.
    b. Krebs spends a lot of time resting in his room. He is still so affected by his wartime experiences that he prefers to be alone.
    c. (Partial credit can be given. Some students may argue that Krebs needs these distractions even though he can't consciously acknowledge that need.)
    d. *(Accept any response that is supported by the selection.)*

17. *(Responses will vary. A sample response follows.)*
    The Battlefield as Krebs's Home: Krebs thinks constantly about the battlefield and his wartime experiences with his buddies. He is nostalgic about being in Europe.
    Krebs's Hometown as his Home: Krebs acknowledges the comforts of his childhood home, but he can't find solace in them.

Written Response

18. Responses will vary. In a model response, students should fulfill the following criteria:
    - demonstrate understanding of the prompt
    - explain that Krebs thinks he is lying because he does not reveal all that he has experienced in war or what he is feeling about hometown life
    - support their ideas with at least two references to specific details in the selection, for example:
      - Krebs's withholding of details about his horrendous experiences in the war
      - Krebs's inability to communicate how alienated he feels from ordinary life
      - Krebs's secretive comparisons between the women in his hometown and the women he met in Europe

The Love Song of J. Alfred Prufrock

SELECTION TEST, page 155

Thoughtful Reading

1. d	**2.** b	**3.** a
4. c	**5.** b	**6.** a

Written Response

7. Responses will vary. In a model response, students should fulfill the following criteria:
   - demonstrate understanding of the prompt
   - clearly identify a passage or image from the poem that communicates a feeling of despair
   - give at least one reason why the passage or image impresses them, for example:
     - The passage about measuring life with coffee spoons creates an image of people who don't have the courage to undertake risky actions.
     - The image of living in a world of illusions (an underground sea chamber) only to be rudely awakened (drowned) conveys a feeling that contemporary life is deadening and threatening.
     - The image of cheap hotels and sawdust restaurants conjures a gloomy, bleak landscape.

The Life You Save May Be Your Own

SELECTION TEST, page 156

Checking Vocabulary

1. d	**2.** f	**3.** c	**4.** h	**5.** i
6. j	**7.** b	**8.** a	**9.** g	**10.** e

Thoughtful Reading

11. c **12.** a **13.** a **14.** b **15.** d

Expanded Response

16. Responses will vary, but students should use at least one example from the selection to support their ideas. The only supportable answers are **a, c,** and **d.** A sample response to each choice follows.

   a. Young Lucynell makes eyes at Shiftlet and acts coy with him.

   b. *(This is not a supportable response.)*

   c. Lucynell's mother tries to use the child's innocence to obtain a steady worker on the farm, and Shiftlet fakes an interest in Lucynell to get money for himself.

   d. Young Lucynell is treated well by her mother and seems content with her life on the farm.

17. *(Responses will vary. Sample responses follow.)*
Shiftlet: thinks only of his own welfare
The Elder Lucynell: considers her daughter's welfare as well as her own
Both: quick to deceive; willing to exploit others

Written Response

18. Responses will vary. In a model response, students should fulfill the following criteria:
- demonstrate understanding of the prompt
- explain their ideas of what the storm symbolizes, for example:
  - warning to Shiftlet that God disapproves of his nefarious ways
  - comment on the egregious transactions between human beings demonstrated in the story
  - punishment for Shiftlet's abandonment of young Lucynell
- support their ideas with at least two references to the selection

COLLECTION 13 TEST, page 158
Responding to Literature

1. *(Responses will vary. Sample responses follow.)*

	Character's Attitudes Toward Modern Life	Your Reactions to the Character's Attitudes
Prufrock	Modern life is dreary and full of difficult decisions.	Yes. Prufrock seems to be searching for meaning in life.
Cheevy	Modern life is unglamorous and unfulfilling.	No. Cheevy is absorbed in self-pity and does nothing to amend his situation.

2. *(Responses will vary. Sample responses follow.)*

Characters	Secret	Result of Not Telling the Truth
Richard Cory	He finds no purpose in life.	He kills himself.
Krebs	The horrors of his war experiences alienate him from those he loves.	He leaves his family and friends.
Shiftlet	He is interested only in his own survival.	He manages to trick both Lucynells.

3. Responses will vary. In a model response, students should fulfill the following criteria:
- demonstrate understanding of the prompt
- explain why people feel heroes are non-existent or hard to find in today's world
- support their opinions with examples from at least two selections in Collection 13, for example:
  - Prufrock's inability to act reflects how difficult it is to be heroic in the modern world.
  - Krebs's feeling that no one understands the horrors he endured in battle shows that heroes may exist but they are unrecognized in today's world.

4. Responses will vary. In a model response, students should fulfill the following criteria:
- demonstrate understanding of the prompt
- discuss how the dramatic monologue technique reveals Prufrock's character by following his rambling thoughts and feelings
- explain the technique by which we come to know Shiftlet or Krebs, for example:
  - We learn about the characters of Shiftlet and Krebs through the omniscient or all-knowing observations of a third-person narrator, who describes the inner thoughts and actions of these characters.

Vocabulary Review

5. a **6.** d **7.** a **8.** b **9.** c

Language Workshop Review

(Responses will vary. Sample responses follow. Subordinating conjunctions are shown in italics.)

10. Heroes need public support *because* they can't work alone in a vacuum.

11. Prufrock acted timidly *because* he expected people to treat him roughly.

12. Krebs didn't do much *until* a discussion with his mother caused him to take action.

13. Perhaps Richard Cory would not have shot himself *if* he had shared his problems with someone.

14. Heroic people sometimes act on impulse, *as if* their own personal welfare doesn't matter.

ANSWER KEY

Collection 14: Shadows of the Past

Richard Bone
Lucinda Matlock
Recuerdo

SELECTION TEST, page 161

Thoughtful Reading

1. b   2. d   3. b   4. b
5. a   6. d   7. c   8. b

Expanded Response

9. Responses will vary, but students should use at least one example from the selection to support their ideas. The only supportable answers are **a, c,** and **d.** A sample response to each choice follows.
   a. Lines 16 and 17 indicate that Bone believes historians sometimes write without knowing the truth.
   b. *(This is not a supportable response.)*
   c. In lines 10–12, Bone notes that living among the people he works for gives him insight into the truth about their lives.
   d. Lines 13–18 indicate that Bone believes historians may write whatever their society wishes them to write.

10. The speaker in "Recuerdo" shows relish for the past by dwelling on romantic scenes and repeating a nostalgic refrain.

    Lucinda Matlock catalogs her accomplishments, one of which is raising twelve children.

Written Response

11. Responses will vary. In a model response, students should fulfill the following criteria:
    - demonstrate understanding of the prompt
    - describe how the theme applies to the three characters in the poems
    - support their ideas with at least one idea or image from each poem, for example:
      - Lucinda Matlock proudly recalls attending to her responsibilities and loving life.
      - The speaker in "Recuerdo" carries into the present warm memories of a past friendship and a nighttime ferry ride.
      - Richard Bone regrets chiseling false epitaphs and not living life more honestly.

The Jilting of Granny Weatherall

SELECTION TEST, page 163

Checking Vocabulary

1. b   2. i   3. e   4. a   5. c
6. h   7. g   8. d   9. f   10. j

Thoughtful Reading

11. a   12. c   13. d   14. b   15. c

Expanded Response

16. Responses will vary, but students should use at least one example from the selection to support their ideas. The best answers are **a, b,** and **d.** A sample response to each choice follows.
    a. Granny Weatherall has never gotten over the shame of being jilted by her first fiancé, George.
    b. Granny Weatherall frets about whether Cornelia has remembered her manners and offered Father Connolly a chair.
    c. (Partial credit can be given. Some students may feel that Granny Weatherall's fate reflects the universal irony that no matter how much fortitude we bring to life, we cannot escape death.)
    d. As she lies on her deathbed, Granny Weatherall believes she is expressing her memories and thoughts to those gathered around her, but all they hear is mumbling.

17. *(Responses will vary. A sample response follows.)*

Granny Weatherall perceives . . .	Others perceive . . .
1. Hapsy coming into the room	1. her daughter Lydia
2. the doctor returning after being gone only five minutes	2. the doctor returning after an entire day has passed

Written Response

18. Responses will vary. In a model response, students should fulfill the following criteria:
    - demonstrate understanding of the prompt
    - explain that Granny may want God to give her a sign of assurance or affirmation
    - note that the sign is not given
    - explain that Granny draws a comparison between God's unresponsiveness and George's jilting of her

A Rose for Emily

SELECTION TEST, page 165

Checking Vocabulary

1. f   2. g   3. i   4. a   5. b
6. d   7. j   8. c   9. h   10. e

Thoughtful Reading

11. b   12. d   13. d   14. a   15. d

Expanded Response

16. Responses will vary, but students should use at least one example from the selection to support

their ideas. A sample response to each choice follows.

a. Tobe's role as a servant reflects an important part of the social setting of the story.

b. An aging Tobe reminds the reader and the townspeople that Miss Emily, too, is growing older.

c. Tobe does all the errands and outside work so that Miss Emily can stay inside and avoid communication with her neighbors.

d. *(Accept any response that is supported by the selection.)*

17. *(Responses will vary. A sample response follows.)*
Emily's father: He keeps Miss Emily from marrying and drives off suitors.
Colonel Sartoris: By excusing her from paying taxes, he encourages her to believe she's above the law.
Homer Barron: He enrages her by rejecting her.

Written Response

18. Responses will vary. In a model response, students should fulfill the following criteria:
   - demonstrate understanding of the prompt
   - explain the importance of the story's setting and note whether they think changing the setting would make a significant difference
   - support their ideas with at least two references to details in the selection, for example:
     - The small-town setting is crucial because of the role of the townspeople. The fact that everyone knows and watches Miss Emily helps the reader understand her pride and her actions. If she were not known by everyone, the thwarting of her desire to marry Homer Barron would not have mattered so much.
     - The southern setting underscores the story's emphasis on social class and gentility.
     - The post-Civil War southern setting also explains the racist attitudes of many of the white townspeople toward the black members of the community.

COLLECTION 14 TEST, page 167

1. *(Responses will vary. A sample response follows.)*
Unhappy Events:
Granny Weatherall: She is jilted.
Miss Emily: She is prevented from having suitors; later, she is rejected by her lover.
Lucinda Matlock: Eight of her children die before she does.
Similarities and Differences: Granny Weatherall and Miss Emily are alike because, unlike Lucinda Matlock, they allow unhappy events to cast long shadows over their entire lives. Granny Weatherall and Lucinda Matlock, unlike Miss Emily, manage to overcome their grief and live productive lives.

2. *(Responses will vary. Sample responses follow.)*

Attitude Toward Past	Character	How Attitude Is Revealed in the Selection
regret	Richard Bone	Bone expresses remorse about chiseling lies onto tombstones.
nostalgia	Granny Weatherall	Granny happily recalls raising her small children.
pride	Lucinda Matlock	Matlock boasts about her hard work and condemns less hearty souls.

3. Responses will vary. In a model response, students should fulfill the following criteria:
   - demonstrate understanding of the prompt
   - describe how the selection they have chosen reflects the characteristics of modernism
   - support their ideas with at least two examples from the selection, for example:
     - The use of stream of consciousness in "The Jilting of Granny Weatherall" is a narrative technique that conveys the inner thoughts of a character.
     - The joyful description of two people staying up all night is a nontraditional subject that reflects the period of the Jazz Age in "Recuerdo."
     - The sense of regret and disillusionment with society and one's place in it is illustrated in "Richard Bone."
     - The use of a collective narrator who speaks as the voice of the townspeople, and the negative portrayal of traditional values, such as a concern for propriety, are two examples found in "A Rose for Emily."

4. Responses will vary. In a model response, students should fulfill the following criteria:
   - demonstrate understanding of the prompt
   - compare and contrast the settings of two selections and explain how the settings are important to the events in the selections
   - include at least two details from each selection, for example:
     - The setting of "A Rose for Emily" is a small southern town, where people are always curious about one another and subscribe to certain standards of behavior, to which Miss Emily does not adhere. The watchful, judgmental nature of the community makes some of Emily's strange actions explicable.
     - The old New York setting of "Recuerdo" provides an array of interesting sights for the characters to see during their all-night adventure. The urban setting fosters a sense of boundless spontaneity.

Vocabulary Review

5. b   **6.** d   **7.** c   **8.** c   **9.** b

ANSWER KEY

Collection 15: I, Too, Sing America

Go Down, Death
America

SELECTION TEST, page 171

Thoughtful Reading

1. c   2. a   3. b   4. d
5. d   6. a   7. c   8. a

Expanded Response

9. *(Responses will vary. Sample responses follow.)*
Comforting: In the poem, the speaker assures Sister Caroline's family that she is resting in the arms of Jesus.
Somewhat Comforting: At the end of the poem, Sister Caroline rests comfortably in the arms of Jesus, but the ride on Death's horse with its foaming mouth seems frightening to me.
Not Comforting: Death takes Sister Caroline into his icy arms. To me it sounds like a nightmare.

10. Responses will vary, but students should use at least one example from the selection to support their ideas. The only supportable answers are **a, b,** and **c.** A sample response to each choice follows.
    a. In lines 1–3, the speaker describes injustices that America has perpetrated and their effect on him.
    b. The speaker says that time will see America sink into the sand like a treasure.
    c. The speaker remarks on America's grand size and energy.
    d. *(This is not a supportable response.)*

Written Response

11. Responses will vary. In a model response, students should fulfill the following criteria:
    • demonstrate understanding of the prompt
    • clearly describe how personification is used in the two poems
    • support their ideas with at least two references to specific details in each poem, for example:
      • In "Go Down, Death," Death is portrayed as a silent man with cold arms who rides a horse.
      • In "Go Down, Death," Death is an obedient servant of God.
      • In "America," America is referred to as a woman who feeds the speaker bitterness and cruelly bites the speaker.

Tableau
Incident

SELECTION TEST, page 173

Thoughtful Reading

1. d   2. b   3. b   4. c
5. a   6. d   7. c   8. a

Expanded Response

9. *(Responses will vary. Sample responses follow.)*

Image or Metaphor	Ideas Conveyed
boys compared to the colors of day and night	conveys the idea that the boys are beautiful and somehow noble
friendship compared to lightning	conveys the idea that the friendship is unique, powerful, and trailblazing

10. Responses will vary, but students should use at least one example from the selection to support their ideas. The only supportable answers are **a, b,** and **d.** A sample response to each choice follows.
    a. (Partial credit can be given.) The Baltimore boy's racial insult was very cruel.
    b. The Baltimore boy's cruel word and gesture surprised and deeply hurt the speaker as a child. The memory of the incident stands out because of the pain and confusion it caused the speaker.
    c. *(This is not a supportable response.)*
    d. *(Accept any response that is supported by the selection.)*

Written Response

11. Responses will vary. In a model response, students should fulfill the following criteria:
    • demonstrate understanding of the prompt
    • compare and contrast the interactions between people of different races in the two poems
    • support their ideas with at least two references to examples from each of the poems, for example:
      • Both poems refer to racial tension. In "Tableau," onlookers express disapproval of a friendship between an African American boy and a white boy. In "Incident," one boy's racism incites him to insult the other.
      • A contrast exists between the interactions portrayed in each poem. The interaction between the two boys in "Incident" causes pain, whereas the interaction between the boys in "Tableau" is friendly.

from *Dust Tracks on a Road*

SELECTION TEST, page 175
Checking Vocabulary
1. d   2. h   3. e   4. i   5. g
6. f   7. c   8. b   9. j   10. a

Thoughtful Reading
11. c   12. a   13. c   14. b   15. c

Expanded Response
16. Responses will vary, but students should use at least one example from the selection to support their ideas. The only supportable answers are **a, c,** and **d.** A sample response to each choice follows.
   a. The women give Zora Neale books because they recognize that she is a talented reader. She can read stories aloud in a way that makes them smile.
   b. *(This is not a supportable response.)*
   c. The women, who are wealthy enough to give Zora Neale gifts of books, clothing, and new pennies, want to help Zora, and probably assume that her family cannot afford to buy her such gifts.
   d. *(Accept any response that is supported by the selection.)*

17. *(Responses will vary. Sample responses follow.)*
   Action: She hails cars on the road and asks for a ride.
   What is revealed about her character: This action shows that Zora Neale is brazen and outgoing. She ignores her grandmother's warning.
   Action: She reads the class reader from cover to cover on her own.
   What is revealed about her character: This action reveals her zest for stories and her strong internal motivation.

Written Response
18. Responses will vary. In a model response, students should fulfill the following criteria:
   • demonstrate understanding of the prompt
   • describe the literary characters that attract Zora Neale. Students do not need to mention the names of the characters. They should, however, describe their personalities. For example, the characters she enjoys are action-oriented, adventurous, brave, and decisive, and the characters that do not attract her are the sweet and gentle girls.
   • support their ideas with at least two references to details in the selection, for example:
      • Thor speeds across the sky in his chariot.
      • Odin plucks out his eye without flinching.
      • Hercules chooses Duty over Pleasure.
      • David is an exciting Old Testament character.

   • Explain why they think Zora Neale is drawn to these characters. For example, they may describe similarities between Zora Neale's character and the literary characters she admires, then suggest that she identifies with characters who share her sense of adventure.

The Weary Blues
Harlem

SELECTION TEST, page 177
Thoughtful Reading
1. a   2. c   3. a   4. b
5. b   6. c   7. d   8. a

Expanded Response
9. *(Responses will vary. A sample response follows.)*
   Past: African American Harlem residents encountered lies, kicks, and the advice, "Be patient." They were denied employment by a racist society.
   Present: They stand on the edge of hell; they remember injustices; the prices of sugar and bread have gone up; they cannot find employment; and they reflect on their bleak future.

10. Responses will vary, but students should use at least one example to support their ideas. The only supportable answers are **a, c,** and **d.** A sample response to each choice follows.
   a. Melancholy sounds include the moan of the piano and the sad tone of the singer's voice. The words of his song are melancholy because they express his lack of satisfaction, his loneliness, and the wish that he were dead.
   b. *(This is not a supportable response.)*
   c. After he sings, the music resounds in his mind and helps him sleep soundly.
   d. *(Accept any response that is supported by the selection.)*

Written Response
11. Responses will vary. In a model response, students should fulfill the following criteria:
   • demonstrate understanding of the prompt
   • clearly describe at least one example of the hardships faced by African Americans that is expressed in "Harlem," for example:
      • the inability to find employment because of racist hiring practices
      • the problem of inflation
      • past encounters with injustice in the form of lies, kicks, and false reassurances
   • clearly describe the musician's experience in "The Weary Blues," which includes feelings of sadness, loneliness, and the desire to escape his troubles

- compare and/or contrast the plight of Harlem residents with the musician's situation, for example:
  - Comparisons may be drawn between the singer's expression of sadness and the hardships suffered by Harlem residents, who live in a racist society.
  - Contrasts may be made between the personal feeling expressed by the lone singer in "The Weary Blues" and the collective suffering of Harlem residents expressed by the speaker in "Harlem."

COLLECTION 15 TEST, page 179

1. *(Responses will vary. Students should analyze two poems; three sample responses follow.)*

Poem Title	Figure of Speech	How It Adds to the Poem's Meaning
"Go Down, Death"	personification: Death is personified as a man on horseback	makes death seem more inviting and easier to comprehend
"Tableau"	metaphor: Two boys are compared to the colors of day and night.	makes the boys seem beautiful and strong
"America"	simile: America is compared to sinking treasures.	conveys the idea that America faces a bleak future if it does not fulfill its promise of equality

2. *(Responses will vary. A sample response follows.)*

Poem Title	Characters or Situations in Conflict	Why the Conflict Arises
"Incident"	two boys	The conflict arises because one boy responds to the other's friendly smile with a rude gesture and a racial slur. Bigotry is at the root of the conflict.
"America"	the speaker and his or her country	The conflict arises because the speaker feels that America has treated African Americans unjustly.

3. Responses will vary. In a model response, students should fulfill the following criteria:

- demonstrate understanding of the prompt
- compare and contrast how two selections address issues of race
- support their ideas with at least two specific examples from each selection, for example:
  - Johnson's poem addresses issues of race by using the style of old-time African American preachers. By using this style, which uses the techniques of repetition and allusion, Johnson affirms a voice that is part of the African American heritage.
  - McKay's poem focuses on the racism and inequality the speaker experiences in American culture. The speaker says that America offers only bitterness and hate and suggests that this unjust treatment will be America's downfall.
  - The excerpt from Hurston's autobiography describes the author's experiences growing up in an African American community in Florida. Hurston portrays school and family experiences and interactions between her young self and various white people.

4. Responses will vary. In a model response, students should fulfill the following criteria:
- demonstrate understanding of the prompt
- demonstrate an understanding of *tone*
- compare and contrast the speakers' attitudes toward the subject matter in two of the selections listed, for example:
  - the speaker in "Go Down, Death" considers death to be a kind of homecoming. The speaker's tone toward the subject is positive, therefore soothing to the audience.
  - The speaker of "America" has conflicting feelings about his country. He describes it as both a fierce tiger and a source of vigor. This speaker's tone is both positive and negative.
  - The speaker of *Dust Tracks on a Road* does not approve of certain aspects of school, like punishment and arithmetic. Her tone is sometimes positive and sometimes negative, depending on the subject. The effect of her attitude is often comic.
- provide examples from the story or the poems to support their opinions

Vocabulary Review
5. c   6. a   7. d   8. d   9. b

Collection 16: Make It New!

The River-Merchant's Wife: A Letter

SELECTION TEST, page 183

Thoughtful Reading

1. a   2. c   3. b   4. a

Expanded Response

5. *(Responses will vary. Sample responses follow.)*

Image	What the Image Communicates
Hair cut straight across her forehead	She is a young girl.
As a child, the wife pulls flowers.	She is mischievous.
Shortly after getting married, the wife looks at a wall and doesn't answer her husband.	She is unhappy and feels trapped in marriage.
The wife desires her dust to be mingled with her husband's.	She loves her husband.
Before her husband leaves, the wife stops climbing the lookout.	She has accepted her marriage and no longer feels restless.
The monkeys make sorrowful sounds.	She is sad.

Written Response

6. Responses will vary. In a model response, students should fulfill the following criteria:
   - demonstrate understanding of the prompt
   - describe the mood of the poem and explain how two images help create that mood, for example:
     - The mood is somber and sad.
     - Images, such as moss growing thick by the gate and two butterflies turning yellow in August, convey a sense of passing time and sadness over the distance between the speaker and her husband.

The Red Wheelbarrow
The Great Figure

SELECTION TEST, page 184

Thoughtful Reading

1. a   2. a   3. d   4. a
5. b   6. c   7. b   8. a

Expanded Response

(Responses will vary. Sample responses follow.)

9. **"The Red Wheelbarrow":**
   Image: red wheelbarrow
   Sense: sight
   Image: white chickens
   Sense: sight
   "The Great Figure":
   Image: howling sirens
   Sense: hearing
   Image: rumbling wheels
   Sense: hearing

10. Responses will vary, but students should use at least one example from each poem to support their ideas. The only supportable answers are **b, c,** and **d.** A sample response to each choice follows.
    a. *(This is not a supportable response.)*
    b. Williams frequently uses details such as colors (white chickens, red wheelbarrow, the gold numeral on a red firetruck) to render objects just as they are.
    c. Both poems contain simple, realistic images but use them in ironic ways. Williams creates a contrast between an image and the words that refer to that image: The thing on which so much depends is only a wheelbarrow; the great figure is only a number.
    d. *(Accept any response that is supported by the selection.)*

Written Response

11. Responses will vary. In a model response, students should fulfill the following criteria:
    - demonstrate understanding of the prompt
    - describe how the two poems by Williams foster an element of surprise
    - support their ideas with references to at least one example in each poem, for example:
      - "The Red Wheelbarrow" creates a sense of expectation in its first line. After reading the first line, the reader expects that the rest of the poem will describe something extraordinary or dramatic, but instead it describes an ordinary scene.
      - The title of "The Great Figure" leads the reader to believe that the poem might be about a famous person or monument. The rest of the poem is surprising because it describes a common occurrence in cities.

Anecdote of the Jar
Poetry

SELECTION TEST, page 186

Thoughtful Reading

1. b   2. d   3. d   4. b
5. c   6. a   7. c   8. d

Expanded Response

9. Responses will vary, but students should use at least one example from the poem to support their ideas. The only supportable answers are **b, c,** and **d.** Sample responses follow.
   a. *(This is not a supportable response.)*
   b. The speaker argues that some poems focus on material that is both important and genuine, while other poems are merely trivial and pretentious. The speaker dislikes the latter type of poetry.
   c. The speaker refers to the importance of imagination in poetry in line 22 and again in line 24. The last stanza emphasizes how the material of poetry should be true and real.
   d. *(Accept any response that is supported by the selection.)*

10. *(Responses will vary. Samples responses follow.)*
    "Anecdote of the Jar": The poem says that art, and human creativity in general, is one of the most powerful forces on earth, capable of taming any environment.
    "Poetry": The poem argues that poetry or art should present concrete images, ones that contain genuine, raw material.
    Similarity: The poems are similar in that both make a case for the importance of art.
    Difference: The poems differ in how they present their messages. Stevens's poem presents a symbolic image of a jar on a hill, whereas Moore's poem seems more like a prose argument at times.

Written Response

11. Responses will vary. In a model response, students should fulfill the following criteria:
    • demonstrate understanding of the prompt
    • offer an opinion about whether Moore would like or dislike Stevens's poem
    • support their opinions with at least one reference to each poem, for example:
      • In Moore's poem, the speaker states that good poems should be concerned with what is both raw and genuine, using concrete images. Students may argue either that Stevens's image of a jar on a hill fulfills this requirement or that it does not.

Chicago
what if a much of
a which of a wind

SELECTION TEST, page 188
Thoughtful Reading

1. b	**2.** c	**3.** a	**4.** a
5. b	**6.** c	**7.** a	**8.** d

Expanded Response

9. **a.** "what if . . ."   **d.** "what if . . ."
   b. "Chicago"   **e.** "Chicago"
   c. "Chicago"

10. Responses will vary, but students should use at least one example from the poem to support their ideas. The only supportable answers are **a, b,** and **d.** Guidelines for sample responses follow.
    a. Students may argue that the use of apostrophe gives the poem more immediacy by making the reader identify the city. The direct address is more dramatic and interesting than straight description. To support this answer, students may refer to the lines in which the word *you* is used.
    b. Similarly, students may argue that the drama and immediacy produced by the use of *you* gives the speaker's voice authority. They may point to the lines in which the word *you* is used and describe how the poet sets up a point-counterpoint between what people say and how the narrator replies. The device enables the speaker to defend the city against perceived arguments.
    c. *(This is not a supportable response.)*
    d. *(Accept any response that is supported by the selection.)*

Written Response

11. Responses will vary. In a model response, students should fulfill the following criteria:
    • demonstrate understanding of the prompt
    • compare the two poems, listing at least two ways that the poems are similar, for example:
      • Both poems give a negative description of their topics.
      • Both poems nonetheless are optimistic in their outlook.
      • Both poems make use of exaggerated language and imagery.

THE AMERICAN LANGUAGE, page 190

1. c	**2.** d	**3.** b	**4.** b	**5.** a
6. d	**7.** c	**8.** b	**9.** d	**10.** c

COLLECTION 16 TEST, page 192

1. *(Responses will vary. Sample responses follow.)*
   • In "Chicago," Carl Sandburg begins with negative portrayals of Chicago. He notes the city's poverty, immorality, and injustice, but he then goes on to say that Chicago's energy, pride, strength, and activity make it unlike other cities. He compares Chicago to a dog eager for action and to a fighter who has never lost a fight.

- In "what if a much of a which of a wind," E. E. Cummings describes universal destruction, but then asserts the invincibility of humanity. The poem argues that even if everything is blown away, humanity will survive.

2. *(Responses will vary. Sample responses follow.)*
   - In "Anecdote of the Jar," Wallace Stevens presents the image of a jar placed on top of a hill. The action itself is trivial; the jar is simply described as round, bare, and gray—its plainness is emphasized. Yet Stevens shows that the jar is significant in that it changes everything in its environment. The jar's taming effect on the hill and wilderness symbolizes how human endeavor changes the world.
   - The humble images and brief length of William Carlos Williams's "The Red Wheelbarrow" appear insignificant at first. The poem presents a wheelbarrow, rainwater, and chickens, and then it ends. The speaker insists, however, that much depends upon these simple things. These images become significant by conveying the message that it is important to appreciate ordinary, immediate objects in our lives.

3. Responses will vary. In a model response, students should fulfill the following criteria:
   - demonstrate understanding of the prompt
   - briefly describe two poets' ideas about poetry
   - clearly explain how a poem by each poet illustrates his or her ideas about poetry, for example:
     - Pound's poem supports the idea that images alone produce an abundance of meaning.
     - Williams's poems illustrate the idea that poetry should focus on concrete, common things and events.
     - Stevens's poem makes an implied case for the power of human creation, including poetry.
     - Moore's "Poetry" communicates ideas about what good poetry consists of—concrete images and raw material that is genuine. The poem's subject and solid imagery reflect these ideas about poetry.
   - support their ideas with references to at least one example from each poem

4. Responses will vary. In a model response, students should fulfill the following criteria:
   - demonstrate understanding of the prompt
   - identify two poems whose images they recall vividly
   - clearly describe the images, for example:
     - the wheelbarrow glazed with rainwater from "The Red Wheelbarrow"
     - a gold 5 on a red firetruck from "The Great Figure"
     - monkeys making sorrowful noises from "The River-Merchant's Wife: A Letter"
     - a wind flaying hills with sleet and snow from "what if a much . . ."

- explain why the images make an impact, for example:
  - the novelty of the image, such as Chicago's being compared to a big dog or a jar being placed on top of a hill
  - the images' strong appeal to the reader's senses, such as the visual image of glazed rainwater or the tactile sense of a critic's twitching skin
  - associated meanings the images convey, such as the monkeys' noise associated with the wife's sadness

Language Workshop Review
5. Cummings's poem describes a very destructive force.
6. A firetruck barrels through the town in Williams's poem.
7. In "Poetry," the speaker says that the subject matter of poetry should be raw and genuine.
8. The jar in Stevens's poem may symbolize human consciousness.
9. Sandburg calls Chicago the city of the big shoulders in the poem titled "Chicago."

LITERARY PERIOD TEST, page 195
Understanding Vocabulary
1. c   2. a   3. b   4. d   5. a

Thoughtful Reading
6. b   7. d   8. d   9. a   10. b

Expanded Response
(Responses will vary. Sample responses follow.)
11. **Image:** swamp mist **Sense:** sight
    Image: clay after rain **Sense:** smell
    Image: hands touching each other like dew **Sense:** touch
    Interpretation: These images create a sense of magical earthiness, beauty, and wonder. The images convey the idea that daybreak in Alabama would be a positive event.

Written Response
12. Responses will vary. In a model response, students should fulfill the following criteria:
    - demonstrate understanding of the prompt
    - offer an explanation of what the poem says about poetry, for example:
      - The poem draws parallels between the poet's creation—the poem—and natural creations such as shrubs. The sun is involved in the creation of both.
      - The poem suggests that poetry should reflect what is distinctive and wondrous in life.

- point out at least one significant similarity and one significant difference between "The Planet on the Table" and a poem in Collection 16, for example:
  - Unlike the poems in Collection 16, "The Planet on the Table" emphasizes that it is

not essential for poetry to endure forever.
- Like Williams's poems, it suggests that poetry should focus on clear, distinct images.
- Like Moore's poem, it states that poetry should be concerned with the greater world and not just the poet's ego.

AMERICAN DRAMA

LITERARY PERIOD INTRODUCTION TEST, page 199

1. c **2.** a **3.** b **4.** a **5.** c
6. c **7.** a **8.** b **9.** b **10.** d

Collection 17: Reaching for the Dream

A Raisin in the Sun, Act One

SELECTION TEST, page 201
Checking Vocabulary

1. d **2.** b **3.** g **4.** c **5.** i
6. a **7.** h **8.** f **9.** j **10.** e

Thoughtful Reading

11. c **12.** a **13.** d **14.** b **15.** b

Expanded Response

16. Responses will vary, but students should use at least one example from the selection to support their ideas. The only supportable answers are **a, b,** and **c.** A sample response to each choice follows.
   a. Beneatha's dream of becoming a doctor will require a lot of money, which puts her in conflict with the desires and needs of other characters. Walter is angry that the insurance money might be spent on Beneatha's education rather than on his dream of opening a liquor store.
   b. Walter wants to open a liquor store with some friends, but Mama opposes his plan on moral grounds. She believes that it is wrong to sell liquor. Walter tries to get Ruth to convince Mama to support him, but Ruth is reluctant to help him. Ruth says that the money is Mama's and that Mama should decide what to do with it.
   c. Mama's conflicts with other characters are central because she is the head of the household and the one who will receive the insurance check. She doesn't seem to understand why Walter is so preoccupied with money and why he doesn't seem to care about his family; nor does she understand her daughter Beneatha's scorn for traditional Christian beliefs, and their disagreements over God are a source of conflict.
   d. *(This is not a supportable response.)*

17. *(Responses will vary. Sample responses follow.)*
   - Walter's dream is to buy a liquor store with Bobo and Willy.
   - Beneatha's dream is to become a doctor.
   - Mama's dream is to have a house with a garden.

Written Response

18. Responses will vary. In a model response, students should fulfill the following criteria:
   - demonstrate understanding of the prompt
   - state what they would do with the $10,000 if they were Mama
   - address the family's situation as it has been presented in the play thus far
   - support their answers with examples from the play, for example:
     - I would use the money to buy a house with a garden because the family needs a more spacious place to live.
     - I would use the money to fund a different kind of store for Walter and Ruth because Walter and Ruth are disillusioned by their current circumstances and need a chance to pursue their dreams.

A Raisin in the Sun, Act Two

SELECTION TEST, page 203
Checking Vocabulary

1. c **2.** g **3.** i **4.** d **5.** j
6. b **7.** f **8.** h **9.** a **10.** e

Thoughtful Reading

11. a **12.** d **13.** c **14.** c **15.** b

Expanded Response

16. Responses will vary, but students should use at least one example from the selection to support their ideas. The only supportable answers are **a, b,** and **d.** A sample response to each choice follows.

a. Walter wants to use the insurance money to start his own business with two friends. He tells Travis that he sees a golden future in which he is the executive of a company and his own boss, and the family lives in a big, beautiful house.

b. Mama places importance on the happiness and health of the family. She worries about Ruth, and when she sees how discouraged Walter is she gives him most of the insurance money to boost his spirits. She wants a home that is comfortable but not necessarily grand.

c. (This is not a supportable response.)

d. Beneatha determinedly pursues her education and dreams of becoming a doctor. She admires those who, like Asagai, are intellectually stimulating. She rebuffs George, who could give her a materially comfortable life, because she discovers that he is not interested in learning for its own sake.

17. (Responses will vary. A sample response follows.)

Character	Walter Lee Younger
Characteristic	pride
What the Character Says	tells Mr. Lindner that his family will not be paid off
What the Character Does	takes the initiative to talk to Mr. Lindner; pursues his dream of running his own business

18. Responses will vary. In a model response, students should fulfill the following criteria:
• demonstrate understanding of the prompt
• explain how what Walter does with the money affects the dreams of the other characters
• support their ideas with at least two references to the play, for example:
    • Walter gives all the money Mama has given him to Willy, who disappears with it.
    • Walter's mistake and Willy's thievery hurt the other characters' chances of fulfilling their dreams.
    • The money that was slated for Beneatha's medical school education is gone because Walter didn't put it in the bank, as Mama had asked him to.
    • The house Mama had hoped to move into may also be jeopardized, since the family still needs to make payments on it and all of the insurance money has been lost.

A Raisin in the Sun, Act Three

SELECTION TEST, page 205

Checking Vocabulary

1. f	2. d	3. e	4. b	5. a
6. h	7. g	8. j	9. i	10. c

Thoughtful Reading

11. c   12. a   13. b   14. c   15. b

Expanded Response

16. (Responses will vary. Sample responses follow.)

Character	Why the Character Is Dynamic	Action That Shows Change
Mama	She learns to respect her children's decisions.	Mama decides to give some of the money to Walter; tells Beneatha not to go out with George if Beneatha thinks he's a fool.
Walter	He realizes his pride and self-respect are more important than money.	Walter tells Mr. Lindner they won't sell the house.

17. Responses will vary, but students should use at least one example from the selection to support their ideas. A sample response to each choice follows.

a. Mama's decision is the hardest because it will probably involve years of conflict with racist white neighbors who don't want a black family to move into the neighborhood. However, her decision also enables the family to live in a more spacious, physically comfortable home.

b. Walter's decision is the hardest because he has been almost entirely focused on doing whatever it takes to make money. His decision represents a major change in his values; he has chosen pride and self-respect over money. He also knows that his decision will mean that he and other family members will have to struggle in order to meet the house payments, but he is willing to accept this responsibility.

c. Mama's decision is the hardest because the money represents her husband's life and values—values that her son may not be capable of sharing or even understanding. She knows he may lose the money, as, in fact, he does.

d. (Accept any response that is supported by the selection.)

Written Response

18. Responses will vary. In a model response, students should fulfill the following criteria:
• demonstrate understanding of the prompt
• explain how A Raisin in the Sun answers the question about deferred dreams posed in Hughes's poem
• support their ideas with at least two references to examples in the play, for example:
    • Having dreams deferred creates tension and bitterness in families, as illustrated by the arguments between Ruth and Walter.
    • Frustration about dreams deferred may encourage family members to consider actions they might otherwise have considered wrong or degrading, such as Walter's

decision to take money set aside for Beneatha to use for his own purposes, or his considering selling out to the racist people of Clybourne Park.

- Dreams deferred can lead to crushing disappointment, but the hope that drives the dreams may survive, as symbolized by Mama's enduring plant.

THE AMERICAN LANGUAGE, page 207

1. b	**2.** c	**3.** a	**4.** b	**5.** c
6. d	**7.** a	**8.** b	**9.** a	**10.** b

LITERARY PERIOD TEST, page 209

Understanding Vocabulary

1. c	**2.** a	**3.** b	**4.** c	**5.** b

Thoughtful Reading

6. c	**7.** b	**8.** d	**9.** a	**10.** b

Expanded Response

11. *(Responses will vary. A sample response follows.)* In Amanda's vision of her past, she was courted by at least seventeen men, most or all of whom, it seems, were rich. Some of them died and left their widows well provided for. One of her beaux kept her photo until he died. Hence, in her memory, Amanda is desired by men who value their wives or girlfriends. In her present situation she has been abandoned by an irresponsible husband. The last they heard of him, he was in Mexico. Amanda's nostalgia affects her relationship with Laura; she seems to be trying to relive her past through her daughter, despite Laura's protests.

Written Response

12. Responses will vary. In a model response, students should fulfill the following criteria:

- demonstrate understanding of the prompt
- describe how Williams uses both realistic and imaginative techniques in the selection
- support their ideas with at least two references to details in the play, for example:
  - The set of the play is both realistic and imaginative. Realistic details include a fire escape, faded curtains, and dark alleys. Nonrealistic images include a blown-up picture of the absent father and the dimness of the interior.
  - The dialogue of the characters is realistic. Amanda, Tom, and Laura speak to each other the way real people do, expressing anger, frustration, and hope.
  - Other imaginative elements include the projection of a phrase in French on a screen; the narrator's monologue at the beginning of the play; and the music in the wings.

CONTEMPORARY LITERATURE

LITERARY PERIOD INTRODUCTION TEST, page 215

1. b	**2.** a	**3.** d	**4.** b	**5.** c
6. b	**7.** c	**8.** b	**9.** d	**10.** a

Collection 18: The Wages of War

Tamar

SELECTION TEST, page 217

Checking Vocabulary

1. j	**2.** h	**3.** b	**4.** a	**5.** i
6. d	**7.** c	**8.** g	**9.** f	**10.** e

Thoughtful Reading

11. c	**12.** b	**13.** d	**14.** d	**15.** a

Expanded Response

16. Responses will vary. The only supportable responses are **a, b,** and **d.** Students should use at least one example from the selection to support their ideas. A sample response to each choice follows.

a. During their dinner conversation, the narrator is clearly impressed by Tamar's self-confidence, her knowledge of many languages, and her fearless belief that she will be able to continue her studies regardless of the war.

b. When the narrator first sees Tamar, her beauty makes him breathless. When he realizes how young she is, evidenced by the wire on her teeth, he recognizes how vulnerable she really is.

c. *(This is not a supportable response.)*

d. The narrator clearly thinks Tamar is beautiful and intelligent, but he recalls a similar situation in the past that made him realize that all connections are temporary.

17. Responses will vary. Students may include the following points in their chart:

- No one in Europe is interested in buying art (even to help escapees) until they realize that the Nazi threat is real. This realization is ironic because it comes almost too late to make a difference.

- The narrator says that, like all men, he is full of speeches he cannot deliver. Instead, he prattles to the children at the dinner table about imagined battles. It is ironic that the narrator has the best of intentions, but he never acts on them.
- The narrator says that being a British Jew in Palestine is like living in a continuous production of "Romeo and Juliet." His comment is ironic because although he and Jews in general are on the verge of catastrophe, the narrator sees all experiences through a romantic filter.
- The story about Erika and the opera parallels the narrator's "relationship" with Tamar. Ironically, although he claims to have learned from the former experience, it is obvious that he is still immature.

Written Response

18. Responses will vary. In a model response, students should fulfill the following criteria:
    - demonstrate understanding of the prompt
    - explain how Helprin defines the concept of vulnerability
    - explain what makes the groups and characters vulnerable, for example:
      - Jews in London have been lulled into a false sense of security.
      - Tamar and the other children are vulnerable because of their youth and naiveté.

The Death of the Ball Turret Gunner

A Noiseless Flash
from Hiroshima

SELECTION TEST, page 219

Checking Vocabulary

1. d	2. i	3. a	4. f	5. b
6. g	7. h	8. c	9. j	10. e

Thoughtful Reading

11. c	12. d	13. a	14. d	15. c

Expanded Response

16. Responses will vary, but students should use at least one example from the selection to support their ideas. A sample response to each choice follows.
    a. Awakened from sleep in his mother's stomach, the speaker finds himself hunched inside the cold, metallic belly of the airplane, facing flak and nightmarish fighters.
    b. The womb represents good and "the dream of life," while the belly of the airplane represents evil, danger, death, and nightmares.

c. The speaker in the poem is loosed from the earth which he describes as a kind of womb, where he was protected. Waking is a nightmare; it brings the end of innocence, followed by death.

d. (Accept any response that is supported by the selection.)

17. (Responses will vary. Sample responses follow.)
    - **Character: Mr. Tanimoto:**
      Details: sick with anxiety; sends his wife and child outside of the city; small man, quick to talk, laugh, and cry; boyish yet wise; moves nervously and quickly; uneasy because he has been questioned by police; graduated from an American college, speaks English, and dresses in American clothes
      Conclusions: He is a cautious, thoughtful, caring man who prepares for what is to come.
    - **Character: Mrs. Hatsuyo Nakamura:**
      Details: long in the habit of doing what she is told but decides not to follow radio instructions and return to parade ground; both annoyed by and moved to pity for neighbor; has had hard life since husband died; first thoughts are for her children
      Conclusions: Even under devastating circumstances, she thinks of others.
    - **Character: Dr. Masakazu Fujii:**
      Details: prosperous and hedonistic, sociable, calm; has no beds for patients but much modern equipment and plenty of people to take care of them
      Conclusions: He is a selfish man who likes having few responsibilities; the portrait of him is the only one that approaches negativity.
    - **Character: Dr. Terufumi Sasaki:**
      Details: sense of duty triumphs over personal condition; idealist distressed by poor medical conditions—gives medical help to poor without permit and worries about the consequences (but probably not enough to stop him)
      Conclusion: He is a caring, giving man who is more concerned about others than he is about himself.

Written Response

18. Responses will vary. In a model response, students should fulfill the following criteria:
    - demonstrate understanding of the prompt
    - explain how *Hiroshima* fits into the nonfiction category, for example:
      - The book is based on fact and filled with statistics and details of the lives of six people. Hersey maintains objectivity, allowing readers to draw their own conclusions. However, he also provides a glimpse of his personal viewpoint in the details he chooses.

- explain how *Hiroshima* fits into the category of fiction, for example:
  - Hersey creates vivid character portrayals and builds suspense.
- support their opinions with at least two examples from "A Noiseless Flash," for example:
  - Hersey's thesis statement at the end of the first paragraph is an example of the author's objectivity: "A hundred thousand people were killed by the atomic bomb, and these six were among the survivors."
  - Hersey builds suspense when he describes Mr. Tanimoto moving furniture. By interposing information about Mr. Matsui, the wealthy man who allows Tanimoto to store his furniture with him, and his friend Matsuo, who helps him move the furniture, Hersey delays telling the reader about what happens to Mr. Tanimoto.
  - By using a combination of nonfiction and fiction techniques, Hersey brings this catastrophic situation to life for readers far more effectively than a collection of statistics and generalized statements would do.

For the Union Dead
Game

SELECTION TEST, page 221
Checking Vocabulary

1. e	2. c	3. h	4. a	5. i
6. d	7. j	8. g	9. f	10. b

Thoughtful Reading
11. b   12. d   13. b   14. c   15. a

Expanded Response
16. *(Responses will vary. A sample response follows.)*
    Image: the boarded-up Aquarium
    Message: The magic of the past is no longer accessible.
    Image: the statue of Shaw
    Message: Valor is no longer valued by "progressive" American culture.

17. Responses will vary, but students should use at least one example from the selection to support their ideas. The best answers are **a** and **b.**
    a. The fact that each is supposed to shoot if he sees the other behaving strangely fuels suspicion. Each is constantly aware of the other's concealed gun and suspects that the other may use it.
    b. They have a lot in common. Although they are both confined to the same space, they rarely speak. They are both part of the "oversight." They both have the same job (to turn

the key when something happens on the console). However, the narrator doesn't know much about Shotwell's personality, background, or feelings.
    c. (Partial credit can be given.) Shotwell refuses to let the narrator play jacks, and the narrator refuses to do with his key what Shotwell requests.
    d. *(Accept any response that is supported by evidence in the selection.)*

Written Response
18. Responses will vary. In a model response, students should fulfill the following criteria:
    - demonstrate understanding of the prompt
    - clearly discuss Lowell's views on contemporary life, providing at least one example from his poem to support their ideas, for example:
      - Historical monuments are not instructive to a culture more interested in the future than the past. Progress, paradoxically, may end up destroying the world.
    - clearly discuss Barthelme's views on contemporary life, providing at least one example from the story to support their ideas, for example:
      - The stressful confinement of the men responsible for operating control panels during nuclear war leads to their childish, paranoid behavior. Barthelme's work exposes the absurdity of life in the nuclear age.

Speaking of Courage

SELECTION TEST, page 223
Checking Vocabulary

1. h	2. e	3. j	4. f	5. c
6. i	7. a	8. d	9. b	10. g

Thoughtful Reading
11. b   12. d   13. c   14. a   15. d

Expanded Response
16. Responses will vary, but students should use at least one example from the selection to support their ideas. The only supportable responses are **b** and **d.** A sample response to each choice follows.
    a. *(This is not a supportable response.)*
    b. His eleven revolutions around the lake seem to be cathartic.
    c. *(This is not a supportable response.)*
    d. Paul gives every indication that he may always wish he had been braver; probably, however, he will learn to live with his unfulfilled expectations.

17. (*Responses will vary. Sample responses follow.*)
- Paul wants to be able to talk to someone about what he experienced in the war, but he has isolated himself from everyone.
- Paul wants to have been truly courageous in the war, but he couldn't bring himself to do something that he was afraid would result in his death.

Written Response

18. Responses will vary. In a model response, students should fulfill the following criteria:
- demonstrate understanding of the prompt
- apply Nixon's comment about peace to Paul's situation, for example:
  - Nixon apparently hoped for a victorious end to the war, while Paul was searching for an inner peace.
- expand on the type of peace Paul needs, for example:
  - Paul's needs for peace include the courage to face not only himself but also the uncaring world to which he has returned.
- cite examples from the text to support generalizations about Paul's search for peace, for example:
  - Paul's car represents a safe, isolated environment for him. By the end of the story, he seems better able to cope when he opens the window and stops for food at the drive-in restaurant.

Monsoon Season

SELECTION TEST, page 225

Thoughtful Reading

1. a **2.** c **3.** d **4.** c

Expanded Response

5. (*Responses will vary. A sample response follows.*)

Sight image:	"wind sways with violet myrtle, beating it naked"
Effect:	The weather destroys even the beauty in the jungle.
Hearing image:	"Dead men slip through bad weather, stamping their muddy boots to wake us."
Effect:	The soldiers' sleep is so light that it can be disturbed by the muted sounds of ghosts.
Touch image:	"My poncho feels like a body bag."
Effect:	The humidity within the rubber material makes the speaker feel as if he were trapped in death.

From "Monsoon Season" from *Toys in a Field* by Yusef Komunyakaa. Copyright © 1986 by Yusef Komunyakaa. Reprinted by permission of **Yusef Komunyakaa**.

Written Response

6. Responses will vary. In a model response, students should fulfill the following criteria:
- demonstrate understanding of the prompt
- state whether Komunyakaa had more of a propagandistic or an artistic purpose in writing the poem
- describe Komunyakaa's purpose, for example:
  - The poet makes no definite or direct statements about the war or how he feels about it. Instead, he compiles a series of images that are suggestive. He leaves it up to the reader to draw conclusions.
- support their ideas with at least two examples from the poem

COLLECTION 18 TEST, page 226
Responding to Literature

1. (*Responses will vary. A sample response follows.*)
"The Death of the Ball Turret Gunner":
Tone: ironic, elegiac
Theme: the suffering and recognition that follow a loss of innocence
Image: womb/belly of the airplane, birth and death
"For the Union Dead":
Tone: ironic, elegiac, nostalgic
Theme: progress has meant little but suffering, loss, and sacrifice
Image: living animals/mechanical beasts, life and death
"Monsoon Season":
Tone: elegiac, nostalgic
Theme: the suffering of war cannot be forgotten
Image: weather/nature, life amid death and death amid life

2. (*Responses will vary. A sample response follows.*)
Fiction techniques: character development; creation of suspense
Effects: makes readers care about the people and want to find out what happens to them
Nonfiction techniques: use of facts and statistics; understatement; detailed chronology of six people's lives preceding the dropping of the bomb
Effects: objectivity; allows readers to draw their own conclusions

3. Responses will vary. In a model response, students should fulfill the following criteria:
- demonstrate understanding of the prompt
- select one piece of literature that made the strongest impact and discuss its impact
- discuss the author's purpose and techniques, for example:

- Jarrell's intention is to force the reader to face the terror of warfare and to ask along with him, "What is it we die for?"
- Helprin wants his readers to realize that outsiders cannot experience the true impact of war because they see only what they want to see.
- Techniques such as compression and imagery in the Jarrell poem and the use of a naive, insensitive narrator to filter experiences in the Helprin story make the selections memorable.

4. Responses will vary. In a model response, students should fulfill the following criteria:
   - demonstrate understanding of the prompt
   - choose an appropriate poem and prose selection to discuss
   - discuss the use of irony in the poem, for example:
     - Lowell uses irony to highlight lost values.

Images of progress are ironically portrayed as lifeless creatures. Fish and birds have been replaced with dinosaur steamshovels while real soldiers have been replaced with unstable bronze statues.
   - discuss the use of irony in the prose selection, for example:
     - While the narrator in "Tamar" believes his own good intentions, the reader sees his blindness and insensitivity.
   - discuss the author's purpose and the ways in which irony advances it, for example:
     - The perverse images of progress in "For the Union Dead" show that growth and change are not necessarily positive.
     - In "A Noiseless Flash,"highlight how fragile life is.

Vocabulary Review

5. c   6. d   7. a   8. c   9. b
10. d   11. a   12. b   13. a   14. c

Collection 19: Discoveries and Awakenings

The Magic Barrel

SELECTION TEST, page 229

Checking Vocabulary

1. g   2. e   3. i   4. c   5. d
6. j   7. a   8. b   9. f   10. h

Thoughtful Reading

11. c   12. b   13. d   14. c   15. a

Expanded Response

16. Responses will vary, but students should use at least one example from the selection to support their ideas. The only supportable answers are **b, c,** and **d.** A sample response to each choice follows.
   a. (This is not a supportable response.)
   b. Leo is very disappointed by his first meeting with Pinye Salzman. He doesn't trust Salzman's enthusiastic descriptions of prospective marriage partners and is dissatisfied with all of the choices Salzman presents. Leo is relieved when Salzman leaves and he regrets calling him in the first place.
   c. Leo sees Salzman as a trickster. After going on a date with Lily Hirschorn, Leo realizes that Salzman lied to both of them, having exaggerated their appealing qualities. However, Leo also seems to think of Salzman as a somewhat mystical figure who is capable of making it snow or who can appear unexpectedly at Leo's door.
   d. (Accept any response that is supported by the selection.)

17. (Responses will vary, but students should note that Leo is a dynamic character because he changes in important ways as the story unfolds. A sample response follows.)

   Leo is a dynamic character because he changes as the story unfolds. He discovers that he does not love God as well as he should because he has never loved another human being. After making this discovery, he experiences another significant change when he falls in love for the first time.

Written Response

18. Responses will vary. In a model response, students should fulfill the following criteria:
   - demonstrate understanding of the prompt
   - discuss their reaction to the tradition of matchmaking as it is described in the selection
   - support their ideas with at least two examples from the story, for example:
     - I think that consulting a professional matchmaker is not a good solution for Leo because Salzman thinks first about the potential partner's social status while Leo hopes to fall in love.
     - Leo succeeds in falling in love only when the photo of Stella is placed in the packet of photos by mistake. Hence, it is serendipity and not the practice of matchmaking that enables Leo to fall in love.
     - The matchmaking tradition described in "The Magic Barrel" seems to be primarily a financial transaction. Men and women are viewed as commodities to be sold off to people who are interested in gaining wealth or status through marriage.

Elegy for Jane
The Beautiful Changes
Homework

Thoughtful Reading
1. c   2. a   3. d   4. b
5. b   6. c   7. c   8. c

Expanded Response
9. Responses will vary, but students should use at least one example from the selection to support their ideas. The best answers are **a, b,** and **d.** A sample response to each choice follows.
   a. The speaker suggests Jane is eloquent when he says that her syllables leapt when she spoke. Her voice is also compared to the song of a wren.
   b. The speaker says that Jane would throw herself down into a deep, solitary sadness at times.
   c. Partial credit can be given. There isn't much evidence to support the idea that Jane was adventurous, except that she was thrown from a horse. Students may infer that Jane was intellectually adventurous since she seems to have been a lively, passionate student.
   d. *(Accept any response that is supported by the selection.)*

10. *(Responses will vary. A sample response follows.)*
   Line: "Your hands hold roses always in a way that says / They are not only yours . . ."
   Two meanings: In the line above, the word *they* is ambiguous because it can refer to either the roses or the subject's hands. The speaker may be saying that his beloved holds roses in a way that implies the flowers are to be shared or that says her hands are not hers alone.

Written Response
11. Responses will vary. In a model response, students should fulfill the following criteria:
   • demonstrate understanding of the prompt
   • discuss the detailed observations or descriptions used by Roethke, Wilbur, and Ginsberg
   • note the primary source of the detailed imagery in each poem and suggest possible reasons that each poet uses these details, for example:
      • The details may be used to look deeply into the subject's character.
      • The details may encourage the reader not to overlook the importance of small things.
   • support their ideas with at least one example from each poem, for example:

   • Roethke is able to tell us something about Jane's character by comparing her to a wren. The details that describe the wren's song paint a vivid picture of Jane's eloquence.
   • Wilbur refers to details from nature, such as a chameleon's ability to blend in with its environment, to emphasize the miraculous, ever-changing aspect of beauty.
   • Ginsberg cites a list of specific environmental and political problems, comparing them to dirty laundry. By referring to details such as oily oceans, he creates strong visual images of problems that need to be addressed.

from *Black Boy*

Checking Vocabulary
1. d   2. i   3. a   4. e   5. c
6. h   7. b   8. j   9. f   10. g

Thoughtful Reading
11. c   12. d   13. b   14. b   15. a

Expanded Response
16. *(Responses will vary. A sample response follows.)*
   Instances of Inaction: He can't finish his soup during the preacher's visit; pull up grass at the orphanage; or blot Miss Simon's envelope.
   Causes of Inaction: Wright finds himself unable to act during these events because he feels angry because of the injustice of these situations and because he is scared and feels helpless.

17. Responses will vary, but students should use at least one example from the selection to support their ideas. The best answers are **b, c,** and **d.** A sample response to each choice follows.
   a. (Partial credit can be given.) Upon seeing the boat, Wright realizes that the boat is not the huge, grand vessel he had imagined. However, this realization is not as important as the other ones he makes.
   b. The departure of his father prompts Wright to realize that his father has been the source of his food.
   c. His mother's refusal to let him in the house until he returns with groceries, despite the fact that he keeps getting beaten up on the way by gangs, makes Wright realize that he has to fight for his own survival.
   d. After seeing his father twenty-five years later, Wright realizes that his father lives in a world different from his own. Wright concludes that the city brought his father failure, while it provided Wright himself with knowledge and opportunity.

ANSWER KEY

Written Response

18. Responses will vary. In a model response, students should fulfill the following criteria:
    - demonstrate understanding of the prompt
    - characterize the young Richard Wright and describe the adult writer's attitude toward his childhood
    - support their ideas with at least two references to examples in the selection, for example:
      - Richard Wright seems to have been a sensitive and resourceful child. He is hurt and frightened when he realizes that his mother will not let him into the house unless he faces the neighborhood gangs and gets groceries, but he manages to fight them off when he has to.
      - The young Wright can be characterized as perceptive and stubborn. He keenly perceives the hypocrisy of adults like the preacher, Miss Simon, and his father, and he resents their bullying. He displays his stubborn pride when he refuses to ask his father for money even though he is extremely hungry.
      - The adult author writes about his childhood experiences with a certain amount of detachment. He describes many harrowing experiences, such as being beaten and being deserted by his father, without self-pity. He seems to recognize the distance between his difficult childhood and his adult life as a successful author when he concludes the selection by saying that the city gave him opportunity and knowledge.

Everything Stuck to Him

SELECTION TEST, page 235

Checking Vocabulary
1. b   2. d   3. e   4. a   5. c

Thoughtful Reading
6. d   7. c   8. a   9. a   10. d

Expanded Response
11. (Responses will vary. A sample response follows.)
    Wife's Desire: She wants her husband to stay with her because she thinks that their baby may be ill.
    Husband's Desire: He wants to go hunting with one of his father's friends.
    Resolution of the Conflict: The husband decides to stay at the apartment, and the wife shows her appreciation by making him breakfast.

12. Responses will vary, but students should use at least one example from the selection to support their ideas. A sample response to each choice follows.
    a. The man says that things change whether or not you want them to. He seems to regret that things did not work out between the two people, despite their good intentions.
    b. At the end of the story, the reader learns that the boy later goes out into the "cold." The man feels nostalgia for the time when the relationship was still warm and the couple could resolve their differences and promise each other that they wouldn't fight anymore.
    c. After he tells his daughter about the past, the man remarks that things have changed without him realizing it or wanting them to. Hence, he feels helpless about what eventually happened.
    d. *(Accept any response that is supported by the selection.)*

Written Response

13. Responses will vary. In a model response, students should fulfill the following criteria:
    - demonstrate understanding of the prompt
    - describe the present situation of the family and note that the situation between the girl and boy described in the story has changed
    - support their ideas with at least two examples from the story, for example:
      - The idea that the young couple's relationship has changed is supported by the man's claim at the end of the story that situations change without people wanting them to.
      - One may infer that the couple is divorced because the daughter is visiting her father in Milan for Christmas and her mother's presence is not mentioned.
      - The impending cold mentioned at the end of the story suggests that the relationship took a turn for the worse.
      - The young woman's request to hear a story about when she was a child suggests that the man telling the story is her father, whom she didn't know while she was growing up.

The Fish Remember

SELECTION TEST, page 237

Thoughtful Reading
1. d   2. c   3. b   4. a
5. c   6. d   7. a   8. b

Expanded Response

9. *(Responses will vary. A sample response follows.)*

	Examples of Personification	Effects of Personification
"The Fish"	hooks in the fish's mouth resemble medals and a beard	makes the fish seem like a weary, noble warrior
"Remember"	the speaker refers to the wind's voice	makes the wind seem like a living creature and emphasizes how people are similar to parts of the universe

10. Responses will vary, but students should use at least one example from the selection to support their ideas. A sample response to each choice follows.
   a. The speaker notices the fish's extraordinary ability to survive several threats to its life. The fish has managed to break loose from at least five fishing lines.
   b. The speaker notices the fish's sullen look, the sea-lice on its body, and the painful hooks stuck in its jaw. The speaker's compassion for the weary fish influences the decision to let it go.
   c. The speaker admires the face and jaw of the fish. In addition, the speaker admires the fish's ability to escape other fishing lines.
   d. *(Accept any response that is supported by the selection.)*

Written Response

11. Responses will vary. In a model response, students should fulfill the following criteria:
   - demonstrate understanding of the prompt
   - describe what kinds of relationships between people and other elements or creatures are expressed in each poem
     - Bishop's poem emphasizes the importance of recognizing other creatures as independent beings, rather than regarding them solely as a source of gratification.
     - In "Remember," Harjo states the need for human beings to remember that they are connected to all other elements of the universe.
   - support their interpretations with at least one example from each poem, for example:
     - After carefully examining the fish, the speaker grows to admire it, recognizing its uniqueness, and she decides to let it go rather than keeping it for food or sport.
     - Throughout the poem, she personifies natural elements such as trees, stars, and animals, emphasizing their similarity to human beings.

The Girl Who Wouldn't Talk

SELECTION TEST, page 239
Checking Vocabulary
1. b   2. d   3. e   4. a   5. c

Thoughtful Reading
6. c   7. a   8. a   9. a   10. d

Expanded Response

11. *(Responses will vary. A sample response follows.)*
   Example of External Conflict: The narrator attempts to force the quiet girl to speak. The quiet girl cries but refuses to speak, despite the narrator's cruel taunting.
   Example of Internal Conflict: The narrator wants to be strong and invincible, but she sees herself as somewhat weak and fragile. She struggles with hating herself because she feels different and therefore vulnerable at times.

12. Responses will vary, but students should use at least one example from the selection to support their ideas. The best answers are **b** and **c**. A sample response to each choice follows.
   a. *(Partial credit can be given.)* The narrator is exasperated because the quiet girl remains silent even when threatened. This makes the narrator even more scornful than before. However, the narrator seems to hate the quiet girl even before the incident.
   b. The quiet girl, like the narrator, is the last one chosen for her team. They both are automatically walked during baseball games. The quiet girl's unpopularity and passivity is even more pronounced than the narrator's. Hence, the narrator despises in the quiet girl what she sees in herself and what she perceives to be weakness.
   c. During the confrontation in which the narrator directly vents her feelings to the quiet girl, she says that speaking means letting others know that one has a brain and a personality. The narrator wants the girl to be tougher and more assertive and resents her for being quiet and meek.
   d. *(This is not a supportable response.)*

Written Response

13. Responses will vary. In a model response, students should fulfill the following criteria:
   - demonstrate understanding of the prompt
   - clearly explain why they think the narrator tries to force the quiet girl to speak, for example:
     - The narrator cannot stand what she sees as her own shortcomings reflected in the quiet girl. Hence, she tries to change her by forcing her to speak up and defend herself.

Perhaps the narrator can only express her frustration to a person she perceives as weaker than herself.
- support their ideas with at least two examples from the story, for example:
  - The narrator and the quiet girl are similar. They both refrain from hitting the ball in baseball.
  - They both are chosen last for their teams.
  - They both demonstrate difficulty in asserting themselves vocally in class; the narrator's teacher refers her to a speech therapist, and the quiet girl doesn't speak.
  - The narrator desperately wants the quiet girl to speak and defend herself. She pulls her hair and offers to buy her candy if she'll talk.
  - The narrator hates what she perceives to be the quiet girl's fragility.
  - The narrator tells the girl that it is important to speak to let others know that you have a brain and a personality.

from *Blue Highways*

SELECTION TEST, page 241

Checking Vocabulary

1. h	**2.** e	**3.** a	**4.** i	**5.** c
6. j	**7.** b	**8.** d	**9.** g	**10.** f

Thoughtful Reading

11. b	**12.** d	**13.** a	**14.** b	**15.** a

Expanded Response

16. *(Responses will vary. A sample response follows.)*
What Harmony Is: a sense of physical and emotional well-being; spontaneous happiness; a feeling that everything is right and good in the universe
Moment of Harmony: While Heat-Moon is visiting with the Watts family, eating buttermilk pie and listening to music, he experiences a sense of well-being and says that this is why he made his journey.

17. Responses will vary, but students should use at least one example from the selection to support their ideas. The only supportable answers are **a, c,** and **d.** A sample response to each choice follows.
a. The Watts family invite Heat-Moon in, feed him buttermilk pie and a delicious lunch, and share their music with him. They also tell him stories about the town.
b. *(This is not a supportable response.)*
c. The Wattses prefer to use old health cures rather than antibiotics and new medicines. They want to sell the store to a churchgoing couple rather than to atheists.

d. *(Accept any response that is supported by the selection.)*

Written Response

18. Responses will vary. In a model response, students should fulfill the following criteria:
- demonstrate understanding of the prompt
- discuss why they think Heat-Moon chooses to take back roads rather than main highways
- support their ideas with at least two examples from the selection, for example:
  - his desire to find seven-calendar restaurants on the back roads
  - his curiosity about the names of small towns located on the back roads
  - the contentment he expresses while sharing pie, music, and conversation with the Watts family
  - his search for harmony, which he seems to find in small, peaceful towns

COLLECTION 19 TEST, page 243

Responding to Literature

1. *(Responses will vary. A sample response follows.)*

Title of the Poem	Connections Between Human Beings and Nature
"Remember"	The speaker says that it is important for people to remember their connections with natural elements. Various aspects of the universe are personified.
"Elegy for Jane"	The subject is compared to a bird and portrayed as being close to nature. The speaker tries to find consolation in the natural world.

2. *(Responses will vary. A sample response follows.)*

Title of Selection	Conflict or Harmony	Example from the Selection
Black Boy	conflict	Wright and his mother need help from his father, but his father refuses to help them.
Blue Highways	harmony	Heat-Moon enjoys hospitality and generosity when he visits with the Watts family.

3. Responses will vary. In a model response, students should fulfill the following criteria:
- demonstrate understanding of the prompt
- discuss the use of dialogue by two authors in the collection
- note how each author's use of dialogue adds meaning to the selection, for example:
  - Heat-Moon's use of dialect helps readers visualize the places he visits and contributes to characterization of the people he describes.

- Malamud's use of Jewish immigrant vernacular helps to create a realistic urban setting.
- Wright's dialogue relates the harrowing events and conflicts of his childhood in a straightforward, realistic manner.
- The one-sided dialogue, or monologue, in Kingston's story emphasizes the nature of the conflict between the narrator and the quiet girl.
- The lack of quotation marks around dialogue in Carver's story gives it a flowing feel. The characters' remarks and thoughts seem to blend together in some instances.

4. Responses will vary. In a model response, students should fulfill the following criteria:
   - demonstrate understanding of the prompt
   - explain the process of discovery presented in one of the selections
   - describe the discovery, the situation leading to the discovery, and the characters or elements involved
   - support their ideas with details from the selection, for example:
     - In "The Beautiful Changes," the speaker relates several discoveries about changes in nature and about the perception of beauty. He or she notices how a mantis changes a leaf's appearance, making it seem more beautiful.
     - In "The Magic Barrel," Leo realizes that he has never loved another human being and becomes despondent for awhile. Soon afterward, he discovers that he has fallen in love with the matchmaker's daughter.
     - At the end of the excerpt from *Black Boy*, Wright recalls seeing his father after twenty-five years. He realizes that there is a vast gulf between them and that his father has changed dramatically from the cruel, forbidding figure he once was to him. His anger toward his father is transformed into pity.
     - In "The Fish," the speaker grows to admire a fish after examining it closely. She or he discovers that the fish is a survivor of past attempts to capture it and realizes that victory lies in letting the fish go.

Vocabulary Review
5. d   **6.** a   **7.** b   **8.** b   **9.** c

Collection 20: From Generation to Generation

Son

SELECTION TEST, page 247

Checking Vocabulary
1. f	**2.** i	**3.** h	**4.** b	**5.** g
6. c	**7.** e	**8.** d	**9.** j	**10.** a

Thoughtful Reading
11. c	**12.** d	**13.** b	**14.** c	**15.** c

Expanded Response
16. *(Responses will vary. A sample response follows.)*

Characters	Conflicts
the narrator's son and his family	The son's perfectionism conflicts with the other family members' lack of perfection.
the narrator as a teenager and his parents	The narrator is disturbed by his parents' quarreling and wants to escape the home.
the narrator's grandfather and himself	internal conflict: He feels ashamed about becoming a minister without having received a call.

17. Responses will vary, but students should use at least one example from the selection to support their ideas. The best answers are **a** and **c**. Guidelines for sample responses follow.

a. Students may cite several examples of conflict in the story, such as the narrator's father's and grandfather's internal conflicts about their professions (teaching and ministry); the narrator's son's conflict with family members over their imperfections; and the son's conflict with his brother and then with his father, the narrator, who tries to punish him.

b. Partial credit can be given. Students may argue that the narrator is mystified by his son's smile in the story's final segment.

c. Students may note the similarities between the narrator's father and grandfather (ambivalence over their professions) and between the narrator and his son (sitting upstairs, escaping from the family) that reflect the repetition of traits through generations.

d. Accept any response that is supported by the selection.

Written Response
18. Responses will vary. In a model response, students should fulfill the following criteria:
   - demonstrate understanding of the prompt
   - describe how the unusual format of the story adds to its theme or message
   - support their ideas with at least two examples from the selection, for example:

ANSWER KEY

- Fathers are sons, and sons are fathers. Updike blurs the boundaries between the characters to emphasize how similar they are.
- By presenting the scenes out of chronological order, the author conveys the message that his father and grandfather are still with him, as much as his son is.

Daughter of Invention

SELECTION TEST, page 249

Checking Vocabulary

1. c   **2.** a   **3.** f   **4.** i   **5.** d
6. e   **7.** h   **8.** j   **9.** g   **10.** b

Thoughtful Reading

11. b   **12.** d   **13.** b   **14.** c   **15.** d

16. *(Responses will vary. A sample response follows.)*
Father's Side: Young people should be respectful toward teachers and others in authority and act with humility.
Daughter's Side: She is inspired by the boldness and individualism of Walt Whitman's poetry. She believes she is doing the right thing by expressing herself unabashedly.

17. Responses will vary, but students should use at least one example from the selection to support their ideas. The only supportable answers are **a, b,** and **d.** A sample response to each choice follows.
a. Cukita's interest in Whitman's poetry and his messages about American individualism puts her into conflict with her father's more traditional ideas about respecting authority.
b. The father's experiences in the Dominican Republic make him wary of authority. This puts him in conflict with Cukita's message, which he fears may place her at risk.
c. *(This is not a supportable response.)*
d. *(Accept any response that is supported by the selection.)*

Written Response

18. Responses will vary. In a model response, students should fulfill the following criteria:
- demonstrate understanding of the prompt
- compare Cukita and her mother
- support their ideas with at least two examples from the selection, for example:
  - They both enjoy the freedom America offers.
  - They are quicker to adapt to a new language than the father is.
  - They both like to invent new things. Cukita enjoys creative writing, while her mother strives to invent something marketable.

The Bells
from *The Way to Rainy Mountain*

SELECTION TEST, page 251

Checking Vocabulary

1. j   **2.** g   **3.** a   **4.** c   **5.** i
6. b   **7.** d   **8.** e   **9.** f   **10.** h

Thoughtful Reading

11. c   **12.** b   **13.** b   **14.** b   **15.** c

Expanded Response

16. **Image:** the thump of elephants **Sense:** hearing
Image: trembling bells **Senses:** sight, hearing
Image: strangers' rough legs **Sense:** touch
Image: pounding breath **Senses:** touch, hearing

17. Responses will vary, but students should use at least one example from the selection to support their ideas. The best answers are **a** and **b.**
A sample response to each choice follows.
a. The Kiowas experienced the most change because they moved from the mountains to the plains. As a result of this move, they evolved into a society of fighters and big-game hunters. Later, as white settlers moved across the plains, the Kiowas witnessed the mass slaughter of buffalo.
b. The selection implies that the changes experienced by the grandmother were similar to the changes experienced by her tribe. Mostly, though, the grandmother is an observer of the changes that the Kiowas experience. The one clear change in the grandmother is her conversion to Christianity late in life.
c. *(Partial credit can be given.)* According to the selection, the only change the land experiences is the loss of the buffalo.
d. *(Accept any response that is supported by the selection.)*

Written Response

18. Responses will vary. In a model response, students should fulfill the following criteria:
- demonstrate understanding of the prompt
- compare and contrast attitudes about the past expressed by the speaker or narrator of each selection
- support their ideas with at least one example from each selection, for example:
  - In "The Bells," the speaker recalls a past experience with pleasure and nostalgia. As a child visiting the circus with her father she felt tremendous love for him.
  - The narrator of the excerpt from *The Way to Rainy Mountain* also is nostalgic about the past. In contrast to descriptions by the

speaker in Sexton's poem, however, Momaday's descriptions of the past are tinged with bitterness about what has been lost.

from *In Search of Our Mothers' Gardens*

SELECTION TEST, page 253

Checking Vocabulary
1. e   2. c   3. b   4. a   5. d

Thoughtful Reading
6. c   7. a   8. d   9. b   10. c

Expanded Response
11. (*Responses will vary. A sample response follows.*)
    Person: Alice Walker's mother
    Creative Work: made clothes, towels, sheets, and quilts; storytelling; gardening
    Person: anonymous African American woman in Alabama
    Creative Work: quilt rendering the Crucifixion
    Person: "Ma" Rainey
    Creative Work: singing and songwriting

12. Responses will vary, but students should use at least one example from the selection to support their ideas. A sample response to each choice follows.
    a. Walker's mother worked hard from before dawn until late in the evening. In addition to working in the fields with her husband, she cooked and cleaned and made everything the family needed—clothing, towels, quilts, and so on. She used the limited resources at her disposal.
    b. Walker's mother defended her children's need to go to school. Her kindness is revealed by all the work she did to keep her children fed and clothed.
    c. Although Walker's mother was busy with many responsibilities, she found the time to express herself creatively by gardening. Working in her flower garden was a daily exercise of her creative spirit.
    d. (*Accept any response that is supported by the selection.*)

Written Response
13. Responses will vary. In a model response, students should fulfill the following criteria:
    • demonstrate understanding of the prompt
    • explain why they think Walker searched for her mother's garden and what they think she discovered in the process
    • support their ideas with at least two examples from the selection, for example:

• Walker is searching for the source of her own creative spark. She discovers that her mother, like herself, was also a storyteller.
• She discovers that art is not merely a product of high culture, but that it also can be discerned in the daily efforts of ordinary people—people like her mother, who created beautiful flower gardens, and the anonymous woman who sewed the quilt of the Crucifixion.

from *Rules of the Game*
What For

SELECTION TEST, page 255

Checking Vocabulary
1. e   2. b   3. j   4. i   5. a
6. f   7. g   8. c   9. d   10. h

Thoughtful Reading
11. b   12. a   13. c   14. d   15. d

Expanded Response
16. Responses will vary, but students should use at least one example from the selection to support their ideas. The only supportable answers are **a, b,** and **d.** A sample response to each choice follows.
    a. Waverly's mother wants her to succeed by being the best at anything she attempts, including chess-playing.
    b. Waverly's mother encourages her talent by relieving her of some household duties so that Waverly will have more time to practice.
    c. (*This is not a supportable response.*)
    d. (*Accept any response that is supported by the selection.*)

17. (*Responses will vary. A sample response follows.*)
    Spoken words: spells, ballads, liturgies, songs
    Interpretation: Some of these words have the power to heal or to soothe the people listening to them.

Written Response
18. Responses will vary. In a model response, students should fulfill the following criteria:
    • demonstrate understanding of the prompt
    • compare and contrast parent-child relationships in "Rules of the Game" and "What For"
    • support their ideas with at least one example from each selection, for example:
      • Both children have somewhat distant relationships with their parents, who are preoccupied with the demands of the outside world; Waverly's mother insists that her daughter be successful, and the father in Hongo's poem is exhausted by hard labor.

COLLECTION 20 TEST, page 257
Responding to Literature

1. (*Responses will vary. Sample responses follow.*)
   Selection: "Son"
   Recalled Event or Situation: The narrator recalls sitting alone upstairs to escape the family.
   Character's Attitude Toward the Past: wistful

   Selection: "The Bells"
   Recalled Event or Situation: A circus poster reminds the speaker of a childhood trip to the circus and its associations of love for her father.
   Character's Attitude Toward the Past: nostalgic

2. (*Responses will vary. Sample responses follow.*)
   Selection: "Daughter of Invention"
   Characters: Cukita and her father
   Nature of Relationship: conflict

   Selection: "What For"
   Characters: the speaker and his or her father
   Nature of Relationship: harmony

   Selection: "Rules of the Game"
   Characters: Waverly and her mother
   Nature of Relationship: conflict

3. Responses will vary. In a model response, students should fulfill the following criteria:
   - demonstrate understanding of the prompt
   - describe the intangible gifts given by older family members to their children or grandchildren
   - support their ideas with at least one example from each selection, for example:

   - Alice Walker's mother gives Walker the gift of creativity. Walker's mother expresses her creativity through gardening and story-telling, while Walker is an accomplished writer.
   - In Tan's piece, Waverly seems to inherit determination and stubborn pride from her mother. Her mother also gives her the gift of encouragement, which enables Waverly to become a chess champion.

4. Responses will vary. In a model response, students should fulfill the following criteria:
   - demonstrate understanding of the prompt
   - compare and contrast two selections in which conflicts occur
   - identify who is involved, what each conflict is about, and the possible reasons for each conflict
   - support their ideas with at least one example from each selection, for example:
     - The conflict in *The Way to Rainy Mountain* involves large groups of people, while the conflict in "Rules of the Game" involves a mother and her daughter.
     - The conflict in *The Way to Rainy Mountain* involves groups who do not know each other well and produces much violence, whereas in "Rules of the Game," the adversaries are in the same family and their conflicts are more personal and subtle.

Vocabulary Review

5. c   6. a   7. b   8. b   9. d

Collection 21: The Created Self

New African

SELECTION TEST, page 261
Checking Vocabulary

1. h   2. f   3. b   4. g   5. i
6. e   7. a   8. d   9. j   10. c

Thoughtful Reading

11. d   12. a   13. c   14. c   15. c

Expanded Response

16. Responses will vary, but students should use at least one example from the selection to support their ideas. The only supportable answers are **b, c,** and **d.** A sample response to each choice follows.
    a. (*This is not a supportable response.*)
    b. Much evidence in the story shows that Reverend Phillips is a strong church leader and civil rights activist: his congregation looks up to him, he had been arrested in Alabama during a civil rights march, his church has a number of white attendees eager to hear his message, he gives radio speeches, and he occasionally appears on television.
    c. The Reverend Phillips's silence about Sarah's decision not to be baptized is not punitive. Rather, Sarah senses a thoughtful, suppressed wistfulness when the topic arises, showing that her parents wish she would be baptized but that they recognize and honor her right to self-determination. She concludes at the end of the story that her father's silence granted her freedom.
    d. (*Accept any response that is supported by the selection.*)

17. (*Responses will vary. Sample responses follow.*)
    Child: she wants to play in a treehouse; she has never been kissed; in church she snaps her elastic hat band, slouches down, and looks at the ceiling; she reads a children's book

Adult: she reads a book about adults and divorce; she refuses to give in to Aunt Bessie's pressure; she doesn't cry when she tells her father about why she didn't choose to be baptized

Written Response

18. Responses will vary. In a model response, students should fulfill the following criteria:
    - demonstrate understanding of the prompt
    - explain Sarah's statement
    - support their ideas with at least two examples from the story, for example:
      - Sarah is obviously an independent person who values freedom. This is clear when she refuses to be pushed into being baptized when she isn't willing.
      - By his silence, her father gives her the freedom to choose what is right for her, no matter what he might want her to do. Sarah understands that the silence is not accidental; rather, it is purposeful.

Autobiographical Notes

SELECTION TEST, page 263

Checking Vocabulary

1. f	2. g	3. j	4. h	5. c
6. a	7. e	8. d	9. b	10. i

Thoughtful Reading

11. d	12. b	13. a	14. d	15. a

Expanded Response

16. Responses will vary, but students should use at least one example from the selection to support their ideas. The best answer is **a.** A sample response to each choice follows.
    - **a.** Baldwin's tone is thoughtful and reflective—he not only considers his own experiences but places them within a larger social context.
    - **b.** (Partial credit can be given.) In the last part of the essay, Baldwin describes some of his interests in a humorous, wry, and self-deprecating way. The tone of the essay, however, is generally serious.
    - **c.** (Partial credit can be given.) Although his tone is even and controlled, Baldwin expresses anger and frustration over the challenges of being an African American and an African American writer. He refers to the irony and dangers of his social situations.
    - **d.** *(Accept any response that is supported by the selection.)*

17. *(Responses will vary. Sample responses follow.)*

    Opinion: The world conspires against the cultivation of a writer's talent.
    Experience: This opinion is based on difficulties Baldwin experienced as a writer.

Opinion: The "Negro problem" has been poorly written about.
Experience: This opinion is supported by Baldwin's reading and reviewing many books about the topic.

Written Response

18. Responses will vary. In a model response, students should fulfill the following criteria:
    - demonstrate understanding of the prompt
    - explain what they think would be the same or different if Baldwin were writing the essay today, for example:
      - Baldwin would not refer to a "Negro problem" as such, although he might argue that there are still racial problems.
      - Writers, both European and African American, continue to face difficulties in America.
      - Baldwin might marvel at the accomplishments and popularity of African American writers since his time.
    - support their ideas with at least two examples from the selection

Mirror
The Fifteenth Summer

SELECTION TEST, page 265

Thoughtful Reading

1. a	2. d	3. b	4. b
5. c	6. c	7. b	8. c

Expanded Response

9. *(Responses will vary. A sample response follows.)*

What Is Personified	How It Is Personified
the mirror	speaks in the first person, describes itself as truthful but not cruel
the candles	the mirror calls the candles "liars"

10. Responses will vary, but students should use at least one example from the selection to support their ideas. The only supportable answers are **a, c,** and **d.** Guidelines for sample responses follow.
    - **a.** References to inlaid gold, a scale, and weight support this idea. Also, by being in the tree, which is compared to the pointer of a scale, the boy is beginning to see his place in the world around him.
    - **b.** *(This is not a supportable response.)*
    - **c.** Students may note that the boy observes and thinks about his environment and his life while he is in the tree.
    - **d.** *(Accept any response that is supported by the selection.)*

Written Response

11. Responses will vary. In a model response, students should fulfill the following criteria:
    - demonstrate understanding of the prompt
    - compare the functions of the subjects of the two poems
    - use at least two examples from each poem to support their ideas, for example:
        - Both the mirror and the tree allow people to see something differently. The mirror provides the woman with an accurate reflection rather than obscuring the truth; the tree provides a perspective from which the boy can consider what he sees—earth, ocean, and cars.
        - Both objects provide a perspective that leads to self-knowledge. The woman sees her past and future in the mirror, the boy sees himself in relation to things around him. His perspective helps him to learn how to value things.

Straw into Gold: The Metamorphosis of the Everyday

SELECTION TEST, page 267

Checking Vocabulary

1. d	2. e	3. h	4. b	5. c
6. f	7. i	8. j	9. a	10. g

Thoughtful Reading

11. c	12. a	13. a	14. a	15. b

Expanded Response

16. Responses will vary, but students should use at least one example from the selection to support their ideas. The only supportable answers are **b, c,** and **d.** A sample response to each choice follows.
    - **a.** *(This is not a supportable response.)*
    - **b.** Cisneros relates many incidents that show how her familial background shaped her writing. She says that her brothers figured largely in her writing. Cisneros also says that her mother's streetwise voice haunts her stories and poems.
    - **c.** Cisneros states that her "Mexicanness" has helped shape her writing. She mentions that frequent trips to her grandparents' house in Mexico City helped to foster a nostalgia for home that would become a theme in her writing.
    - **d.** *(Accept any response that is supported by the selection.)*

17. *(Responses will vary. Sample responses follow.)*

    Characteristics or Behaviors: nomadic, co-conspirator with her brother Henry, not a very

good student, a daydreamer, an avid reader, shy. No, I don't find it surprising that Cisneros became a writer. She was a somewhat introverted dreamer who liked to read and think about things. Her experiences growing up gave her plenty of material to write about.

18. Responses will vary. In a model response, students should fulfill the following criteria:
    - demonstrate understanding of the prompt
    - describe what Cisneros draws upon as subjects for her writing, for example:
        - the women on Mango Street
        - her family
        - her Mexican American heritage
    - explain what these things have in common and why they think Cisneros chooses these things over others, for example:
        - She writes about her personal experiences, to which only she can give a unique voice.
        - She writes about people and circumstances that have influenced her life since childhood.
    - support their ideas with at least two examples from the selection

---

The Latin Deli: An Ars Poetica
The Satisfaction Coal Company

SELECTION TEST, page 269

Thoughtful Reading

1. b	2. c	3. b	4. c
5. d	6. a	7. d	8. c

Expanded Response

9. *(Responses will vary. Sample responses follow.)*

    Examples of spoken language: "a 'glorious return'"; *dólares; Suspiros; Merengues; jamón y queso*

    One message conveyed by these examples might be that the customers of the deli are not alone, that there are others who speak their language and enjoy eating similar foods. The words "glorious return" and *dólares* convey a message of hope.

10. Responses will vary, but students should use at least one example from the selection to support their ideas. The only supportable answers are **a, b,** and **d.** A sample response to each choice follows.
    - **a.** The careful way he sweeps the floor indicates some satisfaction, as does his sitting by the heater. He later recognizes the hard work he did with a sense of wistfulness.
    - **b.** Images of lethargy and confinement support this interpretation. Watching TV, leafing through a magazine, going out to the porch on a freezing day, the neighbor retrieving her mail, a drunk smiling at a tree carving,

a canary singing in its cage, and a gorge "choked" with sumac make him recall a time of greater purpose.

  c. *(This is not a supportable response.)*
  d. *(Accept any response that is supported by the selection.)*

Written Response

11. Responses will vary. In a model response, students should fulfill the following criteria:
    - demonstrate understanding of the prompt
    - compare and contrast the woman in "The Latin Deli" with the man in "The Satisfaction Coal Company"
    - support their ideas with at least two examples from each poem, for example:
      - The woman in "The Latin Deli" functions as a sort of touchstone for immigrants from Latin America, reminding them of their heritage and comforting them with familiarity.
      - The woman in "The Latin Deli" is patient and a hard worker, but we never get to look inside her heart, as we do with the man in Dove's poem.
      - The man in "The Satisfaction Coal Company" has a nostalgic attitude toward his work. He felt useful and productive.
      - Unlike the woman in Cofer's poem, the man in "The Satisfaction Coal Company" is not presented as someone who is still a significant person in the lives of others.

THE AMERICAN LANGUAGE, page 271

1. b	**2.** d	**3.** d	**4.** a	**5.** b
6. c	**7.** a	**8.** b	**9.** c	**10.** c

COLLECTION 21 TEST, page 273

Responding to Literature

(Responses will vary. Sample responses follow.)

1. **Selection:** "New African"
   Character: Sarah
   Change: Sarah has come to an age where she makes adult decisions that are respected by her parents

   Selection: "The Latin Deli"
   Characters: customers in a deli
   Change: The customers have moved from Spanish-speaking countries to an English-speaking one where what they formerly took for granted has become precious.

2. **Selection:** "Autobiographical Notes"
   Character: James Baldwin
   Conflict: The writer expresses internal conflict about his role as an African American writer. He feels that he must establish some distance between his writing and the social problems faced by African Americans; however, he finds that this is a hard goal to accomplish. He also states that the culture which has influenced

him as a writer is not really his, since he is not European American.
   Selection: "New African"
   Character: Sarah
   Conflict: As she grows up, Sarah feels some internal conflict about her decision to not be baptized. She feels both heroic for following her heart and sad because her decision created some distance between her and the rest of her family.

3. Responses will vary. In a model response, students should fulfill the following criteria:
   - demonstrate understanding of the prompt
   - offer an opinion about what the created self is, for example:
     - The created self is what emerges or is molded when people respond to conflicts. Depending on their decisions or actions, they are creating who they will become from that point on.
   - support their ideas with at least one example from each selection, for example:
     - Being an African American in the first part of the 20th century thrust James Baldwin into an arena of conflict. He chose to focus much of his writing on racial issues because he felt those were the subjects he had to ponder before he could move on. Therefore the created self that emerged in his writing came about in response to conflict.
     - In "Straw into Gold" the narrator is shaped by the personal conflicts that she forces herself to face in the pursuit of her educational and professional goals.

4. Responses will vary. In a model response, students should fulfill the following criteria:
   - demonstrate understanding of the prompt
   - identify two selections in which the main character recalls her or his experiences as a younger person, for example:
     - In "New African," the narrator remembers herself as a ten-year-old girl.
     - In "Straw into Gold," the narrator remembers herself as a younger woman.
   - explain how the protagonists seem to regard their younger selves, for example:
     - In "New African" the narrator regards herself as very strong-willed. She refuses to be baptized just to make the congregation of her church happy.
     - In "Straw into Gold" the narrator reflects upon her ingenuity and perseverance in a difficult situation.
   - identify similarities or differences between the younger and older versions of the person
     - As an adult the narrator of "New African" is also very strong-willed. She never gets baptized, and it is hard for her to admit the feelings of loss that she sometimes experiences over never having shared that bond with her family.

- The narrator of "Straw into Gold" compares her current experience of making corn tortillas in France with her experience of writing her master's exam in graduate school and with other experiences in her life. Through perseverance and determination she has managed to accomplish many difficult tasks.
- support their ideas with at least one example from each selection

Vocabulary Review
5. b   **6.** d   **7.** a   **8.** c   **9.** b

Language Workshop Review
(Responses will vary. Sample responses follow.)

10. Nigel said he was not sure whether you called him.

11. A magnificent bear rose on its haunches, sniffed the acrid air, and roared mightily.

12. Arturo Súarez, I would like you to meet my mother, Bonita González.

13. A cloud drifted over the mountain.

14. Please think before you speak.

LITERARY PERIOD TEST, page 276

Understanding Vocabulary
1. b   **2.** a   **3.** a   **4.** c   **5.** c

Thoughtful Reading
6. d   **7.** b   **8.** c   **9.** c   **10.** b

Expanded Response
11. Responses will vary, but students should use at least one example from the selection to support their ideas. The only supportable answers are **a**, **c**, and **d**. A sample response to each choice follows.
   a. When Mah is expressing her anger, she says that the narrator got married without even telling her. She doesn't seem to be upset by the marriage itself, but by the fact that her daughter didn't tell her about her plans ahead of time.
   b. *(This is not a supportable response.)*
   c. The narrator seems to think that Mah's anger is partly due to her own marriage problems. The narrator mentions that Mah married in shame and was unhappy in her marriages.
   d. *(Accept any response that is supported by the selection.)*

Written Response
12. Responses will vary. In a model response, students should fulfill the following criteria:
- demonstrate understanding of the prompt
- discuss how the selection relates to the theme of the created self, for example:
  - The process of self-creation in the excerpt from *Bone* involves communication and confrontation. When the excerpt begins, the narrator has already defied her mother's wishes by getting married without telling her. In order to affirm her right to make decisions about her life, the narrator must tell her mother the upsetting news. However, by the end of the selection the conflict has been resolved and the narrator seems relieved.
- make at least one comparison and one contrast between the selection and two selections from Collections 18 through 21, for example:
  - As in "New African," the process of self-creation in the selection involves external conflict. Both protagonists risk provoking the disapproval of a parent and their community through their actions. However, these conflicts are a necessary part of establishing their independent identities.
  - Although the process of self-creation in the selection involves communication, writing is not a part of that process as it is in "Autobiographical Notes" and "Straw into Gold." Both Baldwin and Cisneros focus on the creation of identity through writing and recall influences on their development as writers.

Standardized Test Preparation

Verbal Expression

Test Passages
Passage I, page 286

1. B	2. C	3. D	4. A	5. D
6. C	7. B	8. D	9. A	10. A

Passage II, page 287

1. B	2. D	3. C	4. C	5. D

Identifying Sentence Errors
Test 1, page 289

1. C	2. A	3. B	4. A	5. D
6. B	7. E	8. C	9. A	10. C

Test 2, page 290

1. D	2. B	3. E	4. C	5. E
6. C	7. D	8. D	9. B	10. C

Test 3, page 291

1. B	2. E	3. B	4. A	5. C
6. C	7. A	8. C	9. D	10. E

Sentence Revision
Test 1, page 292

1. E	2. B	3. C	4. D	5. A

Test 2, page 293

1. B	2. A	3. E	4. C	5. D

Test 3, page 294

1. C	2. D	3. A	4. E	5. E

Critical Reading Test, page 298

1. A	2. D	3. B	4. E	5. D
6. C	7. D	8. B	9. E	10. A

Critical Analysis

Analogies
Test 1, page 303

1. A	2. B	3. C	4. C	5. B
6. D	7. E	8. D	9. D	10. B
11. A	12. A			

Test 2, page 304

1. E	2. D	3. C	4. D	5. A
6. B	7. D	8. C	9. C	10. B
11. A	12. E			

Test 3, page 305

1. B	2. A	3. D	4. E	5. C
6. C	7. C	8. A	9. D	10. B
11. D	12. E			

Test 4, page 306

1. C	2. B	3. A	4. D	5. D
6. E	7. E	8. A	9. B	10. B
11. A	12. C			

Test 5, page 307

1. C	2. D	3. C	4. B	5. B
6. A	7. D	8. E	9. E	10. B
11. A	12. D			

Test 6, page 308

1. E	2. A	3. E	4. A	5. B
6. C	7. D	8. B	9. A	10. B
11. D	12. C			

Logic
Test 1, page 309

1. C	2. D	3. C	4. A	5. D
6. B	7. E	8. B	9. A	10. E

Test 2, page 310

1. D	2. E	3. C	4. B	5. A
6. B	7. D	8. D	9. C	10. E

Test 3, page 311

1. B	2. C	3. C	4. A	5. D
6. E	7. E	8. D	9. A	10. B